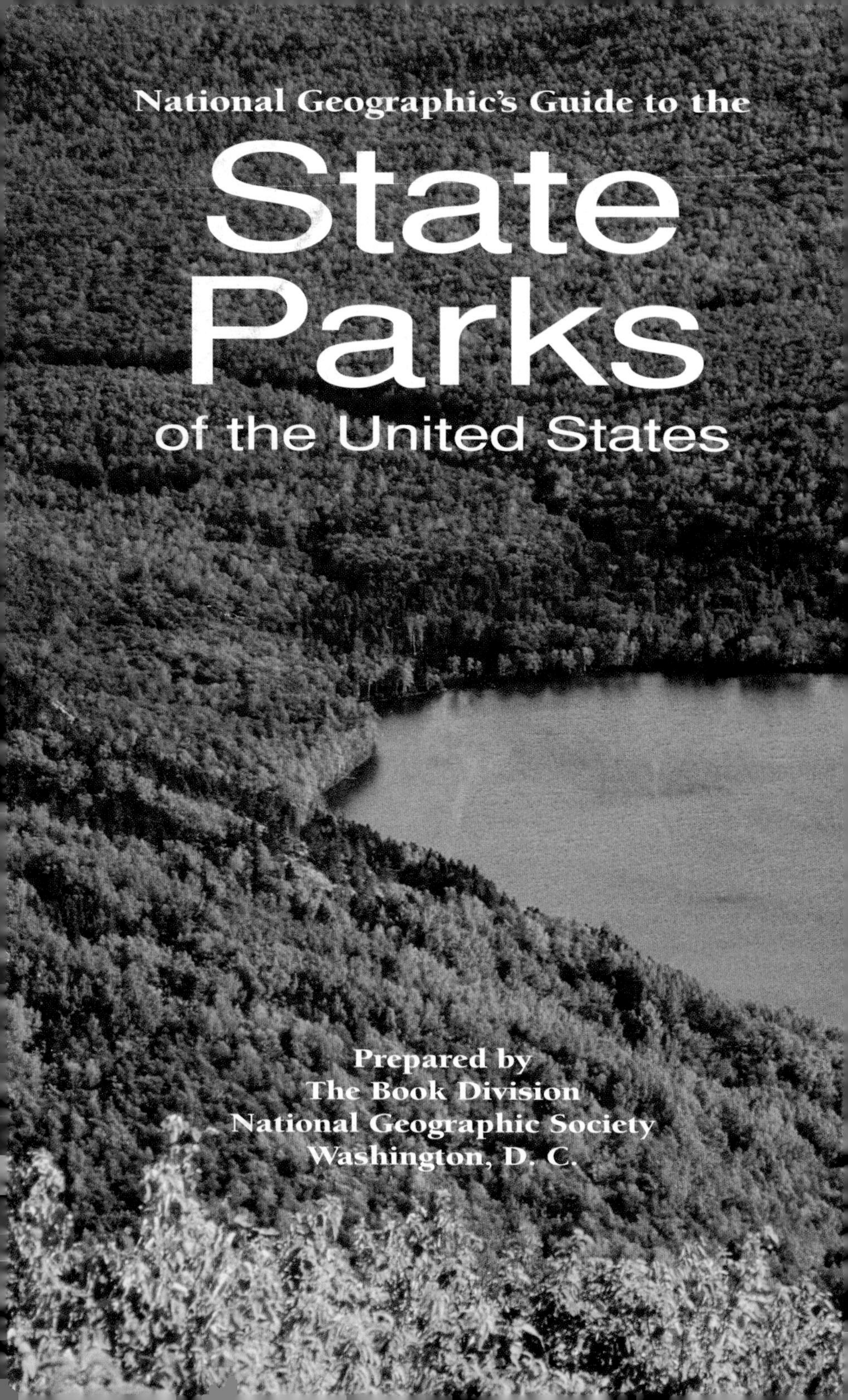

National Geographic's Guide to the

State
Parks

of the United States

Prepared by
The Book Division
National Geographic Society
Washington, D. C.

CREDITS

Published by

THE NATIONAL GEOGRAPHIC SOCIETY

Reg Murphy
President and Chief Executive Officer
Gilbert M. Grosvenor
Chairman of the Board
Nina D. Hoffman
Senior Vice President

Prepared by The Book Division

William R. Gray
Vice President and Director
Charles Kogod
Assistant Director
Barbara A. Payne
Editorial Director

Guidebook Staff

Elizabeth L. Newhouse
Editor and Director of Travel Books
Barbara A. Noe
Project Editor
Suez Kehl
Art Director
Caroline Hickey
Senior Researcher
Mary Jenkins
Illustrations Editor
Carl Mehler
Senior Map Editor and Designer

4

Fly-fishing at Housatonic Meadows State Park, Connecticut

Bob Devine, Jerry Camarillo
Dunn, Jr., Sean M. Groom,
K. M. Kostyal, Mark Miller,
Barbara A. Noe, Geoffrey O'Gara,
Jeremy Schmidt, Thomas Schmidt,
John M. Thompson, Dan Whipple,
Mel White, Susan Young
Writers

Alison Kahn, Mary Luders
Assistant Text Editors

Susan A. Franques, Sean M. Groom,
Michael H. Higgins, Mary E.
Jennings, Keith R. Moore
Researchers

Margaret Bowen
Copy Editor

Louis J. Spirito
Map Production Manager
Mapping Specialists, Ltd., Thomas
L. Gray, Michelle H. Picard
Map Research/Production
Tibor G. Tóth
Map Relief

Meredith C. Wilcox
Illustrations Assistant
Richard S. Wain
Production Project Manager
Lewis R. Bassford, Lyle Rosbotham
Production
Kevin G. Craig, Mark Fitzgerald,
Dale M. Herring, Peggy J. Purdy,
Robert Weatherly
Staff Assistants

Susan Fels
Indexer

Wallace Council, Joan Wolbier
Contributors

**Manufacturing
and Quality Management**

George V. White, *Director*
John T. Dunn, *Associate Director*
Vincent P. Ryan, *Manager*
Polly P. Tompkins, *Executive Assistant*

Cover: Na Pali State Park, Hawaii
Previous pages: Baxter State Park,
Maine

Facing page: Anza-Borrego Desert State
Park, California

CONTENTS

6

7

Canoeing at Stephen C. Foster State Park, Georgia

Niagara Reservation State Park, New York

The United States has over 5,000 state parks, totaling nearly 12 million acres. Their annual visitation numbers are staggering—750 million, three times the number of visits made to national parks. State parks comprise a multitude of scenic wonders—mountains, lakes, rivers, deserts, and seacoasts; abundant and diverse wildlife; and profusions of wildflowers in season. They display the ancient imprints of glaciers, volcanoes, and floods. Yet few state parks are known beyond their immediate areas. This guidebook introduces you to more than 200 of the wildest and most scenic of the parks, as well as to some that stand out for their cultural or historical significance.

As you set out to explore these public treasures, it's worth reflecting on the role of the Civilian Conservation Corps in their evolution. Back in the 1930s, fewer than half the states had any kind of state parks program. In those Great Depression years, President Franklin D. Roosevelt created the CCC to put unemployed but able-bodied young men to work. Their job was to improve the public lands that had been ravaged by logging and by the Revolutionary and Civil Wars. It was also hoped that such a program would preserve the rapidly diminishing recreational acreage.

In Armylike settings throughout the country, these men rose at dawn to operate stone quarries, dig drainage ditches, cut trails, reintroduce wildlife, and fight forest fires—for as little as a dollar a day. They cleared ridges to reveal spectacular vistas, planted thousands of tree seedlings, and from native materials built handsome lodges and cabins, many still in use today. The coming of World War II effectively disbanded the CCC, but in its nine years more than three million youths had laid the foundation for many of our state parks. And their rich legacy is still ours to cherish and enjoy.

About the Guide

Our staff selected the parks to include in this guide with the generous help of the state park directors, who made recommendations for their states. Our regional travel writers explored every park to report on their findings; they were helped immeasurably by the individual park staffs. Ney Landrum, Executive Director of the National Association of State Park Directors, deserves our greatest thanks for his support and advice throughout the project. Without his help we never could have produced the guide in the time we had.

Most parks are open daily year-round. Campgrounds are common in state parks. We have listed the number of tent and RV sites; call the park for specific hook-up information. Most campgrounds admit visitors on a first-come, first-served basis, but often accept reservations. Each park's camping section tells you when these are advised.

Information about every park has been checked and, to the best of our knowledge, is correct as of press date. However, call ahead when possible, as visitor information often changes.

MAP KEY

▢	State Park Site		▬▬▬	State Park Boundary
■	Point of Interest		———	State or International Boundary
♟	Ranger Station, Visitor Center, Park Headquarters		(294)(12)	Interstate, U.S. Federal, or Principal Highway
△	Campground, Campsite		(36) [29]	State or Local Road
⛺	Park Cabin		———	Unpaved Road
⊏	Picnic Shelter		- - - -	Jeep Trail
🕱	Picnic Area		········	Bike Trail
⛳	Golf Course		·········	Major Trail
◇	Downhill Ski Area		·········	Local Trail
⛵	Boat Launch or Dock		··············	Ferry
�	Canoe Launch or Take-Out		———	Aerial Tram
➤	Airboat Tours			
⚑	Observation Tower		ABBREVIATIONS	
•→	Gate		Cr. — Creek	
)(	Tunnel		Fk. — Fork	
✻	Vista, Overlook		HWY. — Highway	
			I. — Island	
✗	Rapid		Mt.-s. — Mount-ain-s	
↗	Waterfall		PKWY. — Parkway	
			Pt. — Point	
○	Spring		R. — River	
•	Well			
⍑	Palm Springs		National Park	Wildlife Area
•	Town, Village		State Park	
I	Dam		Forest	Swamp

Maine

Baxter
Cobscook Bay
Lily Bay
Grafton Notch
Rangeley Lake

New Hampshire

Franconia Notch
Mount Washington
Robert Frost Farm
Odiorne Point

CANADA
U.S.

MAINE

BAXTER

95

LILY
BAY

201

6   16

RANGELEY
LAKE

16

ISLAND
COMPLEX

2   91

17   2   1A   1

COBSCOOK BAY

SMUGGLERS NOTCH

VT.

GRAFTON
NOTCH

MOUNT PHILO

89

Augusta

BUTTON
BAY

Montpelier

MOUNT
WASHINGTON

100

FRANCONIA
NOTCH

1

N.H.

302

4

16

89   93

95

7   91

Concord

4

ODIORNE POINT

9

ROBERT FROST
FARM

MOUNT
GREYLOCK

2

MASS.

SKINNER

WACHUSETT
MOUNTAIN

WALDEN POND

Boston

7   TALCOTT
MT.

90

95   3

PILGRIM
MEMORIAL

HOUSATONIC
MEADOWS

84   395   R.I.

Hartford

CONN.

Providence

COLT   195

SLEEPING GIANT

95

BLUFF
POINT

1

FORT ADAMS

BEAVERTAIL

DINOSAUR

GODDARD
MEMORIAL

0   50 mi
0   100 km

Massachusetts

Walden Pond
Mount Greylock
Wachusett Mountain
Pilgrim Memorial
Skinner

Rhode Island

Fort Adams
Beavertail
Colt
Goddard Memorial

Vermont

Island Complex
Smugglers Notch
Button Bay
Mount Philo

Connecticut

Housatonic Meadows
Talcott Mountain
Dinosaur
Sleeping Giant
Bluff Point

11

Franconia Notch State Park, New Hampshire

Baxter

18 miles from Millinocket on park access road

● **204,733 acres** ● **207-723-5140** ● **Mid-May to mid-Oct.,
Dec. through March** ● **Non-resident vehicle fee** ● **No pets,
RVs, or motorcycles** ● **New England's largest state park**
● **Maine's highest mountain** ● **Wildlife viewing** ● **Hiking,
boating, fishing (license required)**

Mount Katahdin from Sandy Stream Pond

12

As he watched the vast Maine woods being gobbled up
by paper companies and developers after the turn of the century, Gov. Percival Baxter determined that a portion of his
home state be set aside as a wilderness area. In 1930 the
wealthy lawyer began buying plots at the edge of the rugged
land known as the North Woods and giving them to the
state. Thirty-two years and 28 purchases later, the governor
had built up the empire of mountains, lakes, and wildlife
that would bear his name.

Today, the park is administered by a special Baxter
State Park Authority, which still maintains it in strict adher-
ence to Baxter's will. He stipulated that preservation of the
park's wild character be the top priority, with recreational
use a secondary concern.

The park's skyline is dominated by Mount Katahdin,
actually a cluster of mountains whose highest point, called

Baxter Peak, is named in honor of the governor. "Man is born to die. His works are short-lived. Buildings crumble, monuments decay, wealth vanishes but Katahdin in all its glory forever shall remain the mountain of the people of Maine," Governor Baxter wrote of the 5,267-foot peak, the state's highest.

He was not the first person to be impressed by the great gray mountain, which rises abruptly from the wooded plain. America's early environmental writer, Henry David Thoreau, traveled by foot, train, boat, and horse and buggy to reach Katahdin in 1846. He was among the first white men known to have scaled the mountain's steep rocky slope, which he immortalized as "vast, titanic, inhumane" in his 1864 book, *The Maine Woods*.

Baxter State Park is still best seen by walking. Short, flat trails follow rivers or lead to ponds frequented by moose. Longer trails will take you to waterfalls and lakes, and strenuous trails climb to the tops of the park's many mountains, including Mount Katahdin, the northern terminus of the Appalachian Trail.

What to See and Do

If you have only a day to spend at Baxter, a drive along the **park loop road,** with stops for short walks and wildlife viewing, will give you a good flavor of the rugged region. With a little advance planning, you can stretch this trip and stay overnight at one of the campgrounds or in cabins along the way. Before journeying into the park, fill up your gas tank and stock up on food and water, because there are no

13

stores, gas stations, and drinking water sources in the park. At the **Visitor Center** at the park's south entrance, register and obtain a map of the park. Here park staff can also tell you if certain popular parking lots are full. If this is the case, they will suggest alternatives.

Just beyond the Visitor Center, you'll reach a fork; go right to **Roaring Brook,** a popular starting point for treks up Mount Katahdin. Even if you don't want to go all the way to the top, try to take the steep, 3.3-mile trail to **Chimney Pond,** a picturesque moose watering hole in the shadow of Baxter Peak. Many hikers stay at the campsites or in the bunkhouse at the pond before making the final ascent of Mount Katahdin.

Backtrack to the main park loop road and head in the direction of Abol Campground. Your first stop is **Abol Pond,** a popular feeding ground for moose, with a small sandy beach and picnic area. About 2 miles up the road, you'll find the wooded Abol Campground. From here, the steep, rocky **Abol Trail** climbs up the south face of Mount Katahdin. This rugged, 7.6-mile round-trip trail—visible as a wide slash on the mountainside—is the shortest route to Baxter Peak. It also closely parallels the route Thoreau took.

Bull moose and visitors at Beaver Falls

About 4.5 miles farther up the road, turn left on Daicey Pond Road to popular **Daicey Pond.** A loop trail edges the water, offering excellent views of Mount Katahdin. Several small cabins also offer great mountain and lake views. You can rent canoes at Daicey and more than a dozen other ponds.

Nearby **Kidney Pond,** which can be reached by trail or the park road, is also well worth a stop. The cabins here face the water, where loons nest and moose visit frequently. At sunrise or sunset or on a moonlit night, enjoy the quiet beauty by canoe.

From Kidney Pond, several trails lead to more remote ponds, including **Celia** and **Jackson,** where canoes are available for a leisurely paddle. A popular 2.5-mile trail wends from Kidney Pond to the top of **Sentinel Mountain,** which offers commanding views. Both ponds are home to brook trout, which can be caught by fly-fishing only.

Four miles up the road, swimmers enjoy sliding down the slippery rocks of **Ledge Falls.**

Further Adventures

Most one-day visitors to Baxter get only as far as Nesowadnehunk, about 17 miles into the park. But if you have more time and want to get away from the crowds, a journey to the park's remote northern end is worth the effort. It is about 17 miles from Nesowadnehunk to the turnoff for the **Branch Ponds,** two small ponds nearly ringed with mountains. Here you'll find tent sites and a bunkhouse, as well as canoes for rent and a variety of hiking trails. A short path leads to **South Branch Falls,** while more strenuous trails climb **Black Cat** and **Traveler Mountains. Grand Lake Matagamon,** home to eight types of fish including salmon and yellow perch, is a few miles up the road. For a good view of the 4,000-acre lake, climb the mile-and-a-half to the summit of **Horse Mountain,** capped by a lookout tower. From the park's north entrance gate, you can follow the paved road to Patten and back to I-95.

In winter the park is open for snowshoeing, cross-country skiing, and snowmobiling. To camp or to climb above timberline, you must register two weeks in advance, have proof of winter mountaineering experience, and travel in groups of four or more.

Camping and Lodging

Baxter has ten campgrounds, with a range of accommodations. Many offer tent sites as well as wooden lean-tos. Kidney and Daicey Ponds have cabins, while the sites at Chimney Pond and Russell Pond can only be reached by backpackers.

Reservations are strongly advised, especially in July and August. The park accepts reservations for the summer season beginning January 2, when people line up outside headquarters to reserve the best spots. You can also send in your requests to park headquarters, at the address below. No phone reservations taken; however, visitors can call the main number for information. A couple of dozen sites are available on a first-come, first-served basis.

❏ *Baxter State Park, 64 Balsam Dr., Millinocket, Maine 04462*

A State Park By Any Other Name

In addition to donating more than 200,000 acres of land to the state of Maine, Gov. Percival Baxter, upon his death in 1969, left more than 7 million dollars to run the park he had created. The money, invested in a trust, pays for operation and maintenance. This way, Baxter reasoned, the park would not fall victim to the whims of state lawmakers or the budget-cutting ax. The park is run by a three-member park authority that includes the state attorney general, director of forestry, and commissioner of fish and wildlife.

15

Cobscook Bay

5 miles south of Dennysville on US 1

Atlantic puffin

16

● 871 acres ● 207-726-4412 ● Mid-May to mid-Oct., trails open year-round ● Day-use fee in summer ● Walking trails ● Clamming

Cobscook Bay State Park has the look of the Maine coast before the birth of ubiquitous outlet malls and restaurants. Far from the hub-bub of the southern part of the state, you'll discover a quiet seaside retreat dominated by towering spruce trees. Whether just stopping for a picnic lunch or pitching your tent for the night, Cobscook is a good jumping-off point for further exploration of Down East Maine.

What to See and Do

You've set up camp at a site with sweeping views of **Whiting Bay,** and realize you've forgotten to pack dinner. No problem. Cobscook Bay is Maine's only state park with a clamming area where visitors are allowed to dig. Bring a big pot and plan to get dirty as you try your hand (at low tide) at this popular Maine activity. After tending to your scraped knuckles, watch the setting sun cast a pink glow over the shimmering waters as you dine on your handpicked steamers.

If you're an early bird, scramble up **Cunningham Mountain** for views of the sun rising over secluded Whiting Bay, part of the larger Cobscook Bay. Leaving from Broad Cove Road, the 0.2-mile trail climbs up the granite hill. From this vantage, you may be one of the first people in the lower 48 states to see the sunrise. If you hike up in the pre-dawn darkness, don't forget a flashlight since the trail is rocky. This trail connects to a nature trail that follows the park's western edge through the woods.

Another path, the .75-mile **Anthony's Beach Trail** meanders through the woods and along the rocky shore to a large wharf. Be sure to follow the trail blazes; it's easy to get lost.

The park's jagged shoreline and many coves lend themselves to sea kayaking. Numerous islands and small bays may be easily reached by small motorboat or canoe. Boat launch facilities are found near the middle of the park and in the park's northwest corner. There are no boats for rent in the park.

More than 200 species of birds have been sighted at Cobscook Bay, including bald eagles. The park office has bird lists, as well as a collection of field guides available for visitor reference.

Reversing Falls

The local Maliseet and Passamaquoddy Indians called the area Cobscook, or waterfall, for the reversing falls that are a short distance from the park. The best time to see the falls is a couple of hours before high tide, when the incoming water is as much as 24 feet higher than at low tide. This causes the flow of water in the bay to temporarily reverse direction. Ask the park ranger for directions and a tide chart.

Camping

Cobscook Bay offers 106 and RV tent sites, with nearby shower facilities. Four secluded spots at the end of Cobscook Point are accessible only by short trail. A couple of dozen sites are available on a first-come, first-served basis. A few sites have wooden Adirondack shelters. Reservations advised in season; call 207-287-3824 or 800-332-1501 (Maine only). Camping fee.

Nearby Sights

The picturesque fishing village of **Lubec,** located about 10 miles from Cobscook Bay, is the easternmost town in the United States. Follow the signs to **West Quoddy Head,** the easternmost point of land in the contiguous U.S., guarded by a candycane-striped lighthouse (now closed).

From Lubec, cross Franklin D. Roosevelt Memorial Bridge to Campobello Island and **Roosevelt Campobello International Park** (*506-752-2922. Mem. Day–early Oct.*), the New Brunswick, Canada, vacation home of President Franklin D. Roosevelt's family. Sitting amid a 2,800-acre memorial park, the large wooden

Cobscook Bay

cottage's 34 rooms are furnished much as they were when FDR spent his boyhood summers here in the early 1900s.

❏ *Cobscook Bay State Park, R.R. 1, Box 127, Dennysville, ME 04628*

Lily Bay

9 miles north of Greenville, along eastern shore of Moosehead Lake

● 925 acres ● 207-695-2700 ● May to mid-Oct., trails open year-round ● Day-use fee ● Largest lake in New England
● Fishing (license required), boating, wildlife watching

At the southern end of the undeveloped expanse known as the North Woods, the area around **Moosehead Lake** offers wilderness adventure coupled with nearby creature comforts. Within the confines of Lily Bay, a 1.6-mile one-way trail snakes along the lakeshore, a swimming beach, and boat docking facilities. But you'll likely spend most of your time outside the park.

One of the best ways to see the largest lake in New England—measuring 74,890 acres—is to take a **floatplane ride.** There are several flying services in Greenville *(Chamber of Commerce 207-695-2716)*, which can also arrange a stay at one of the lake's remote camps. For a more down-to-earth adventure, troll the lake in a motorboat for its trout or landlocked salmon. Boats are available for rent near the park or in Greenville. Also in town, you can book a lake tour on the **Katahdin** *(Waterfront. 207-695-2716. July-Aug. Tues.-Thurs. and Sat.-Sun., Sat. in June, Sept.–Columbus Day Sat.-Sun.; fare)*, a refurbished steamboat. As the lake's name suggests, many moose inhabit the area. For the best moose watching, drive slowly on the back roads, especially along boggy areas.

Rising sharply from the lake's floor, **Mount Kineo**'s 800-foot cliff towers over the clear water. Technically a peninsula, Kineo is accessible to visitors only by water; rent a canoe or catch a water taxi *(Old Mill Campground 207-534-7333. Fare)* from Rockwood on the lake's western shore for the 1-mile journey. Steep paths lead to a lookout tower, and a shore path rings the rocky formation.

Camping

Lily Bay has 90 primitive tent and RV sites. Reservations advised in season; call 207-287-3824 or 800-332-1501 (Maine only). Camping fee.

❑ *Lily Bay State Park, HC 76 Box 425, Greenville, Maine 04441*

Grafton Notch

8 miles north of Newry on Maine 26

● 3,192 acres ● 207-824-2912 ● Mid-May to mid-Oct., trails open year-round ● Day-use fee ● No camping
● Waterfalls ● Hiking

The Bear River carved this narrow passageway through the mountains of far western Maine. In late spring, with the help of melting snow, the river rages through the gorge, forming several waterfalls only a short walk from the road. The largest cascade is **Screw Auger Falls,** at the park's southern end. Over the years, the falling water has gouged rounded potholes in the boulders that stand in the river's path. A couple of miles north, a .25-mile trail leads to **Moose Cave,** where water flowing under huge slabs of granite gurgles eerily.

Elsewhere in the park, many trails including the Appalachian Trail scale the peaks surrounding the notch. Try the 2-mile Eyebrow Loop Trail, which climbs to Eyebrow Precipice for spectacular views. A strenuous day hike ascends Old Speck Mountain, offering views of the Mahoosuc Range and White Mountains. ❏ *Grafton Notch State Park., HCR 61 Box 330, Newry, Maine 04261*

Screw Auger Falls

19

Rangeley Lake

Southern shore of Rangeley Lake between Maine 4 and Maine 17, on South Shore Rd.

● 748 acres ● 207-864-3858 ● Mid-May through Sept., trails open year-round ● Day-use fee ● Boating, swimming, fishing (license required)

Nestled in the heart of western Maine's mountains, this lakeside park is popular with fishermen for its trout and landlocked salmon. Listen carefully at night and you'll hear the haunting call of loons. At dusk, drive slowly on the roads along the lake and you're apt to see a moose out for a stroll.

Whether from shore or aboard a boat on the lake, you'll enjoy nice views of the surrounding mountains. Boat tours and rentals are available in the town of Rangeley (*Chamber of Commerce 207-864-5364*), on the lake's northern shore. Trails lead up nearby **Bald** and **Saddleback Mountains,** both offering excellent views of the whole area. In winter, the **Saddleback ski area** (*207-864-5671*) draws thousands of visitors to the region.
Camping
The park has 50 tent sites, with showers. Reservations advised in season; call 207-287-3824 or 800-332-1501 (Maine only). Camping fee.
❏ *Rangeley Lake State Park, HC 32 Box 5000, Rangeley, ME 04970*

Franconia Notch

I-93 between Lincoln and Franconia

● 6,440 acres ● 603-823-5563 ● Year-round ● Old Man of the Mountain ● Waterfalls ● Aerial tramway ● Hiking, biking, skiing, snowmobiling, fishing (license required)

In a narrow valley in the White Mountains, Franconia Notch was formed by glaciers thousands of years ago. The slow-moving snow and ice also sculptured the craggy granite face known as the Old Man of the Mountain, the state symbol and centerpiece of the park. Immortalized by Nathaniel Hawthorne in a 1850 tale, the stone face began drawing visitors to the park in the late 19th century. Stagecoaches and the railroad brought people from all over the East Coast to stay at the luxurious Profile House.

20

Sentinel Pine Bridge

When the inn burned down in 1923, efforts to rebuild failed, and timber on the 6,000-acre parcel owned by the hotel was put up for sale. The Society for the Protection of New Hampshire Forests began a nationwide campaign to save Franconia Notch. The group raised 200,000 dollars, which was matched by the state legislature and, in 1928, the notch became a state park and forest reservation. Now a scenic parkway (I-93) edged with hiking trails and other natural attractions runs through the long, skinny park, showcasing the timbered notch to perfection.

The park is best seen in the fall, when the brightly colored trees offset the notch's gray granite walls. Beware, however, of hordes of leaf peepers and their accompanying tour buses. Plan to start your day early to stay ahead of the crowd.

What to See and Do

Begin at the parkway's southern end at **The Flume Gorge** (*Mid-May–Oct.; adm. fee*). During an 1808 fishing trip, 93-year-old Aunt Jess Guernsey discovered this narrow, rocky canyon, threaded by rushing Flume Brook. Stop first at the large **Visitor Center,** where a video presentation, photographs, and other memorabilia recount the history of the notch.

Then ride the shuttle bus or walk along the well-groomed trail to Boulder Cabin, where a scenic hike into the The Flume Gorge begins. Stroll along the boardwalks that cling to 90-foot granite walls, then climb numerous steps out of the chasm. Farther along, the trail wends downhill through the woods, then crosses the Pemigewasset River in Sentinel Pine Bridge, built in 1939 from a huge pine tree that was felled by a hurricane from a nearby cliff. The covered bridge overlooks a large stone pool created by glaciers at the end of the Ice Age. Edged with numerous rain shelters, the trail circles back to the Visitor Center.

The next stop on the northbound park road is **The Basin.** A short, paved trail leads to a large, rounded rock basin carved by the Pemigewasset River. Here, naturalist and writer Henry David Thoreau watched the gently cascading water and proclaimed, "This pothole is perhaps the most remarkable curiosity of its kind in New England."

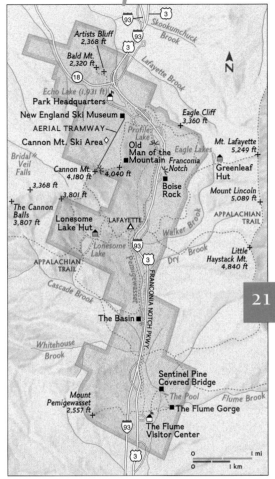

Cannon Mountain aerial tram

Giving the Old Man a Face Lift

Imagine you're made of several tons of granite and your chin begins to sag. A little epoxy and the deft touch of David Nielsen and you'll look forever old. Recently taking over for his father, Nielsen is responsible for keeping up the Old Man of the Mountain's stony profile. Each year, he and his son—rappelling down the face from the summit—cover cracks, remove leaves and other debris, and paint the turnbuckles, which prevent pieces of the craggy face from falling to the valley floor.

Among several hiking trails that explore nearby **Lonesome Lake** and the surrounding mountains is a popular 6-mile loop that follows the Cascade and Cascade Brook Trails to the tree-fringed lake. From here, head downhill on the Lonesome Lake Trail to Lafayette Campground and then along the Pemi Trail back to The Basin. The loop can also be done from the campground.

The **Old Man of the Mountain,** the profile-shaped rock formation that clings to the hillside more than 1,000 feet above the valley floor, is the crown jewel of the park. The profile is visible from an overlook along the parkway and from **Profile Lake,** a popular spot for summer visitors during the 19th century. Today, the lake is well-known for its brook trout and is open to fly-fishing only. Overlooking the lake, a **museum** details the history of the Old Man of the Mountain.

At the park's north end lies the **Cannon Mountain ski area** (603-823-5563). In summer and winter, an **aerial tram** (Fare) whisks visitors up the mountain, where trails lead to a summit observation tower. There are over 25 miles of trails for skiers and snowboarders. The area, site of North America's first aerial tramway, began operation in 1938. Nestled at the mountain's base, the **New England Ski Museum** (603-823-7177. Mem. Day–Columbus Day, Dec.-March) displays skis dating from the 1890s, the ski parka of Minnie Dole (founder of the National Ski Patrol), and more.

Across from the ski area, a steep, rocky trail leads atop **Bald Mountain,** a spot to watch the sun set over the White Mountains. The loop trail winds to **Artists Bluff,** which overlooks Echo Lake before heading back to the parking lot.

Extending the length of the park, a paved bike trail runs 9 miles between The Flume Gorge and Cannon Mountain. Many bikers take their time, visiting sights on the northbound, slightly uphill journey, then whiz back southward for a full day's ride. Snowmobilers and cross-country skiers use the trail in winter.

If you have a boat or canoe, enjoy the placid waters of **Profile** or **Echo Lake.** Both lakes also offer fishing, and Echo Lake has a small swimming area.

Camping

The park has 97 tent sites (mid-May–early Oct.), with shower facilities (fee). Primitive camping, with no water or facilities, available in winter. No pets. Reservations advised in season; call 603-271-3628. Camping fee. Nearby Echo Lake RV Park has 7 RV sites, open year-round. Reservations advised; call 603-823-5563. Camping fee.

❑ *Franconia Notch State Park, Rte. 3, Franconia, NH 03580*

Mount Washington

Via Mount Washington Auto Road, on N.H. 16 in Gorham; or Mount Washington Cog Railway, off US 302 near Bretton Woods

● 59 acres ● 603-466-3347 ● Mid-May to mid-Oct. ● No camping ● Highest mountain in New England ● Weather observatory ● Historic hotel

Ammnonoosuc River and Mount Washington

23

The 6,288-foot summit of Mount Washington is lashed with weather reputed to be the worst in the world. In 1934 meteorologists recorded on its summit the highest wind velocity ever measured on earth—231 mph. Winds in excess of hurricane force (75 mph) sweep across the mountain more than

100 days per year. So why venture to the top? Simple, the views. On a clear day (less than 180 days a year), you can see more than 90 miles to Vermont, Massachusetts, Maine, Quebec, and the Atlantic Ocean.

What to See and Do

Getting to the top of New England's highest mountain is half the fun. Whatever route you choose, remember that the weather can change quickly and it is always cooler on top of the mountain than at its base, so bring warm clothing.

You can drive up the 8-mile **Mount Washington Auto Road** *(Fee)*, which opened in 1861 as a carriage road. Beginning on N.H. 16 in Gorham, putter up the steep, winding road to the summit in your own car, or catch a ride with one of the many vans *(fee)* that provide guided tours. For a more interesting experience, take the **Mount Washington Cog Railway** *(603-278-5404 or 800-922-8825. Sat.-Sun. in May, daily Mem. Day–Oct.; fare)*. The 3-mile railway, one of the steepest in the world, made its first run up the mountain in 1869. A unique rack-and-pinion system together with coal-fired steam engines push wood-and-aluminium railway cars up the mountain. The railway base station is located off US 302, near Bretton Woods.

At the mountain summit, visit the Mount Washington Observatory's **museum** *(603-356-8345. Mid-May–mid-Oct.; adm. fee)*, which features exhibits about the mountain's natural and human history. At the **observatory** *(Tours for observatory members only)*, staff monitor the harsh weather.

The mountain's first recorded climb was made in 1642 by Darby Field, from Exeter, New Hampshire. Today, several hiking trails including the **Appalachian Trail** lead up the steep slopes. Only experienced hikers should attempt an ascent.

By the mid-1800s, tourism was a flourishing industry on the mountaintop, where two hotels competed to accommodate visitors, and a daily newspaper was published. A fire in 1908 virtually destroyed the "City Among the Clouds," sparing only the stone **Tip-Top House** *(Now defunct, but open for tours)*, believed to be the world's oldest mountaintop hostelry. The hotel was built in 1853 using only native stones and wood.

Nearby Sights

The famed Bretton Woods area is located at the mountain's western base, on US 302. The picturesque **Mount Washington Hotel** *(603-278-1000 or 800-258-0330. Guided tours)* opened in 1902 as a European-style spa, attracting trainloads of wealthy visitors during its heyday. In 1944 representatives from 44 countries met here to sign the Bretton Woods Accord, a post-World War trade and financial assistance plan that established the World Bank and International Monetary Fund. The hotel's elegant rooms are still open to guests.

❑ *MOUNT WASHINGTON STATE PARK, P.O. BOX D, GORHAM, NH 03581*

Why is the Weather So Bad?

Imagine water rushing over a small boulder in a raging stream. That is the same effect the wind has on Mount Washington. Not only is the mountain the tallest mass of rock around, it also happens to lie in the path of the three major storm tracks that affect the Northeast. This turbulent air is pushed over the lofty peak, gaining speed as it rises from the valley below, just as a river gains velocity as it passes over a rapid.

24

Robert Frost Farm

2 miles south of the Derry Circle on N.H. 28

● 64 acres ● 603-271-3556 ● Late June to Columbus Day Thurs. to Mon., weekends spring and fall ● User fee ● No camping ● National Historic Landmark ● Nature-poetry trail

Overlooking Franconia Notch at Derry Farm, poet Robert Frost tried his hand at farming in the early 1900s. Inspired by the plants, animals, and landscapes that surrounded him, his writing flourished— later bringing him critical acclaim and four Pulitzer prizes.

25

Derry Farm in autumn

In a 1952 letter, Frost commented, "I might say the core of all my writing was probably the five free years I had there on the farm down the road from Derry Village . . . The only thing we had plenty of was time and seclusion."

The family sold the farm in 1911. It passed through many hands before becoming a garage and auto junkyard in the 1940s. The state acquired the land in 1964 and began restoring the white clapboard New England farmhouse and farmland to its turn-of-the-century condition. The house was refurbished with the guidance of Frost's eldest daughter, Lesley Frost Ballantine, who selected furnishings representative of ones the family had owned.

Retrace Frost's steps on the farm's footpaths, which he shoveled himself in winter, by taking a stroll along the **Hyla Brook poetry and nature trail.** You will pass many of the farm's man-made and natural features that appear in Frost's poems. "Mending Wall," for example, lyrically recalls how each spring Frost and his neighbor Napolean Guay replaced the stones that had fallen off the rock wall separating their properties. In the poem "Hyla Brook," Frost describes the seasonal creek he named for its peepers, tiny tree frogs of the genus *Hyla*.

❏ *Robert Frost Farm State Historic Site, P.O. Box 1075, Derry, New Hampshire 03038*

Odiorne Point

3 miles south of Portsmouth, on US 1A in Rye

● 330 acres ● 603-436-7406 ● Year-round ● Adm. fee
daily May to late Oct. and weekends year-round ● No
camping ● Seacoast Science Center ● Remnants of
Army fort ● Walking and biking trails

Tidal flats at Odiorne Bay

In 1623 British settlers landed on this windy point of
land and built a small fishing and trading community—the
first European settlement in New Hampshire. They dubbed
it Pannaway Plantation. John Odiorne and his family joined
the settlement in 1660, which by that time had become a
thriving farm center for the nearby town of Portsmouth.
Two hundred years later, the point had grown into a popular seaside retreat. Among the posh hotels and summer cottages that cropped up along the shore was a 1920 residence
built by the Sugden family, which now houses the park's
Seacoast Science Center.

At the outbreak of World War II, the U.S. Army requisi-
tioned the strip of land to protect the nearby Portsmouth Naval
Shipyard. The point was turned into Fort Dearborn, the Sug-
dens' stone farmhouse became officers' quarters, and many of
the area's seaside estates were demolished. After the war, a legal
technicality prevented the families from returning to their land.

In the late 1950s, the Army declared the land surplus property and in 1961 sold it to the state of New Hampshire, whereby it became a state park. Remnants of the fort, including bunkers and machine gun emplacements, can be found in the hills overlooking the Atlantic Ocean.

What to See and Do

Kids of all ages will enjoy learning about marine life at the **Seacoast Science Center** (*603-436-8043. Adm. fee*), located at the park's south end and managed by the Audubon Society. Daily programs teach children and their parents about lobsters and other sea dwellers, as well as about the plants and animals that live in the marshes and woodlands of Odiorne Point—the largest undeveloped seashore on New Hampshire's 18-mile coastline. Kids can peer into a thousand-gallon tank swarming with sea creatures, as well as feel and study a plethora of specimens in a touch-tank.

The science center is built around the Sugden House, where the family lived until 1942. Displays describe the point's history from the early settlers to its use as a World War II fort to its current educational mission. Large picture windows overlook the Gulf of Maine and Portsmouth Harbor.

After learning about the point's landscapes and habitats in the science center, go out and see them firsthand. Walk along the rocky shore and examine tide pools for sea urchins, crabs, and other animals temporarily trapped in the shallow waters by the receding tide. In the center of the park, a man-made freshwater pond offers a good place for birdwatching, and along the ocean, the rocky shore gives way to a pebble beach and a freshwater marsh. A saltwater marsh lies at the park's northern border.

A paved hike-and-bike trail runs the length of the park, while several dirt trails pass by batteries, bunkers, and other remnants of Fort Dearborn. You can also see the remains of formal gardens dating from the point's heyday as a resort community.

At the park's northern entrance, a short trail leads to **Frost Point.** One of the area's early settlers, George Frost, owned a house on this spit of land that juts into the sea and offers commanding views of the length of the park.

❏ *ODIORNE POINT STATE PARK, P.O. BOX 606, RYE BEACH, NEW HAMPSHIRE 03871*

Fruitful Shores

Shortly after New Hampshire's first European settlers landed at Odiorne Point, another group of travelers came ashore in 1630 a few miles north along the Piscataqua River. Since the riverbanks were covered with strawberry plants, they called their fledgling settlement Strawbery Banke. With a ready supply of timber, the town—renamed Portsmouth in 1653—soon became known for shipbuilding. Today, **Strawbery Banke Museum** (*Marcy St. 603-433-1100. Late April–early Nov. Adm. fee*) comprises many restored buildings from the town's long history.

27

Lobsterman

Island Complex

7 miles west of St. Albans off Vt. 36, via ferry from Kamp Kill Kare

● 563 acres ● 802-524-6353 (Burton Island) ● Mid-May to Labor Day ● Day-use fee ● No cars ● Remote islands ● Hiking and nature trails ● Fishing (license required)

A string of bucolic islands in Lake Champlain, Vermont's Island Complex comprises three unusual state parks. Accessible only by state-run ferry or private boat, these three isles provide different levels of escape for day and overnight visitors.

Burton is the string's largest and most developed island, where most visitors head. If you're searching for a more remote experience, try Knight Island, dotted with small ponds and primitive camping sites, or undeveloped Woods Island—reachable only via private boat.

All three islands were farmed extensively from the early 1800s to the early 1960s, and today contain trails that pass by remnants of fences, abandoned corn and bean fields, and other evidence of cultivation.

What to See and Do

Much of what you do on these islands depends on your

Peaceful Knight Island, Lake Champlain

mode of transportation and how long you stay. If you plan to camp, 253-acre **Burton Island,** which has potable water, hot showers, and a small store that sells basic supplies, is a good base of operations. To get here, take the state-run ferry (*contact park for information; fare*) from Kamp Kill Kare, a former boys camp on the Lake Champlain shore. Or slide your own boat up to one of the marina's 100 boat slips or 15 moorings—often full during peak summer weekends. You can rent a canoe or rowboat at the marina, the heart of island activity, and explore the island's wooded, rocky coves.

Remember that once you get to Burton Island, you'll travel by foot, so pack lightly. Park staff will cart gear to campsites for a small fee.

Away from the marina's hubbub, the island is mostly quiet and undeveloped. A short distance away, a small wooden building houses the island's **Nature Center,** where a resident naturalist conducts programs. In the 1800s, turkeys, sheep, and milk cows roamed the pastoral landscape. Farmwork was done by horses or tenant farmers, many of whom were Abenaki Indians. You can see rusted implements and other artifacts from the farming days in the Nature Center. A short **nature trail** that begins nearby passes through abandoned fields, offering good views of the town of St. Albans Bay, a thriving shipping community in the late 18th century.

Two short walking trails leave from the camping area. The 0.8-mile **North Shore Trail** parallels the island's rocky shoreline. A brochure recounts the island's geological history and describes the plants and animals that now inhabit it. Take the Eagle Bay Trail back to the campground.

The 185-acre **Knight Island** was also heavily farmed before being turned into a private primitive campground in the 1980s. All but 10 acres on the island's southern tip was acquired by the state in 1990. Arrangements must be made on Burton Island for a ferry ride (*fare*) to and from Knight Island, or you can take a private boat. Strong paddlers can reach the island by canoe or sea kayak from North Hero and Knight Point State Parks, both located west of the island and accessible by car on US 2; overnight parking is permitted at these parks.

A **hiking trail** rings Knight Island, passing small ponds and rocky outcroppings with views of Lake Champlain and northwestern Vermont.

Further Adventures

To truly get away from the crowds, head to 125-acre **Woods Island,** a short motorboat ride or an invigorating paddle by canoe or kayak from Burton Island. Many developers had grand visions for this small island, which was also

---

Fishing For Supper

While staying on one of Vermont's remote islands, why not enjoy a supper of fresh fish cooked over an open fire? Lake Champlain offers some of the best fishing and the greatest variety of freshwater fish in the Northeast. A two-decades-old restoration program has successfully reintroduced landlocked salmon to the lake, and the chilly waters are stocked annually with trout and salmon.

a tenant's farm in the 1800s. An abandoned, uncompleted airstrip runs down the island's center, a remnant of a developer's dream to build a secluded business retreat.

Today, only foundations of a farmhouse and a few weatherworn pieces of farm equipment recall past development. One hiking trail follows the shoreline around the entire island, while another cuts across the island and the abandoned airstrip.

Camping

Burton Island has 17 tent sites and 26 wooden lean-tos, with shower facilities. Reservations advised on weekends from July to mid-August.

Knight Island has 7 tent sites, with no potable water or facilities. A camping permit must be obtained from Burton Island. Call ahead to reserve space on state ferry.

Woods Island has 5 primitive tent sites, with no potable water or facilities. A camping permit must be obtained from Burton Island.

Campsite reservations for all islands may be obtained by calling the Northwest Region supervisor at 802-879-5674 from January and mid-May. From mid-May to Labor Day, call Burton Island directly. Camping fee.

❑ *Burton Island State Park, P.O. Box 123, St. Albans Bay, VT 05481*

Smugglers Notch

Between Stowe and Jeffersonville on Vt. 108

● **4,000 acres** ● **802-253-4014** ● **Mid-May to Columbus Day**
● **Mountain pass** ● **Rock formations** ● **Hiking**

A giant slice between Mount Mansfield and Sterling Peak, Smugglers Notch runs north to south between the towns of Jeffersonville and Stowe. Some geologists believe that a glacial-melt river carved the notch about 12,000 years ago. In more recent years, the notch became a smugglers route. An 1807 embargo forbidding trade with Great Britain and Canada prompted northern Vermonters to sneak cattle and other goods through the narrow passageway to their neighbors in Quebec. Later, fugitive slaves are said to have used the notch as an escape route to Canada. During Prohibition, locals brought in whiskey from Canada over a makeshift road that had been built through the gap in 1922.

Comprising a campground and picnic area, the state park is part of the surrounding Smugglers Notch Natural Resource Area, a wild landscape of rumpled mountains and thick hardwood forest. Narrow, two-lane Vt. 108 (*closed winter*) winds through the gap, visiting several interesting attractions along the way.

What to See and Do

From the south, begin your journey in the quaint town of **Stowe,** Vermont's oldest ski resort. A short distance away, on Vt. 108, you come to the **Mount Mansfield Toll Road** *(802-253-3000. Spring–first snowfall; toll),* a steep auto road that winds up to

View through Smugglers Notch

the southern summit, or "nose," of Vermont's highest mountain. There, spectacular views of much of the Green Mountain State, neighboring New York, New Hampshire, and Quebec await you. You can also ride the **Stowe Mountain Resort Gondola** *(802-253-3000. Mid-June–Oct. and ski season; fare)* to the 4,393-foot summit and its mountaintop eatery.

Heading north again on Vt. 108, you'll pass the **State Ski Dormitory** *(802-253-4010. Mid-Sept.–early May),* which has been offering bunks and hearty meals to skiers since 1933.

Just south of the park information booth, stop at **Big Spring,** the site of a 1920s restaurant where customers were invited to catch a trout in the pool and have it fried up for dinner. Now returned to its natural state, the spring offers cool, fresh drinking water. From here, the road enters the shadows of Smugglers Notch, where 1,000-foot cliffs block out the sun. The rocky cliffs are the ideal home for the peregrine falcons that have recently returned to Vermont after a 30-year absence.

A short distance above the information booth, you will see the **Old Smugglers Face,** a miniature version of New Hampshire's Old Man of the Mountain. Other odd rock for-

Cross-country skier

The Nose Knows

The summit of Mount Mansfield is often referred to as the nose. This is because the mountain's profile is said to resemble the outline of a reclining man's face. Following the mountain ridge, you will also see the forehead, chin, and Adam's apple.

32

mations such as the Elephant's Head and the Hunter and His Dog can also be found in the notch. But don't just look up in this mountain passage; some of the park's more interesting features may be under your feet. Because of the notch's often Arcticlike conditions, many rare alpine species of plants thrive here, including the butterwort, a tiny yellow, carnivorous flower.

Several hiking trails ascend from the notch to the surrounding peaks. One of the most popular routes climbs along a 1.25-mile section of the **Long Trail** to the **Lake of the Clouds,** on the side of Mount Mansfield.

From the notch, Vt. 108 descends out of the mountains and passes the **Smuggler's Notch Resort** *(800-451-8752),* a popular ski area, before reaching the small town of Jeffersonville.

Camping

A campground with 24 tent or RV sites, 14 lean-tos, and showers is located 2 miles south of Smugglers Notch. Reservations advised in season; call 802-253-4014 (summer) or 802-479-4280 (winter). Camping fee.

Nearby Sights

While in the Stowe area, don't pass up the **Trapp Family Lodge** *(42 Trapp Hill Rd. 802-253-8511 or 800-826-7000).* The Austrian-style lodge and cross-country ski center was started by Maria von Trapp, the former nun immortalized in *The Sound of Music.* Indulge yourself in the lodge's delicious Austrian pastries and traditional fare.

Another place to indulge, just 15 miles south of the park in Waterbury, is Vermont's ice-cream mecca—**Ben & Jerry's** *(802-244-8687. Fee for tour).* Take a tour of the brightly colored factory, then sample the rich, creamy product.

❑ *SMUGGLERS NOTCH STATE PARK, 7248 MOUNTAIN RD., STOWE, VT 05672*

Button Bay

6 miles northwest of Vergennes, on Lake Champlain

● 253 acres ● 802-475-2377 ● Mid-May to Columbus Day ● Day-use fee ● Fossils ● Nature Center ● Swimming pool, boating, fishing (license required)

Many geological events have occurred in the very small area where Button Bay currently exists. Nearly 500 million years ago, Button Bay was part of a continental shelf submerged in a warm shallow sea full of life. The park's limestones and limey shales preserve many fossils dating from that time; its fossilized coral is among the world's oldest. About 12,000 years ago, the region was covered by a chilly ocean called the Champlain Sea—predecessor of Lake Champlain. A clam species living today in Button Bay has been traced back to a species that existed here in those times.

To explore the geology, follow the nature trail to **Button Point,** where you can see large, fossilized sea snails, as well as the park's namesake buttonlike concretions, formed when calcium mixed with clay in the Champlain Sea. The nearby **Nature Center** details the bay's geologic history. The park also offers boat rentals and a swimming pool.

Camping

The park has 59 tent or RV sites and 13 lean-tos, with shower facilities. Reservations advised in season; call 802-475-2377 (summer) or 802-483-2001 (winter). Camping fee.

❑ *Button Bay S.P., Rd. 3, Box 4075, Vergennes, Vermont 05491*

Mount Philo

2 miles north of North Ferrisburg, off US 7

● **168 acres** ● **802-425-2390** ● **Mid-May to Columbus Day**
● **Day-use fee** ● **Mountain and lake views** ● **Hiking**

Like nearby Button Bay, the beehive-shaped Mount Philo—established as Vermont's first state park in 1924—was created by the former Champlain Sea. Several thousand years ago, chilly waters surrounded the mountain, creating an island; if you look closely, you'll see evidence of a wave-cut terrace halfway up the mountain slope.

33

A narrow, one-way loop road winds up the 968-foot mountain to a view that takes in the Adirondacks across

Champlain Valley and Lake Champlain, from Mount Philo

Lake Champlain in New York. Hiking trails also ascend the mountain. You can swim and boat on Lake Champlain at nearby **Button Bay State Park.**

Camping

A summit campground has 5 tent sites; plus there are 7 tent and RV sites and 3 lean-to sites on the mountain's northern edge. Reservations advised in season; call 802-425-2390 (summer) or 802-483-2001 (winter). Camping fee.

❑ *Mount Philo S.P., Rd. 1, Box 1049, North Ferrisburg, VT 05473*

Walden Pond

On Mass. 126, in Concord

- 333 acres ● 508-369-3254 ● Year-round ● No camping
- National Historic Landmark ● Walking trails ● Boating, fishing (license required)

Fishing in Walden Pond

In 1845 Henry David Thoreau began his two-year experiment in simple living in the woods beside Walden Pond. He spent $28.12—half on supplies—and built a tidy, one-room wooden cabin on land loaned to him by Ralph Waldo Emerson, a friend from his days at Harvard College. Thoreau spent his time in the Walden Woods reading, studying nature, and gardening. Drawing on experiences during an 1839 trip with his late brother, he drafted his first book, *A Week on the Concord and Merrimack Rivers*. He also made the first accurate survey of the glacially formed pond, where he sometimes sat in a boat playing the flute. Far from being a hermit, Thoreau often entertained visitors at his rustic home and walked the short distance to Concord.

In September 1847, Thoreau completed his experiment and returned to Concord, where he continued to study and write, as well as to lecture audiences throughout New England. *Walden,* the book that describes his life at the pond, was published in 1854. Thoreau died of tuberculosis in 1862 at the age of 44.

What to See and Do

"I went to the woods because I wished to live deliberately, to front only the essential facts of life, and see if I could not learn what it had to teach, and not, when I came to die, discover that I had not lived," Thoreau wrote in *Walden*. While he came to the remote pond to discover life, thousands of visitors now make the short trek from Boston to capture a bit of the aura of one of America's first conservationists. Whether you are a Thoreau fan or not, it's hard not to be caught up in the contemplative nature of the park—but be warned that you won't be contemplating alone. For a more peaceful visit, come in the late fall, winter, or early spring, or early in the morning. At these times, you can sit on a rock with the crystal-clear water lapping at your feet as Thoreau must have done more than 150 years ago. The pond is a popular spot with families, who enjoy shoreside picnic dinners while watching the sun set over the tall, straight pine trees.

Begin your tour of the park with a walk around the pond. On the far side, follow the signs to the site of Thoreau's long-vanished cabin. A half century ago, an amateur archaeologist located the remnants of the fireplace that had provided the writer with both heat and companionship. A fieldstone marker and plaque mark the spot of one of the most visited former homesites in America.

A re-creation of Thoreau's tiny cabin is located near the parking lot across Mass. 126 from the pond. Peer through the windows to see what a cozy little home 28 dollars would buy in 1845. Nearby, a small store sells books and trinkets that commemorate the writer.

For a different perspective, paddle around the pond (*no rentals*), or try your hand at fishing. In Thoreau's day the pond didn't hold many fish, but now it's stocked with trout.

In winter, the many trails that wind through woods and meadows are popular with cross-country skiers, and ice skaters glide atop the frozen pond.

❑ *WALDEN POND STATE RESERVATION, RTE. 126, CONCORD, MA 01742*

> ### Writers' Resting Place
>
> A short distance from Walden Pond, in the town of Concord, many of America's best-known authors have come to rest at the **Sleepy Hollow Cemetery** *(Mass. 62.)*. In addition to Henry David Thoreau and his family, Ralph Waldo Emerson, Louisa May Alcott, and Nathaniel Hawthorne are buried in the graveyard's Author's Ridge.

35

Re-creation of Thoreau's cabin, Walden Pond

Mount Greylock

Accessible via Mass. 2 in North Adams or US 7 in Lanesborough

● 12,500 acres ● 413-499-4262 ● Year-round, but limited road access Nov. to early May ● Highest point in Massachusetts ● War Memorial ● Historic lodge ● Hiking, skiing

36

Potter Mountain from Mount Greylock

"It was such a country as we might see in dreams, with all the delight of paradise," Henry David Thoreau proclaimed upon reaching Mount Greylock's summit in 1844. The 3,491-foot mountain, the highest in Massachusetts, also inspired awe in Ralph Waldo Emerson and Herman Melville. Some believe the snow-capped, rounded mountain was the inspiration for Melville's famed white whale in *Moby-Dick*.

Later in the 19th century, concern over heavy logging on the mountain prompted a group of local residents to purchase land on the summit for recreational purposes. When that venture failed, Mount Greylock was turned over to the Commonwealth and became Massachusetts' first state park in 1898. The park is planning a centennial celebration on June 20, 1998.

What to See and Do

Today's visitors have a much easier time reaching the summit of Mount Greylock than did Thoreau and his counterparts.

In 1906 an auto road that ascended the mountain from the south was completed. Most visitors still begin their trip at the park's southern entrance, where a modern **Visitor Center** (*Mid-May–mid-Oct.*) offers maps, snacks, and nature programs.

From the Visitor Center, the road heads up the mountain, passing **Rounds Rock,** where a short trail leads through a field of blueberries to an overlook with views of Connecticut and New York. The road continues up through thick forest to the summit, crowned by an enormous granite pillar. The **War Memorial,** originally designed as a lighthouse for the Charles River, was erected atop the mountain in 1932 to commemorate the Massachusetts men and women who served in World War I. A dozen search lights, together forming the most powerful beacon in Massachusetts, honor fallen heroes. The "perpetual light" was extinguished during World War II so as not to attract enemy aircraft. The lights still shine today except during spring and fall bird migrations. An observation deck on the tower (*mid-May–mid-Oct*) offers 360-degree views of five states. Some people think the mountain's name comes from the fact that it's often locked in dark grey clouds.

The Civilian Conservation Corps in 1935 built the rustic stone **Bascom Lodge** on the summit. With its stone fireplaces, hand-cut oak beams, and large porch, the lodge provides a welcome summer retreat for diners and overnight guests. Nature walks are also available.

From the summit, the auto road snakes down the mountain's steeper north face, passing **The Hopper,** a large basin that resembles a grain hopper, and into the town of North Adams.

Further Adventures

Mount Greylock has 50 miles of hiking and cross-country skiing trails of varying difficulty. Departing from the Visitor Center, the 2-mile **Brook and Berry Trail** cuts through an abandoned farm. Popular with hikers and skiers alike, the relatively flat 1.5-mile **CCC Dynamite Trail** skirts Saddleball Mountain, where dynamite boxes discarded by CCC workers in the 1930s can be seen along the way. The strenuous 3.7-mile **Bellows Pipe Trail** is the route Thoreau took to the summit in 1844.

Camping

Mount Greylock offers 35 primitive tent and RV sites (Mem. Day–mid-Oct.), with showers. Reservations advised in season; call 413-499-4262. Camping fee. Bascom Lodge (mid-May–mid-Oct.) accommodates 36 guests, and has a restaurant serving dinner only. For reservations phone 413-443-0011.

❑ *MOUNT GREYLOCK STATE RESERVATION, ROCKWELL RD., LANESBOROUGH, MASSACHUSETTS 01237*

Quick Descent

Mount Greylock was a downhill skiing mecca in the 1930s and '40s, when the Civilian Conservation Corps built a steep run on the mountain's east face. Skiers came from Boston and New York to tackle the bone-rattling Thunderbolt Trail. In 1948 Norwegian Per Klippgen made the 1.6-mile run in a record speed of 2 minutes and 9 seconds. Today, the trail is used mostly by hikers, but each year a few daring skiers schuss down the treacherous slope.

Wachusett Mountain

Between Princeton and Westminster, off Mass. 140

● 2,018 acres ● 508-464-2987 ● Year-round, but road closes mid-Oct. to Memorial Day ● No camping ● Scenic views ● Hiking, downhill skiing

Before white settlers arrived in the mid-1600s, the Nipmuc tribe lived "by the great hill," which in Algonquin, their native language, sounds like "wachusett." In 1675 King Philip's War broke out between European settlers and New England Indians, who used the mountain as a staging area for attack on the nearby town of Lancaster. Soon after the war ended, much of the Indian land, including Wachusett Mountain, became the property of the Massachusetts colony.

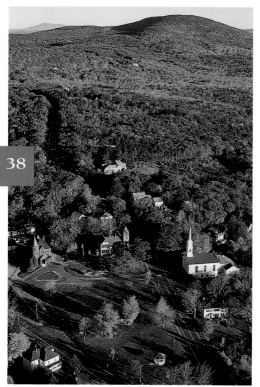

38

Princeton nestled at base of Wachusett Mountain

Throughout the 19th century, the mountain's sweeping views lured visitors to its summit, including Henry David Thoreau, who in 1843 walked here from Concord. Grand hotels crowned the summit by the turn of the century, when the state purchased the land for public use. Wachusett became Massachusetts' second state natural reservation in 1900.

Today, a paved road winds to the 2,006-foot mountaintop, which is much less developed than it was a century ago. From here, the city of Boston is sometimes visible nearly 50 miles to the east. Sixty miles to the west, the light atop Mount Greylock shines this far at night.

Nearly 20 miles of hiking trails crisscross the wooded mountain. Try the steep, 1-mile **Mountain House Trail,** which visits the remnants of one of the old summit hostelries. The gentle **Dickens Trail** connects the park with the adjacent Wachusett Meadows Wildlife Sanctuary.

On the mountain's northern slope, the **Wachusett Mountain Ski Area** (508-464-2300) has 18 trails, lit for night skiing.

❑ *Wachusett Mountain State Reservation, P.O. Box 248, Princeton, Massachusetts 01541*

Pilgrim Memorial

Off US 44, in Plymouth

- 9 acres ● 508-866-2580 ● Year-round
- No camping ● Plymouth Rock

Monument above Plymouth Rock

In 1620 English settlers known as the Pilgrims came ashore at Plymouth Harbor and established a small colony based on their quest for religious and political freedom. The large grey rock on which they're supposed to have stepped rests along the waterfront beneath a canopy designed in 1921 by McKim, Mead & White. The ***Mayflower II,*** a full-size reproduction of the ship that brought the settlers to America, is anchored nearby. "Sailors" and "passengers" in period costumes discuss their journey from England.

Plimoth Plantation (*Plimoth Plantation Hwy., S of Plymouth. 508-746-1622. April-Nov.; adm. fee*), a detailed recreation of the pilgrim settlement as it appeared in 1627, sits on a hill overlooking Plymouth. The stories of costumed residents will take you back to the beginning of American history. ❏ PILGRIM MEMORIAL STATE PARK, P.O. BOX 66, S. CARVER, MA 02366

39

Skinner

Off Mass. 47, in Hadley

- 390 acres ● 413-586-0350 ● Year-round, but road closes mid-Nov. to mid-April ● Adm. fee Mem. Day through Oct.
- No camping ● Historic mountain inn ● Scenic views

Spectacular views of the Connecticut River Valley have lured visitors to the top of **Mount Holyoke** since the 1800s. At the turn of the century, Joseph Allen Skinner built the Summit House, drawing crowds of diners and dancers to enjoy the views. When a powerful hurricane destroyed part of the hotel in 1938, Skinner donated the inn and 375 mountaintop acres to the state. Restored to its early 19th-century appearance, the defunct Victorian inn is open for tours. Visitors can drive to the 942-foot summit (*mid-April–mid-Nov.*), or hike up one of the trails.

Skinner is located within the nearly 3,000-acre **Holyoke Range State Park** (*413-586-0350*), which stretches the length of the mountain range and offers over 45 miles of hiking, cross-country skiing, and horseback riding trails. In April and September, you can watch migrating hawks as they ride the hot air thermals rising from the mountains. ❏ SKINNER STATE PARK, P.O. BOX 91, HADLEY, MASSACHUSETTS 01035

Fort Adams

3 miles south of downtown Newport on Ocean Dr.

● **105 acres** ● **401-847-2400** ● **Year-round** ● **No camping**
● **Historic fort** ● **Yachting museum** ● **Sailing center**

After the nation's capital was burned during the War of 1812, the military decided a fort was needed to protect the entrance to Narragansett Bay and Newport Harbor, one of

Aerial view of Fort Adams

40

the East Coast's most strategic ports. Construction on a fort named after the second president, John Adams, began in 1824 under the direction of Lt. Col. Joseph Totten, the foremost military architect of the day. The huge stone fortification, which was intended to garrison 2,400 men and hold nearly 500 cannons, took 33 years to build. By the time it was completed, the threat of an oceanborne attack had passed, so it was never used to defend the Rhode Island coast's thriving shipping ports.

What to See and Do

During the summer, you can tour the imposing structure, with its commanding view of the bay and the posh town of Newport. Notice the masonry of the gray stone walls—a mason traveled from Scotland just for this task. He later built other fine stone houses in the area.

Newport, long a playground of the rich and a mecca for yachtsmen, is well known for its excellent sailing. In the shadow of the fort, the **Museum of Yachting** *(401-847-1018. Mid-May–Oct.; adm. fee)* houses all kinds of restored yachts and memorabilia that celebrate the sport of sailing. Each year the museum hosts several regattas. The largest, held over Labor Day, is the **Classic Yacht Regatta,** which attracts more than 100 vintage yachts.

If you want to hit the water in your own boat, head over to the state park's sailing center. **Sail Newport** *(401-846-1983. Mem. Day–Columbus Day)*, a non-profit community agency, offers sailboat and windsurfing rentals and instruction. Another community group, **Shake-A-Leg** *(401-849-8898)* provides sailing instruction and boats specially equipped for the physically handicapped.

Located on a hill overlooking the park, the fort's former commanding officer's quarters became the summer home of President Dwight Eisenhower. The two-story clapboard house, built in 1873, is now available for conferences and weddings. Each August, the park's sprawling lawn plays host to the **Newport Jazz Festival** *(401-847-3700)*.

Nearby Sights

The fort is located along the heavily traveled **Ocean Drive,** site of some of the nation's most opulent estates. After leaving the park, turn right to continue along the drive. The childhood summer home of the late Jacqueline Kennedy Onassis, **Hammersmith Farm** *(401-846-0420. Mid-March–mid-Nov.; adm. fee)*, is located next to the park. The former working farm was the site of Jacqueline and John Kennedy's 1953 wedding reception and later became a summer White House. The drive then passes **Castle Hill Lighthouse** and **Brenton Point State Park** *(401-847-2400)*, a popular kite-flying spot with stunning views of the Atlantic Ocean. Follow the Ocean Drive loop back toward Newport to see the best known mansions, or "cottages," including **The Breakers** *(401-849-4470. April-Oct.; adm. fee)*, Cornelius Vanderbilt's lavish estate. The largest of the Newport cottages, it was built in 1895, a copy of an Italian palace. Contact the Preservation Society of Newport County *(401-847-1000)* about touring other mansions.

For free exterior views of the lavish houses, stroll along the 7-mile round-trip **Cliff Walk** *(From Newport Beach to Bailey's Beach)*, sandwiched between the estates' well-kept grounds and the pounding ocean surf.

❑ FORT ADAMS STATE PARK, HARRISON AVE., NEWPORT, RI 02840

Pineapple Port

Travel around Newport and you're sure to notice pineapple motifs and flags decorating a lot of buildings. The tropical fruit became the town's symbol of hospitality in the 18th century. Sea captains brought pineapples home from the West Indies, where they also obtained molasses and sugar to make rum. A captain would place a pineapple on his front steps to indicate that he had returned from his voyage and that his home was welcoming visitors.

41

Beavertail

4 miles south of Newport Bridge, on southern tip of Conanicut Island

● **153 acres** ● **401-884-2010** ● **Year-round** ● **No camping**
● **Lighthouse museum** ● **Scenic overlooks** ● **Biking, fishing (license required)**

Jutting into Narragansett Bay, this rocky point of land was notorious among early sailors. More than 30 vessels were destroyed or ran aground on what became known as Shipwreck Rock. To aid wary sailors, a lighthouse was built on the rocks in 1749. Even with the aid of the light, however, ships still met with disaster. If you look closely among the jumble of rocks on the east side of the lighthouse, you can find some of the granite blocks that were being carried aboard the H.F. *Payton* when the vessel sank in 1859. The blocks, decorated with flowery designs, sat beneath the shallow water until a 1938 hurricane hurled some of them up on shore. The fierce hurricane also exposed the foundations of the original lighthouse, burned by the British in 1779. The foundations can still be seen across the road from the present-day lighthouse, built in 1856 and now fully automated, which stands watch over the crashing waves.

A **lighthouse museum** *(Mid-June–Labor Day)* in the assistant keeper's house recounts the treacherous early days of Beavertail and other Rhode Island lighthouses. It also details the technological changes that have made the seas safer for shipping.

Harbor seal pup

In summer, park naturalists lead walks along the rocky shore. The paved loop road paralleling the shore is popular among cyclists and roller-bladers.

❏ BEAVERTAIL STATE PARK, C/O GODDARD MEMORIAL S.P., IVES RD., WARWICK, RI 02818

Colt

On Hope Street in Bristol, off R.I. 114

● **464 acres** ● **401-253-7482** ● **Year-round** ● **Entrance fee May to Labor Day** ● **No camping** ● **Historic farm** ● **Open-air chapel and ornamental gardens** ● **Biking and horseback riding trails**

Entering Colt Farm, you pass between bronze statues of Jersey bulls perched on marble pedestals—a fitting entrance to a farm that once was centered around cows. Samuel Colt, nephew of the Samuel Colt of revolver fame, began buying up old family farms in Bristol at the turn of the century to create an estate overlooking Narragansett Bay. A centerpiece of the farm was a heated stone barn with rubber and cork floors, built to house Colt's prized herd of Jersey cows. A grand champion bull, immortalized in the statue on the left side of the farm entrance, was one of Colt's favorites until it killed a farm worker and had to be shot. It is buried behind the stone barn, which still stands.

Colt believed his estate, including a lavish residence and two guest cottages, should be enjoyed by the public, even when he lived there. He had the words "Private Property, Samuel P. Colt, Public Welcome" inscribed in the marble gates.

Summer nature programs focus on the farm's history and its diverse plant and animal life. A 3-mile bike path circles the farm, passing by ornamental gardens and an open-air chapel popular with wedding parties.

❏ *Colt State Park, Hope St., Bristol, RI 02809*

Colt State Park along Narragansett Bay

43

Goddard Memorial

On Ives Road in Warwick, off US 1

● **489 acres** ● **401-884-2010** ● **Year-round** ● **No camping**
● **Hiking and horseback riding trails** ● **Beach** ● **Performing Arts Center** ● **Golfing, boating**

Once called the "finest example of private forestry in America," this former tree farm now resembles an overgrown city park. In 1874 Henry Russell began planting acorns on the barren sand dunes along Greenwich Bay. After Russell's death, his cousin Col. Robert Goddard acquired the land and continued to plant oaks. Goddard built a large mansion on the bayfront property. The lower floors of the estate housed the country's first insect zoo. Although The Oaks, as the house was known, was destroyed by fire in 1973, many outbuildings remain on the grounds. Goddard's family donated the estate to Rhode Island for a park in 1927.

The stable now houses a riding academy, and a bathhouse built early in this century is still in use on the swimming beach. An octagonal building made to hold a carousel was moved to the park in 1931 and serves as a performing arts center.

Today, 18 miles of horseback riding and hiking trails wind through thick woods; the information station has trail maps.

❏ *Goddard Memorial State Park, Ives Rd., Warwick, RI 02818*

Housatonic Meadows

1 mile north of Conn. 4 on US 7, near Sharon

● 451 acres ● 860-927-3238 ● Year-round ● Fly-fishing (license required) ● Hiking, canoeing

Located in the hilly northwest corner of the state, Housatonic Meadows State Park nestles in the curves of the Housatonic River. The park lies at the northern end of a stretch of US 7 designated as a scenic drive and is surrounded by the upland hills of Housatonic State Forest.

The Civilian Conservation Corps originally developed the park as a recreation site during the Great Depression. The centerpiece of the park, the Housatonic River, provides a host of aquatic activities. Meadows along the river's western bank contain two camping areas in an upper unit of the park and a recreation area in the lower unit. Along the riverbank, copses of evergreens and mixed hardwoods offer shade and solitude to the camper and angler, the swiftly running current invites canoeists, and the hills of the park and adjoining state forest beckon hikers.

What to See and Do

If you like to fly-fish, then Housatonic Meadows is your kind of park—head directly to the water. The **Housatonic River** runs shallow, cold, and swift, ideal for the trout lazing in the eddies of the boulder-strewn river bottom. A 2-mile stretch of the river, including the portion that runs through the park, is dedicated to catch-and-release fly-fishing. As the park awakens from winter and the spring runoff begins to recede, fly-fishermen wade in from the park's shore, gracefully casting their lines in long, looping figure-eights. Just as increasingly elongated arcs of fishing line begin to collapse, the angler's fly settles effortlessly on the water—an irresistible lure to trout scanning the passing flow for insects.

Fly-fishing enthusiasts are not the only ones attracted to the valley's waters. By turns easy flowing and then roiling rapids with names such as **Pencil Sharpener,** the Housatonic attracts canoeists and kayakers of varying abilities. The stretch from West Cornwall (5 miles north of park) to the park's southern unit, known as the "covered bridge section," offers Class II to III waves and ledges. Several commercial outfits provide trips along this section of the river. Contact the park for information.

From the western edge of US 7, the park's meadows give way to the forested rise defining the Housatonic Valley. Inviting those who wish to stretch their legs and keep their feet dry, the trailhead of the 2.5-mile **Pine Knob Loop Trail** lies approximately half a mile south of the campground driveway. After fording **Hatch Brook,** follow the

Covered Bridges

Three traditional wooden, single-lane covered bridges along US 7 evoke the Yankee character of the towns near Housatonic Meadows. North of the park, the bridge at West Cornwall has spanned the Housatonic River and been in continuous use since 1864. At Kent Falls State Park (860-927-3238), you cross a second bridge on the short walk to a 250-foot-high series of cascades. Just south of the upscale village of Kent, at Bulls Bridge, a third covered bridge crosses the Housatonic, complete with a riverside parking area and short hiking trails. During the spring runoff, the roaring water under the bridge challenges some of New England's best kayakers.

loop trail clockwise, climbing steeply uphill among pine trees. The thick underbrush and the running water of the brook seem to absorb all outside sounds as you wind to the trail's high point at **Pine Knob Summit** (1,120 feet).

Catch your breath at the rocky overlook and survey the expansive vista: The river lies at your feet, and beyond rises the stippled terrain of the Litchfield Hills—verdant in spring and summer and a palette of colors in autumn. Joining the Appalachian Trail for half a mile, you come to **Pine Knob** and another river valley before descending back toward the trailhead. After some initial scrambling down small crags, the descent eases and soon picks up the path of

Day lilies along the Housatonic

a creek, which has worn a flume several hundred feet long as it drops to river level at the meadows.

Camping

The park has 102 tent and RV sites (mid-April–Dec.), with showers. Reservations advised in season; write the park at the address below. Camping fee.

☐ HOUSATONIC MEADOWS S.P., P.O. BOX 77, CORNWALL BRIDGE, CT 06754

Talcott Mountain

1.5 miles east of Conn. 10 on Conn. 185, near Simsbury

● 557 acres ● 860-242-1158 ● Year-round ● No camping
● Heublein Tower ● Hiking

Farmland and forest from atop Talcott Mountain

In northern Connecticut, the Farmington River meanders southward, seeking the path of least resistance through the tobacco fields and affluent towns around Hartford. The riverside meadows of the eastern floodplain quickly yield to talus piles below the exposed, greenish-black, basaltic rock of Talcott Mountain, which rises dramatically to nearly 1,000 feet. A familiar landmark in the Farmington area interrupts the mountain's wooded ridgeline: Heublein Tower.

In 1914 food and beverage importer Gilbert Heublein constructed a summer home atop Talcott Mountain. Not 30 feet from the house's entrance, the exposed rock of the mountain drops away, providing a bird's-eye view of the valley. Built like a Bavarian alpine castle replete with a 165-foot tower, the house has unparalleled views of five states—an estimated 1,200 square miles. In 1965 the structure and

surrounding 557 acres became Talcott Mountain State Park.

What to See and Do

Park along the access road or across Conn. 185 at Penwood State Park and look for the well-marked trailhead of the **Tower Trail.** The 1.25-mile trail delivers you, like Heublein's guests earlier in the century, to the stone patio of Heublein Tower. Beginning with a steep, .25-mile climb, the trail levels off, closely following the mountain edge. Numerous outcrops overlook the river valley, a riot of reds and oranges in autumn. The stunted, gnarled evergreen trees along the ridge attest to the regular winds that buffet the rock face and carry the hang gliders you may spy soaring off to the west. Farther ahead, the trail gradually winds away from the cliffs, revealing an unusual pond in Talcott Mountain's upland forest. In sheltered, cooler pockets along the trail you will find stands of white birch among the chestnuts, oaks, ashes, and hemlocks.

A rock outcrop appears to your left as you approach the tower. Covered with lichen and home to Dutchman's-breeches, this damp crag allows close examination of the mountain's visible, but not easily accessible, basalt cliffs. **Heublein Tower** has tables and a covered bandstand where you can picnic or rest your legs. Then climb the stairs to the top of the tower and enjoy the panoramic view. On a clear day Hartford and Springfield, Massachusetts, are visible on the horizon, yet the noise and bustle remain far removed. From this perch watch for turkey vultures and hawks and, in winter, the occasional bald eagle. The tower and house *(call park for tour schedule),* restored to its 1925 condition, showcase the eclectic Victorian and art nouveau furnishings and decor of the Heublein family.

Further Adventures

If you have some time and do not mind a more rugged, less traveled path, look for the blue blazes that cross the Tower Trail just north of the tower. Part of a large trail network that stretches throughout the state, the **Metacomet Trail** runs along the park's eastern border and allows a better opportunity to see white-tailed deer, wild turkey, rabbits, and other wildlife than the more traveled Tower Trail. Listen for the loud, slow knocking of the shy pileated woodpecker. Large for a woodpecker, this variety is reclusive, so stop and look carefully if you hear one at work in the trees. The trail crosses Conn. 185 and continues into adjacent **Penwood State Park** *(800-242-1158).* In addition to the Metacomet Trail, five other hiking trails explore this 767-acre park, including a mile-long **nature trail** with a brochure *(available at park office)* describing the process of succession from meadow to forest.

❑ *Talcott Mountain State Park, c/o Penwood State Park, Gunn Mill Rd., Bloomfield, Connecticut 06002*

King Philip

The rocky face of Talcott Mountain contains a shelter used by another, earlier, resident. A hollow in the cliff face north of Heublein Tower is known as King Philip's Cave. Sachem of the Wampanoug Indians and the leader of the Algonquin uprising bearing his name, King Philip is rumored to have watched Simsbury burn on March 26, 1676, from this cave. King Philip's War (1675-1676) cost the colonies of southern New England dearly; approximately 2,500 colonists were killed, 13 settlements were entirely destroyed, and New England's expansion forestalled for nearly a century. The war also devastated the Algonquin and destroyed the national identities of Native Americans throughout the region.

47

Dinosaur

5 miles south of Hartford, in Rocky Hill

Dinosaur footprint

● 60 acres ● 860-529-8423 ● Year-round ● No camping ● North America's largest dinosaur track site ● Footprint casting ● Nature trails

In 1966 a bulldozer disturbed an ancient lake bed beneath the soil of the Connecticut Valley. Excavations revealed nearly 2,000 dinosaur tracks from the early Jurassic period, about 200 million years ago. Most of these imprints have been reburied to prevent erosion, but the Exhibit Center's geodesic dome protects about 500 tracks. Extremely popular with children—be prepared for screams of "dinosaurs!" punctuated with "oohs" and "ahhs"—the park's exhibits begin at the parking lot. A 92-foot-long time line in the sidewalk leading to the Exhibit Center recounts the geological and paleontological history of the planet. (*Homo sapiens* don't appear until the last few inches.)

At the **Exhibit Center** (*Closed Mon.; adm. fee*), visitors circle a portion of the building's interior along a wide boardwalk just above the exposed bedrock containing the dinosaur tracks. Displays and interactive exhibits along the way explain the geological events that formed the lake and the sequence of events required to preserve the tracks. Other displays discuss how to interpret dinosaur travel behavior from footprint patterns. A 20-foot-long reconstruction of a *Dilophosarous* and several other period creatures are posed in a diorama depicting the shore of the long dried-up lake.

To make casts of dinosaur tracks in the **outdoor casting area** (*May-Oct.*), bring ten pounds plaster of paris, a quarter-cup of vegetable oil, a mixing bucket, and cloth rags. Instructions are posted. **Nature trails** traverse swamps, woodlands, and meadows typical of the Connecticut Valley. Among the flora, look for ginkgo trees in fall: As if in fear of a lumbering, leaf-eating *Brontosaurus*, these trees drop all their leaves in a single day.
❑ *Dinosaur State Park, 400 West St., Rocky Hill, CT 06067*

Sleeping Giant

East of Conn. 10 on Mt. Carmel Ave., in Hamden

● 1,500 acres ● 203-789-7498 ● Year-round ● Vehicle fee weekends mid-April through Oct. ● No camping ● Hiking, cross-country skiing

As if you have entered the world of *Gulliver's Travels*, a range of hills north of New Haven creates the silhouette of a distinctly human figure lying on his back. The Sleeping Giant Park Association has labored since 1924 to protect the giant from quarrying and development by donating land to the park. With more than 30 miles of trails, the park provides a wooded retreat for the suburban communities surrounding New Haven. The popular 1.6-mile **Tower Path** climbs up the giant's arm and beneath the jutting chin before traversing the length of the torso to a stone tower planted on his left hip. Built during the 1930s, the tower offers views of New Haven County and a pleasant place to picnic.

The 1.5-mile **Nature Trail,** keyed to a pamphlet available at the trailhead, branches off from the Tower Trail. In winter, the park opens several trails for cross-country skiing and snowshoeing. The **Mill River,** a fine place to fish, slices through a grove of pine trees and a picnic area east of the resting giant.

❑ *Sleeping Giant S.P., Mt. Carmel Ave., Hamden, CT 06518*

Sleeping Giant's hip

Bluff Point

Depot Road in Groton, 1/2 mile south of US 1

● 806 acres ● 860-445-1729 ● Year-round ● No camping
● Birdwatching ● Hiking ● Wetlands and beach

Bluff Point protects a 1.5-mile-long peninsula, one of the last major parcels of undeveloped land on the Connecticut shoreline. A 3-mile **loop trail** allows for reflective walks along rambling stone walls, through wooded stands, and past estuarial wetlands to the rocky promontory of **Bluff Point.** Here the surf crashes 40 feet below against the jumble of boulders that trail into Long Island Sound. Look westward for the rocky top of Bushy Point, a small island just beyond the sandy spit curving off the peninsula. The erosional forces of the surf and wind now slowly eat away at the beach—an ice age remnant.

Birders seeking to add shorebirds to their sightings list flock to the Coastal Reserve. Ospreys nest beside the **Poquonock River** on the western side of the park, sharing the habitat with smaller feathered friends, including loons and buffleheads that feed in the sea.

Returning you to your car, the trail's eastern leg skirts the stone foundation of the Governor Winthrop residence, built in the early 1700s for the state's first governor and located on a slight rise amid stone walls and an overgrown orchard.

❑ *Bluff Point State Park and Coastal Reserve, c/o Fort Griswold Battlefield State Park, 57 Fort St., Groton, Connecticut 06340*

Pennsylvania
Ohiopyle
Presque Isle
Cook Forest
Ricketts Glen

New York
Niagara Reservation
Taughannock Falls
Letchworth
Allegany
Connetquot

West Virginia
Pipestem Resort
Blackwater Falls
Canaan Valley Resort
Watoga

CANADA
U.S.

Lake Ontario

81   N.Y.   87

Hudson
River

NIAGARA RESERVATION

390

190   LETCHWORTH   TAUGHANNOCK   ★ Albany

90   89   FALLS

PRESQUE
ISLE

90   ALLEGANY   17   88   87

Lake Erie

17

Allegheny
River

6   RICKETTS
GLEN   84   RINGWOOD

79   COOK
FOREST   180   HIGH
POINT   CONNETQUOT

76   80   80   495

Pittsburgh ●   381   81   78   New York

70   70   76   Harrisburg   Trenton ★   N.J.   ALLAIRE   51

PA.

OHIOPYLE   WHITE CLAY
CREEK   ISLAND BEACH

83   Philadelphia   GARDEN STATE PKWY.

SWALLOW FALLS   PATAPSCO   FORT DELAWARE

BLACKWATER FALLS   VALLEY   Dover ★   GUNPOWDER FALLS

CANAAN VALLEY   50   66   DEL.

Ohio   64   79   219   13   CAPE HENLOPEN

Charleston ★   W.VA.   81   MD.   50   TRAP POND

77   WATOGA   Washington,   3   ASSATEAGUE

64   DOUTHAT   D.C.   50

PIPESTEM   WESTMORELAND   13

360   VA.   64

Richmond

460   ★

BLUE
RIDGE
PKWY.   85   95   64   FIRST LANDING/SEASHORE

GRAYSON   58   FALSE CAPE
HIGHLANDS

0   100 mi
0   200 km

Maryland
Assateague
Gunpowder Falls
Patapsco Valley
Swallow Falls

New Jersey
Island Beach
High Point
Ringwood
Allaire

Virginia
Grayson Highlands
Douthat
False Cape
First Landing/Seashore
Westmoreland

Delaware
Cape Henlopen
Trap Pond
Fort Delaware
White Clay Creek

Rhododendron bushes, Grayson Highlands State Park, Virginia

Niagara Reservation

20 miles north of Buffalo on Robert Moses Pkwy.

● 138 upland acres; 296 underwater acres ● 716-278-1770 ● Year-round ● Entrance fee for Prospect Point ● Entrance fee for Goat Island Memorial Day to Labor Day ● No Camping ● Observation Tower ● Boat tour ● Viewmobile ● Geological museum

Maid of the Mist beneath Horseshoe Falls

Visitors beware, the mist, thunder, breadth, and height of Niagara Falls may overwhelm you. Yet each year eight to ten million people come to Niagara Reservation, the oldest state park in America, and one of the most popular. Few preserves claim so many attractions in such a small area, but the essence of this park remains the sound and fury of the Niagara River rushing downhill from Lake Erie toward Lake Ontario.

At the heart of this drama lies Goat Island, where the river splits to plunge more than 175 feet over the brinks of Horseshoe, Bridal Veil, and American Falls at a rate of 750,000 gallons per second. Heavily wooded, with landscaped trails and bridges that follow the rapids to islets and all three falls, Goat Island is little more than a half-mile long and a quarter-mile wide. The river and shore west of here fall into Canadian territory, while the Prospect Park section of the reservation lies on the eastern shore, or what is commonly called the "American side."

More than a century ago the reservation's land belonged to private entrepreneurs who charged tourists money to view the falls, sometimes through peep holes in fences. After more than 15 years of lobbying by painter Frederick Church and landscape architect Frederic Law Olmsted, leaders of the "Free Niagara" movement, the state began to buy the land in 1885. Olmsted, who designed New York City's Central Park, let his love of trees and water direct his plan for the reservation.

What to See and Do

To avoid crowds, try to arrive at the falls before 8:30 a.m. or after 5 p.m., taking the American Rapids Bridge to **Goat Island** and parking in one of the two lots. In spring through fall, depending on the weather, Viewmobile trains stop at both lots and, unless you like to hike, it's worth purchasing a Viewmobile ticket. Head to the island's northwest end, following the wooded trails along the rapids and across the footbridge to tiny **Luna Island,** where you can stand and see **Bridal Veil Falls** trailing into the void to your west, **American Falls** fuming to the east, and the *Maid of the Mist* tour boats chugging through the spray below. Now take the Viewmobile (or walk) counterclockwise around Goat Island to **Terrapin Point,** which juts to the edge of Canada's **Horseshoe Falls.**

Next travel to the **Prospect Park** section, where you can overlook the gorge, learn about the falls at the **Visitor Center,** climb up the **Observation Tower** *(Fee),* or book passage on a *Maid of the Mist (fare).*

If you have more time, visit the **Schoellkopf Geological Museum** *(Adm. fee)* or descend 279 steps from Goat Island to the **Cave of the Winds** at the base of Bridal Veil Falls.
❏ *Niagara Reservation State Park, P. O. Box 1132, Niagara Falls, NY 14303*

53

Experiencing American Falls

Taughannock Falls

8 miles north of Ithaca on N.Y. 89

- 783 acres ● 607-387-6739 ● Year-round ● Parking fee
- Highest vertical single drop falls east of the Rockies
- Rim and gorge trails ● Summer concerts ● Swimming,
boating, fishing (license required), cross-country skiing

Enjoying the waters of Taughannock Falls

Viewed from the rim, the gorge—almost 400 feet deep
and at least as wide—snakes through the forest plateau west
of Cayuga Lake, a landscape ripe for legends about Indian
massacres and leaping lovers. Near the head of the gorge,
Taughannock Creek cascades in a silver ribbon into the
cataract, falling 215 feet—30 feet farther than Niagara. From
above you can hear the soft wash and warble of the falls and
gaze on a fairyland set amid the hemlocks and white pines.

One legend claims the falls bear the name of a Delaware
chieftain who, with 200 warriors, stood his ground along the
gorge before powerful Cayuga cornered and killed them all.
The falls also tell a vivid tale of geological history. During the
last million years, moving glaciers gouged the troughs that
eventually became the Finger Lakes. Streams such as Taughannock Creek that flow toward the lakes traveled over sand-

stone plate until reaching the steepened lake valley walls, which expose a thick layer of underlying shale. As this shale eroded faster than the sandstone, the result was the falls and the gorge, which is deepening to this day.

Modern history begins here after Native Americans vacated the area following the Revolutionary War. Mills grew up along the creek before the Civil War. Taughannock Falls first became a tourist attraction in the 1870s, when steamboats and a railroad started bringing visitors, and Victorian hotels sprouted up on the high ground. After the hotels failed, the state began acquiring the land for a park in 1925.

What to See and Do

First, stop at the parking lot just off N.Y. 89 and obtain a park brochure and trail map from the attendant. These will direct you up Park Road to the **Falls Overlook,** the only place you can drive to see the falls.

For a more dramatic perspective on the falls, take the interpretive **Gorge Trail,** an easy 1.5-mile round-trip hike leading to the base of the falls. This trail begins at the gorge parking lot and heads west along the creek bed. Walking along, note how the sky seems to shrink overhead as the canyon walls rise and the gorge fills with a mix of tall hemlocks, maples, birches, and locusts. The rush of the stream masks the sound of the falls almost until you break from the forest and cross a footbridge. Now the falls tower ahead, exhaling mist. At trail's end, you stand in what has been called a natural amphitheater, where the falls spew from a frowning lip and crash into a basin.

Adventurers with more time and plenty of stamina should tackle the **Rim Trail** (*Closed in winter*), which loops about 2.6 miles around the gorge. This is a steep walk on undulating trails—be prepared with the proper footgear and a supply of water.

After your workout, or if you just want to take it easy and catch a breeze off **Cayuga Lake,** head to the beach for a swim or some sunning.

Camping and Lodging

Taughannock has 76 tent and RV sites, with shower facilities; and 16 cabins. Late March–mid Oct. Reservations advised in season; call 800-456-2262. Camping fee.

❏ *Taughannock Falls State Park, P. O. Box 1055, Trumansburg, New York 14886*

Taughannock Cookie Monster

In 1879 workmen near the Taughannock House resort unearthed a "stone man" from under the driveway. Weighing 800 pounds, with a height of nearly 7 feet and a shoulder span of 18 inches, the "fossil" drew large crowds who paid 25 cents a look at what was dubbed the Taughannock Giant. Eventually, word got out that the hotel owner had made the giant from a mixture of ox blood, iron filings, sand, sugar, eggs, sulfur, salt, and phosphorous, baked in an oven.

55

Letchworth

**40 miles south of Rochester off I-390,
near Mount Morris**

● 14,350 acres ● 716-493-3600 ● Year-round ● Entrance
fee Memorial Day through Oct., and weekends May and
late Dec. through Feb. ● Grand Canyon of the East
● Museum ● Historic inn ● White-water rafting ● Hot-air
balloon rides ● Hiking, swimming, cross-country skiing
● Hunting, fishing (license required for both)

Late on any given sunny afternoon, from one of the
many lookouts over the Big Bend on the Genesee River
Gorge, you can watch the shadow of the western rim flood
across the canyon floor, cross the river, and rise 600 feet up
the eastern wall to announce dusk. In fall, the red, yellow,
and orange leaves of maples, oaks, and beeches sway in the
canyon drafts, painting the landscape with shifting colors.
This is probably the East's most auto-accessible gorge park,
as evidenced by the number of visitors on peak-color weekends. But on a weekday, the shadows, trees, and waterfalls
seem to exist for you alone.

After millions of years of work, the swift and sometimes
swollen Genesee River continues carving the 17-mile gorge,
which has been called the Grand Canyon of the East and

October view from Inspiration Point

stands at the heart of Letchworth State Park. The 1797 Treaty of Big Tree established reservations for the Seneca in this region that included areas now part of the park. Later, in 1859, nature lover and Native American admirer William Pryor Letchworth acquired the first parcel of what was to become the 1,000-acre centerpiece of this long, narrow park shouldering the gorge. He also renovated and expanded a building for his home. In 1907 he donated his property for the park.

What to See and Do

The most dramatic way to see Letchworth is to enter from the north, picking up a park map at the entrance. Your first stop is the **Mount Morris Dam Overlook,** where you can view the gorge twisting to the south. The steep, tall dam may look misplaced in the nearly dry gorge—unless you are here during winter thaws or spring runoff. From here, continue south along **Park Road,** stopping along the way at such overlooks as **Hogs Back,** where the river makes a horseshoe. If you want to feel your heart pound, check out the views of the **Big Bend** from the **Great Bend** and **Archery Field** vistas. On calm evenings, you are likely to see deer in the cornfields by Castile Entrance. The **William Pryor Letchworth Museum** (*Mid-May–Oct.; donation*) houses Letchworth's collection of Native American and pioneer artifacts. Across the road his former home, now the **Glen Iris Inn,** offers fine dining. On a nearby hillside stands the **Seneca Council House,** the oldest known council house east of the Mississippi.

Don't miss the drive down into the gorge to the **Middle Falls Area.** Here you can park near the river and walk an easy half-mile section of the **Gorge Trail.** The trail links 107-foot **Middle Falls** with **Upper Falls,** which tumble 70 feet from beneath a soaring railroad trestle. Those with more time and energy can follow this sometimes steep trail downstream to the **Lower Falls Bridge** and beyond for 5 miles.

Camping and Lodging

Letchworth has 270 tent or RV sites (mid-May–mid-Oct.), with showers; and 82 cabins (some year-round). Reservations advised in season; call 800-456-2267. Camping fee. The Glen Iris Inn offers 15 rooms, and meals are available; call 716-493-2622.

❏ *Letchworth State Park, Castile, New York 14427*

Hot-air balloons

57

White Woman of the Genesee

Mary Jemison was born at sea in 1743, as her family made its way to settle in the wilds of Pennsylvania. In 1758, during the French and Indian War, Delaware Indians killed her family and kidnapped her. She was adopted by the Seneca and chose to remain with them. When the 1797 Treaty of Big Tree established Seneca reservations, Mary was given 18,000 acres of her own land, near the part of the gorge called Gardeau, now part of Letchworth State Park. Her grave lies at the Seneca Council Grounds, near the inn.

Allegany

7 miles south of Salamanca, off N.Y. 17

Thunder Rocks

● 65,000 acres ● 716-354-9121 ● Year-round ● Entrance fee ● 2,200-foot peaks ● Deep valleys ● Hardwood forest ● Hiking, boating, swimming, mountain biking, cross-country skiing

It's tempting to lose yourself among the steep valleys, thick forest, and stream-carved mountains of this park. Popular with campers in summer and leaf peepers in autumn, Allegany is actually more dramatic in winter, when snow squalls sweep through the hollows, leaving fresh powder for skiers, snowmobilers, and alpine romantics.

Since its origins in 1921, the park has shared a common border with the Seneca Indian Reservation. Their struggle against the federal government's nearby Kinzua Dam Project, which attracted national attention, is reported at the **Seneca-Iroquois National Museum** (*794-814 Broad St. 716-945-1738. Feb.-Dec.; adm. fee*), just outside the park in Salamanca.

The best views of the mountains come from the **Stone Tower** at the Summit Cabin Area, near the park's north entrance. After a stop here, head south to the Red House Administration Building and pick up a map for the 25-mile auto tour. Follow this route in a clockwise direction, continuing south on Park Route 2, and making a stop at **Thunder Rocks** to see the house-size boulders. From here, your route leads through oil and gas fields along the Pennsylvania border, past **Science Lake,** and on to the **Old Quaker Store Museum,** where exhibits highlight park history. On your way back north, visit **Stony Brook Overlook** for autumnal vistas, and **Big Basin** for 220-year-old hemlocks.

If you have more time, consider a swim at **Quaker Lake,** renting a boat at **Red House Lake,** or hiking the popular 1.5-mile round-trip **Bear Caves Trail.** In winter, skiers will also find excellent trails and rentals.

Camping and Lodging

The park has 315 tent or RV sites, with showers; and 380 cabins (April–mid-Dec., with 150 for year-round use). Reservations advised in season; call 800-456-2267. Camping fee.

❏ *Allegany S.P., 2373 ASP Rte. 1, Suite 3, Salamanca, NY 14779*

Connetquot

On N.Y. 27 (Sunrise Hwy.) near Oakdale

- 3,473 acres ● 516-581-1005 ● Year-round ● Entrance
fee ● Access by permit only ● No pets ● No camping
- Gristmill and tavern ● Trout hatchery ● Stocked streams
- Hiking, fly-fishing (license required)

An oasis of wetlands, meandering trout streams, and
pine barren forest in the middle of suburban Long Island,
Connetquot preserves what F. Scott Fitzgerald called the "old
island here that flowered once for Dutch sailors' eyes—a fresh,
green breast of the new world." To visit Connetquot is to
enter a sanctuary with deer, hawks, owl, eastern bluebirds,
brown creepers, and winter wren. Anglers share the fishing
with ospreys and great blue herons.

The site of an 18th-century gristmill and the Snedecor
Tavern (circa 1820), **Connetquot River** has long been valued
for its resources and beauty. In 1866 a group of sportsmen
formed a club to maintain the river area for the propagation
of game birds, fish, and animals, and the State Park Service
has continued the tradition since 1973.

Only visitors over 60 years old or
those with handicaps can drive to the
hatchery, so come prepared to walk. Start
by the mill pond dam at **Snedecor Tavern,** enlarged as the sportsman's club,
and the **Nicoll Gristmill.** The buildings
(516-581-1072. By appointment) house
exhibits on milling, hunting, and fishing,
as well as mounted animals.

If you have the time for an easy
2-mile walk, follow the **Yellow Trail**
through the woods to the trout hatchery.
From here, cross the bridge and return
along the river and pond via the **Red
Trail.** While walking the trails, keep an
eye out for trailing arbutus and orchids in
their natural habitat. For information on
nature programs, call 516-581-1072.

The park requires a permit, obtained
in advance, for hikers (good for one
year), and reservations for fishing sites
and boats. Requests should be sent to the
address below; include your name,
address, telephone number, and number
of people to be included in the permit.

Fishing the Connetquot River

❏ *Connetquot River State Park Preserve, P.O. Box 505, Oakdale,
New York 11769*

Ohiopyle

15 miles west of Uniontown on Pa. 381

● 19,046 acres ● 412-329-8591 ● Year-round ● Wild river gorge ● Ferncliff Natural Area ● White-water rafting ● Hiking, biking ● Hunting, fishing (license required for both) ● Snowmobiling, cross-country skiing

Youghiogheny River

A Native American word *ohiopehhle*, meaning "white, frothy water," probably gave this park and the village it surrounds their names. They stand at the gateway to the rugged Laurel Mountains, where the Youghiogheny River has carved a 1,700-foot-deep gorge. Within the park, thick oak and maple forest rises on both sides of the "Yough" (YOCK), surrounding the gorge for more than 14 miles. The park's focal point is 25-foot Ohiopyle Falls, which spews foam and spray at the heart of the park and village, where the river carves a horseshoe through the gorge. Across the river, high above the gorge on a peninsula formed by the bend in the river, stands Ferncliff Natural Area, a designated National Natural Landmark with scenic overlooks and nature trails. More than 100,000 white-water boaters a year launch here, making the Yough one of the most heavily used recreational rivers in the country.

Although the state only began acquiring parklands here in the mid-1960s, Ohiopyle has been well-known through the ages. Long ago the Delaware, Shawnee, and Iroquois used the area as a hunting ground. And in 1754, before the French and Indian War, George Washington came down the Yough looking for a water route to the Forks of the Ohio (near present-day Pittsburgh), but he turned back at the falls. In the 19th century, the Baltimore & Ohio Railroad followed Washington's path through the gorge to reach Pittsburgh and the West. By the beginning of the 20th century, the railroad was running summer excursion trains to the small resort that developed here.

What to See and Do

Start your visit at the well-marked **Visitor Center**
(*April-Nov.*) in the train station on the north side of Ohiopyle
village. Here you can pick up a map, brochures about park
and local attractions, and information on river and moun-
tain-bike outfitters.

If you are on a tight schedule, drive straight to **Ohiopyle
Falls.** Although the cascade is not especially high, it does span
the river, causing clouds of mist, rainbows, and an eerie rum-
ble. Take pictures from the observation decks, stroll along the
river, or grab a snack at the park concessionaire. Outfitters
have their shops across the street, and you can watch them
launch raft loads of life-jacketed paddlers onto the Lower
Yough from the ramp just downstream of the falls. To view the
first set of rapids, follow the riverside trail south.

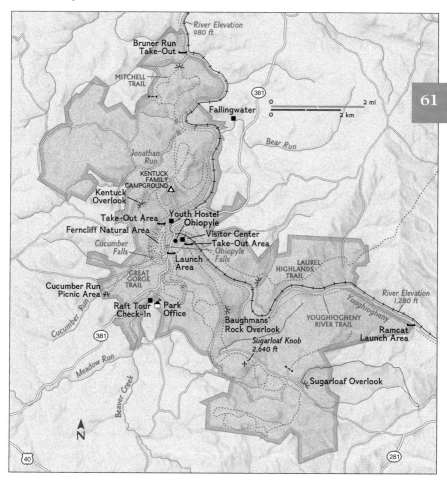

Rafting the "Yough"

Fallingwater

Architect Frank Lloyd Wright caught the drama of the Laurel Highlands forest gorges and rushing water within the design of his 1936 masterpiece, **Fallingwater** (Pa. 381, 2 miles N of Ohiopyle. 412-329-8501. April–mid-Nov. Tues.-Sun.; adm. fee). Acclaimed by the American Institute of Architects as the "best all-time work of American architecture," Fallingwater employs local stone, poured concrete, glass walls, and cantilever construction to blend with the wooded hillside and thrust above the waterfalls of Bear Run.

62

For a different view of the gorge, drive north across the bridge on Pa. 381 to **Ferncliff Natural Area.** Short, easy nature trails follow the rim of the Ferncliff Peninsula and afford bird's-eye vistas of the falls, gorge, and river runners careening through six sets of rapids. In June the trails bloom with rhododendron, mountain laurel, and partridge berry.

If you have time, head south to the top of **Cucumber Run** where, in April and May, the ravine bursts forth in blankets of wildflowers, joined by blooming rhododendron in June. Walk the half-mile downhill on **Great Gorge Trail** to **Cucumber Falls,** or drive to a lot near it. Cap your day with a hike or drive up to **Kentuck Knob** to watch the sun set on the gorge.

Further Adventures

● If day hikes are your thing, the park has 85 miles of trails to chose from. Both **Sugarloaf** and **Baughman Trails** climb about 900 feet over 3.5 miles through the woods from the gorge to the mountain-biking and snowmobile area near **Sugarloaf Knob.** Serious backpackers can head north for 70 miles along the **Laurel Highlands Trail,** which starts here.

● Hike or bike the popular **Youghiogheny River Trail** that passes through the park as it follows an abandoned railroad bed paralleling the river. Mountain biking along all or part of the 28 miles of this trail is the best way to lose yourself to the power of the place. (Bike rentals are available in village of Ohiopyle.)

● For white-water aficionados, the 9-mile **Middle Yough** upstream from the village has excellent canoeing water with some Class I and II white water. The Class III and IV rapids of the **Lower Yough,** a 7.5-mile segment below the village, challenges enthusiasts in white-water rafts, kayaks, and decked canoes. The popularity of the Lower Yough has made a series of guidelines necessary. All boaters must have a launch permit from April through mid-October. Reservations required (call park) on weekends and holidays; recommended during popular times. Boaters should request a specific white-water brochure for details and safety requirements.

Note: The Lower Yough can be dangerous. Boaters without the services of one of the four authorized park outfitters should be experienced paddlers with proper equipment *and* thorough knowledge of the area.

Camping

The park has 237 tent or RV sites (March through antlerless deer season in late fall), with shower facilities. Call 800-63-PARKS for reservations. Camping fee.

❑ *Ohiopyle State Park, P.O. Box 105, Ohiopyle, PA 15470*

Presque Isle

4 miles west of Erie on Pa. 832

● 3,200 acres ● 814-833-7424 ● Year-round ● No camping
● Coastal wilderness ● Birdwatching ● Boat tours ● Ice
fishing, skating, kite and cross-country skiing, hiking,
boating ● Hunting, fishing (license required for both)

To a migratory bird, Presque Isle must look good
enough to eat. This 7-mile-long sand spit rises above the
waves of Lake Erie like a giant crayfish with its tail just
brushing the lake's south shore. Here, a walk of any dura-
tion along the beaches and marsh trails is rewarded by
crashing waves, cooling breezes, and flocks of shorebirds
wheeling and cackling overhead. Built by the action of wind
and waves, Presque Isle is here because of a ridge of sediment deposited as a glacial moraine 13,000 to 14,000 years
ago. Since that time, breezes and surf have driven the
peninsula ever eastward. Shore life of every kind thrives
amid such dynamic geology, including sandhill cranes,
golden eagles, and Swainson's hawk. Presque Isle has been
identified as one of the best
birding areas in America.

According to the legends
of Erie Indians who first
inhabited the south shore of
Lake Erie, Presque Isle forms
the silhouette of the left arm
of the Great Spirit who
reached into the lake to shelter the Erie from a storm.

In the 1720s, French
explorers named the land
Presque Isle, meaning
"nearly an island." Later,
during the War of 1812,
Misery Bay served as the
home of Commodore Oliver
Hazzard Perry's fleet (his brig
Niagara is docked across the
bay from the park, near the
Erie Public Dock). Recog-
nizing the undeveloped
peninsula's value as a wildlife habitat and recreation
area, the state bought the
land to form a park and
began developing it during
the 1920s.

Cottonwoods along Lake Erie

"We Have Met the Enemy..."

On Sept. 10, 1813, Commodore Perry and his fleet of nine ships defeated the British near Sandusky, Ohio. A turning point in British control of the Lakes region, the battle cost Perry 123 casualties, and disabled his flagship, the *Lawrence*. Undaunted, Perry transferred to the brig *Niagara*, raised his "Don't Give Up the Ship" battle flag, and fought on. Afterward he wrote his famous dispatch to Gen. William Henry Harri-son: "We have met the enemy and they are ours."

What to See and Do

With no camping facilities, Presque Isle lures day trippers . . . again and again. Before driving the 14-mile road that loops around the park, orient yourself with a stop at **Stull Interpretive Center,** about a mile inside the gate. Here, you can pick up park brochures, watch a video about Presque Isle's geology, handle displays of flora, fauna, and marine life, or join one of the daily *(April-Oct.)* environmental lectures and walks. You may also consider picking up a tour tape at the center's **Presque Isle Nature Shop.** Before you leave the center, make sure you sign up for the park's most popular warm-weather attraction—the free pontoon boat tour *(June–Aug.).* After leaving from Grave Yard Pond, passengers are treated to a 45-minute narration as they cruise through inland ponds. Wildlife you may see along the way includes great blue herons, painted turtles, muskrats, beavers, and deer.

If you have time for a walk, the 1.25-mile **Sidewalk Trail** starts near the boat livery and crosses the peninsula from Misery Bay to the lakeside and 74-foot-tall **Presque Isle Lighthouse.** Those who choose to combine the pontoon boat tour with this walk can observe ecological zones ranging from marsh to climax forest to beaches.

Don't miss the lake vistas from the **Sunset Point** and **Budny Beach** shores at the northeast end of the park. From here, you can walk the easy 1.5-mile **Gull Point Trail** loop, which stops at an observation platform overlooking the restricted management area of Gull Point. From this vantage point, birders can spot concentrations of migratory shorebirds and waterfowl, including wood ducks and tundra swans, as well as easily witness migrating falcons preying on the shorebirds.

Green-backed heron

If you have the time for some serious leisure, 11 beaches beckon you for a lakeside picnic or a swim *(swimming permitted Mem. Day–Labor Day).* Or launch your boat and tie up at the 500-slip **Presque Isle Marina.** If you didn't bring your own, motorboat and canoe rentals are available at the Livery *(814-838-3938. Mem. Day–Labor Day).* For information on scenic boat tours, call 814-833-3680.

You can end your visit with a trip to Erie's revitalized waterfront and Perry's flagship, the U.S. Brig **Niagara** *(814-452-2744. Adm. fee)* by traveling across the bay via the ferry from the Waterworks ferry dock *(Mem. Day–Labor Day. Call the park or stop by the Stull Interpretive Center for schedule. Fare).* See sidebar this page.

❑ *Presque Isle State Park, P.O. Box 8510, Erie, PA 16505*

Cook Forest

12 miles north of I-80/Brookville on Pa. 36

● 6,668 acres ● 814-744-8407 ● Year-round ● Sawmill
craft center and theater ● Canoeing, tubing, hiking, swimming, cross-country skiing ● Fishing, hunting (license
required for both)

Forest Cathedral

Picture 200-foot-tall stands of virgin timber on gentle slopes, and you will grasp the lure of Cook Forest and how it came to be nicknamed the Black Forest of Pennsylvania. The first Pennsylvania state park acquired to preserve a natural landmark, Cook Forest lies south of the Allegheny National Forest, where an upheaval of the earth's crust created open valleys and rounded hills reaching 1,600 feet within the park. Once a primary means of shipping rafts of timber south to Pittsburgh, the shallow Clarion River has carved the valley that bounds the park to the east.

In the 19th century, the need for lumber made Pennsylvania the largest timber-producing state in the Union. The boom persisted into the 20th century, when most stands of old-growth forest had been cleared from the state's northern highlands. Beginning in 1910, environmentalists bent on saving the remains of the Pennsylvania woods campaigned to buy this forest from the A. Cook Sons lumber company on the grounds that "the East possesses few scenes more impressive than this magnificent area of primeval white pine surrounded by giant hemlocks and hardwoods." In 1927 Cook

65

Forest became a state park and by 1934 President Roosevelt's Civilian Conservation Corps had set up camp here and begun building roads, trails, and cabins, as well as working to save the giant white pines from blister rust, a serious fungal disease.

What to See and Do

Cook Forest is a place to feel humble in the face of nature. If you only have a short time to spend here, go straight to the **Log Cabin Inn Visitor Center** (*Mem. Day–Labor Day*) and pick up a park map. From here, about a mile of easy walking will take you to the heart of the **National Natural Landmark old-growth forest.** Following the **Longfellow Trail** (1.2 miles one way) from the Visitor Center, you will traverse a forest floor of pine needles. Giant hemlocks and white pines, sometimes called "cork pine" because of their thick spongy bark, loom above the gently sloping trail until you arrive at a glade known as the **Forest Cathedral.** A canopy of eastern hemlock and white pine more than 300 years old, this is a place where you hear nothing but the songs of wind and bird.

Next, pause at the **Sawmill Craft Center and Theater** about a half-mile west of the Visitor Center. Here, in a former CCC facility, craftspeople display and sell their creations and offer demonstrations and classes in arts ranging from bird carving to quilting. The theater hosts plays and musicals each weekend of the summer.

Your trip will not be complete without a tour through the woods on **Forest Drive** as it swings northeast, joins Coleman Run Road, and meets the **Clarion River.** The river got its name from trail blazers in 1817, who thought "the ripple of the river sounds like a distant clarion," or trumpet call. Your drive follows this slow-moving river as it twists south for 5 miles to the Park Office and Cooksburg Bridge. Picnickers, anglers, waders, and canoeists love this section of the park. For those so inclined, outfitters in Cooksburg can supply canoes (ask park for information).

Before you leave, climb up the **Cook Forest Fire Tower** (*Fire Tower Rd.*) for photographs of the Clarion River Valley from 1,600 feet, the park's highest point. Here at **Seneca Point** you will also see a site where erosion has exposed beds of massive sedimentary rocks as large as houses.

Camping and Lodging

Ridge Camp has 225 tent or RV sites (limited number in winter), with shower facilities; and 24 rustic cabins (mid-April–mid-Dec.). For reservations call 800-63-PARKS. Camping fee. Swimming pool open Memorial Day to Labor Day (fee).

❑ *Cook Forest State Park, P.O. Box 120, Cooksburg, PA 16217*

How Much Wood Can a Woodhick Log?

More than 100 years ago when A. Cook Sons lumber company ruled over the Clarion Valley, the woods echoed with the sighs of saws and thousands of men—many unemployed Civil War veterans—who sought a living as "woodhicks," or loggers. Life in the logging camps began at 5 a.m. and ended at 9 p.m. Men worked six days a week, 11 hours a day. But room and board were free and a man could earn $1.50 a day . . . if he didn't get his head snapped off by a hemlock bucking as it fell.

66

Ricketts Glen

30 miles north of Bloomsburg on Pa. 487

- 13,050 acres ● 717-477-5675 ● Year-round
- Glens ● Waterfalls
- Giant trees ● Lake
- Fishing (license required), boating, swimming, hiking, cross-country skiing

Stairway to Harrison Wright Falls

Ricketts Glen is the undiscovered gem of Pennsylvania parks. For those approaching from the south, the park is recognizable by its escarpment spanning part of the Allegheny Front and rising up to 1,200 feet above the surrounding hills. Here you find 245-acre Lake Jean and the **Glens Natural Area,** where waterfalls and giant trees epitomize the "forest primeval." The park is named for Col. Robert Bruce Ricketts, who once owned the land and distinguished himself at the Battle of Gettysburg.

To visit beautiful **Adams Falls,** pick up a map at the park office and follow Pa. 487 and Pa. 118 to the south side of the park. The falls are just a few steps from the parking lot. Most sites, however, are not this easy to get to. For the full effect of the glen area, you need the stamina and foot gear to hike steep trails for a minimum of 3 miles, as they follow **Kitchen Creek**'s 1,000-foot plunge.

Start south of the park office and take the **Falls Trail,** which travels down through Ganoga Glen to 94-foot **Ganoga Falls,** the highest in the park. Along the way, you will pass a score of named cascades as you descend among giant pines, hemlocks, and oaks. Where the creek branches join at Waters Meet to form **Ricketts Glen,** the trees, many older than 500 years, often span 5 feet in diameter. The return climb is equally rewarding, as it loops through **Glen Leigh** and skirts eight more falls.

Lake Jean offers quieter waters, where you can bring your own non-powered or registered electric-powered boats, rent a canoe or a rowboat lakeside, or swim at the guarded beach (*mid-May–Labor Day*).

Camping and Lodging

There are 120 tent or RV sites, with showers, and 10 cabins; all open year-round. Most sites first come, first served. For reservations, call 800-63-PARKS. Camping fee.

❑ *RICKETTS GLEN STATE PARK, R.R. 2, BOX 130, BENTON, PA 17814*

67

Island Beach

On N.J. 35, in Seaside Park

● 3,000 acres ● 908-793-0506 ● Year-round ● Entrance
fee ● No camping ● Barrier island ● Surf fishing
● Birdwatching ● Swimming, canoeing, sea kayaking

This protected place on the Jersey Shore thoroughly transports you back to a time before humans ruled the world. The last significant remnant of the barrier island

Goldenrod and dune grasses

ecosystem that once existed along more than 150 miles of the state's Atlantic coast, Island Beach stands as an oasis amid massive coastal development. The park stretches for more than 9 miles, sandwiched between the Atlantic Ocean and Barnegat Bay, a collage of white beaches, dunes, and marsh constituting the southern tip of the barrier island that ends at Barnegat Inlet. While summer heat draws crowds of bathers, the guarded bathing area constitutes less than a mile of the beach, leaving the rest of the park to wildlife, surf fishermen, beach walkers, and birders drawn to observe the large populations of migratory fowl as well as the state's largest osprey colony.

For centuries, Island Beach has defied human encroachment. Henry Hudson steered clear of the island, noting large shoals in his log of 1609. In 1735 the British king ceded a large holding, including Island Beach, to the First Earl of Sterling . . . who kept his distance. During the 19th century, a few squatters shared the island with the U.S. Life Saving Service. Then, in 1926, Andrew Carnegie's partner, Henry C. Phipps, purchased the land with the intent of developing an exclusive resort. After Phipps built three model homes, the Depression brought an end to that dream. The state bought the property in 1953, opened the park in 1959, and today Ocean House, in the Northern Natural Area, serves as summer residence for the governor of New Jersey.

What to See and Do

Make your first stop the **Aeolium Nature Center** (908-793-1698), about a mile inside the park entrance. Here, pick up a map and study the host of brochures highlighting park flora, fauna, geology, and the various special programs. If you are lucky enough to visit during July or August, or on a weekend in spring or fall, someone at the center will tell you how to join one of the naturalist-guided birding and marine life tours. Naturalists also lead free canoe tours (*Mem. Day–Labor Day Tues., Thurs., and Sun.*) of the Sedge Islands, where the ospreys nest and fish. Space on these three-hour tours is limited, so call ahead for reservations.

If you don't have time for a canoe tour, drive to the south end of the park and walk the short **Bird Blind Trail** through the bayberry until you reach the blind. You might see bold red foxes along the way, and this is the best place in the park to watch nesting and fishing ospreys. And, when the marigolds bloom here in early September, waves of migrating monarch butterflies arrive to feast.

For a dramatic beach hike, head south from the parking lot in the Southern Natural Area to **Barnegat Inlet.** The 1.5-mile trek through soft, white sand lands you in view of the 172-foot-high **Barnegat Lighthouse** across the inlet, marking treacherous shoals offshore. If you come here during the winter, expect to see gray and harbor seals. Dolphins arrive to feed when the herring run in May.

Surf anglers enjoy the wild beaches of the Northern Natural Area, where you can fish for striped bass right outside the governor's front door.

❏ *ISLAND BEACH STATE PARK, P.O. BOX 37, SEASIDE PARK, NJ 08752*

Flying Litmus Test

Because ospreys are at the top of the food chain in estuaries such as Barnegat Bay, their prevalence correlates with the health of the environment. Ospreys suffer from poor reproductive rates due to chemical pollutants from feeding on contaminated fish. Before the elimination of DDT, Island Beach's osprey population had dwindled to five nesting pairs. Today, the Sedge Islands are home to 22 nesting pairs and the fishing is good.

69

High Point

On N.J. 23, in Sussex

● 14,056 acres ● 201-875-4800 ● Year-round ● Entrance fee Memorial Day to Labor Day ● Observation monument ● Appalachian Trail ● Birdwatching ● Hiking, swimming, fishing (license required), boating, cross-country skiing

70

On the way to High Point

The crown jewel of the Delaware Water Gap region, High Point State Park sits in the northwest corner of the state atop the tallest knob in New Jersey (1,803 feet), attracting leaf peepers, hikers, cross-country skiers, migrating birds, and bears. On a clear day you can see 220-foot High Point Monument from 20 miles away, towering like the Washington Monument above the forest on Kittatinny Ridge. And from the monument's observation deck you can see even farther . . . to the steep Catskill peaks in the north and the Pocono summits to the west. But it's the view to the south that takes most people's breath away. Here, where the Delaware River carves a nearly straight canyon for more than 40 miles, state and federal lands on both sides of the river valley preserve an unbroken swatch of hardwood forest, filling hundreds of square miles.

High Point had its first serious fling with humans in 1888 when the plush High Point Inn was developed on the shores of Lake Marcia. But by 1909 the resort had gone bankrupt and Col. Anthony Kuser picked up the mortgage, making High Point his summer home before handing the property over to the state in the 1920s.

What to See and Do

High Point attracts a crowd each October to traverse its forest, alive with autumn colors of maple, oak, and sassafras. Whether or not leaf-peeping is your reason for visiting, stop at the **park office** on the south side of N.J. 23 and pick up current maps, trail guides, and brochures. Then head north on **Scenic Drive** to **High Point Monument** (*Daily mid-May–Labor Day, then weekends through Oct.*), dedicated to New Jersey war heroes. Dating from 1930, the obelisk is a serious climb, but if you are not up for the trek, you will find the view from the base is almost as good.

With a little more time for nature, take the easy 1.5-mile **Cedar Swamp Trail** from the end of Cedar Swamp Road. This loop leads through the boggy remains of a 30-acre glacial lake, where you find a rare upland growth of Atlantic white cedar. The trail guide (available at the park office) will tell you what you are seeing, and you can enjoy a rest on the benches along the way and, in spring and fall, listen to the songs of migrating warblers. Deer, porcupines, and black bears pass this way, too, so keep one eye open.

The 4-mile **Iris Trail** is the first choice of many day hikers. Many backpackers join the Appalachian Trail in the park, following it 42 miles south to the Water Gap. Snow-making facilities, ski rentals, and some 10 miles of groomed trails draw cross-country skiers each winter—they later lounge before the fire in the new lodge at Lake Marcia. This is also a popular spot for swimmers during the summer.

Camping

The park has 50 tent sites (April-Oct.), without showers. Two group sites, 2 small cabins, and a group cabin are open mid-May to mid-Oct. Half of sites are first come, first served; the other half can be reserved by writing park. Camping fee.

❏ *High Point State Park, 1480 N.J. 23, Sussex, NJ 07461*

Guess Who's Coming for Dinner?

Far-ranging black bears find the hundreds of square miles of public forest in the Delaware Water Gap region, including High Point, to be attractive habitat. Normally furtive, the lumbering ursines lack all self-control when it comes to food and possess noses that can scent grub from long distances. In recent years, hungry-bear invasions into campsites have been nearly a nightly occurrence at High Point. Some animals have been so bold as to walk right up in the middle of a picnic and scoop lunch from the table. Be forewarned: If you don't keep your food in sealed containers and stored in a vehicle, you too might find yourself with large, obstreperous dinner guests.

Ringwood

Off County Rd. 511, in Ringwood

● 6,196 acres ● 201-962-7031 ● Year-round ● Vehicle fee Memorial Day to Labor Day ● No pets ● No camping ● Botanic gardens ● Historic manors ● Swimming, boating ● Hunting, fishing (license required for both)

Winter at Ringwood Manor

Driving up the winding road toward the stone tower and Gothic windows of Skylands Manor House, visitors may have the sense of venturing to the threshold of novelist Emily Brontë's *Wuthering Heights*. Thickly wooded, rugged, and windy, the very terrain of the Ramapo Mountains looks like Brontë's native Yorkshire. And like the setting for Brontë's famous novel, Ringwood State Park defines itself by the juxtaposition of two manors divided by a wilderness as well as social ranking. Beginning in 1936, the estates began a slow merger to form this unusual park, which includes the 96-acre **New Jersey State Botanical Gardens** and the 74-acre **Shepherd Lake,** where you can rent a boat or take a swim.

The best place to start seeing the natural and material splendor that money can buy is **Ringwood Manor.** From Sloatsburg Road, you can spot the mansion on the slopes above Sally's Pond. Embracing several architectural styles, this 78-room manor house is part of a National Historic Landmark District; it was home to some of America's most powerful iron makers for nearly 200 years. Furnished with an impressive collection of Americana, 21 of the rooms have been restored and opened for tours *(Wed.-Sun.; adm. fee)*. The grounds also make a baronial picnic site.

After learning about Ringwood's history, head east through the forest and follow Morris Road to the **Skylands Manor** *(Open first Sunday of month; adm. fee)*. The palatial facade of this 44-room Jacobean mansion, a stockbroker's fantasy from the 1920s, makes a dramatic focal point for the Botanical Gardens. Pick up a map at the park headquarters, and head off to explore your favorite gardens. Come in late May to see the magnolias, crab apples, lilacs, and tulips in flower.

❑ *Ringwood State Park, P.O. Box 1304, Ringwood, NJ 07456*

Allaire

4 miles west of Spring Lake, on County Rd. 524

● 3,068 acres ● 908-938-2371 ● Year-round ● Parking fee
weekends Memorial Day to Labor Day ● 19th-century
iron-making village ● Steam train ● Hiking, canoeing
● Hunting, fishing (license required for both)

If you like prowling around the relics of the past, enter this
park in the heart of an oak, pine, and holly forest, where the
narrow Manesquan River meanders toward the sea. On the
river's north bank sits the ghost of a company town that thrived
by smelting bog iron ore over a century ago. Yet from the looks
of the carpenter shop, blacksmith shop, general store, bakery,
church, and houses, the citizens just left on the steam train you
might hear chuffing through the woods to the west.

Allaire Village traces its roots to a circa 1790s iron
forge. During the early decades of the 1800s, under the guidance of James P. Allaire, the business grew into a community
of as many as 500 people. But when the iron business failed
in 1848, the town declined. During the 1950s, state and
local citizens united to develop the park and preserve the
deserted village, and in the 1960s railroad buffs, interested in
steam railroading, set up operations at the park, resulting in
the 3-foot-gauge **Pine Creek Railroad.**

73

On weekends between Memorial Day and Labor Day,
Allaire Village comes alive
with historical interpreters.
The season for the trains
(fee) is a little longer, weekends from April through
October and daily in July
and August, when they
carry passengers twice
around a .75-mile loop
through the woods, using
steam power on weekends
only. True romantics visit
on weekdays, to roam the
empty village or train
yards, and populate the
scene in their imaginations.

Allaire Village wash day

Nature lovers might best see the park by canoeing or hiking
along the river in the spring, when the floodplain blooms with
violets, ginseng, and white Dutchman's-breeches.

Camping

There are 55 tent and RV sites, with shower facilities. No
RV hookups. Write park for reservations. Camping fee.

❏ *Allaire State Park, P.O. Box 220, Farmingdale, NJ 07727*

Cape Henlopen

1 mile east of Lewes, off Del. 9

● 4,000 acres ● 302-645-8983 ● Year-round ● Entrance
fee ● No fires on beach ● Wild maritime landscape
● Bountiful wildlife ● Dune trail ● Birdwatching ● Hiking,
biking ● Surf fishing, hunting (license required)

Phragmite at sunset

74

Jutting out into the sea, the thumb-like projection of
Cape Henlopen separates the Atlantic Ocean from Delaware Bay—a discernible landmark since the Spanish first identified it around 1544. Though the Dutch in the next century founded a small fort on this wild, windswept land, and the military maintained one of its key posts here during World War II, no permanent settlement took root. So today Cape Henlopen—preserved in 1964 as a state park—appears much as it did centuries ago.

Rimmed by a wide, sandy beach and containing sand dunes and forests of pine, cherry, oak, and cedar, Cape Henlopen has a dynamic, ever-changing landscape. Though the cape itself has existed for thousands of years, winds and waves have tirelessly chipped, chiseled, and resculptured its profile, slowly changing its shape. The peninsula's seashore is creep-

ing westward, while the tip marches north about 50 feet
a year.

Despite this ever-shifting environment, life holds on.
You may not see the velvet ants, pine lizards, hairy wolf spiders,
rabbits, snakes, mice, or voles—they stay mostly hidden by
day—but look for their tracks that etch the sand early in the
morning. The birdlife, however, is awesome. A stop along the
Atlantic flyway, the cape lures hundreds of species each year:
sanderlings, red knits, ruddy turnstones, pelicans, eider ducks,
even bald eagles and ospreys, to name just a few.

Of all the cape's wildlife, however, two species put on
the most intriguing seasonal displays. In spring, horseshoe
crabs—a species unchanged for 300,000 years—sidle onto
the bayshore, where they dig shallow holes and lay tiny, pea-
green eggs. Half-starved migrating shorebirds, somehow tim-
ing their arrival just right, swarm to the scene, jab the sand
for eggs to devour, and double their weight in two weeks. For
months after, thousands of helmetlike crab shells, stranded at
high tide, litter the beach like the aftermath of a battle.

Between mid-April and mid-July, the piping plover—
sweet little shorebirds the color of dry sand—nest among the
dunes. Endangered, these little birds are protected by park
rangers (access to certain portions of the dunes and easternmost tip of the cape is limited during nesting season).

As you approach the park on Del. 9 past condominiums
and high-rises, you may doubt a lonely, isolated realm could
beckon ahead. Just before the fee booth, the road forks; to the
right are campgrounds, hiking trails, and the Observation
Tower, while straight ahead lies the Nature Center, hiking
trails, and access to the point—some of the most beautiful,
desolate land around.

What to See and Do

Begin at the small **Seaside Nature Center** (302-645-
6852), full of aquariums displaying local denizens. This is a
good place to pick up park information and trail brochures,
and to perhaps sign up for an interpretive program. Then, to

75

Cape Henlopen's oceanside

sample the cape's diverse habitats, take three short trails through beach, pine forest, and dune environments. The first, the 0.7-mile **Seaside Nature Trail,** begins next to the Nature Center and wanders through low dunes dotted with markers keyed to a brochure available at the Nature Center. The trail comes to the sandy shores of gentle Breakwater Harbor and follows the bayshore a bit before looping back through the woods.

Across the road from the Nature Center lies the 1.6-mile **Pinelands Nature Trail.** Meandering through a sandy pine forest, this trail passes several cranberry bogs that support club mosses and tiny, insect-eating sundew plants. To reach the last short trail, drive back to the fork before the fee booth and turn left, into the park's southern portion. Before you reach the trailhead, consider stopping at the **Observation Tower,** built on an old military bunker. At the top awaits an extraordinary vista: a mosaic of pinelands, marshes fingered with tidal creeks and piney ridges, the endless blue Atlantic, and rippling sand dunes.

Just down the road is the start of the **Walking Dune Hiking Trail,** offering an intimate look at "walking" dunes— mounds of sand that blow with the wind, moving forward bit by bit. They once traveled 60 feet a year, but the growth of vegetation has hampered their speed. Look closely: The "dwarf" pines along the sandy peaks may actually be the topmost branches of 30-foot trees!

For another panoramic vista, drive to the end of the southern park road, where **Herring Point Overlook** takes in a sweeping scene of the crashing Atlantic. A short trail leads down to the ocean beach, where you can picnic, swim, or sunbathe.

Further Adventures

Hardy hikers won't want to miss the 1.8-mile **Beach Loop Trail** (*Closed during piping plover nesting season*), beginning from The Point parking lot and following the cape's contour around its lonely, easternmost point. Be forewarned: Walking on sand is tiring; only those in good shape should attempt this hike. Wandering along the bayshore, where a lighthouse overlooks placid **Breakwater Harbor,** the trail heads east past sand dunes inhabited in summer by nesting piping plover, black skimmers, and least and common terns. You soon reach the wide open point where land and bay and ocean meet. Just offshore, a lighthouse flashes warnings to ships and boats. Chances are, flocks of shorebirds, and perhaps a brown pelican or two, will be the only signs of life. Return along the ocean, where the Atlantic surf rolls onto a wide, seashell-strewn beach.

Camping

Set among pine-covered dunes are 159 tent and RV sites (April-Oct.). Available first come, first served. Call 302-645-2103 for information. Camping fee.

❑ *Cape Henlopen S.P., 42 Cape Henlopen Dr., Lewes, DE 19958*

War Stories

Standing atop the 83-foot concrete Observation Tower, it's easy to understand the Cape's strategic importance to shipping along the Atlantic. That's why the Army built Fort Miles Military Reserve in the early 1900s, and why, during World War II, soldiers from here kept watch for enemy activity off shore. Indeed, more than 400 allied ships were sunk in these waters by German U-boats. And, in one of the last actions of the war, a German U-858 submarine surrendered here five days after V-E Day. The lands have since been returned to the state.

Trap Pond

5 miles east of Laurel via Del. 24 and Cty. Rd. 449

● 2,109 acres ● 302-875-5153 ● Year-round ● Entrance fee
in summer ● Bald cypress trees ● Nature Center ● Hiking,
biking, swimming, canoeing, fishing (license required)

Among the neat rows of corn and soybeans on the Eastern Shore rises a great stand of bald cypress trees, their moss-draped limbs and buttressed trunks more reminiscent of a Southern bayou than mid-Atlantic woodlands. The remnants of an ancient swampland that once covered much of the Atlantic coastal plain, these harbingers of another time form the heart of Trap Pond State Park.

In the late 1700s, colonists discovered that the rot-resistant bald cypress wood was ideal for building boats, posts, and shingles. They excavated Trap Pond to power their mills . . . and down came the tall, shaggy trees. As more and more trees toppled, opening up the tree canopy, the sun dried the underlying peat bogs, making the whole swamp susceptible to fire. One blaze in the 1930s raged for eight months.

The cypresses of Trap Pond are the mere shadows of a once vast forest, but still they evoke an aura of mystery. In winter,

Trap Pond morning

flocks of overwintering Canada geese and whistling swans sit by the water's edge, and the Southern-dwelling trees stand locked in ice—quite a sight to behold. Acquired by the federal government in the 1930s, Trap Pond and its surrounding forest became Delaware's first state park in 1951.

What to See and Do

Stop by the **Bald Cypress Nature Center** (*302-875-5163*) in the main section of the park, where you can learn about Trap Pond's natural history, plus pick up park literature and a schedule of interpretive programs. Then hop in

Amphibian Symphony

As night falls on the springtime swamp, a small reedy voice breaks the silence, soon joined by more voices: humming trills and bassline grunts and plunks like twanging rubberbands. It's the amphibian symphony—an integral part of the frog and toad courtship. Each species has its own sound, enabling males to call across the darkness for mates.

your car, exit the park, and proceed down County Rd. 449 to the first road you come to (Cty. Rd. 450). Turn right and continue about 100 yards to the campground entrance. You're headed for the other side of the pond and the **Cypress Point Trail,** the park's most intriguing hike. Just a mile long, the trail wanders beside the shore, where bald cypresses congregate in all their splendor.

One point, where a short boardwalk juts out across the tea-colored waters, offers a good spot to examine these odd trees. Deciduous conifers, they lose their needles each autumn (hence the name "bald" cypress). Their "knees," thought to be part of their aerial root system, poke above the standing water like probing periscopes. Watch for wildlife, too: eastern painted and spotted turtles sunning on gnarled logs, bull frogs, and green tree frogs. One resident, the carpenter frog, is also known as the bog frog because of its preference for the sphagnum wetlands of cypress swamps. Birders will be interested in the wide variety of southern birds, including prothonotary, parula, and yellow-throated warblers, as well as the elusive Swainson's warbler, one of the least-known of North America's birds because it favors dense swamps. After about half a mile, the trail returns through woods embracing 12 different species of oaks—including black jack, normally not found near swampy land—and four different pines.

While hiking provides a good introduction to the cypress swamp, nothing beats a canoe trip through a labyrinth of flared trunks and knobby knees. (*Canoes may be rented in summer season from the park concessionaire.*) Try the popular trail leading southeast from Trap Pond to Records Pond along the **James Branch River,** deep into the swamp's interior. Floating silently past venerable stands of cypress, including one giant more than 500 years old, you'll feel like you've traveled into centuries past. You can detour to **Trussum Pond,** whose smooth, ebony waters are dappled in spring with snowy water lilies, and great bald cypresses reach toward the sky.

End your warm-weather exertions with a dip in the pond. A small **beach** in the main section of the park is guarded in summer. Shaded by loblolly pines, picnic tables dot the lakeshore, and there are several other hiking trails you may wish to explore. In summer, a concessionaire rents rowboats and paddle boats, and on summer weekends the park interpreter narrates pontoon boat tours (*fee*).

Camping

The park has 152 tent or RV sites (April-Nov.), with showers. Call 302-875-2393 for reservations. Camping fee.

❏ *Trap Pond State Park, R.D. 2, Box 331, Laurel, Delaware 19956*

Buckeye butterfly on goldenrod

Fort Delaware

Via ferry from end of Clinton St., Delaware City

● 190 acres ● 302-834-7941 ● Ferry operates Wed.-Sun.
mid-June to Labor Day, weekends late April to mid-June
and Sept. ● No pets ● No camping ● Historic fort
● Civil War camp with interpreters ● Heronry ● Hiking

Cattle egret

A 10-minute ferry ride *(fare)* brings you to **Pea Patch Island**—named for a boatload of peas that ran aground in the 1700s and sprouted—and the castlelike **Fort Delaware,** complete with drawbridge and moat. Built in 1848 to defend the sea approach to Philadelphia, and later garrisoned during the two World Wars, the bastion's most famous era is the Civil War, when it imprisoned Southern soldiers. Established in 1951 as one of Delaware's first state parks, Fort Delaware remains possibly the country's best preserved Civil War camp. Soldiers dressed in period garb *(daily in season)* march, fire guns, and chat about those trying times when 2,000 soldiers were jammed into the tiny rooms through freezing winters and humid summers, while in the **museum,** swords and cannon balls recall the fort's past.

The **Prison Camp Trail** loops through the island's north end, with markers keyed to an interpretive brochure *(available at gift shop)* detailing prison life. Midway, an observation platform looks out on the largest heronry north of Florida—as many as 10,000 herons and egrets nest here. Watch the great birds glide over the marshlands; with binoculars you can pick out their large nests in the trees across the marsh.

❏ *Fort Delaware S.P., P.O. Box 170, Delaware City, DE 19706*

79

White Clay Creek

2 miles northwest of Newark on Del. 896

● 2,300 acres ● 302-368-6900 ● Year-round ● Entrance fee
May through Oct. ● No camping ● Hiking, biking,
fishing (license required)

Showcasing the beauty of Delaware's piedmont, this park has three different entrances accessing 20 miles of trails that explore lush farm valleys and thick woods. Take the Hopkins Road entrance for the **Nature Center,** a good place to begin a visit. Nearby, the 2.1-mile **Preserve Trail Loop** traverses a stone-strewn creek. And the mile-long **Possum Hill Trail,** off Smith Mill Road, wanders through rolling farmland, passing a weathered Mason-Dixon Line monument. Off Del. 896, the **Logger's Trail** looks at the area's lumbering history.

❏ *White Clay Creek State Park and Preserve, 425 Wedgewood Rd., Rte. 896, Newark, Delaware 19711*

Wild horses of Assateague

Assateague

8 miles south of Ocean City via US 50 and Md. 611

● 800 acres ● 410-641-2120 ● April through Nov.
● Entrance fee Memorial Day to Labor Day ● No pets
● Nature Center ● Wild horses ● Birdwatching ● Shell
collecting ● Swimming, boating, fishing

Created and dominated by the sea, Assateague Island is a narrow barrier island of golden sand stretching 37 miles off the coasts of southern Maryland and northern Virginia. A stark contrast to the neon lights of nearby Ocean City, its wild, natural beaches and bird-filled marshes are virtually undeveloped.

One of the thousands of barrier islands and spits protecting the Atlantic coast from the ocean's brutal onslaught, Assateague is a sandy, vulnerable place of constant change—growing and shrinking and moving as the sea adds sand here, washes it away there. Many geologists believe the barrier islands—including Assateague—were created after the last ice age, some 15,000 years ago. As glacial ice melted, rivers carried ice-scoured rocks and sands to coastal estuaries, where offshore ocean currents and waves redeposited them in new configurations along the shoreline.

Humans have tried to possess this difficult land, from early-day colonists to modern entrepreneurs, who built roads and buildings in hope of creating a beachfront resort. Nature won out: The great March storm of 1962—also dubbed the Ash Wednesday Storm—blew away every last hope for human habitation, leaving the island to revert to its natural state.

However, most summers the ocean is calm, the beaches warm. Created in 1964 and one of Maryland's most visited parks, the state park joined two other entities in preserving the entire island: Assateague Island National Seashore, which encircles the state park; and Chincoteague National Wildlife Refuge, lying at the southern part of the island.

What to See and Do

The park's premier attraction is, of course, the **beach.** Less crowded than Ocean City, the 2-mile sandy shoreline lures thousands each summer to swim, collect oyster shells and clamshells, picnic, and simply bask in the sun's warm rays. Check out the **Nature Center,** which has aquariums full of local species, as well as innovative interpretive programs.

Along quieter parts of the beach—especially to the north—you glean a true sense of what the Eastern Seaboard was like centuries ago: Churning surf rolls onto empty sand, tall oatgrass rustles in a salty breeze, and pines and bayberry shrubs create a dense thicket along the island's spine. Keep walking north and you'll cross into Assateague Island National Seashore, void of any signs of 20th-century life. Here the wildlife is out in full force. You may not see the nocturnal red foxes, hognose snakes, or wolf spiders, but in early morning you can spot their tracks in the sand. And you can't miss the fabled wild horses. Legend dictates that the ancestors of these small creatures swam ashore after a Spanish galleon sank in the 1700s. Possibly—but more likely they descend from horses that were placed on the island in colonial times for free grazing.

And then there are the birds. More than 200 different species have been spotted on this rest stop along the Atlantic flyway—ranging from the common gull to herons and egrets to endangered peregrine falcons and bald eagles. Birders come from all over to watch the show: Terns divebombing the water to catch fish, gulls dropping clams to break them open on a paved road, flocks of sandpipers flirting with the surf on long, strawlike legs, and protected piping plovers nesting in the sand dunes. The best viewing times are spring and autumn, during the annual migrations. Don't forget the binoculars.

Further Adventures

● Consider hopping in a canoe and paddling down **Chincoteague Bay** *(Canoe rentals at end of Bayside Dr.).* You glide past golden marshes filled with wading birds—egrets, herons, perhaps even a brown pelican or two. In early morning, muskrats and white-tailed deer feed near the water's edge. The National Park Service also operates four backcountry canoe-camping sites along the way.

● For a primer on the island's three ecosystems—dunes, forests, and marshes—drive (or bike) south about 3 miles along Bayberry Drive to **Assateague Island National Seashore**'s *(410-641-1441. Vehicle fee)* developed area, with campsites and several excellent, short hiking trails. The **Life of the Dunes Trail** explores the ever-shifting world of sand, teaching how different plants have adapted to the harsh, unstable dune conditions, where temperatures can reach more than 120°F. For example, the leaves of dusty miller, a gray-green plant with yellow flowers, are covered with thick white "hairs," which serve as heat insulators. The **Life of the Marsh Trail** offers a good chance of spotting wild horses, their stomachs bloated by salty marshgrass. (Remember, it's illegal to feed and pet them.) And the **Life of the Forest Trail** visits a maritime forest, inhabited by the Delmarva fox squirrel, an endangered subspecies twice the size of its common gray cousin, with foxlike ears.

● The fascinating **Chincoteague National Wildlife Refuge** *(757-336-6122. Vehicle fee; no camping)* lies 50 miles away. (You'll have to exit the island, drive south to Va. 175, and reenter the island via Chincoteague.) Established in 1943, the refuge's 14 freshwater impoundments provide a haven for shorebirds. In winter, thousands of greater snow geese descend, offering one of the most breathtaking natural spectacles around. The **Wildlife Loop,** closed to cars until 3 p.m. daily, gives hikers and bikers a chance to spot birdlife up close.

Camping

The park has 311 tent and RV sites (April-Oct.), with showers. Reservations highly recommended in summer. For reservations call 410-641-2120, ext. 22. Camping fee.

❑ *ASSATEAGUE S.P., 7307 STEPHEN DECATUR HWY., BERLIN, MD 21811*

Assateague's Inlets

Early explorers noted that the island of Assateague extended some 60 miles along the coastline. Great storms have since whittled through the weak spots, forming inlets. The most recent example occurred in 1933, when the power-packed Inlet Storm severed present-day Assateague from Fenwick Island, site of Ocean City. Nature would probably have closed the inlet since, had humans not intervened by building a jetty.

Rose mallow

Gunpowder Falls

3 areas in Baltimore and Harford Counties

- 18,000 acres ● 410-592-2897
- Year-round ● Scenic river valley
- Hiking, biking, swimming, boating

Surprisingly close to Baltimore, this state park embraces the banks of a beautiful river and its two tributaries as they race across a mosaic of open meadows and gentle forested slopes, encountering rocky bluffs, a freshwater marsh—and no waterfalls. The term "falls" dates back to colonial times, when swift-moving streams that emptied into a tidal river were considered that river's falls; in this case, Big and Little Gunpowder Falls flow into the tidal Gunpowder River. Established in response to the rapid suburbanization of Baltimore County in the late 1950s, this is Maryland's largest state park, scattered across three different recreation areas. Make a point to get a map from the Visitor Center in Monckton.

83

Canoeing the Big Gunpowder Falls

The **Hammarman-Dundee Area** near the Chesapeake Bay contains picnic tables and a swimming beach (*Mem. Day–Labor Day; adm. fee*). For a fee, motor boats may be launched here, and canoeists may explore the marsh at the river's mouth—a birder's paradise. Try entering this world of giant cattails and wild rice in early morning, when deer, raccoons, and muskrats feed along the river's edge.

In the more remote **Hereford Area,** 35 miles upstream, some hundred miles of hiking trails await. A rocky, 1.5-mile segment of the **Gunpowder Falls South Trail** (*Off Mount Carmel Rd.*) best showcases Big Gunpowder Falls, which dances through a narrow valley draped in lush greenery. The fast-moving water supports a large population of trout—evidenced by the many fly-fishermen in sight.

The new 21-mile **North Central Railroad Trail** allows hikers and bikers to meander north from Ashland into Pennsylvania, through plush green pastures and rural towns. Pick up information at the **Visitor Center** (*410-472-3144*) in Monckton.

Camping

The park has 22 primitive sites on Hart-Miller Island (Mem. Day–Labor Day), 6 miles south of the Hammarman Area in Chesapeake Bay; accessible only by private boat. No showers. Available first come, first served. Camping fee.

❏ *GUNPOWDER FALLS S.P., 2813 JERUSALEM RD., KINGSVILLE, MD 21087*

Patapsco Valley

5 different areas; call for directions

Bridge over Patapsco River in Hollofield Area

● 17,000 acres ● 410-461-5005 ● User fee weekends March-Oct.; Avalon Area, user fee daily March-October ● Scenic river valley ● Hiking, fishing (license required)

A long, skinny wilderness area popular among Baltimoreans, the Patapsco River winds 32 miles from its source near Woodbine to the Baltimore Harbor, as lovely as it was when Capt. John Smith first set eyes on it in 1608. It wasn't always so. Early this century, lumbermen denuded the area; then in the 1970s, the dumping of sewage and industrial waste turned the river into a cesspool. Thanks to clean water legislation, fish once again swim its depths, songbirds fill the tree canopy, and coyotes roam the forests. In the early 1980s the state bought the narrow greenbelt flanking both sides of the river and created this linear park.

Patapsco Valley encompasses five different recreational entities. Three areas—**Hollofield, Pickall,** and **Hilton**—are mostly for picnicking and camping; the **Avalon-Orange Grove** and **McKeldin Areas** stand out for their hiking and biking trails. Stop by **park headquarters,** on US 40 near Ellicott City, to pick up maps and information about all portions of the park.

The Avalon Area includes the 1.3-mile **Grist Mill Recreational Trail,** a paved path that wends along the alluvial floodplain. Along the way, bikers and hikers visit the ruins of the 1856 **Orange Grove Flour Mill** and the landmark steel-and-cable **swinging bridge.** To explore the surrounding forested ridges, take the 2.1-mile **Valley View Trail,** with spectacular overlooks of the silvery ribbon of water far below.

For more hiking and biking, head for the McKeldin Area, 20 miles upstream. The popular 4.8-mile **Switchback Trail** sashays between dense woods and the Patapsco, which at one point splashes prettily over shaded ledges into a green pool.

Camping

The Hollofield Area has 73 tent and RV sites (April-Oct.), with showers. Call the park for reservations. Camping fee.

❏ PATAPSCO VALLEY STATE PARK, 8020 BALTIMORE NATIONAL PIKE, ELLICOTT CITY, MARYLAND 21043

Swallow Falls

9 miles northwest of Oakland, off US 219

- 300 acres ● 301-387-6938 ● Year-round ● Entrance fee
- Old-growth hemlocks ● Maryland's largest waterfall
- Nature programs ● Hiking, swimming

The Youghiogheny River pounds through Swallow Falls State Park, spilling over two falls—including Maryland's largest (Muddy Creek Falls)—and through a deep, rocky canyon before continuing its tempestuous journey across the Appalachian plateau. Surprisingly, this striking scene is not what led to the formation of the state park.

On the river's bank stands a magnificent grove of virgin hemlock and white pine, centuries-old giants that have never been logged thanks to the foresight of one Henry Rug, who owned the forest at the turn of the century. The 40-acre grove and surrounding forest were donated to the state in 1906, and around this gift the Civilian Conservation Corps developed Maryland's tiniest state park.

People come from far and wide to walk the 1.25-mile **Canyon Trail** along the river gorge. The hike begins from the main parking area, delving deep into regal hemlocks. Follow the sign to **Muddy Creek Falls,** which splashes 54 feet over a wide stone ledge into a big green pool. From here, a wooden staircase leads down to a narrow cliff-shaded path winding beside the furious, churning river. Ahead stands two-tiered **Swallow Falls,** flanked above and below with large flat boulders; sun worshipers dot them in summer. Note the large plinth below the falls, where thousands of cliff swallows once nested, lending the park their name.

Most people stick by the river, but for the adventurous, a 5.5-mile hiker-biker trail—poorly marked by faint white blazes—winds through sylvan woods, connecting Swallow Falls to nearby **Herringbone Manor State Park** *(301-334-9180)*. Here a small lake with boat rentals and swimming beach make for a quiet respite.

Camping

The park has 65 tent and RV sites (April–mid-Dec.), with shower facilities. Reservations recommended in summer; call 301-387-6938. Camping fee.

❏ *Swallow Falls State Park, 222 Herringbone Ln., Oakland, Maryland 21550*

Youghiogheny River

Grayson Highlands

Between Damascus and Independence, on US 58

● 4,935 acres ● 540-579-7092 ● Year-round ● Entrance fee ● Alpine scenery ● Access to Appalachian Trail and Mount Rogers NRA ● Horse camping ● Hiking, fishing (license required), mountain biking, cross-country skiing

Sitting high atop the Appalachian Mountains in southern Virginia, Grayson Highlands crowns lofty Haw Orchard Mountain, offering some of the most spectacular alpine scenery around. Flanked by the state's two highest peaks—

Jones Homestead

5,729-foot Mount Rogers and 5,520-foot Whitetop Mountain—this is the northern realm of red spruce and fir, Ice Age relics that still flourish in the high elevation and abundant moisture. Trout-filled streams roll off the mountainside, wild horses graze flower-dotted meadows, and blooms of purple and white rhododendron festoon the understory in June and July.

With its cool summer temperatures, sophisticated horse-camping facilities, and miles of hiking trails, it's surprising that just 160,000 people visit this scenic corner annually.

Long before the park was established in 1965, hardy pioneers of Scotch-Irish descent settled the region. They left behind their names in such park features as Massie Gap and Wilburn Ridge. Celebrating this heritage is a fall festival held in late September, complete with live bluegrass music and molasses-making.

What to See and Do

From the contact station at 3,698 feet, follow Grayson Highland Lane up Haw Orchard Mountain, with supreme mountain vistas in every direction. At **Wildcat Overlook,** about halfway up, a short walk is rewarded with a splendid vista of farm fields cradled by rows and rows of towering, tree-covered ridges. As you climb higher, the forest around you changes to northern hardwood sprinkled with spruce and red fir. The temperature here may be 10 degrees cooler than at the contact station, and you may very well be in the clouds. The **Visitor Center** (*Mem. Day–Labor Day*), located at 4,958 feet, remembers the region's rich heritage with exhibits on pioneer life, including such items as hand tools, moonshining apparatuses, and musical instruments, as well as on the region's natural history. Local artisans sell their handicrafts—quilts, musical instruments, and delicate art glass, among others—at the adjacent **Mountain Crafts Shop** (*Late May-Sept.*).

The popular 1.6-mile-loop **Twin Pinnacles Trail** leaves from behind the Visitor Center. Hiking through mountain ash, yellow birch, and spine-covered hawthorns—which gave the mountain its name—you soon come to Little Pinnacle, an igneous rock outcrop with 360-degree views of surrounding crags, including regal Mount Rogers. Hike a half-mile farther and you'll reach the top of Big Pinnacle, with views down into Massie Gap.

To visit a restored homestead, drive down the hill to the picnic area and walk the 1.2-mile **Rock House Ridge Trail.** Wandering through a pretty meadow, you'll soon come to the **Jones Homestead,** complete with oak-log cabin, spring house, cane mill (to grind sorghum), and old cemetery surrounded by a crumbling rock wall.

Mountain Balds

Gazing across the panoramic sweeps of mountains in the southern Appalachians, you'll note rocky, treeless spots among the forested slopes. Called balds, some are said to have been created by Native Americans, who set fires for game clearings, while others resulted from logging in the 1800s. For hikers, these balds can be a source of revelation: In spring many balds become blooming gardens of deep-pink rhododendron.

87

Further Adventures

Adjacent to the spectacular **Mount Rogers National Recreation Area** (*540-783-5196*), Grayson Highlands provides the shortest hike to the top of **Mount Rogers**—4.5 miles from Massie Gap via the Rhododendron Gap and Appalachian Trails. The hike shows off the area's beauty to perfection—overlapping mountains marching off into the distance, grassy balds, thickets of sweet blueberries (ripe in August), and acre upon acre of Catawba rhododendron, quite a sight when they bloom in June. Keep an eye out for wild horses. Dense with the state's only spruce and fir forest and often fogged in, the summit itself has no views; but mosses and ferns, which thrive in this moist environment, create a dark, magical realm.

Camping

The park has 73 tent and RV sites, with showers; plus 24 horse-camp sites adjacent to horse barn. March-Nov. Call 804-225-3867 or 800-933-PARK for reservations. Camping fee.

❏ *GRAYSON HIGHLANDS STATE PARK, 829 GRAYSON HIGHLAND LN., MOUTH OF WILSON, VIRGINIA 24363*

Douthat

7 miles north of Clifton Forge on Va. 629

● 4,493 acres ● 540-862-8100 ● Vehicle fee ● Spectacular mountain setting ● Nature programs ● Hiking, fishing (license required), boating, swimming

White-tailed deer

Driving deep into the Alleghenies, the cars thin out, massive ridges crop up, and a splendid sense of isolation envelops you. Hidden in this lofty mountainous realm lies Douthat State Park, where forested, wind-swept peaks ring an indigo-colored lake—the domain of black bear and white-tailed deer, wild turkey and whippoorwill. This park isn't meant for a whirlwind tour; spend at least a weekend here, sampling the 40 miles of interconnecting hiking trails, fishing in the trout-filled lake, or simply gazing into the night sky at extremely bright stars.

Established in 1936 as one of Virginia's first six state parks, Douthat—on the National Register of Historic Places since 1986—is a veritable memorial to the Civilian Conservation Corps, which built most of the park's rustic cabins, restaurant, and two lodges. The Depression-era artistry of its 600 workers still is evident in such details as hand-carved doors and hinges.

What to See and Do

From Clifton Forge, Va. 629 winds beneath a canopy of oak and hickory along clear-running Wilson Creek, providing a taste of what lies ahead. Beyond the entrance gate, stop by the **Visitor Center** (*Mem. Day–Labor Day*) for good exhibits on the area's history, flora, and fauna. Of particular interest are the rounded-off shovels, worn leather boots, and grainy photos that detail the CCC legacy. This is also the place to pick up park maps and information.

The park has two easy nature walks. To reach the **Buck Lick Interpretive Trail,** drive a mile or so farther into the park and leave your car at the Lake View Restaurant and Country Store; the trailhead lies across the road. Winding beside a rock-riven stream, the woodsy path highlights many of the park's trees, which are typical of the Appalachians: dogwood, black oak, white oak, white pine, sassafras, American chestnut, hemlock, and the tulip poplar—decorated in spring with yellowish-green blooms the shape of tulips. Here, as elsewhere in the park, mountain laurel and rhododendron form the understory—adorning the forest with brilliant blooms of pink and white in spring.

The easy 0.8-mile **Heron Run Trail,** beginning inside Campground A, hugs the shoreline of Douthat Lake, a perfect vantage to admire the shimmering reflections of high mountain peaks and maples crowding the shoreline. Along the beginning of the trail stands a magnificent stand of dark-green hemlocks. Walk quietly: You have a good chance of spotting a beaver or two. The narrow trail wends to the dam, at which point you'll have to retrace your steps.

If you'd like a different perspective on the park and have a lot of stamina, drive back to the Bucklick Interpretive trailhead (the Buck Hollow Trail also begins here) and take the 5.6-mile loop formed by the **Buck Hollow, Mountain Top,** and **Mountain Side Trails.** This rugged, hilly hike winds through a pretty hollow to the top of Beards Mountain, offering far-off views of rumpled ridges extending as far as the eye can see. Then, diving off the mountain's other side, you spy Douthat Lake, a little sparkling gem nestled far below at the base of the mountains. Along the way, tree-filled coves burst into flames of color in autumn.

After all this hiking, you're probably ready for a swim. Head for **Douthat Lake,** where a sandy beach occupies a small cove dotted with picnic tables. A concessionaire rents paddleboats and johnboats; a unique self-guided **paddleboat tour** of the lake has seven interpretive stops focusing on the fish funnel (fish-stocking point), cattails, beavers, and more. You can fish here, or at nearby **Wilson Creek.**

Camping

The park has 116 tent and RV sites, with showers, in 3 areas; and 30 cabins. March-November. Call 804-225-3867 or 800-933-PARK for reservations. Camping fee.

❑ *DOUTHAT STATE PARK, RTE. 1, BOX 212, MILLBORO, VIRGINIA 24460*

Autumn Color

The heralding of autumn begins at Douthat in late September with the slightest hints of color—a few precocious maples or oaks flashing gold or red. Then, at startling speeds, the whole forest explodes in a brilliant mosaic: Flowering dogwoods turn crimson and sassafras burnt orange; aspens and birches become yellow; while oaks blaze in yellows, oranges, or bronzes; and sugar maples— the forest highlight— glow intense scarlets, oranges, and golds.

89

Appalachian wildflowers

False Cape

**5 miles south of Sandbridge, southeast of
Virginia Beach. No vehicular access.**

● 4,321 acres ● 757-426-7128 ● Year-round ● Entrance fee
to Back Bay NWR ● No cars ● No pets ● Beautiful barrier
spit ● Hiking, biking, swimming, fishing (license required)

Primitive, windswept, and wildly beautiful, False Cape isn't easy to get to—you must hike or bike 5 miles to reach its gates. But isolation is also one of its virtues. Located along a mile-wide barrier spit between the Atlantic Ocean and Back Bay, the unspoiled coastal environment embraces beach, dunes, marshlands, and maritime forest as pristine as they were centuries ago. Walking the trails and sunning on the beach, you'll likely be alone.

90

Wind-rippled dunes

The park's most exceptional feature is its abundant wildlife: red foxes, white-tailed deer, feral pigs and horses, raccoons, nutria, and hundreds of loggerhead turtles—the only sea turtle that nests in Virginia. Birders are in paradise at this remote perch along the Atlantic flyway, where up to 300 species—egrets, swallows, flocks of ducks, trumpeter swans—stop by each year. Be sure to bring binoculars.

False Cape first became known as a shipping graveyard; ships aiming for Cape Henry just north often became confused by this landmass—hence the cape's name—and sank in shallow waters. Using cypress-wood debris, the survivors of one such wreck in 1895 built the fishing community of Wash Woods, which thrived until sand engulfed it in the 1950s. The least-visited of Virginia's state parks, False Cape opened in 1980.

Be forewarned: There is no food service or drinking water in the park; carry at least one gallon of water per person, per day. Mosquitoes and biting flies are pesky in summer, so bring repellent.

The only access to the park is through Back Bay NWR (757-721-2412. *Entrance fee; trails closed Nov.-March),* and cars are prohibited in both the refuge and the park; so park at the Back Bay Visitor Contact Station, don your walking shoes or hop a bike, and head south into the refuge.(You can also enter along the beach or by canoe along Bay Bay. Contact the park for information.)

Collecting seashells

What to See and Do

Back Bay is a glorious refuge, a wonderful introduction to life on a barrier spit. Mostly marshland, it harbors abundant birdlife. Follow signs along the dike road; by the time you reach the state park in 5 miles, you'll have entered the maritime forest—live oaks, hollies, and loblolly pines. The scenery indicates that you're on the spine of the barrier spit, where vegetation has managed to take root in the sandy soil. To the west, toward Back Bay, lies marshland; to the east, golden dunes undulate to the Atlantic and a seemingly endless beach. Continue straight ahead on the park's only road, which splices the spit. You'll soon reach the **contact station,** where you can pick up brochures and maps, as well as a guide to the 2.4-mile **Barbour Hill Interpretive Trail.** This nature loop explores the different features of the barrier spit, including loblolly pines, walking dunes, and thickets full of wildlife.

Now you have a choice. If you've had enough exercise, take the 0.7-mile **Barbour Hill Beach Trail** to the Atlantic Ocean—and a beautiful, desolate beach sprinkled with shells. Or continue 2.4 miles down the main road to **False Cape Landing,** with pretty views of **Back Bay.** On the east side of the road, the 0.6-mile **False Cape Landing Trail** provides another chance to reach the Atlantic. Two miles farther down the main road lies **Wash Woods,** site of an educational center *(visit by advance reservation only)* and a tangle of short trails. Try the 0.5-mile **Cemetery Trail,** which visits the remains of the early settlement: a church steeple and shaded cemetery dotted with crumbling tombstones.

From here, head to the beach on the **Wash Woods Interpretive Trail;** or delve even deeper into solitude along the 3-mile **Dudley Island Trail** *(Hikers only).* Wandering to the North Carolina line, this trail promises good odds at sighting some of the region's wild horses, and perhaps even a red fox.

Camping

The park has 12 primitive sites, with no showers. March-Nov. Available on a first-come, first-served basis. Camping fee. Permits must be obtained in person at First Landing/Seashore S.P., 2500 Shore Drive, Virginia Beach, VA; 757-481-4836.

❏ *FALSE CAPE S.P., 4001 SANDPIPER RD., VIRGINIA BEACH, VA 23456*

Life of a Loggerhead

Most common to Florida's beaches, endangered loggerhead turtles nest as far north as False Cape— a ritual that can be observed between May and October. After dark the female loggerhead crawls ashore, where she digs a nest and buries about 110 leathery eggs, then heads back to the water. Hatchlings pop through the sand 50 to 70 days later, and with flailing flippers race for the waves. The next time anyone sees these little guys they're 4 inches long and living somewhere near the Azores. Researchers have suggested that the loggerheads may return to their birth site to nest—commencing the cycle all over again.

91

First Landing/ Seashore

US 60 at Cape Henry, in Virginia Beach

Bald cypress swamp

92

● 2,889 acres ● 757-481-2131
● Year-round ● Vehicle fee
● Cypress swamp ● Varied eco-
systems ● Hiking, biking, boating

Those who judge this little park—tucked between high rises on the tip of Cape Henry—for its beach alone are in for a big surprise. For here you'll find an astonishing medley of northern and southern ecosystems, including cordgrass-filled marshlands, forested dunes, and a bald cypress swamp.

Lacking fertile farmland, much of the cape was settled only recently. Indeed, when Capt. John Smith landed here in 1607—memorialized in the recent addition of "First Landing" to the park's name—he chose to push farther up the James River to found America's first permanent English settlement, at Jamestown. In 1936 more than 2,000 acres of the pristine land became one of Virginia's first state parks, now the state's most popular.

On the south side of US 60, the **Visitor Center** (*757-481-4836. April-Nov.*) offers exhibits on the region's ecosystems. Next, head for the **Bald Cypress Trail** along a boardwalk above tannin-stained waters, where bulbous-trunked bald cypresses stand draped in Spanish moss. You may glimpse pileated woodpeckers or the endangered chicken turtle, whose neck extends longer than the length of its shell. The hike can be extended by the 3.1-mile **Osmanthus Trail,** wandering beneath olive trees. The longer, less crowded 5-mile **Long Creek Trail** moves through bird-filled salt marshes. The 6-mile **Cape Henry hiker-biker trail** cuts across the park to the **Narrows** (*Accessible by auto via 64th St.*) and its small beach. There's a boat launch here, but no swimming. To cool off head to the **bayshore** (*Registered campers only in summer*).

Camping and Lodging

The park has 235 tent and RV sites, with showers; and 20 housekeeping cabins. March-November. For reservations call 804-225-3867 or 800-933-PARK. Camping fee.

❑ *First Landing/Seashore State Park and Natural Area, 2500 Shore Dr., Virginia Beach, Virginia 23451*

Westmoreland

40 miles east of Fredericksburg, off Va. 3

● 1,300 acres ● 804-493-8821 ● Year-round ● Entrance fee ● Fossil-filled cliffs ● Nature Center ● Hiking, swimming, boating, birdwatching

Overlooking the Potomac River on Virginia's remote Northern Neck, Westmoreland's multihued Horsehead Cliffs provide more than a scenic backdrop for visitors who come to swim, boat, fish, and sun. Embedded with billions of fossils of sea creatures dating back 15 million years, the cliffs recall a time when porpoises, sharks, and whales cavorted in a warm, shallow sea. Protected for millions of years by sand and silt, these relics—including shark teeth and whale bone—are only now being exposed through erosion. Cast upon the rocky beach, they're here for finding and keeping.

Beyond the cliffs, the park's pretty woodlands cover deep-gouged ridges, and frogs bellow in a cattail-filled marsh. Crisscrossed with 6 hiking trails, this forested realm lures more than 100 species of birds, including wild turkeys and—soaring above—ospreys and bald eagles.

Get an introduction to the area at the **Visitor Center** *(Mem. Day–Labor Day),* located in the heart of the park. Be sure to check out the samples of fossils—so you know what to look for later on. From here it's a short walk to the park's most popular spot, the beach. The easy 0.4-mile **Beach Trail** leads to a rocky expanse on the Potomac. Families picnic, kids splash, and everyone keeps their eyes peeled for that coveted fossil. *(Fossil collecting permitted along beach between the cliffs and marsh; digging in the cliffs themselves is illegal and dangerous.)*

To explore the marsh and woodlands, take the interpretive **Big Meadows Nature Trail,** located about half a mile east of the Visitor Center. About midway (0.3 mile), a short spur leads to the river and a magnificent view of the cliffs. Farther along is Yellow Swamp, cloaked in spring with the tender shoots of cattails. The path dead-ends at the **Turkey Neck Trail,** where you can either backtrack the way you came or make a loop by turning right.

Camping

The park has 138 tent and RV sites, with showers; and 25 cabins. March-Nov. Call park or 800-933-PARK for reservations. Camping fee.

❏ *WESTMORELAND STATE PARK, RTE. 1, BOX 600, MONTROSS, VIRGINIA 22520*

93

Wild turkey

Pipestem Resort

12 miles south of Hinton on W. Va. 20

● 4,026 acres ● 304-466-1800 or 800-CALL-WVA
● Year-round ● Bluestone River Gorge ● Mountain
scenery ● Nature Center ● Horse rentals and trails
● Hiking, tennis, swimming, golf, boating, mountain biking

In one aspect a wilderness oasis with remote hiking trails, a clear-running river, and plenty of wildlife, Pipestem is also a "resort" state park—containing such urbane offerings as golf courses, restaurants, swimming pools, and modern conference facilities. Whether hiking or golfing, you can't miss the park's spectacular setting. Sitting prettily on a plateau high above the Bluestone River Gorge, the park's surrounding ridges roll off in every direction, changing moods with the time of day. White-tailed deer nibble bushes along the park road, wild grouse and wild turkeys rummage the understory, and the occasional golden eagle soars in the blue sky above—everywhere a sense of splendid isolation pervades.

Springtime profusion on a Pipestem ridge

In summers long past, Algonquin, Shawnee, and Iroquois came to this remote spot in the Appalachians to fish and hunt. These people were probably the first to use the hollow, woody stems of the native "pipestem" bush (commonly known as meadowsweet) to fashion their pipes, a practice that continued with later European colonists. The region's beauty was threatened around the turn of the century, when the Bluestone River ran black with the coal dust of nearby industries—a blemish that since has been cleaned up. The park opened its gates to the public in 1970.

What to See and Do

With all the activities and facilities, you could easily spend a week at Pipestem and still have lots to do. If time is short, begin near the entrance station with the popular .33-mile walk to **Pipestem Knob Tower,** which offers a 360-degree view of Bluestone Lake and scattered farms, lush green mountains and valleys. Next, drive along the 3-mile **park road,** which bisects the plateau, extending the length of the park. Several pullouts provide a chance to pause and take in the spectacular mountain setting.

Along the way you pass the **stables** *(Closed Mon. Labor Day–Mem. Day; fee),* where horses may be rented. If you're here for more than a couple of days, consider signing up for an overnight trail ride into Bluestone Canyon, complete with cookout beneath the stars and a berth in a rustic 1910 cabin. Near the stables, the **Nature Center** has exhibits on natural history and wildlife—stop by if only to check out what programs are going on, perhaps a salamander hunt, bug walk, or winter tree identification stroll.

Make a point to visit the **Canyon Rim Center,** near park headquarters. Housing the **Mountain Artisans Shop** *(Closed Mon.-Tues. Labor Day–Mem. Day),* full of locally made handicrafts, the center serves as the upper terminus for an **aerial tramway** *(April-Oct.; fare)* that shoots into 1,200-foot Bluestone Canyon to **Mountain Creek Lodge** *(April-Oct.),* a romantic getaway featuring an elegant restaurant. The views alone are worth the trip, though the portion of the **River Trail** that wanders along the rugged, rock-strewn river at the bottom is first-rate. Consider walking as far as Pilots Knob, 2 miles away, which provides picturesque views of the area.

If you don't take the tramway (or even if you do), don't miss the hike along the .75-mile **Canyon Rim Trail,** which leaves from the center and drops 500 feet off the plateau to Heritage Point. This large sandstone outcropping juts out over the gorge, offering sweeping views of pure mountain scenery. Along the way, sassafras and dogwood, maple and oak shade the rocky trail.

Just before you reach McKeever Lodge along the park road, leave your car and walk the short, steep trail to **Long Branch Lake,** a serene body of water nestled in the woods. Stocked with trout, the lake is popular with fishermen, canoeists, and paddleboaters *(rentals available at dock near Long Branch Lake Dam).*

At the end of the park road, seven-story **McKeever Lodge** sits on the lip of the canyon, offering stupendous

New River

Flowing from Hinton northwest to Fayetteville, the **New River Gorge National River** promises some of the East's best white-water rafting—no great secret, judging by the floods of thrill seekers who take to inflatable rafts mid-March to October. Lesser known are the river's landside treats: mountain biking, rock climbing (1,400 different course choices), plus 25 hiking trails that explore waterfalls, geological formations, and old coal and railroad towns. Stop by the Canyon Rim Visitor Center in Lansing *(304-574-2115)* for the best views of the gorge, as well as exhibits that describe its geological and cultural history. You can also obtain information on how to arrange a white-water rafting trip.

Trail riding

views as well as an extravaganza of facilities. Even if you're not staying here, at least take a cup of coffee in the window-walled restaurant—preferably early in the morning, when purplish peaks float above gossamers of fog.

Further Adventures

Hardy hikers should consider taking the 4-mile one-way **River Trail,** an old road that begins near McKeever Lodge and winds to the bottom of Bluestone Gorge through a thick canopy of tulip poplar, oak, black locust, hemlock, and rhododendron. The trail passes the remains of a long-gone farmstead, and offers plenty of chances to spot rabbits and white-tailed deer. Birders will appreciate the abundance of birdlife: 161 bird species have been spotted at Pipestem, including tundra swan, Bonaparte's gull, American wigeon, black-bellied plover, and 24 types of warblers. In September hawks and other migratory raptors fly by. The fun part comes at the bottom of the canyon, where you must wade across the cool, green river (*before starting, check with park staff to see if river is running high*). Walk downstream to Mountain Creek Lodge, and let the aerial tram whisk you back up to the canyon rim.

Another popular, albeit arduous, trail traces a rugged, unspoiled segment of the Bluestone Gorge, protected as the Bluestone National Scenic River. Hike the 7 miles to lovely 2,100-acre **Bluestone State Park** (*304-466-2805*), where misty mountains ring boat-dotted Bluestone Lake, and watch for great blue herons and kingfishers, which favor the warm-water stream. (During summer, park rangers sometimes lead groups on this beautiful foray into the wilderness.) If you're not up to the hike, drive to Bluestone via W. Va. 20 and sample the lake's beauty along one of the park's short trails, through stream-laced woods inhabited by flocks of wild turkey, white-tailed deer, woodchuck—and the elusive bobcat. The popular 2-mile **Boundary Trail** ambles to a cave in the forest.

Camping and Lodging

The park has 82 tent and RV sites, with shower facilities; and 25 housekeeping cabins. Camping fee. McKeever Lodge offers 113 rooms; the rustic Mountain Creek Lodge has 30 rooms (summer only; access by tram). Call 304-466-1800 or 800-CALL-WVA for reservations.

❑ PIPESTEM RESORT STATE PARK, P.O. BOX 150, PIPESTEM, WEST VIRGINIA 25979

Blackwater Falls

Off W. Va. 32, near Davis

● 1,688 acres ● 304-259-5216 or 800-CALL-WVA ● Year-round
● Blackwater River Canyon ● Hiking, cross-country skiing,
fishing (license required), horseback riding, mountain biking

Promontory above Blackwater River Canyon

One of the most dramatic gorges east of the Mississippi
slices through the Potomac Highlands in this park. Half a
mile wide and 8 miles long, the canyon was cut by the
tannin-stained Blackwater River, whose five-story-high falls
are justifiably famous. Hugging the rims of the canyon, the
park provides endless views of the gorge, and trails lead
you close enough to the falls to let you feel their cool, misty
breath on your face. One of West Virginia's signature "resort
parks," Blackwater boasts a beautifully situated stone-and-

wood lodge overlooking the canyon and an active Nordic center, with 20 miles of cross-country skiing trails.

What to See and Do

Obviously, **Blackwater Falls** are the park's major attraction, and maps available in the lodge information center list a number of relatively short trails weaving down into the gorge. The most accessible and therefore the most popular is the paved .25-mile **Gentle Trail,** which begins on Blackwater Falls Road before reaching the lodge and leads to an observation platform above the falls. Or, if stairs don't bother you, you can follow the more than 200 steps from the Trading Post parking lot to the roaring water. A final platform at the base of the falls offers a good sense of their power and beauty. The distinctive red-brown river water is stained by leaching from upcountry hemlocks and spruce. Hemlocks, spruce, and rhododendron also frill the canyon edges, buffeting them in greenery year-round. In winter, mist from the falls veil the surrounding greenery in a lace of ice.

Two other trails worth following lie just west of the lodge on Blackwater Falls Road. If you take the mile-long **Balanced Rock Trail,** you'll come to a large sandstone boulder that seems to perch precariously on a smaller rock. As you leave the rock, you can take the trail spur to your left and make a quick loop around the **Rhododendron Trail,** especially appealing in spring. The nearby **Elakala Trail** will take you down to a footbridge across the **Upper Elakala Falls.** From here you weave back through a garden of huge boulders and equally impressive hemlocks. For hikers looking for something a little more challenging, pick up the 8-mile (one-way) **Blackwater/Canaan Trail** at the horse stables and follow it south through mountain scenery and into the wide-open Canaan Valley Resort State Park.

In the northwest corner of the park, **Pendleton Lake** offers a cooling alternative to mountain hiking, and keeps swimmers and boaters occupied all through the summer months. In winter, cross-country skiers flock to the park to take advantage of evergreen-overhung trails and the area's predictably abundant snowfall. A toboggan run and rope tow (fee) provide more winter sport.

Camping and Lodging

The park has 65 tent and RV sites (May-Oct.), with shower facilities. Camping fee. Blackwater Lodge offers 54 rooms and 25 cabins. Reserve far in advance by calling the park at 304-259-5216 or 800-CALL-WVA.

❏ *BLACKWATER FALLS STATE PARK, P.O. DRAWER 490, DAVIS, WEST VIRGINIA 26260*

The Art Co-op of Davis

The little crossroads hamlet of Davis, situated at 3,200 feet, once looked to lumber for its livelihood. The lumber boom ended decades ago, however, and now tourism fuels the town's coffers. Two state parks, Blackwater and Canaan Valley, flank Davis, and the Monogahela National Forest wraps in and around the area, so the town keeps busy with mountain bikers, hikers, and the anglers who come to try their luck on the Blackwater. Davis also has its own bit of culture. The town's former pool hall and bowling alley have been put to good use as an artists' cooperative. More than a hundred artists now display their paintings, woodwork, textiles, pottery, and photography there.

Autumn-bedecked country road

Canaan Valley Resort

10 miles south of Davis, off W. Va. 32

● 5,910 acres ● 304-866-4121 or 800-CALL-WVA
● Year-round ● Mountain-ringed valley ● Interpretive
programs ● Skiing, ice skating, hiking, swimming, golf

Gazing for the first time upon Canaan Valley's rugged
beauty, a group of fur traders in the 18th century were
reminded of Canaan, the promised land of milk and honey.
Hunters who later ventured into the valley, however, formed a
different opinion: Filled with bears, panthers, tangled growth,
and dangerous cliffs, the place literally swallowed humans
whole. These days, visitors here still feel like explorers,
enduring narrow, winding, mountainous roads to reach this
isolated pocket in central West Virginia. But those who perse-
vere discover a mecca for outdoor recreation—and in the
heart of it all sits Canaan Valley Resort State Park.

The main reason people come here is to ski. Cradled by
tall peaks of the Alleghenies, the valley—actually the largest
and highest plateau (3,200 feet) east of the Rockies—catches
storms and collects an abundance of snow, heralding long
winters and skiing from Thanksgiving into April. The state
park boasts a decent ski area with 16 runs, plus a cross-
country ski center and many miles of trails. Mountain biking,
hiking, golfing, and canoeing on the Blackwater River take
precedent in other seasons.

The charm of Canaan lies in its undisturbed wilderness, where animals outnumber the people. The thick stands of red spruce that once filled the valley are long gone, thanks to loggers in the 1920s; but in their wake flourishes a realm of meadows, balsam swamps, marshes, ponds, and bogs that swarm with such wildlife as black ducks, green herons, minks, raccoons, and skunks, to name just a few. Douglas-fir, beech, birch, and maple cloak the surrounding mountain ridges—the domain of white-tailed deer and snowshoe hares, mountain lions and black bears.

What to See and Do

If you're game for exploring the valley beyond the ski lifts, take the interpretive **Deer Run Trail,** which begins near the lodge *(ask for trail map at front desk)* and wanders for 1.5 miles through hemlocks, thickets of rhododendron and mountain laurel, and a balsam swamp. Watch for white-tailed deer and red squirrels (locally called "fairy diddles"), as well as golden crowned kinglets, hermit thrushes, vireos, and warblers. At trail's end, you can visit the tiny **Nature Center and Ski Touring Center,** where mounted local animals are displayed, then loop back to the lodge via the **Abe Run** and **Mill Run Trails,** past an active beaver pond (best viewing at dusk). Another easy hike, the 1-mile **Blackwater River Trail** *(Trailhead at golf course parking lot),* ambles along the slow-moving Blackwater River, past some of the park's most beautiful bigtoothed aspen.

Those wanting a more rugged experience—hiking or cross-country skiing—should head for the **Bald Knob Trail** *(From lower lot of ski area, cross road and walk up gravel drive to smaller parking area and the trailhead).* The steep, 2.5-mile climb through hardwood forest brings you to 4,308-foot Bald Knob, offering a stupendous overview of the entire Canaan Valley. (For an easier route, pay a few dollars for the ski lift, which brings you to the ridgetop, then hike a short way to the knob.)

Another option is the 8-mile (one-way) **Canaan/Blackwater Trail,** which climbs up and over Canaan Mountain to Blackwater Falls State Park, a popular trek especially among cross-country skiers. But be forewarned: The terrain is quite difficult. It is suggested that you stop by the Nature Center for additional information. At the end of the day, put up your feet at the lodge, which beckons with a snapping fire, hearty meals, whirlpool bath, and perhaps some live entertainment.

Camping and Lodging

The park has 34 tent and RV sites, with shower facilities. Camping fee. The Canaan Valley Lodge offers 250 rooms and 23 cabins. Call 304-866-4121 or 800-CALL-WVA for reservations.
❏ *Canaan Valley Resort State Park, HC 70, Box 321, Davis, West Virginia 26260*

Winnowing Woodcocks

The wetlands of Canaan Valley are the courtship grounds of the woodcock—a bird typically found much farther north in Canadian peatlands. From March into June, at dawn, dusk, and night, the males fly high into the sky then divebomb the ground, their swept-back wings creating an odd humming sound loud enough to be heard—even by humans—half a mile away. The bird repeats this "winnow," up to eight times before dropping beside the female of his choice.

Chestnut-sided warbler

Watoga

17 miles south of Marlinton on US 219

- 10,100 acres
- 304-799-4087 or 800-CALL-WVA
- Year-round
- Appalachian highlands ● Hiking, fishing (license required), skiing

Flame azalea

West Virginia's first and largest state park, Watoga sprawls across the forested Appalachian highlands near the eastern border with Virginia. Established in 1934, the park was developed by the Civilian Conservation Corps, and a museum to their efforts, as well as the quaint stone-and-chestnut cabins they built, still stand in the park. The shallow **Greenbrier River** that meanders along the park's western boundary accounts for its name—*watauga* is Cherokee for "river of islands." Ensconced in lush, green hardwood forest, the park's 11-acre **Lake Killbuck** is a classic West Virginia paradise. Most park facilities are located in its northern half, while the southern portion, adjacent to both the vast Monongahela National Forest and the Calvin Price State Forest, remains mostly wild.

Pick up information at the park's rustic headquarters, then, for a long overview of the park, head up to the **T.M. Cheek Overlook.** For hikers and tree-lovers, the **Brooks Memorial Arboretum** offers several walks through forests of birch, hemlock, maple, beech, and tulip trees. A 3-mile round-trip hike on the **Dragon Draft Trail,** which begins at the aboretum entrance, will take you to more views. Along the way, especially during spring, listen for the unmistakable thrumping of wild grouse hidden in the forest. Take a row across the wide open waters of **Lake Killbuck,** or try your hand at a little fishing, perhaps at **Laurel Run.** Evenings are a good time to stroll along part of the **Greenbrier River Trail,** a 75-mile-long corridor following the path of the former C&O Railroad. Watch for beavers busy at work in the fading glow of sunset.

Camping and Lodging

The park has 88 tent and RV sites (mid-April–Nov.), with showers; plus 33 cabins (a few open year-round). Call 304-799-4087 or 800-CALL-WVA for reservations. Camping fee.

❑ *WATOGA STATE PARK, HC 82, BOX 252, MARLINTON, WV 24954*

101

Tennessee

Fall Creek Falls
Roan Mountain
Pickett
Reelfoot Lake

Kentucky

Cumberland Falls
Natural Bridge
Carter Caves
John James Audubon

Mississippi

Tishomingo
Winterville Mounds
Natchez
Percy Quin

Alabama

DeSoto
Cheaha
Joe Wheeler
Gulf

Georgia

Stephen C. Foster
Tallulah Gorge
Fort Mountain
Cloudland Canyon
Providence Canyon

Florida

John Pennekamp
  Coral Reef
Myakka River
Wekiwa Springs
Paynes Prairie
St. Joseph Peninsula

North Carolina

Hanging Rock
Stone Mountain
Hammocks Beach
Fort Macon

South Carolina

Mountain Bridge
Devils Fork
Huntington Beach
Hunting Island

Map labels

CARTER CAVES
Louisville · Frankfort
Lexington
JOHN JAMES AUDUBON
Ohio
NATURAL BRIDGE
K Y.
CUMBERLAND FALLS
STONE MOUNTAIN
REELFOOT LAKE
Nashville
HANGING ROCK
TENN.
PICKETT
ROAN MOUNTAIN
N.C.
FALL CREEK FALLS
Memphis
Raleigh
MOUNTAIN BRIDGE
FORT MACON
Mississippi River
CLOUDLAND CANYON
TISHOMINGO
DEVILS FORK
HAMMOCKS BEACH
JOE WHEELER
DeSOTO
Columbia
WINTERVILLE MOUNDS
FORT MOUNTAIN
TALLULAH GORGE
S.C.
MISS.
Birmingham
CHEAHA
Atlanta
HUNTINGTON BEACH
ALA.
GA.
Jackson Montgomery
NATCHEZ
PROVIDENCE CANYON
HUNTING ISLAND
PERCY QUIN
GULF
Tallahassee
STEPHEN C. FOSTER
Jacksonville
ST. JOSEPH PENINSULA
Gainesville
PAYNES PRAIRIE
WEKIWA SPRINGS
Orlando
Tampa
FLA.
MYAKKA RIVER
Miami
JOHN PENNEKAMP CORAL REEF

0   200 mi
0   400 km

Sunrise at John Pennekamp Coral Reef State Park, Florida

Hanging Rock

4 miles northwest of Danbury, on Moore's Spring Road (N.C. 1001)

● 6,457 acres ● 910-593-8480 ● Year-round ● 400-foot cliffs ● Waterfalls ● Hiking, rock climbing ● Boating, fishing (license required), swimming ● National Historic Landmark

View from Hanging Rock

Exposed knobs and peaks, high rock cliffs and promontories characterize this rugged park lying in one of the easternmost mountain ranges in the state. The Sauratown Mountains, named for the Saura Indians, rise some 50 miles east of the Blue Ridge, hence their nickname "mountains away from the mountains." Hanging Rock, Moore's Wall, Cook's Wall, Wolf Rock, and other prominent outcrops are supported by a foundation of quartzite that resisted the erosive effects of ice, wind, and water over the eons. The resulting stone caps and ridges climb to 400 feet and range nearly 2 miles long on a mountain system that dramatically towers more than 1,500 feet above the surrounding countryside.

Nearby mineral spring resorts attracted well-heeled vacationers to the area in the decades following the Civil War, but by the 1930s the resorts' appeal had declined. In 1936 a citizens group working through the Winston-Salem Foundation donated 3,096 acres for the creation of a park. During the late 1930s and early 1940s, the Civilian Conser-

104

vation Corps put in a road, trails, parking and picnic areas, a stone bathhouse, and a sand beach, the latter to accompany the new 12-acre lake formed by damming Cascade Creek.

What to See and Do

Drive to the **Visitor Center** and pick up a trail map, which indicates length and degree of difficulty for each hiking trail. The 0.7-mile **Chestnut Oak Nature Trail** offers a quick primer on the local forest as it gently winds along the lake through a canopy of oak and pine. More than 300 species of flora grow in the park, including rhododendron, mountain laurel, galax, azalea, and numerous ferns. At higher elevations you'll find delicate wildflowers such as lady's slipper, bird's-foot violet, and fire pink.

For waterfalls, park in the first lot and walk 0.3 mile to **Upper Cascades,** then take **Indian Creek Trail** down to **Hidden Falls** and **Window Falls** (0.6 mile from parking lot). The trail continues downhill, crossing the stream on big rocks, and pushing through the rhododendron understory another 3 miles to the Dan River. To return you must retrace your steps or have someone pick you up on the dirt road at trail's end. To get a good look at the park's signature rock formations, try **Hanging Rock Trail,** a 2.4-mile up-and-back hike that takes you to the top of the 200-foot cliff for which the park is named. From up here, savor fine views of the country all around—Moore's Knob shows itself to the west and Winston-Salem is visible on clear days to the southeast. If time allows, take the more strenuous, 4.2-mile **Moore's Wall Loop Trail,** which provides wonderfully close encounters with Moore's Knob, Balanced Rock, and Indian Face, and offers a rewarding mountain vista from a 60-foot **observation tower.** Rock climbers test their agility and strength on Moore's Wall as well as on nearby **Cook's Wall.**

The unnamed impoundment **lake** is fully outfitted with a snack bar, stone-and-timber bathhouse, beach, and diving platform. In the summertime, chill out in the roped-off swimming area or fish for bass and bream. You can rent a rowboat or canoe and paddle around enjoying views of encircling forest and distant Moore's Knob. Also, check for regularly scheduled ranger programs on geology and mountain flora and fauna. Among the forest denizens you may be lucky enough to see are white-tailed deer, gray fox, and eastern screech owl.

Camping and Lodging

The park has 73 tent and RV sites, with showers, available on a first-come basis. Eight group campsites offer more primitive arrangements; reservations required. Camping fee. There are also 6 cabins. For reservations call the park at 910-593-8480.
❏ *Hanging Rock State Park, P.O. Box 278, Danbury, NC 27016*

Layered Look

As you walk the park's trails and gaze up at its sheer cliffs, you can read the rock walls for a history of time and movement on the earth. Sand and mud from an inland sea were packed down to sandstone and shale, then metamorphosed with tremendous pressure and heat into hard quartzite and mica schist. Piled up like a stack of papers, the layers—each with its own color and texture—were then rumpled and bent, the stress so great that here and there they fractured.

105

Stone Mountain

7 miles southwest of Roaring Gap, off N.C. 1002

Rock climbers on face of Stone Mountain

● 13,560 acres ● 910-957-8185 ● Year-round ● 600-foot granite dome ● Hiking ● Waterfalls ● Rock climbing, trout fishing (license required) ● Historic structures

More than 300 million years ago, molten lava blistered up under the earth's surface and hardened into a 25-square-mile mass of igneous rock here in what would become the edge of North Carolina's mountain region. Part of that mass, Stone Mountain swells 600 feet above the ground, its rounded bald front obscured from view until you are well into the park. The forces of erosion continue to sculpture the granite dome, rivulets of water clawing dark grooves down its face and standing pools leaving potholes on the top. Surrounding Stone Mountain, a forest of oak, maple, hickory, and pine gives cover to a host of wildlife, while a network of streams carves out valleys, in one case growing from a high trickle to a series of plunging falls.

Little is known of the earliest inhabitants of the area. The Catawba lived here long before the arrival of white settlers, who made their living by farming and logging. The mountain folk used to point out scars on the rock face and claim that they were made by the devil's chariot; a split in a gigantic boulder they said was caused by a shaking of the earth on the day Christ was crucified. Long aware of the beauty and natural resources of the area, locals campaigned in the 1960s for the formation of a state park. At their prompting, the North Carolina Granite Corporation—which owned much of the desired property—donated 418.5 acres that included Stone Mountain, and agreed to sell more to the state. Stone Mountain State Park came into being in 1969 and was designated a National Natural Landmark six years later.

What to See and Do

Begin at the **Visitor Center,** a small but up-to-date facility loaded with interesting displays on pioneers and natural history. Among the exhibits are an 1865 muzzle-loader, an 1870s loom, a 1930s mail-order banjo with calfskin head, and a copper moonshine still. A deck offers a fine view of the mountain. Pick up a map here and drive 2 miles down to the parking lot, where an easy stroll (wheelchair accessible) affords splendid views of the broad southwest face of Stone Mountain.

By all means, try to make time for **Stone Mountain Trail,** one of the most gorgeous in the Southern mountains. The 4-mile loop opens with an adrenaline-pumping sign: "Area contains hazards associated with rocks, steep slopes and cliffs. INJURY OR DEATH POSSIBLE. Stay on Marked Trail!" You then ascend a precipitous trail, shooting straight up through the forest and out across tremendous slabs of granite. In less than a mile you're at the top, taking in magnificent mountain panoramas. You could turn around and go straight back down, but staying with the loop brings you to another park highlight—**Stone Mountain Falls,** a 200-foot water slide. A series of steps and boardwalks offers safe viewing. Continue around to the base of the dome, fringed with pine woods and high-grass meadow where deer often graze. At this point you can take another trail up to **Cedar Rock** (1 mile) and **Wolf Rock** (1.5 miles) granite outcrops. Or head back to the car, passing the 1855 Hutchinson Homestead with its log cabin and tin-roofed barn.

Hone your fly-fishing technique on one of the managed sections of Bullhead and Rich Mountain Creeks, where a limited number of anglers are allowed to fish on a catch-and-release basis *(fee)*. Other streams in the 17-mile system are open for take-home fishing. Finally, if you take the gravel road out, you'll drive past the quaint 1898 Garden Creek Baptist Church, one of the oldest in the county.

Camping

The park has 37 tent and RV sites, with showers; and 6 backcountry sites. Available first come, first served. There are also 6 primitive tent sites suitable for groups; for reservations call the park. Camping fee.

❑ *Stone Mountain State Park, 3042 Frank Pkwy., Roaring Gap, North Carolina 28668*

Bug Lady

Betty Lou Wallace of nearby Mountain Park began collecting insects in the 4th grade. Pretty soon she was winning awards in state and national science fairs. Caught mostly in the 1950s, her butterflies, moths, and other insects eventually numbered 9,000. Calling herself the "buggiest" girl in the state, Betty Lou raised many of her catches from egg to larva to pupa to adult. Part of her collection is on display in the Stone Mountain State Park Visitor Center—the handsome cases were built by her father, cabinetmaker I.O. Wallace.

107

Hammocks Beach

4 miles south of Swansboro, via N.C. 1511 and passenger ferry

● 227 acres ● 910-326-4881 ● Year-round ● No pets on ferry ● Barrier island ● Canoe trail ● Swimming, shelling, fishing

Located on unspoiled Bear Island, Hammocks Beach offers an intimate sojourn with nature—its estuarine creeks and salt marshes, high dunes, and white-sand beaches paint a picture of coastal serenity. The 3.5-mile-long slip of land attracts nesting loggerhead turtles from mid-May to late August, while egrets and herons stalk the tidal creeks and bottle-nosed dolphins sport offshore. Originally named in the 1700s for its lack of vegetation, Bare Island became Bear Island by a simple spelling change. The island was a haven for pirates in the early 18th century; later Confederate forces used it as a defense post. During World War II the U.S. Coast Guard patrolled here against U-boats. Donated to a black teachers organization, the island became a park in 1961 for blacks only; after the Civil Rights Act of 1964 the park was opened to the general public.

A 25-minute ferry (*Mem. Day–Labor Day daily, May and Sept. Wed.-Sun., April and Oct. Fri.-Sun.; fare*) runs from the mainland. During the off-season you can take a water taxi from Waterway Boat Rentals (*910-326-1861*), which also rents boats. Once on the island, you'll have a 15-minute walk out to the **beach**—bring good shoes, a hat, insect repellent, and plenty of sunscreen. A concessionaire sells drinks and snacks, and the bathhouse has showers and changing rooms.

You can fish for flounder, trout, bluefish, and puppy drum. Or you can stroll along the beach, scattering sandpipers and gulls, then take to the water in a designated swimming area. Or just park yourself on a plot of sand and soak up the salt air and warm sun.

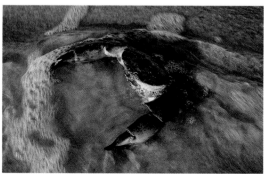

Stone crab

Camping

The park has 17 backcountry sites, 14 with a maximum capacity of 6 people, 3 with a maximum capacity of 12. Sites closed during summer full moons to minimize disturbance of turtle nests. Available first come, first served. Camping fee.

❏ *HAMMOCKS BEACH STATE PARK, 1572 HAMMOCKS BEACH RD., SWANSBORO, NC 28584*

Fort Macon

4 miles east of Atlantic Beach on N.C. 58

- 385 acres ● 919-726-3775
- Year-round ● No camping
- Civil War-era fort ● Nature trail
- Ocean swimming, fishing

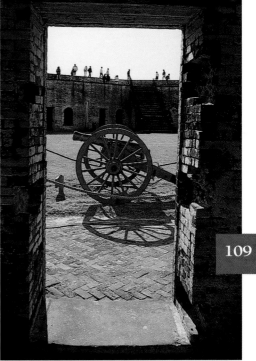

Fort Macon

On the eastern tip of Bogue Banks, where the Atlantic crashes into Bogue Sound, a young Lt. William Eliason engineered the construction of a tremendous masonry bastion called **Fort Macon** to guard Beaufort Inlet. Earlier forts on the same strategic site dated back to 1756. The present fort was built between 1826 and 1834, and named for a North Carolina senator. On April 25, 1862, Union batteries bombarded the Confederate-held bastion for 11 hours, their rifled cannon battering the fort. The Confederate surrender underscored the futility of 1820s defenses against 1860s military technology.

After the war, Fort Macon served as a military and civil prison for about ten years, then was regarrisoned in 1898 during the Spanish-American War. Abandoned for more than two decades, the fort was sold to North Carolina for one dollar in 1924 for use as a park. During World War II, coast artillery troops once again occupied the old fort. Since 1945, it has functioned as a major drawing card for area tourism, its one million-plus annual visitors making it North Carolina's most visited state park.

Guided tours (*Mem. Day–Labor Day*) of the pentagonal fort explore local military history and ramble through the vaulted casemates, gunpowder magazines, and counterfire galleries. You can also pick up a self-guided tour brochure at the fort entrance. Afterwards, take the 0.4-mile **Elliott Coues Nature Trail** behind the fort through a maritime forest of yaupon, live oak, cedar, and beach holly.

A lovely beach has a protected swimming area, as well as a bathhouse and refreshment stand. And there are picnic shelters and outdoor grills. If you bring your rod and reel, you're likely to catch flounder, bluefish, or spot.

❏ *Fort Macon State Park, P.O. Box 127, Atlantic Beach, NC 28512*

109

Mountain Bridge

Jones Gap Station: 25 miles northwest of Greenville, off US 276. Caesars Head Station: 30 miles northwest of Greenville on US 276

Rock pinnacle, Caesars Head Station

● 10,813 acres ● 864-836-6115 ● Year-round ● Mountain vistas ● Waterfall ● Hiking, fishing (license required)

Tucked into the mountainous northwest corner of the state and linked by hiking trails, Caesars Head and adjacent Jones Gap State Parks were in 1996 combined into one entity—Mountain Bridge State Natural Area. Containing the land that connects Greenville's two watersheds, this is where the Blue Ridge suddenly drops 2,000 feet to South Carolina's piedmont region, forming a high rock escarpment that gives wonderful views of the endless foothills to the south. Low-lying Jones Gap embraces the Middle Saluda river valley, lush home to more than 400 plant species, while Caesars Head spreads over the highlands, its granite outcrop namesake somewhat resembling the Roman emperor's profile.

One of the earliest settlers here, planter and merchant Col. Benjamin Hagood bought 500 acres just before the Civil War. He herded livestock up the mountain in spring and stayed in his cabin until fall. Another pioneer, Solomon Jones is said to have laid out a road in the 1840s without surveying instruments, relying instead on his instincts for contours and grades. The Jones Gap toll road went from River Falls up to Caesars Head and on to Cedar Mountain, North Carolina. Now used by hikers, it's the easiest footpath from Jones Gap to Caesars Head.

From the 1860s to the early 1900s, the toll road stayed busy with guests of a Caesars Head resort hotel. A journalist in 1895 wrote that "the way up is torturous, and possibly could be improved, but it is no child's play to build a road through these gorges and along the precipitous mountain sides." Nevertheless, one "finds rich compensation in the bracing atmosphere and the boundless views." People came

South Carolina

from as far away as China for those views, and for dancing, dining, tennis, and swimming. Only the views remain—the hotel burned in 1954, and the old dance hall is now a private club just down from the Visitor Center. The park land was privately owned until the state bought it in the late 1970s.

What to See and Do

Both Jones Gap Station and Caesars Head Station lie far off the beaten tourism path, and most people come through either for a quick look or for serious hiking or backpacking. If you want to look *up* at towering cliffs, go to Jones Gap; for views *out* from the clifftops, drive up the twisty road to Caesars Head.

JONES GAP STATION

Starting with Jones Gap, park in the lot and take the path to the hiker check-in station. A footbridge crosses the loud Middle Saluda, and leads to a wide, shady picnic area and to the pools of the old Cleveland Fish Hatchery, which operated here from 1931 to 1963. The rainbow, brook, and brown trout swimming in the pools provide a visual sample of what you might catch in the streams. Look up from here to the heights—forested mountains and steep rock walls rising more

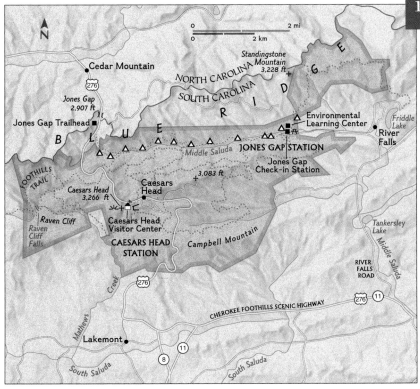

Keeping It Clean

With the rise in back-country use over the last several years, low-impact camping has become more important than ever. To keep the wilderness wild, Mountain Bridge permits camping only in designated sites and allows no fires. Dig toilet pits as far from water sources as possible, and burn your toilet paper. If you really want to help, take along an extra plastic bag and pick up any stray trash you see.

112

than 1,500 feet from the valley floor. Directly ahead looms Cleveland Cliff, a towering stone bulwark.

Walk over to the **Environmental Education Center,** a stone-and-log building that served as the fish hatchery superintendent's house. Take in the nature exhibits and purchase trail maps here. If you're backpacking, ask where the trailside campsites are. Among the many trails from here, **Hospital Rock Trail** zigzags up Standingstone Mountain and east around to Friddle Lake—4.4 miles one way (then another 2 miles back along the road). It's a tough 1.2 miles up to Hospital Rock itself, a 30-foot-long shelter that was reputedly used by Confederates to stash medical supplies, but you don't need to hike all the way for good views. For the best nearby views, take **Rim of the Gap Trail,** then connector #22 to **Pinnacle Pass Trail,** a 6-mile round-trip.

The easiest way from here up to Caesars Head is to hike west on the **Jones Gap Trail,** then hook up with connecting trails. Considered very strenuous, the relatively new **Rim of the Gap Trail** is a 5-mile walk up to Caesars Head, which affords excellent views of the mountains to the north. Unless you're in extremely good condition and want to walk back, have somebody drive around and meet you at the top.

CAESARS HEAD STATION

As you crest the mountain from the south, the parking lot for Caesars Head appears abruptly on the left. There's only one entrance before you start heading down the other side of the mountain—drive slowly. The **Visitor Center** has a gift shop and some interesting photographs from the resort hotel days. From here it's a short scramble out to the fenced-in overlook from atop the **Caesars Head promontory,** at an elevation of 3,266 feet. The panorama takes in Table Rock to the southwest, Table Rock reservoir, and long stretches of undulating hills that subside to plains. Hawks and ravens glide over this vast space.

Take the wooden stairway down through a crevice in the rock, a cool passageway known as **Devil's Kitchen.** Another viewpoint from down here allows you to look up at the profile of Caesars Head. If you can't see it, don't worry—the chin fell off 50 years ago, and anyway some people say the mountain was named for a hunting dog that fell to its death.

If you have time for only one hike, drive a mile north and park at the trailhead for **Raven Cliff Falls,** a moderately difficult walk of 2 miles (one way). The worthwhile effort brings you to a series of cascades that plummet a total of 420 feet down a narrow valley. Wildflowers you may see along the way include columbine, showy orchids, and jack-in-the-pulpit.

Camping

There is primitive trailside camping only. Available first come, first served. Register at either station. Camping fee.

❑ MOUNTAIN BRIDGE STATE NATURAL AREA, 8155 GEER HWY., CLEVELAND, SOUTH CAROLINA 29635

Raven Cliff Falls, Caesars Head Station

Devils Fork

4 miles northeast of Salem, off S.C. 11

● 622 acres ● 864-944-2639 ● Year-
round ● Lake swimming, fishing
(license required), hiking

One of a string of lovely parks just off
the Cherokee Foothills Scenic Highway
(S.C. 11), Devils Fork hugs the shore of
Lake Jocassee, a 7,565-acre reservoir created in 1973 by Duke Power Company for
hydroelectric energy. The park nudges into
the Blue Ridge mountains, giving height-
ened pleasure to lake activities. Named for
an area creek, the park dates only from
1991. The state is currently trying to raise
between 30 and 40 million dollars to buy
33,000 acres of wilderness surrounding
the lake so that the area's gorges and hills
will never be developed.

Stop in first at park headquarters for
information and a trail map. From here
take the 1.5-mile **Oconee Bell Nature
Trail** through pine and hardwood forest.
The trail is named for a wildflower that
blooms white in March; about 95 percent

113

Lake Jocassee

of the world's population grows here. Over in the picnic area,
the moderate 3.5-mile **Bear Cove Trail** courses through
mountain laurel and rhododendron thickets to a fine view of
the lake and surrounding mountains. Wild turkey and white-
tailed deer are common, as are bloodroot, trout lily, and other
wildflowers. Bird species include the recently reintroduced
peregrine falcon, while songbirds such as red-eyed vireo and
scarlet tanager fill the woods with live music.

The park's focal point, **Lake Jocassee** has a 75-mile shoreline and deep, clear water just right for boating and fishing—
among likely catches are brown and rainbow trout, and
smallmouth bass. The lake holds six state fishing records,
including a brown trout of nearly 18 pounds. Boat rentals are
available at Hoyetts Bait and Tackle *(0.5 mile before park
entrance)*—they'll deliver and pick up the boat. Near the picnic
area, the beach offers a bathhouse, refreshment stand, and
supervised swimming area *(Mem. Day–Labor Day)*; you can
swim anywhere else in the lake at your own risk.

Camping

There are 84 tent or RV sites, with showers; and 20 villas.
Reservations advised in season; call 864-944-2639. Camping fee.

 Devils Fork State Park, 161 Holcombe Circle, Salem, SC 29676

Huntington Beach

3 miles south of Murrells Inlet on US 17

● 2,500 acres ● 803-237-4440 ● Year-round ● Day-use fee
● Beach ● Marsh boardwalk ● Nature trail ● Historic house

Wind-rippled dunes at Huntington Beach

114

One of the most well-preserved stretches on the increasingly popular Grand Strand, Huntington Beach occupies 3 miles of gorgeous beach washed by warm seas. Extensive dunes and salt marsh shelter a wide variety of plants and animals on this life-preserving length of South Carolina coast. In 1930 sculptress Anna Hyatt Huntington and her husband, railroad heir Archer Milton Huntington, bought a large tract of land that once belonged to four rice plantations. When the Huntingtons made their purchase, the property was a hunting and fishing preserve. Their idea was to study and protect the local flora and fauna as well as to build a winter home and studio on the beach—the Moorish-style Atalaya (Spanish for "watchtower") is open for tours just off the parking lot.

The Huntingtons continued to visit here until 1947. After Mr. Huntington's death in 1955, Mrs. Huntington moved her studio across the highway to Brookgreen Gardens and most of the furniture to New York, where she died in 1973. The Brookgreen Trustees leased the 2,500-acre parcel to South Carolina in 1960.

What to See and Do

The park road winds at first through dense forest, then emerges to a lovely causeway. On your right, a freshwater **lagoon** plays host to coots, marsh hens, grebes, and migratory ducks. Cattails, duckweed, and other grasses edge this impoundment. Pull off after you cross the causeway and look for alligators lurking in the water. On the other side of the road, the saltwater **marsh** with its tall grasses and rushes is where you can spot snowy egrets, great blue herons, and other waterfowl.

Take the road to the right and drive a short way to the main park area. A park store here sells camping supplies and snacks, and a 2-story beachside pavilion has changing rooms and showers. From the parking lot, the lowlying gray building to the south may look somewhat forbidding, but it's actually the Huntingtons' unique winter home, **Atalaya.** Acting as his own CCC, Huntington hired local labor during the lean years of the early 1930s to construct Atalaya and Brookgreen Gardens. The 30-room mansion forms a square surrounding an open courtyard planted with Sabal palmettos and Bermuda grass. In here you might imagine you're in some Mediterranean villa, its pierced brick walls, crumbling in places, covered with fig vines. The 40-foot tower held a 3,000-gallon water tank that, with the help of gravity, supplied the house with water. The empty rooms around the courtyard include Mrs. Huntington's spacious studio on the southern wing; a 25-foot skylight flooded the room with natural light.

After touring Atalaya, walk up to the **beach** and find a place to plant your umbrella. If you want neighbors, stay close by; if you want a whole beach to yourself, take a short walk north or south.

Driving to the left after the causeway brings you to a parking area at the **boardwalk,** which extends 500 feet out to a covered deck where you can spy on wildlife. Back where you left the car, the 1.5-mile **Sandpiper Pond Nature Trail** goes into the woods opposite the marsh. Following a 100-year-old abandoned road, the trail enters a forest of live oak and loblolly pine, then crosses the dunes and heads north along the beach to a picnic area. Taking the trail gives you a look at the park's various ecosystems. From here you can continue out to the jetty at the north end of the beach. If you don't want to walk the whole way, take the park road. There's a picnic area and good fishing for flounder, spottail bass, and croaker.

Camping

The park has 184 tent and RV sites, with showers; 40 available by reservation. Call the park. Camping fee.

❏ *Huntington Beach State Park, Murrells Inlet, SC 29576*

115

Sculpture by the Sea

Directly across from the park lies one of the South's greatest cultural treasures. Started by Archer Milton and Anna Hyatt Huntington in the 1930s, **Brookgreen Gardens** *(US 17. 803-237-4218. Adm. fee)* now displays more than 500 works of American sculpture in landscaped settings defined by lily pools, azaleas, dogwoods, and mossy live oaks. The rearing horses at the entrance are by Mrs. Huntington.

Hunting Island

16 miles east of Beaufort on US 21

● 5,000 acres ● 803-838-2011 ● Year-round ● Beach ● Historic lighthouse ● Nature trails ● Fishing

A semi-tropical barrier island spreads its ample skirt of sandy beach for 3 pristine miles along the Atlantic shore, while back in its salt marsh mussels and fiddler crabs hide in mudflats, and herons and egrets pose in tall cordgrass. Giving the island its name, nearby plantation owners started the tradition of deer hunting here in the early 18th century, a tradition that continued until the island became a public park in the 1930s. Despite the hunting, deer remain abundant, and more than 125 species of birds have been spotted in the park.

116

In 1938 the Civilian Conservation Corps began the daunting task of constructing a 2-mile causeway over the marshes to connect Hunting Island to the mainland. Fierce mosquitoes, a forest fire, and a hurricane hampered, but didn't defeat, their efforts. During World War II the CCC moved out and the Coast Guard moved in. The park reopened to the public after the war, and in the 1950s electricity and segregated bathhouses were installed. In 1966 all the park facilities were desegregated.

Though the causeway remains, nearly all the original CCC buildings have been wiped out by hurricanes and steady erosion. As coastal sands shift north to south, some 10 feet of the island's land are lost each year. Large shoals

Palms at sunrise on Hunting Island

in St. Helena Sound just north claim much of the sand that would otherwise flow down to Hunting Island, causing the unusually high rate of erosion. A prominent island landmark, the 1875 lighthouse was first located in a place now awash with breakers, and an earlier light was destroyed during the Civil War. To counteract the inevitable forces of wind and waves, more than four million cubic feet of sand have been pumped in from offshore since 1968, but nature continues to make quick work of such stopgap efforts. Erosion has happened so quickly in places that you can see tree skeletons standing in the surf where forest once grew.

What to See and Do

Entering the park, you drive through a dense forest of live oak, bayberry, wax myrtle, and palmetto. The boardwalk across a swamp to the **Visitor Center** is one of the best places for spotting alligators. The center itself has good exhibits on cultural history, beach habitats, and the lighthouse. To make sure you don't miss it, drive around to the **Hunting Island Lighthouse** *(Fee),* a 135-foot sentinel that operated until 1933. You can climb to the top and enjoy peerless views of the beach, the ocean, and the edges of the island.

Hunting Island Lighthouse

117

From here it's a short walk out to the beach—prickly sand spurs in the dune area make shoes a necessity. Picnic shelters, restrooms, and a concessionaire are handy to the swimming area. Shells common along the beach include angelwings, cockles, lettered olives, and knobbed and channeled whelks.

Just off the park road, a **nature trail** courses 2.3 miles (one way) through an aromatic maritime forest, home to deer, raccoons, and other animals. If you encounter an alligator, give it a wide berth—they're unpredictable. The trail meanders for a while along the lagoon, once a freshwater marsh but now connected with Fripp Inlet. Across the highway, a short **marsh boardwalk** gives you access to what many would say is the island's most beautiful side. Come here at sunset for an enchanting view of golden grasses and long-legged birds.

To cast for whiting, spot, sea trout, and other saltwater fish, take Sea Island Parkway down to the southern end of the island, where a fishing pier *(April-Oct.)* extends 1,120 feet into the inlet. Crabbing is also popular here. A tackle shop at the pier entrance sells bait and supplies.

Camping and Lodging

The park has 200 tent and RV sites, with showers; reservations available for 40 sites. Camping fee. There are also 15 furnished cabins. For reservations call 803-838-2011.
❏ *Hunting Island State Park, 2555 Sea Island Pkwy., Hunting Island, South Carolina 29920*

Tidal Change

Those dreamy backwaters fringed with rich mud and cordgrass, the Carolina marshes change character depending on the time of day—or, more accurately, on the tide. At low tide, fiddler crabs scurry out of their holes, while egrets and raccoons take advantage of low water to catch a meal. When the waters of high tide stream in from the ocean, the marsh becomes still and smooth as a mirror. But underneath is a food-chain hierarchy of microscopic nutrients, as well as shrimp, blue crabs, even bottlenosed dolphins.

Stephen C. Foster

18 miles northeast of Fargo on Ga. 177

● 80 acres ● 912-637-5274 ● Year-round ● Fee for wildlife refuge ● Okefenokee Swamp tours ● Boardwalk nature trail ● Boating, fishing (license required)

Bald cypresses

118

Tall cypress trees dripping with Spanish moss make mirror-perfect reflections in the clean, black waters of an ancient swamp visited by alligators and water moccasins, bears and otters. An anhinga breaks the surface of the water, a fish speared on its beak, and flies to the nearest tree . . . then all is still again. Named for the songwriter who penned the line "Way down upon the Swanee [sic] River," the park occupies 80-acre Jones Island, which lies entirely inside the 396,000-acre **Okefenokee National Wildlife Refuge** *(912-496-3331)*.

In reality more of a watershed than a swamp, the Okefenokee is a shallow basin from which an inland sea retreated long ago, leaving a reservoir of water that gives rise to the Suwannee River on this (west) side and the St. Marys on the east. The Suwannee flows to the Gulf of Mexico, the St. Marys to the Atlantic. That original basin of water collected enough dead vegetation over thousands of years that layers of peat several feet thick began to form. As seeds blew onto these floating mats, aquatic plants and trees took root and islands appeared. But unlike most islands, these actually hang above the swamp floor—the thinner ones are spongy and shake if you walk on them, hence the Indian term *okefenokee* ("land of the trembling earth").

Georgia

In the early 1900s, the Hebard Cypress Company drove 20-foot pilings deep into the muck and laid 35 miles of railroad track through the swamp. From 1908 to 1927 it harvested virgin cypress, employing up to 2,000 men and creating a lively community. The wildlife refuge was established in 1937 and now covers more than 90 percent of the 600-square-mile swamp. The state park was established on Jones Island within the national wildlife reservation in 1954.

What to See and Do

A good way to explore the swamp is to take a 90-minute **boat tour** (*Fare*). In spring and summer, visitors should sign up for a tour at the park office as soon as they arrive. Traveling lily-speckled waterways, you'll see gators, egrets, herons, turtles, and healthy stands of cypress. Tannic acid from decayed vegetation gives the water a dark tea color.

While waiting for a tour, or after it's over, walk across to the **Museum** and adjoining **Interpretive Center** (*Mon.-Fri.*). The museum focuses on local flora and fauna, while the center holds informative exhibits on moonshining, turpentining, beekeeping, and other historical associations.

Some time while you're here, take the .25-mile **Trembling Earth Nature Trail** out behind the park office. A new addition to the trail, an elevated **boardwalk** weaves 3,704 feet into the swamp, past mossy cypress, freshwater ponds, and wetlands. You'll probably see alligators and herons, and you have a good chance of spotting deer, egrets, and sandhill cranes as well. In all, there are 234 species of birds in the refuge, and a resident population of 12,000 alligators. Interpretive

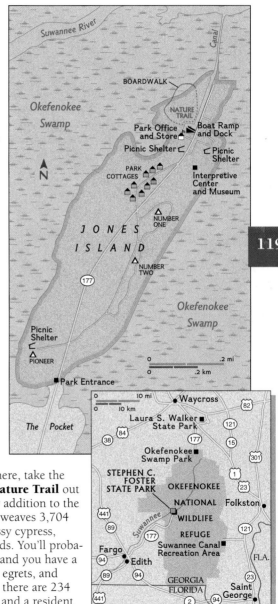

119

Down the Drain

In 1890 an Atlanta lawyer named Capt. Harry Jackson had the bright idea of draining the Okefenokee Swamp. He bought up half the swamp and planned to dig a series of canals that would direct the water down the St. Marys River, leaving a dry Okefenokee worth millions in timber and fertile land. Not until a few years into the project did Jackson realize the enormity of the undertaking. By 1895 an 11.5-mile main canal and about 8 miles of branches were complete, but Jackson estimated it would take 300 miles to do the job. With funds drying up quicker than the swamp, Jackson gave it up and died shortly thereafter.

120

markers and benches punctuate the loop, and a covered pavilion makes a fine perch for resting and studying the primordial scene.

Further Adventures

If you want to venture into the swamp on your own, there are 25 miles of marked waterways for exploring. Rent a motorboat or canoe for a day. The boat basin adjoins the park office and information center. While here, you can buy camping, fishing, and picnicking supplies and, most importantly, pick up a trail map.

A canal leads from the boat basin out to **Billy's Lake,** the largest of some 60 named lakes in the Okefenokee. The 3.5-mile-long lake measures only 300 to 750 feet wide. Paddling or motoring west takes you to a 3-mile **Day Use Canoe Trail** (*Currently closed*). At the end of the trail is the Suwannee River Sill, a 5-mile-long earthen dam; you can make a 10-mile loop by heading back via the River Narrows.

If you go east on Billy's Lake, you come to **Billy's Island** (*3 miles from boat basin*). You can tie up at the dock here and take a 1-mile walking trail. The Hebard Cypress Company bought the island from a pioneer family and used it as their main interior camp. Houses sprang up on the 4-mile island, as well as streets, a hotel, and a movie theater. Lush new growth has erased nearly all signs of civilization, making it hard to imagine a thriving community of 600 people existing on this jungly outpost. But you can see an old cemetery, a couple of Indian mounds, a railroad bed, and a curiosity—the rusting frame of a car with a right-hand steering wheel.

To the north of Billy's Island lies **Minnie's Lake** (*5 miles from boat basin*), which connects to another finger of water called **Big Water Lake** (*12 miles from boat basin*). Big cypresses punctuate the narrow waterway, which opens to a grassy prairie. Then at Big Water, you see more cypresses and scrub underbrush. In addition to alligators and herons, look for red-shouldered hawks, vultures, and otters. There are two rest-stop shelters along the way.

Camping and Lodging

The park has 66 tent and RV sites, with showers; and 9 cottages. Reservations advised in season; call 800-864-7275. Camping fee.
☐ *STEPHEN C. FOSTER STATE PARK, RTE. 1, BOX 131, FARGO, GA 31631*

Boating on the Suwannee River

Tallulah Gorge

On US 441, in Tallulah Falls

● 3,000 acres ● 706-754-7970 ● Year-round ● Parking fee
● Wild gorge ● Rim trail, overlooks ● Lake swimming, tennis

121

Tallulah River

A river that drops as sharply as the Tallulah River does from the northeast Georgia mountains can do a lot of landscaping over thousands of years. In less than a mile it plunges 500 feet, sawing its way through dense quartzite and leaving a spectacular legacy of sheer cliffs, waterfalls, rock formations, and cascades. One definition for the Indian word *tallulah* is "unfinished," since the river does not level out. The river's business as a land shaper also remains unfinished. As you stand on the edge of the 2-mile-long Tallulah Gorge and peer down nearly 1,000 feet to the river, it's as though you were looking far back in time, down to the earliest rock layers.

The human history, by contrast, is relatively brief. A few decades before the Civil War, about the time the area's Indians were being forced out, the first white sightseers began coming to have a look at the gorge. By the late 19th century, the town of Tallulah Falls boasted 20 hotels, making it one of the most popular resorts in the South. Against the protest of early environmentalists, a dam was installed above the falls in 1912 to generate electricity for

Atlanta and other towns. As the novelty of the gorge wore off, resort businesses waned and by 1921 fires had virtually wiped the little town off the map. For many years, the area remained almost unknown to tourists; *Deliverance* and other movies filmed here portrayed a place of untamed and dangerous beauty. Then in 1992 the Georgia Power Company leased acreage to the Georgia Department of Natural Resources, and a new state park was born.

What to See and Do

If you're traveling north, follow signs to the right for the **Jane Hurt Yarn Interpretive Center,** a spiffy 16,000-square-foot facility that opened in 1996. Here you can pick up maps and information and easily spend an hour browsing two floors of exhibits on the cultural and natural history of the gorge area. Highlights here include a birdwatching station, equipped with binoculars; information on the persistent trillium, an endangered wildflower that grows only here; panels and dioramas on the park's eight distinct ecosystems—from the cliff tops to the bottom bogs; and an absolutely must-see 15-minute film with dramatic footage of rock climbers and kayakers.

The film almost, but not quite, replaces the experience of actually going out to see the gorge for yourself. Less than a mile long, the **North Rim Trail** takes about 45 minutes to walk both ways. Since the park is new, you may encounter some trail construction along the way. The trail leads to breathless views of plunging waterslides, blue-green pools, and vertiginous cliffs where you can watch birds tilt and wheel in a wide chasm of air. Named sites include Hawthorne Pool, Tempesta Falls, and L'Eau d'Or Falls. The west end of the trail provides a fine vista of the spillways of **Tallulah Dam;** just beyond the east end is the area rock climbers go *(permit required; 20 issued per day).* You also need a permit *(100 issued per day)* if you plan to hike to the bottom of the gorge—check at the Interpretive Center. There is also a trail of about the same length, with some slightly different views, on the **South Rim.** If you want to bike or take a longer walk, inquire about access to more than 20 miles of trails.

Five weekends a year (in April and November) the power company releases enough water to turn the river into a frothing rampage, suitable for expert kayaking. For those who prefer more peaceful waters, the 63-acre **Tallulah Falls Lake** has a beach with a guarded swimming area.

Camping

The park has 45 tent and RV sites and 5 tent-only sites, with showers. Reservations advised in season; call 706-754-7979. Camping fee.

☐ *TALLULAH GORGE S.P., P.O. BOX 248, TALLULAH FALLS, GA 30573*

Walking on Air

Tallulah Gorge stepped into the national spotlight on July 18, 1970, when Karl Wallenda walked across it on a 2-inch-thick steel cable stretched 750 feet above the river. Some 35,000 spectators turned out to watch the 65-year-old circus family patriarch make the 1,000-foot crossing. During a high-wire stunt eight years later in Puerto Rico, he fell to his death. The remains of the towers from which the cable was suspended are visible on the north and south rims. Amazingly, local lore claims that Wallenda was not the first—a Professor Leon ropewalked across in 1886.

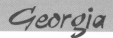

Fort Mountain

8 miles east of Chatsworth on Ga. 52

- **3,428 acres ● 706-695-2621**
- **Year-round ● Park pass fee**
- **Mountain wilderness ● Hiking, swimming, fishing (license required)**

123

Autumn at Fort Mountain

Some of Georgia's prettiest scenery can be found in the rolling hills, gentle farms, and meadows of the Chattahoochee National Forest, where Fort Mountain crests to 2,800 feet at the southern end of the Appalachians. On this prominent lookout, Woodland Indians built a mysterious 855-foot-long rock wall around 2,000 years ago, perhaps as a fortification against hostile tribes or for use in ceremonies. Framed by cliffs, the wall snakes around the mountain's south slope. In 1934 Dalton resident Ivan Allen donated 1,930 acres of land, including the wall, to the state, and the Civilian Conservation Corps then developed the area into a park.

Stop off at the park office for maps and information, then proceed up the road to the parking lot for the **Old Fort Wall.** An overlook here provides a good view of the Indian ruin, or you can take the 1.8-mile **Old Fort Trail** around the structure and to a 50-foot stone **lookout tower.** Though tower views are obscured by tall trees, there's a great view on the ground nearby of Dalton, Chatsworth, and Lookout Mountain to the west. Just before the parking lot, **Cool Springs Overlook** faces east over the Cohutta Wilderness Area.

Back at the main park area, the 0.7-mile **Big Rock Nature Trail** diverts out to a westward view of low-lying mountains rippling into purple haze. The trail follows the creek that issues from **Fort Mountain Lake.** You can take the **Lake Loop Trail** 1.2 miles around the lake, then head down to the beach (*May-Sept.*). Or, you might prefer to rent a paddle or fishing boat. If you feel the need for a really good workout, head for the 8.2-mile **Gahuti Backpacking Trail** that loops nearly the entire park.

Camping and Lodging

The park has 70 tent and RV sites, with showers; 4 walk-in tent sites; and 15 cabins. Reservations advised in season; call 800-864-7275. Camping fee.

❏ *Fort Mountain State Park, 181 Fort Mountain Park Rd., Chatsworth, Georgia 30705*

Cloudland Canyon

8 miles southeast of Trenton on Ga. 136

● 2,219 acres ● 706-657-4050 ● Year-round ● Park pass fee ● Hiking trails ● Swimming pool, tennis

A gift of endless space characterizes this rugged mountain park. Standing at the canyon overlook where the ground drops away 1,000 feet, you feel the immense power of nature to make massive changes over time. Here at the western edge of Lookout Mountain, streams have chiseled away at the layers of shale and sandstone over the eons to create a deep gorge embellished by craggy cliffs and cascading waterfalls.

The state began acquiring land from local owners in 1938 for the establishment of a park; the completion of Ga. 136 the following year meant visitors no longer had to travel through Alabama or Tennessee to reach the canyon.

If you have just a short time at Cloudland Canyon, park at the **Canyon Overlook** (the Point) and in just a few steps enjoy the finest view in the park. Bear Creek (on your right) and Daniel Creek (left) join in the gorge below to form Sitton Gulch Creek, or Cloudland Canyon. Peering out to the wide open valley north—the direction of the streams—you look toward the oldest rocks in the area.

With more time you can take the **Waterfalls Trail** to the left, down into Daniel Creek Canyon. You pass through a hardwood forest and along walls of sandstone—in places deeply undercut by the more easily eroding shale. Two prominent waterfalls are about half a mile from the parking lot; the one to the right drops nearly 100 feet. Over time, these cascades will wear down their rock ledges and retreat farther upstream, eventually disappearing altogether as the slopes gradually smooth out. You can return to the parking lot, or continue up and along the west rim of Cloudland Canyon through hemlocks, dogwoods, and mountain laurel and back around for a 4.5-mile loop.

After your journey into the natural world, drive south from the parking area to get to the swimming pool and tennis courts. A short walk from the pool, a new wildlife-viewing area is planted with clover, wheat, rye, and other goodies to tempt the appetites of deer, turkey, rabbits, quail, and more. From the 16-foot observation tower you can watch animals enjoy hassle-free garden raiding.

Camping

The park has 75 tent and RV sites, with showers; 34 walk-in tent sites; and 16 cottages. Reservations for all advised in season; call 800-864-7275. Camping fee.

❏ CLOUDLAND CANYON STATE PARK, 122 CLOUDLAND CANYON PARK RD., RISING FAWN, GEORGIA 30738

Providence Canyon

7 miles west of Lumpkin on Ga. 39C

● 1,108 acres ● 912-838-6202 ● Year-round ● Park pass fee ● Hiking

Thank the area's early settlers for Georgia's "little Grand Canyon," a striking network of 16 fingerlike gullies etched deep into the red-clay hills. Those early 19th-century farmers had no idea that clearing the trees for fields would set up an unstoppable erosion process. By 1850 water had cut ditches 5 feet deep in the soft, sandy soil. Today, there is a canyon 150 feet deep. The state park was created in 1971 to preserve and protect the canyon's unusual beauty.

The bright oranges, reds, violets, and whites of the castellated ridges and naked walls make an arresting sight, particularly from July to September when wildflowers such as the rare plumleaf azalea add yet more color to the scene. At the **Interpretive**

Providence Canyon

125

Center, learn more about the canyon's formation through films and exhibits. Then hike out along the rim for views down into the gullies. If you only have a short time, drive to the picnic area and take the **rim walk** to the left for the best overlooks. You'll see where watercourses have planed the canyon walls. Sunrise and sunset fine-tune the salmon and scarlet tones.

You can also start from the Interpretive Center and descend into the canyon for the 3-mile **White Blaze Loop** that returns along the rim. The 7-mile **Red Blaze Backcountry Loop** explores canyons on the park's back (west) side, with campsites for backpackers.

Camping

The park has 6 backpack sites. Reservations advised in season; call 800-864-7275. Camping fee.

❏ PROVIDENCE CANYON STATE CONSERVATION PARK, RTE. 1, BOX 158, LUMPKIN, GEORGIA 31815

John Pennekamp Coral Reef

Mile Marker 102.5 on US 1, in Key Largo

● 56,097 acres ● 305-451-1202 ● Year-round ● Living coral reef ● Snorkeling ● Glass-bottom boat tours ● Scuba tours ● Nature and canoe trails ● Boat rentals

Scuba diver on the reef

One of the great natural treasures of the Southeast, John Pennekamp's colorful coral reef flashes with brilliant color in the Straits of Florida. More than 95 percent underwater, the park stretches 25 miles along the shore and about 3 miles

into the ocean, protecting a portion of the only living coral reef offshore the continental United States. Trade winds and warm waters of the Gulf Stream bless this invaluable ecosystem, as well as the park's other intriguing communities—the seagrass beds, mangrove swamps, and tropical hammocks.

If you take a boat out to the patch reefs, you'll behold an undersea garden that has taken from 5,000 to 7,000 years to grow. The reefs are actually complex communities formed by living polyps that secrete a limestone substrate around themselves. Over several generations, these substrates develop into a large, hard mass that not only anchors new polyps but shelters sponges, crabs, shrimp, and nearly 600 species of fish.

Early visitors to the reef could not resist taking home souvenirs in the form of live corals and seashells—what they couldn't break off they went after with hammers, chisels, even dynamite. As the demand for marine trinkets increased, commercial vendors stepped up the harvest. At a biological conference in 1957, Dr. Gilbert Voss of the Marine Institute of Miami predicted that without restricted access the reef would soon be dead. An assistant editor for the *Miami Herald,* John Pennekamp became the reef's most outspoken champion. Pennekamp had helped in the creation of Everglades National Park, and now he and Voss set out to marshal support from local government. So began a three-year battle against commercial businesses that depended upon plunder from the reef. The real winner was the reef itself, and in 1960 the country's first underwater park was dedicated.

What to See and Do

First off, head over to the **Main Concession building** *(305-451-1621)* and check out boat tour times. If the weather is good, there are usually three glass-bottom and three snorkeling tours *(fee)* a day. Tours last about 2.5 hours; the snorkeling tours offer about 90 minutes in the water. You can also opt for a combination sailing and snorkeling tour on a 38-foot catamaran. Heading out to the reef, these tours show you the highlight of the park—the kaleidoscope of tropical life under the surface. Among the most colorful fish you'll see are angelfish, parrot fish, snapper, and triggerfish. Brain and star corals are accented by softer corals such as sea fans, plumes, and whips that sway gently in the currents. In all, the reef harbors 40 different kinds of coral, and on days of good visibility you can see for more than 100 feet underwater.

Above the surface is worth a look, too—the park and adjacent **Key Largo National Marine Sanctuary** *(305-451-1644)* cover a total of 178 square nautical miles, a dazzling sheet of blue-green water lined by mangroves. The park stretches nearly the entire length of Key Largo, longest of the keys.

If you're stuck on land waiting for a tour, walk over to the

Christ of the Deep

Graced by pillars of sunlight, the most well-known landmark at John Pennekamp stands on the sea floor under 20 feet of water, its uplifted arms and flowing robe a familiar sight to hosts of snorkelers and fish. A 1961 gift from the Underwater Society of America, the nine-foot bronze is a copy of "Il Christo degli Abissi," placed in the Mediterranean Sea near Genoa as an inspiration to those who work or play in the ocean.

127

Visitor Center. In addition to its friendly and knowledgeable staff, the center has a 30,000-gallon saltwater aquarium filled with a rainbow spectrum of fish, coral, sponges, and anemones. You can study the exhibits and watch films here to get a feel for what you'll see out on the water. One worthwhile display, a tank of dead coral littered by trash, underscores the need to treat the fragile reef system with care—touching or standing on coral can harm it and is against the law.

After a tour, you'll probably be ready to idle the rest of the day away on your own. You can rent snorkeling equipment at the concession building, then head over to **Cannon Beach** or the **Family Fun Area.** The rocky beach is typical of the Upper Keys, where the reef traps sand before it reaches the shore. You don't see much coral this far in, but there are tropical fish. A reconstructed Spanish shipwreck lies in shallow water about 130 feet offshore, complete with cannons, anchor, and ballast stones. Another fun thing to do is to rent a canoe, kayak, or seacycle at the Main Concession and explore the network of mangroves and tidal creeks on a 2.5-mile canoe trail that leads to the Far Beach Area. There are showers and a swimming area here. Note: If you swim outside the designated swimming areas, you must display a Diver Down flag (*available at Dive Shop*).

Two short walking trails are easy to fit into a busy day and will give you an appreciation for the variety of Keys vegetation. The **Wild Tamarind Trail** loops through a hardwood hammock that includes tropical plants such as thatch palm, strangler fig, gumbo-limbo, and West Indian mahogany. Over near the water, the **Mangrove Trail** follows a boardwalk through red, black, and white mangroves, trees that can actually live in saltwater—their cagelike roots provide sanctuary to young fish and help stabilize the shoreline.

Further Adventures

If you have more than one day to spend here and want to try scuba diving, the dive shop at the marina (305-451-6322) offers scuba tours both for novices and experienced divers. A non-certification resort course has you diving down to 20 feet within four hours, and an open-water certification class takes three to four days to complete.

To accommodate those wishing for more deep-sea adventure, the marina rents fishing boats. You need to study your navigation charts and know what the channel markers mean.

Camping

The park has 47 tent and RV sites, with showers, about half available by reservation; call the park at 305-451-1202. Camping fee. Mid-fall through spring is the busy season.

❏ *John Pennekamp Coral Reef State Park, Mile Marker 102.5, P.O. Box 1560, Key Largo, Florida 33037*

Myakka River

14 miles east of Sarasota on Fla. 72

● 28,875 acres ● 941-361-6511 ● Year-round ● Entrance fee ● Boat and tram tours ● Hiking, birdwatching, fishing (license required), biking

Cabbage palms along Myakka River

One of Florida's oldest and largest state parks spreads along the gentle Myakka River for 12 miles, presenting a wonderfully varied landscape of marsh-fringed lakes, oak and palm hammocks, pine flatwoods, and palmetto prairies. In general, as you drive the park road, deep woods lie to your right, while to your left are open views of marshes and Upper Myakka Lake. Deer, bobcat, and wild turkey find good cover in the woods and hammocks; alligators, turtles, and wading birds may be spotted out in the wetlands to the left.

129

The state purchased the land in 1934, and for the next seven years the Civilian Conservation Corps and the U.S. Army, with guidance from the National Park Service, developed the park with trails and facilities. Opened to the public in 1942, the park preserves one of Florida's most diverse natural areas. In 1985 the state legislature declared the Myakka a State Wild and Scenic River, giving special protection status to a 34-mile section and making it one of only two rivers in the state so designated. South of the highway sprawls the 7,500-acre wilderness preserve, a portion of the park completely unspoiled by any development.

What to See and Do

Myakka is a big park, and even though it's very popular—particularly on weekends—you can find a quiet corner without going to much trouble. You'll be handed a brochure and a tour schedule at the entrance gate. If you want more specific information—for instance, on backpacking, horseback riding, or the wilderness preserve—ask for it here. It's odd that such a large park has very little in the way of a Visitor Center. The wooden CCC building off to the left has a few taxidermic displays of waterbirds and reptiles, and the introductory video here is worth seeing. But the center is seldom staffed and has no restrooms. If you need more details on tours and rentals, you'll get plenty of help down at the Boat Basin.

Park Drive winds 7 serpentine miles along the edge of the river and lake. The drive is itself a major attraction, affording fine views of the marshes and hammocks and offering plenty of pulloffs for further study. Most drivers travel below the 25-mph limit. Just after the road crosses the river, pull over to the right for an unmarked **fisherman's trail.** This sandy path under rattling cabbage palms and moss-hung oaks follows the river downstream about a mile back toward the highway. Few people seem to be aware of this lovely trail that offers good views of the peaceful river and wetlands. A bit farther down the road is a designated 1-mile **nature loop.** The trail explores a pretty section of open forest, and interpretive markers provide interesting commentary on local flora and fauna.

As you continue down the road, you'll see several places

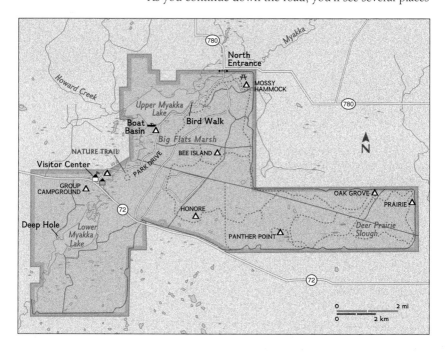

along the right to pull off for more hiking. The trails, nearly 40 miles total, loop out under dense hammocks and across dry prairies. You can walk out as far as you like, but to really get into the wilderness you'll need to backpack.

The busiest area in the park, the **Boat Basin** lies about 3.5 miles from the entrance. Sign up here for the highly popular **airboat tours** *(Fee)* and **tram safaris** *(Fee),* running several times a day. The 70-passenger boats cruise around Lake Myakka for about an hour, while a guide outlines the ecological scene. The trams carry up to 50 passengers through the forested areas, and provide a running narration. To help you explore on your own, the Boat Basin rents canoes, and the store sells picnic, fishing, and camping supplies. An invasion of hydrilla, an exotic weed, has reduced fish catches somewhat, but you can paddle quietly along the edges of the lake and observe alligators and long-legged birds.

A good alternative is to rent a bike here and pedal up to the north entrance (3.5 miles). The road is flat and scenic, and traffic is light. After about 2 miles, pull left for the **bird walk,** a boardwalk out to a viewing platform in the grassy marshes. Panels here help you put names to the birds you see, such as great blue herons, snowy egrets, roseate spoonbills, and various ducks. Just before the north entrance, you can pull right into a picnic area by a creek called **Clay Gully.**

Further Adventures

Considered one of the most beautiful places in the park, **Deer Prairie Slough** lies far to the east, its groves of giant maple and oak forming a high ceiling for a lush garden of ferns and subtropical plants. But since it's 10 miles one way from the trailhead, only hardy backpackers get to see it. In the wet season (late spring to early fall) the ground soaks up a lot of water—bring plenty of socks.

If you don't want to camp out, you can still experience primitive Florida by heading across the highway to the **Myakka River Wilderness Preserve.** More than a quarter of the park's total acreage lies in this sanctuary of marshes and hammocks around **Lower Myakka Lake.** A limited number of visitors are allowed in each day; register at the Ranger Station *(entrance gate)* and drive over to the parking area. A dirt track leads 1.5 miles down to the lake; from here it's another half mile to **Deep Hole,** a 140-foot-deep sink favored by anglers.

Camping and Lodging

The park has 76 tent or RV sites, with showers. Half available by reservation. Camping fee. There are also 5 log cabins. For reservations call 941-361-6411.

❏ *Myakka River State Park, 13207 Rte. 72, Sarasota, Florida 34241*

Smart Burn

Florida's steamy inland prairies, vast grasslands dotted with wildflowers and saw palmettos, began to disappear as a result of fire exclusion practices encouraged early in this century and implemented only until recently. The absence of fire nearly spelled disaster for Myakka's prairie. Without natural fires, trees and shrubs crept in on the prairie's turf and animals dependent on this system vanished. To restore the open range, the park uses frequent prescribed burns and removes the feral pigs that are destroying prairie plants and animals.

131

Wekiwa Springs

3 miles north of Apopka, off Fla. 434 or Fla. 436

● 6,900 acres ● 407-884-2009 ● Year-round ● Natural springs ● Swimming, canoeing, hiking

132

Canoes on Wekiwa Springs

Birds call from unseen perches and fish flap the surface of the water as your canoe glides through an ancient wilderness. From the low river swamps to the dry sand ridges, this inviting park presents a picture of Florida's wild and jungly interior almost as it looked before the arrival of Europeans. The presence of eight shell mounds within the park indicates that Timucuans—early hunter-gatherers—lived here on abundant fish and shellfish. The park takes its name from the Creek word for "spring of water." To complicate matters, Wekiwa (we-KI-wa) Springs forms the headwaters of Wekiva (we-KI-va) River, the Creek term for "flowing water."

White settlers began moving into the area in the 1840s, following the Second Seminole War. They cut down the cypress and farmed cotton and other crops, using the Wekiva River to ship their goods and turn their grist- and sawmills. It was not long before tourists discovered the springs and their soothing mineral waters, and by the 1890s a resort hotel was in full swing in a town called Clay Springs. When the Great Depression killed off the tourism trade, the town ceased to exist. After the hotel burned in 1953, it gradually melded back into the wilderness as locals began scavenging—first the doors and windows, then the wiring, plumbing, even the foundations. What remains from that era are railroad grades used by loggers, and hundreds of large cypress stumps. But you won't see many cypress trees—the loggers were very thorough.

The Apopka Sportsmen Club bought the land in 1934 and held it as a fishing and hunting preserve until 1969. About that time, local real estate developers were envisioning subdivisions of houses and condominiums. But the state stepped in, purchased the property, and opened it as a park in 1970. The adjacent Rock Springs Run State Reserve and Lower Wekiva River State Preserve combined with Wekiwa Springs, make a total of more than 44,000 acres collectively called **Wekiva Basin Geopark** (See sidebar this page).

What to See and Do

The **Ranger Station** at the entrance will get you started with brochures and maps. Most people come to paddle or take a dip in the cool, clear spring waters, which maintain a temperature of 68 to 72°F year-round. Put on your suit in the changing room and walk out to the **Wekiwa Springs** bathing area. Enhanced by a boardwalk, ramp, and steps, the 3-acre swimming hole has a shallow and deep end; you can swim down toward the cave from where the water issues—the spring is so forceful it pushes you away. Afterwards, spread a blanket on the grassy area and grab a snack from the concessionaire. When you get hot, jump back in again. The nearby **Visitor Center** here outlines the natural and cultural history of Wekiva Basin.

For a nice, leisurely outing, rent a canoe or kayak and paddle down **Wekiwa Springs Run** to Wekiwa Marina, have lunch, then head back. Allow two hours' paddling time for the 2-mile round-trip. For a longer excursion, drive up to King's Landing *(407-886-0859)*, where you can rent a canoe and paddle 8.5 miles (about 6 hours) down **Rock Springs Run** to the Wekiwa Marina. The King's Landing operators will pick you up here. There are several other possibilities for day and overnight trips that include the Little Wekiva and lower Wekiva Rivers through Katie's Landing *(407-628-1482)*.

If you want to give your arms a rest, try some of the 13.5-mile **Main Hiking Trail.** A shorter loop, the 5.3-mile **Volksmarch Trail** offers much of the same scenery—riparian wetlands, then a climb up to pine flatwoods and a sandhill area, the remnants of dunes from before the last ice age.

Camping

Wekiwa Springs has 60 tent or RV sites, with showers. Half available by reservation; call the park at 407-884-2009. There are also 2 canoe camps and 2 backpack camps, available first come, first served. Camping fee.

❑ *Wekiwa Springs State Park, 1800 Wekiwa Circle, Apopka, FL 32712*

What's in a Name?

Adjoining the state park on the north are **Rock Springs Run State Reserve** and **Lower Wekiva River State Preserve,** with the three entities combining to create the Wekiva Basin Geopark. Why the different designations? In Florida a "state park" ranks low on protection level (just above a "state recreation area") and high on development—up to 20 percent of its land. A "reserve" means almost no development, and a "preserve" means none at all. There are no facilities on the preserve and few trails—deep in these dense river swamps live bears and bobcats, far from the eyes of most humans.

133

Blue flag iris

Paynes Prairie

1 mile north of Micanopy on US 441

● 21,000 acres ● 352-466-3397 ● Year-round ● Entrance fee
● Hiking ● Observation tower ● Fishing (license required)

One of the most significant natural areas in Florida sprawls over an 8.5-mile-wide basin that resulted from the sinking of the terrain's limestone foundation. The ponds, marshes, wet prairie, and pine woods that characterize the preserve are home to large numbers of alligators, wading birds, and otters, as well as wintering sandhill cranes and bald eagles. During his travels here in 1774, naturalist William Bartram described the basin as the great Alachua Savannah. The preserve takes its name from King Payne, a Seminole chief.

Start at the **Visitor Center** *(352-466-4100)*, which has a wide window onto the marshy prairie where bison once roamed. The basin fills with water from time to time. During a dry period in the late 17th century, the largest cattle ranch in Spanish Florida operated here, and during a wet spell two centuries later there was enough water to form a lake that served as a steamboat route. You can gain an even broader perspective by taking the 0.3-mile **Wacahoota Trail** from here out to a 50-foot observation tower. The

White ibises

wild horses and bison you may see were reintroduced in the mid-1980s.

Also in this part of the preserve, **Lake Wauberg** features a boat ramp and picnic area. You can fish for bream, bass, and speckled perch, but you'll need your own boat. Across the park road, **Chacala Trail** makes a loop of about 6 miles through pine flatwoods and shaded hammocks.

Driving around to the North Rim area, stop off at the **Bolen Bluff** trailhead (US 441). This pleasant 2.9-mile walk covers open marsh and shady hammock, taking you out to a wildlife viewing platform on the edge of the prairie. The **North Rim** has an Interpretive Center and the 3-mile **LaChua Trail,** which repays walkers with scenic views of the marsh, Alachua Sink, and Alachua Lake.

Camping

The park has 35 RV and 15 tent sites, with showers; reservations taken up to 60 days in advance. Call the park at 352-466-3397. Camping fee.

❏ *Paynes Prairie State Preserve, Rte. 2, Box 41, Micanopy, Florida 32667*

St. Joseph Peninsula

26 miles west of Apalachicola on County Rd. 30E

● 2,516 acres ● 904-227-1327 ● Year-round ● Beaches ● Nature trails ● Boating

Sand dunes and sea oats along the Gulf shore

A long fishhook off the elbow in Florida's panhandle, St. Joseph cuts into the Gulf of Mexico, its remoteness giving it a rarefied beauty. More than 9 miles of white quartz sand drape the park's Gulf shore, while a 10-mile bayside embraces mudflats, tidal marsh, and more sandy beach. Early Indians lived on shellfish from these warm waters. A Spanish fort was established here in the 17th century. But, except for a training stint by the U.S. Army during World War II, the peninsula has remained fairly peaceful over the centuries. It was leased from the Bureau of Land Management in 1964.

Birdwatching—serious and incidental—is one of the favorite activities here. In addition to the usual long-legged shore- and wading birds, thousands of hawks fly through during fall migrations—you can see dozens a day, flying *north* as they follow the peninsula's hook back toward the mainland. They then arc down the Gulf coast toward Mexico. Monarch butterflies and peregrine falcons wing their way through in fall.

Three nature trails, totaling about 5 miles, offer a look at the various coastal communities—beach, bayshore, dunes, flatwoods, and sandpine scrub. One of these paths, the **Barrier Dunes Trail,** explores the large dune system and its sea oats, yaupon holly, saw palmetto, rosemary, and other plants; a brochure corresponding to 14 numbered markers points out highlights. If you want to poke around the shallow bay area, rent a canoe at the entrance station. And if you really want to get away from it all, a protected wilderness on the peninsula's north end makes up nearly two-thirds of the park's total acreage. You can pitch a tent out here, walk on 8 miles of trails, and absorb the sanctity of an untamed seashore.

Camping and Lodging

The park has 118 tent or RV sites (half may be reserved), with showers, and 8 cabins. Call 904-227-1327. Camping fee.

❏ St. Joseph Peninsula State Park, Star Rte. 1, Box 200, Port St. Joe, Florida 32456

135

DeSoto

8 miles northeast of Fort Payne on County Rd. 89

● 5,067 acres ● 205-845-0051 ● Year-round ● Day-use
fee ● 22-mile canyon drive ● 15 waterfalls ● Hiking
● Lodge ● Swimming, tennis

Riding the back of long, flat Lookout Mountain, DeSoto
State Park sprawls some 40 miles north to south, its upland forest laced by streams that make their way down to the deep
canyon slashing along the park's eastern border. Union Gen.
Andrew May had a tough time crossing the canyon in 1864,
leading his troops to join Sherman in Georgia. Confederate
snipers on his rear encouraged him to find a quick route across.

As you approach from the tiny resort town of Mentone
to the north, you'll take County Rd. 89, part of the scenic
Lookout Mountain Parkway that stretches from Chattanooga
to Gadsden. Vacation cottages and country stores intersperse
with park land, making it sometimes hard to tell when you're
actually within park boundaries.

Seven miles before you reach the main part of the park,
signs direct you left (east) to DeSoto Falls, where a self-educated engineer named Arthur Miller built a dam in the
mid-1920s to supply power to Fort Payne, Mentone, Valley
Head, and Menlo. Though it no longer generates electricity,
the project was a marvel of mountain community resourcefulness—Miller himself often had to jump up from supper

DeSoto Falls

to take care of power outages. Miller and a partner bought 300 acres of land surrounding the falls and planned to develop a vacation resort, divided into 266 building lots. But the Depression brought Miller's dream to a halt.

The Civilian Conservation Corps arrived here in 1935, put in cabins, a lodge, trails, and other facilities, and the new state park was dedicated in May 1939 and named for the Spanish explorer who made forays into the area in 1540 on a search for gold.

What to See and Do

An old-style park, DeSoto does not have the slick Visitor Center and organized roster of activities that some parks offer. You need to make inquiries at the **Country Store** or **Lodge** *(205-845-3580 or 800-568-8840),* and pick up maps. The maps, however, are not to scale and present a confusing tangle of roads and trails. Instead of describing neat loops, the trails meander all over the main park area, and are prosaically called by their corresponding blaze (Blue, Gold, Orange). Ask for suggestions on hikes and drives, then get specific directions. The trouble is well worth it—DeSoto offers a sense of

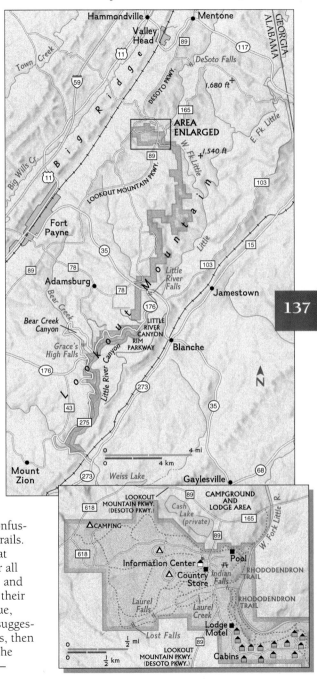

Granny Dollar

People around here still recall the legendary woman who was born sometime in the 1820s and lived until 1931. Local papers back then found good material in Granny Dollar, the pipe-smoking part-Cherokee whose father had two wives and 26 children. She could remember her father hiding in a cave to avoid the 1830s Indian Removal. Near the end of her life she looked back with sadness: "Another race has taken our fields, our forests and our game... The trouble with the white race is that they lay up so much for old age that they quit work at 50 and 60 years. When they stop working, they get out of touch with nature; all wear shoes in summer which keeps them from God's good earth; then they begin to fail, and soon they are dead."

138

untamed wilderness rare for a state park in this region of the country.

The 8 miles of trails wind along unusual geological formations, past endangered plant life, and over rustic footbridges. Start by walking along the bluff just behind the lodge. You can hike up and down just about as far as you like and get good views of Little River and its high rock cliffs. The **Rhododendron Trails,** located along here, take you past Indian Falls and other falls, and in May and June the rhododendron and mountain laurel burst into a pageant of color.

Back up at the Country Store area you can play tennis, take a swim in the Olympic-size pool (*Mem. Day–Labor Day*), or set up in one of the stone picnic shelters. This is also the play area—check out volleyballs, horseshoes, and other recreational equipment at the Country Store. The small **Doyle Benefield Interpretive Center** (*Mem. Day–Oct.*) next door has mounted animals, live snakes, a pet skunk, and other displays on the area's natural history. From here you can drive the 6 miles north to spectacular 100-foot-high **DeSoto Falls.**

Further Adventures

The **Little River Canyon Rim Parkway** takes you down 22 twisty miles, dipping in and out of the park and the boundaries of the **Little River Canyon National Preserve** (*205-845-9605*). One of the deepest canyons east of the Mississippi, Little River descends to 700 feet in its 16-mile-long run, its sheer walls and churning cascades a boon to rock climbers and white-water enthusiasts. If you plan to scale cliffs or boat the waters, contact the national preserve.

Those who prefer to explore by car should drive 5 miles down County Rd. 89 from the Country Store; at Ala. 35 turn left, and travel another 5 miles to the beginning of the parkway, Ala. 176. Park here and get out for a look at **Little River Falls,** a 60-foot plunge at the head of the canyon. After the first 3 or 4 miles along the parkway, you'll find yourself pulling over every few minutes to gaze down into the gorge and out to the layered cliffs. The road at one point cuts far to the northwest to maneuver around **Bear Creek Canyon,** a tributary gorge adorned by **Grace's High Falls.**

The parkway's first 12 miles are on a good gravel-and-asphalt road. After that, the going gets rougher, with patches and potholes to slow you down. You can bail out after 12 miles (*follow Ala. 176 west*) and return on back roads to the lodge area.

Camping and Lodging

There are 78 tent and RV sites, with showers; several primitive sites; 22 cabins; and 25 lodge rooms. Camping fee. For reservations call 205-845-5380 (campsites) or 800-252-7275.
❏ *DeSoto State Park, 13883 County Rd. 89, Fort Payne, AL 35967*

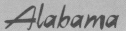

Cheaha

29 miles south of Anniston on Ala. 281

● 2,719 acres ● 205-488-
5111 ● Year-round ● Adm.
fee ● Mountain vistas
● Hiking ● Swimming,
fishing (license required)

Wild Cheaha Mountain

Not much has
changed at this easygoing
state park since the early
1940s. That's when the
Civilian Conservation
Corps finished building the
lodge and disbanded. The
CCC started work here in
1933 when only a mule
trail went to the top of
Cheaha (CHE-ha) Moun-
tain, the highest point in
the state. After putting in a
road, they erected an
observation tower using
only native stone and hand
tools, then turned to building cabins and a 50-foot-
long dam for a reservoir.
The park still has the same
benign charm, and the same
fine mountain views that
attracted the earliest visitors.
You can still spend a night in the lodge or cabins and walk the
trails laid out by those industrious young men in the 1930s.

Indian for "high," Cheaha makes a final exclamation
point in the Appalachian Mountains as they peter out in
northern Alabama. Chestnut oaks and scrub pines cover the
summit, and in autumn the red maples fire up the woods.
Since Cheaha is located within Talladega National Forest, the
overlooks give a sense of almost unlimited wilderness in all
directions. Looking out from the cliffs, you may see turkey
vultures and red-tailed hawks circling the heights.

What to See and Do

First stop by the park office or **Country Store** for a
park map. Just across Ala. 281, the **Nature Center** (*Mem.
Day–Oct.*) displays a handful of Indian artifacts, a few aquariums, bee hives and yellow-jacket's nests, and some mounted
animals. After taking a look, return to the park's entrance gate

and drive the 2.5-mile **Bunker Loop** around the top of Cheaha Mountain. Along the way you'll want to stop for walks and overlooks, particularly for the 30-foot **Observation Tower** on the state's highest point. The 1930s stone tower beckons with terrific views of timbered hills rolling into the hazy distance— the 2,407-foot elevation may not sound like much, but you're so far above the surrounding landscape that you'll feel high up. The adjoining **CCC Museum** (*May-Oct. Sat.-Sun.*) displays photos and tools of the Civilian Conservation Corps camps.

Continue around to **Bald Rock Trail,** a 1-mile loop through boulder-strewn woods on a high ridge. For the best overlook, you need only walk a quarter-mile out to a cliff with a grandstand vista of the soft green hills and hollows. Down the road, **Pulpit Rock Trail** is another nice short walk out to a similar westward exposure, but you also have a good southern vantage here and a view down to the park lake. This makes a fine place to picnic, or sit with the sun on your face and the scent of pine in the air.

One more walk up here, the .25-mile **Rock Garden Trail** brings you to fine overlooks of a cliff favored by rock climbers and rappelers. This trail continues as the Lake Trail for a mile, down to **Cheaha Lake** (or you can drive around). From May through August the lake and sandy beach are open for swimming, sunning, and fishing. Bring your own bait and tackle; paddle boats are available for rent. Further adventures may be found on the challenging new 6-mile **Cheaha Mountain Express Bike Trail.**

Camping and Lodging

The park has 73 tent or RV sites, with showers. Camping fee. There are also 10 cabins and 5 chalets; a 31-unit motel; plus 30 rooms at the lodge (currently closed for restoration). Reservations advised in season; call 205-488-5115 or 800-846-2654.
❏ CHEAHA STATE PARK, 19644 ALA. 281, DELTA, ALABAMA 36258

Talladega Scenic Byway

One of the state's prettiest drives winds its way along Ala. 281 from just north of I-20 down through the state park, then to Adams Gap. Sprinkled with views similar to those on Cheaha Mountain, the 27-mile byway follows the narrow ridge of Horseblock Mountain south toward the tail end of the Appalachians. You have fine views of the Coosa River valley to the west before the steep climb up Cheaha. The 80-mile **Pinhoti Trail** parallels the route, and there are plenty of places to get out and hike.

Joe Wheeler

2 miles west of Rogersville, off US 72

● 2,550 acres ● 205-247-5466 ● Year-round ● Day-use fee
● Lake ● Golf, tennis, swimming, fishing (license required)

Named for a Confederate cavalry commander whose house stands nearby, this well-developed resort park hugs the shores of **Wheeler Lake,** a 74-mile-long reservoir created by a dam that stretches more than a mile across the Tennessee River. Activities focus around the lake and the handsome stone-and-redwood **Resort Lodge,** complete with a dining room that overlooks the lake. A pool and swimming area in the lake are reserved for lodge guests only.

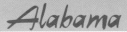

If you're not staying overnight, a special day-use area *(fee)* near the wooded campground offers a beach, bathhouse, picnic tables, tennis courts, and 5 miles of hiking trails. To get out on the lake, go up past the lodge to the **marina** and rent a paddle boat, canoe, fishing boat, or pontoon boat.

Camping and Lodging

The park has 116 tent or RV sites, with showers; and 40 primitive tent sites. Reservations advised in season; call 205-247-1184. Camping fee. For reservations at the 23 cottages, call 205-685-3306. There are also 2 group lodges and 74 units at Resort Lodge; call 205-247-5461 or 800-544-5639 to reserve.

❑ *Joe Wheeler State Park, Rte. 4, Box 369-A, Rogersville, AL 35652*

Gulf

Just east of Gulf Shores on Ala. 182

● 6,150 acres ● 334-948-7275 ● Year-round ● Day-use fees ● Gulf of Mexico beach ● Pier ● Lake ● Nature trail ● Golf, swimming, tennis

141

The wide welcome mat of this sunny park, a sparkling white-sand beach, runs for 2.5 miles along the Gulf of Mexico. First developed by the Civilian Conservation Corps in the 1930s, Gulf State Park was upgraded to resort status with new facilities in the 1970s. If you're planning an overnight stay in the summer, make reservations early.

Starting on the beach side of the highway, walk out onto the 825-foot **fishing pier** *(Fee)*, the longest in the Gulf. Just up the beach in a separate parking area, the **Resort Hotel** is fully loaded with a pool, snack bar, lounge, and all-you-can-eat buffet. A bit farther east, the beach pavilion is the place to go if you just want an afternoon on the sand.

On the other side of the highway, **Lake Shelby** offers freshwater fishing and swimming. At the store here rent an aluminum jonboat in summer and explore the lake, then row east through a canal to the smaller **Middle Lake,** where a campground sprawls on the north shore. A **Nature Center** on this lake's edge has exhibits on shore ecology and 4 miles of woodsy trails.

Great blue heron

Camping and Lodging:

The park has 368 RV sites and 100 tent sites, with showers. Camping fee. There are also 21 cabins, and 144 hotel rooms. Reservations advised in season; call 334-948-6353 (campsites only), 800-544-4853 or 800-ALA-PARK.

❑ *Gulf State Park, 20115 Ala. 135, Gulf Shores, Alabama 36542*

Tishomingo

2 miles south of Tishomingo, off Miss. 25

● 1,530 acres ● 601-438-6914 ● Year-round ● Day-use fee ● Natchez Trace Parkway ● Indian artifacts ● Float trips ● Hiking, swimming, fishing (license required)

142

A ride down Spring Hill

An old-fashioned state park, Tishomingo nestles in the Appalachian foothills on the border of Alabama, presenting a rugged contour unusual in this low-lying state. Tremendous sandstone cliffs vie for attention with moss-covered boulders strewn about the hillsides, while woodland trails explore cool glades lined by ferns and colorful wildflowers.

Named for a Chickasaw chief, the park was the site of paleo-Indians as early as 7000 BC. The Indians relied on the high-quality chert and sandstone for making tools, and they used the local clay for ceramics.

The park straddles the Natchez Trace Parkway, the fabled highway extending nearly 500 miles from Nashville to Natchez that began as a bison trail followed by prehistoric hunters. By the early 18th century, the Trace was well worn by Indians, French and Spanish traders, trappers, soldiers, and missionaries. Cutthroats and vagabonds found easy prey on the long, lonely stretches, darkened by tree tunnels, prompting early travelers to call the road the "devil's backbone."

The Civilian Conservation Corps started building a park here in the mid-1930s, putting in trails and facilities with rock quarried in the park. The pond just south of the Trace was created for the park's main water supply, and if you continue a bit farther on the park road, you can see the remnants of the old CCC camp off the trail on the right. Other reminders of their work can be found here and there throughout the park, including the swinging bridge across Bear Creek. In 1997 the park sponsored a crew from the new service organization Americorps to refurbish trails and facilities.

What to See and Do

Stop first at the **park office** for a brochure and trail map. A small museum here houses a collection of spear points, grinding stones, pottery fragments, and other artifacts from various periods of Indian occupation.

Then get some exercise outside on the 13-mile system of trails that range from short loops to sections 6 miles long. One of the best walks to acquaint yourself with the terrain and its subtle interplay of rocky ridges and shallow defiles is the **Bear Creek Outcroppings Trail,** a 3.5-mile loop that begins on the swinging bridge near the pool. Cross the 186-foot-long bridge, suspended high above frothy, boulder-tossed Bear Creek, and continue up through the woods. You can get a drink from a cool, clean spring, and take a look at the park's largest rock shelter, the 62-foot-high **Jean's Overhang.** (The park's many overhangs average 25 to 30 feet.)

Though the park in general lacks overlooks and broad vistas, it specializes in close-ups—look carefully and you'll see a spectacular variety of plant life. Among more than 600 kinds of ferns and wildflowers are rare purple cliff brake and walking ferns, delicate fire pinks, spring beauties, and mayapple mandrakes, their blossoms like little umbrellas. In spring look for the blooms of oak-leaf hydrangea, wild azalea, and mountain laurel. Returning along Bear Creek, the path offers fine views of cypress knees bent at the water's edge and the stream rushing and churning northward, building momentum on its way to the Tennessee River.

You can also walk on the other side of the creek, all the way up across the Trace to 45-acre **Haynes Lake** (*2 miles from the pool*). About halfway along this pretty walk, a trail to the left leads across the park road to a copy of an 1840s log cabin, donated by local families in the late 1970s. A short trail loops the old CCC pond behind the cabin. Popular with photographers, the scenic pond is edged with wildflowers and lilies, and it flows to a waterfall set about with boulders. A footbridge crosses the stream. Of course, if you prefer not to walk, you can drive up to the lake. Though there's no swimming here, visitors may rent paddle boats,

143

canoes, and flat-bottom fishing boats. The fishing is good for catfish, bream, crappie, and bass.

Whereas the lake area dates from the 1960s, the **Horseshoe Bend area** was the work of the CCC in the 1930s. In addition to the cabins, the CCC built the old **Loōchapōlo Lodge** of wood and native Highland Church sandstone, which serves as a focal point for various activities. Part of the rustic scenery, the people you see rocking on the wide front porch are locals who partake in an eldercare program. In operation for some 25 years, the program doesn't just provide meals, it keeps seniors busy with quilting, pitching horseshoes, and the like. In addition to the eldercare, the lodge serves as a rental facility for family reunions, church groups, Boy Scouts, and so forth. Among annual events that take place here is a reunion of the state's CCC laborers; recently, 89 former CCC men attended and shared their memories of creating the state parks in the 1930s and '40s.

Paddling the Horseshoe Bend area

Further Adventures

To cool off on a hot day, take a swim in the pool (*Mem. Day–Labor Day; fee*), or sign up at the park office for a canoe trip down **Bear Creek** (*Mid-April–mid-Oct. Reservations strongly recommended through park; fee*). The three-hour excursions begin 8 miles upstream (transportation provided), then meander back to the swinging bridge, offering pleasant, woodsy scenery. It's mostly a lazy float, but there are some Class I ripples and a few treetop rope swings that give you a chance to get wet. Offered twice a day in season, the trips take up to 16 canoes.

Camping and Lodging

The park has 62 RV sites, with showers; some may be

reserved. There are also primitive tent and group cabin sites. Camping fee. There are also 6 cabins; reservations advised in season. For information and all reservations, contact the park at 601-438-6914.

❏ *TISHOMINGO STATE PARK, P.O. BOX 880, TISHOMINGO, MISSISSIPPI 38873*

Winterville Mounds

3 miles north of Greenville on Miss. 1

● **43 acres** ● **601-334-4684** ● **Year-round Wed. to Sun.**
● **Entrance fee** ● **No camping** ● **Prehistoric Indian mounds**
● **Museum**

One of the numerous ceremonial settlements strung along the Mississippi River, the village that flourished near here about 1,000 years ago traded, farmed, fought, and played until suddenly dispersing around the year 1440, perhaps because the stream connecting it to the river dried up. Of the villagers' activities, the most fascinating (and obvious) to modern civilization was their mound building. Thirteen of the original 35 to 39 earth mounds remain, including the 60-foot-high **Temple Mound.** Here the chief lived in a grass and cane hut, which was burned during an annual ceremony. Lesser authorities occupied the smaller mounds. Whereas common villagers were buried in cemeteries, those of rank were interred within their mounds, so that, in effect, the chiefs sat atop big mausoleums where their predecessors lay buried.

Modern farmers did their share of damage to these archaeological mines—bulldozing them flat when they were in the way. But in some cases, they accidentally preserved them from erosion by planting them with hay. Winterville operated as a small local park from the late 1950s until 1971, when it opened as a state park.

The **Museum** has been undergoing extensive renovations, but it should be open by now. Built in the shape of a mound, the museum displays a dugout canoe, pottery, ax heads, spear points, bone and stone tools, pipes, and bead and shell ornaments. Exhibits outline Mississippian trade, agriculture, and daily life, focusing on the culture that existed within the immediate vicinity. Films help re-create a world far removed from ours.

Outside, a short trail with interpretive markers takes you around the grassy **mounds.** Evidence exists for occupation here as early as 500 BC. Interrupting the quiet woods and fields, the mounds serve as reminders of America's long past.

❏ *WINTERVILLE MOUNDS HISTORIC SITE, 2415 HWY. 1N, GREENVILLE, MISSISSIPPI 38703*

145

Natchez

10 miles north of Natchez, off US 61

- 3,411 acres ● 601-442-2658
- Year-round ● Entrance fee
- Antebellum history ● Lake
- Hiking, fishing (license required)

Located near the southern terminus of the Natchez Trace Parkway, this secluded, peaceful park dates only from 1979. The park's 33,000 annual visitors generally fall into two categories—tourists from Natchez and serious anglers. The sun-worshiping Natchez Indians lived in a nearby village until the arrival of the French in 1716. By the early 19th century, not only were the Indians and French gone, so were the later-arriving English and Spanish. The era of spiral staircases and skyhigh ceilings was at hand. Built by rich cotton planters, dozens of the region's neoclassical mansions have survived and are on tour year-round.

Built in 1985, the 230-acre **Natchez State Park Lake** was stocked with bass, bluegill and red-ear bream, crappie, and catfish. That one time was enough to produce the state record largemouth bass—an 18.15-pound catch. You'll need your own fishing gear, but if you don't have any you can still get out on the lake by renting a flat-bottom, aluminum jonboat. You can paddle around and explore the marshy edges—only 50 acres of the lake are open water, the rest occupied by standing dead timber and stumps. Rental cabins hide among the woods at lake's edge. In addition to fish, the lake and nearby areas provide a home to alligators, water moccasins, and rattlesnakes. And you might want to note that in summer it's a good idea to bring insect repellent.

Pick up a snack at the boat rental pavilion and take a walk out into the pine and hardwood forest. There are no set loop trails, but you can wander old logging roads as far as you like. The gentle terrain supports oak, hickory, poplar, and gum trees, and you may catch a glimpse of a deer or wild turkey.

146

Walking the Natchez Trace

Camping

The park has 6 tent and 21 RV sites, with showers; and 10 cabins. Reservations advised in season; call the park at 601-442-2658. Camping fee.

❏ NATCHEZ STATE PARK, 230 B WICKLIFF RD., NATCHEZ, MISSISSIPPI 39120

Percy Quin

6 miles south of McComb, off I-55

● 1,700 acres ● 601-684-3938 ● Year-round ● Entrance fee ● Deep South scenery ● Lake ● Watersports ● Fishing (license required), golf, swimming ● Nature trail

During the Great Depression, a local newspaper editor stirred up interest in buying devalued land for the creation of a state park. By 1935 a brigade of 200 Civilian Conservation Corps laborers, working for a dollar a day, had begun cutting timber for the construction of a lodge and cabins. Within three years the work was done, a dirt dam erected with wheelbarrows and shovels. The lake park was named for U.S. Congressman Percy Edwards Quin, whose ancestors were original Pike County settlers. In 1942 the dam that had been built with backbreaking labor broke, and the lake dried up for three years, until 75,000 dollars were raised for rebuilding.

Percy Quin centers around 700-acre **Lake Tangipahoa,** edged by loblolly pines and magnolias and set amid a peaceful landscape of rolling hills. The best way to get a feel for this Deep South park is to take part or all of the 4-mile **nature trail** that circles the lake. The trail offers the opportunity for spotting a variety of wildflowers and birds.

147

Most people want to get right onto the lake. Park at the boat rental pavilion, pick up a snack, and rent a canoe, paddle boat, or fishing boat—ideal for lazing around the lake. The marina is for people who want to launch their own boats, and you'll need your own if you want to water-ski. A public swimming area is located near the **Lodge.** Positioned near the park entrance, the lodge no longer serves meals, but you can pick up information here. Nearby are the swimming pool and miniature golf course *(fee for both).*

For those who need to follow through on their swing, there are 27 holes of golf at the Quail Hollow Golf Course *(601-684-2903. Mem. Day–Labor Day; greens fee).*

Camping and Lodging

The park has 101 RV and 40 tent sites, with showers; group sites; and 22 cabins. Reservations advised in season; call 601-684-3931. Camping fee.

❏ *PERCY QUIN STATE PARK, 1156 CAMP BEAVER DR., McCOMB, MS 39648*

Big leaf magnolia

Fall Creek Falls

14 miles northwest of Pikeville on Tenn. 284

● 21,135 acres ● 423-881-3297 ● Year-round ● Waterfalls
● Hiking ● Lake ● Nature Center ● Scenic drive ● Resort
lodge ● Golf, tennis ● Swimming, horseback riding, biking

Tennessee's largest and most popular state park lies on the western edge of the Cumberland Plateau, a forested area sliced by giant gorges and tumbling waterfalls. Though developed into a major resort park, Fall Creek Falls maintains more than two-thirds of its acreage in a natural state; you can behold some of Tennessee's most spectacular scenery just off a scenic drive that loops along Cane Creek Gorge.

Fall Creek Falls

The exposed rock layers you see were laid down 250 to 325 million years ago, the remains of ancient dunes, tidal plains, and swamps. The park's main stream, Cane Creek, then began cutting through the terrain, leaving flat-topped hills. The three tremendous falls here were formed when tributaries eroded soft shales underlying sandstone ledges from which the water now cascades. The park's centerpiece, Fall Creek Falls plunges 256 feet, the highest falls east of the Rockies.

In 1935 the National Park Service made the place a recreation demonstration area, with the Civilian Conservation Corps and Works Progress Administration adding bridges, trails, and facilities. Old farmlands were reverted to forest, while other large fields were planted with pines. Turned over to the state in 1944, the area began a period of steady growth and popularity. The state park officially opened in 1972.

What to See and Do

Whether you enter the park from the north or south, well-marked signs direct you to the Information Center and visitor's lounge. Pick up trail maps and park literature here and plan your visit. If you're staying at the Fall Creek Falls Inn or one of the cabins, you may want to check in. At any rate, driving around this way (west) will take you across the dam and give you a fine view of **Fall Creek Lake**. Nestled beside the lake, the 3-story cinder block-and-concrete inn may not have great visual appeal from the outside, but the rooms are quiet and comfortable. The spacious dining room serves good country buffets at reasonable prices—picture windows look onto the lake and its resident geese.

Just up the road, turn right for the 6-mile **Gorge Scenic Drive,** a wonderful loop that takes you past the park's highlights. The first pulloff is for **Fall Creek Falls** itself, where a short walk ends at a thrilling cliffside overlook. Nature must have been proud of her falls to have created this perfectly situated viewing platform. From here you look down on a semi-circular amphitheater of stone over which the water plummets

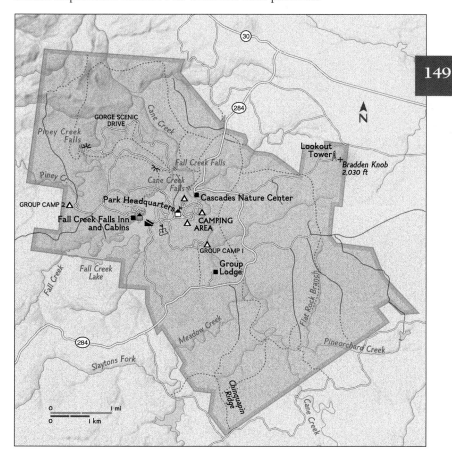

to a big plunge pool. As you drive around, pull over again for breathtaking views of the 600-foot-deep gorge, as wide as a mile in places. The sound of wind and water thunder up from the valley floor, and sundown tints the rock walls russet and ash. A good place to watch birds soaring the updrafts is from **Millikan's Overlook,** named for a naturalist who fell to his death climbing here in 1947. At **Piney Creek Falls Overlook,** two short paths lead out to another impressive waterfall, this one a 75-foot plunge. Virgin stands of Eastern hemlock, yellow birch, and yellow poplar surround this secluded redoubt of stone terraces and pulpits. The path on the left takes you over a suspension bridge on the upper creek.

Hiking trails begin at the **Nature Center.** First, take a look inside at the exhibits on local geology, flora, and fauna. Included are a live honeybee hive, taxidermic animals, and several worthwhile films—the 14-minute film on the park gives you a good overview. Then take a walk. A bouncy suspension bridge over Cane Creek brings you to trailheads for Fall Creek Falls. The easy **Woodland Trail** is the quickest way there—about 20 minutes. Or you can swing out on the **Gorge Trail,** which takes a little longer because of its many overlooks. Both trails end up at the same overlook for Fall Creek Falls that you had on the scenic drive. If you have time and stamina, continue down a switchback trail for a little less than half a mile to the base of the falls. A good option is to head out on Gorge Trail and return on Woodland, for a total walk of about 90 minutes.

A longer, yet easier stroll, the 4.6-mile **Paw Paw Trail** starts at the Nature Center, pauses for views of **Cane Creek Falls** and Fall Creek Falls, and winds back through the forest.

Further Adventures

If you have all day to hike, or want to do an overnight backpack, the **Cane Creek Lower Loop** courses around the gorge for about 12 miles. There are two designated camping areas *(permit required)*. For another workout, the 13-mile **Cane Creek Upper Loop** offers an in-depth exploration of the creeks and forest of the park's southeastern corner.

You can rent bicycles at the camper check-in station at park headquarters; more than 4 miles of paved trails skirt the lake from the inn to Fall Creek Falls and out to Piney Creek Falls. **Fall Creek Lake** is stocked with bass, bream, and catfish. You can rent paddle boats, canoes, and motor boats from the boat dock.

Camping and Lodging

The park has 227 tent and RV sites, with showers; and 20 cabins. Some reservations taken; call 800-250-8611. Camping fee.

❏ *Fall Creek Falls State Resort Park, Rte. 3, Pikeville, TN 37367*

Winter World

The 256-foot Fall Creek Falls are perhaps at their magical best in the dead of winter. Frozen to a trickle, the mighty falls take on a strange silence, the high ledge hung with fangs of ice two stories tall, the plunge pool turned into an immense iceberg. In winter, you have nearly the whole park to yourself.

Rhododendron leaves droop, curling against the cold, while the mist of creek water rimes low shrubs that clatter like heavy wind chimes as you push past. And a warm noontime sun can send 10-foot icicles crashing to the valley floor.

Roan Mountain

20 miles southeast of Elizabethton on Tenn. 143

● 2,006 acres ● 423-772-3303 or 800-250-8620
● Year-round ● Natural rhododendron garden
● 6,285-foot peak ● Highlands drive ● Hiking,
swimming, cross-country skiing

Every June, the top of Roan Mountain bursts into brilliant purples, pinks, and reds as the rhododendron garden on the 6,285-foot peak comes into blossom. Catawba legend claimed that the shrubs would bloom red after a bloody battle. As far back as the 18th century, a famous botanist, John Fraser, made a journey to the summit and reported back on the "new plant," *Rhododendron catawbiense.*

151

Such was the appeal of Roan Mountain that in 1877 Gen. Thomas Wilder erected a 20-room inn on the mountaintop, replacing it a mere eight years later with the 166-room Cloudland Hotel. A carriage bumped along a steep, narrow trail, ferrying guests from the railroad station up to the hotel. Early advertising beckoned visitors to "magnificent views above the clouds where the rivers are born." Buying up large tracts of land on area mountains, Wilder went about mining the hills for

Rhododendron adorning Roan Mountain

iron ore. But by 1900, with the mines played out, Wilder had sold his holdings and the hotel was abandoned and later dismantled. Stands of mature balsam fir and spruce were cut down, and the rhododendron was dug up for sale to nurseries.

Left alone, the natural gardens began coming back to life, as thick and healthy as ever. In 1941 the U.S. Forest Service acquired mountaintop acreage and began to manage the gardens, controlling the surrounding 850 acres of Fraser fir and spruce and thinning the rhododendron when necessary. The annual Rhododendron Festival, held the third weekend in June, draws crowds of admirers.

What to See and Do

You'll want to start at the **Visitor Center,** which, in addition to maps and information, has varied displays on area culture and natural history. You can sit in a rocking chair by the wood-burning stove planning your visit, then browse at the cases of Indian tools, Civil War relics, the gourd dulcimer, crazy quilt, clay pipes, and other crafts. Stretch your legs out back on the 1-mile **Cloudland Nature Trail,** and get a taste for the mountain air before driving to higher elevations. Among 150 species of wildflowers—in bloom early May to early fall—are orchids, trilliums, and larkspur. Deer, bobcat, fox, and numerous songbirds make homes here. The adjoining 0.4-mile **Peg Leg Mine Trail** takes you past a mill wheel on the Doe River and back to the site of a 19th-century ore production works.

Dave Miller Homestead

It's a 10-mile drive south to the top of Roan Mountain, the views growing ever wider and more beautiful as you ascend. On the way up, stop off at the **Dave Miller Homestead** (*Mem. Day–Labor Day Wed.-Sun.*), a farm with a log house, root cellar, and other dependencies dating from 1870 to 1919. Continue up to the parking and picnic area on your right. Here you can play tennis, swim (*fee*), and run the kids through the playground. The cross-country skiing trail across the road is part of the park's 8.5-mile network. Trails from this parking lot include the delightful **Raven Rock Overlook,** a 0.6-mile huff-and-puff up through hemlocks and rhododendron to nice views down to the pool and out upon the mountains to the west. From the top, you can swing around to make a 2-mile loop, or head back north and down to the restaurant and cabins.

Drive on up to Carver's Gap, where the road intersects the Appalachian Trail. Turn right for Roan Knob and the **rhododendron gardens.** You're now actually well beyond the park boundary and into Pisgah National Forest (*704-682-6146*). Crest the mountain, park, and get out to savor splendid views.

Camping and Lodging

The park has 87 tent or RV sites and 20 tent-only sites, with showers; and 30 cabins. Reservations advised in season; call 423-772-3303. Camping fee. No tent camping mid-Nov. to mid-April.

❏ *ROAN MOUNTAIN S.P., RTE. 527, HWY. 143, ROAN MOUNTAIN, TENNESSEE 37687*

Roan Mysteries

No one knows how the mountain got its name. One version maintains that Daniel Boone left a roan horse up here, while some folks hold it was called after a "rowan tree" that grows bright red berries in late fall. Another enigma is the eerie music sometimes heard on the mountain. Scientists speculate that electrically-charged air currents brush each other near the summit, filling the air with the sound of buzzing bees.

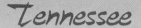

Pickett

12 miles northeast of Jamestown on Tenn. 154

● 16,752 acres ● 615-879-5821 ● Year-round ● Natural
bridges and overhangs ● Hiking ● Lake swimming
● Fishing and hunting (license required for both)

Bobcat

In a secluded corner of Tennessee, Pickett holds some of
the state's most striking geological features. Natural arches, cave-
like overhangs, and graceful waterfalls await those who venture
just off Tenn. 154 into the hilly forests. In the early 1800s, white
settlers began moving into the area that had once sheltered prehistoric Indians. By the early 1930s, the Civilian Conservation
Corps had arrived, putting in trails, a boathouse, office, picnic
shelters, rustic cabins, and a lodge made with locally quarried
stone. The park opened to the public in 1940.

What to See and Do

Stop at the park office for trail maps and information. If
you're on a time budget, take two or three of the shorter
trails that lead to the park's many arresting geological points
of interest. Driving just past the office and over Thompson
Creek, you come to a pulloff on your right for **Crystal Falls.**
This is a vigorous, 10-mile loop trail, but if you walk just
over a mile you come to **Hidden Passage,** a big rock overhang where the trail momentarily disappears into the cave-

like dark, and then you wind around to lovely Crystal Falls. Mountain laurel and rhododendron line the trail, and if you hike quietly you have a good chance of surprising a deer. A dozen black bears were recently released with tracking devices into the adjacent Big South Fork backcountry; unfortunately, several wandered off and one was hit by a car.

Even shorter trails are just off Tenn. 154 between the office and the park entrance: .25-mile (one-way) **Indian Rockhouse,** a tremendous overhang, was used by prehistoric Indians; on the other side of the road, **Hazard Cave**—the park's largest overhang—was named for CCC officer James E. Hazard. If you move far enough back in this cavernous auditorium of rock, the opening seems to close down like a giant eyelid. Walk back up to the road, or continue on until you link up with the network of trails around the lake and cabins. Driving toward the lake, pull over for **Natural Bridge.** You can walk across and under this 50-foot-long stone arch.

Down at the boat dock, rent a canoe or rowboat and paddle around 15-acre **Arch Lake.** There's a supervised swimming area and fishing for trout and other species. Just behind the lodge, walk over the lake on the popular **swinging bridge,** originally built by the CCC. Also don't miss the natural bridge connecting the "island" (a loop in the lake) to the mainland. Though it doesn't serve meals, the lodge has a snackbar and bathhouse. From the park office, you may check out equipment for badminton, archery, horseshoes, tennis, and volleyball. During the summer, a naturalist conducts free guided tours and campfire programs.

Camping and Lodging

The park has 40 tent and RV sites. Available first come, first served. A group camp can handle up to 144 persons. Camping fee. The park also has 5 villas, 5 chalets, and 10 cottages. Reservations advised; call 615-879-5821.

❏ *PICKETT STATE PARK, ROCK CREEK RTE., BOX 174, JAMESTON, TN 38556*

Big South Fork

On Pickett's eastern border, the **Big South Fork National River and Recreation Area** encompasses a sprawling 119,000 acres in Tennessee and Kentucky. Over the ages, the Cumberland River's Big South Fork carved a rugged wonderland of spires, pinnacles, and sheer cliffs. Once ransacked by logging and mining operations, nature has begun reclaiming this gorgeous back-of-beyond. In addition to the many trails, adventurous souls seek out the 80 miles of streams, ranging from placid to dangerous white water. *(Visitor Center, on Tenn. 297, 15 miles W of Oneida. 615-879-3625).*

154

Reelfoot Lake

5 miles southeast of Tiptonville on Tenn. 21

● 280 acres ● 901-253-7756 ●Year-round ● Boat cruises ● Bald eagle tours ● National Wildlife Refuge ● Wildlife drives ● Nature Centers ● Lakeside inn ● Hiking ● Fishing and hunting (license required for both)

Named for a legendary Indian, this appealing lakeside park is comprised of ten segments situated among the 25,000-acre Reelfoot Lake Wildlife Management Area, 60 percent of it water and wetlands. Ancient cypresses haunt the margins of Reelfoot Lake, while waterbirds and eagles add to a picture of primitive beauty. Only 5 miles from the Mississippi River, the lake was born during the New Madrid earthquakes in the winter of 1811-12, when violent landslides and sinks reshaped the area's topography.

The **Reelfoot Lake Visitor Center** is a good place to familiarize yourself with the area and its offerings. Take in the excellent exhibits on the lake's formation and the area's natural history. Included here are an earthquake simulator

Reflecting bald cypresses

and a boardwalk out through a cypress forest. Narrated pontoon boat tours (*fee*) operate May through September. Pick up an auto tour map and plan your itinerary. The 37-mile drive loops the lake and offers several miles of side excursions, plus 10 miles of hiking trails.

Next drive northeast on Tenn. 22 to the Visitor Center for the **Reelfoot Lake National Wildlife Refuge** (*901-538-2481. Mon.-Fri.*), where you can learn more about local flora and fauna. Some 125,000 Canada geese and 215,000 mallard ducks stop here during winter migrations. A 5-mile round-trip excursion from here, by car or foot, brings you to an observation platform on **Grassy Island,** a great place for viewing wildlife and sunsets. Up at the **Reelfoot Lake State Airpark Inn** you can arrange to join an eagle-watching tour (*901-253-7756. Dec.–mid-March; tour fee*). Continuing back around to the Visitor Center, there are several possibilities for short hikes, including the **Keystone Trail,** which edges the lake for about 1.5 miles through old-growth cypresses and offers views of waterfowl and wading birds.

At the park dock you can rent a boat (*April-Sept.*) and fish for crappie, bream, largemouth bass, catfish, bluegill, and many other kinds of fish in **Reelfoot Lake,** one of the largest natural fish hatcheries in the country.

Camping and Lodging

The park has 102 tent and RV sites, with showers. Available on a first-come, first-served basis. Camping fee. There are also 20 motel units; call 901-253-7756 for reservations.

❑ *Reelfoot Lake State Resort Park, Route 1, Box 2345, Tiptonville, Tennessee 38079*

155

Cumberland Falls

20 miles southwest of Corbin on Ky. 90

● 1,657 acres ● 606-528-4121 ● Year-round ● Waterfalls
● Moonbow ● Hiking ● Swimming, fishing (license required), horseback riding ● White-water rafting

Swing Time

Put on your checkered shirts and cowboy boots, grab your partners, and head down to the poolside dance pavilion. A time-honored tradition at Cumberland Falls, square dancing takes place several nights a week during the summer. It's all right if you don't know a do-si-do from an electric slide—the caller will set you straight. And you don't have to pay a cent.

156

On a boulder-tossed bend in the Cumberland River, a sheer curtain of water 125 feet across drops nearly seven roaring stories, spraying the gorge with so much mist that on moonlit nights an eerie arc of light shimmers out from the falls. The only regularly occurring moonbow in the Western Hemisphere, the rare phenomenon works best during a full moon that is fairly close to the horizon. You should be able to catch a glimpse at least five nights a month (if the weather cooperates). But even if you miss the moonbow, there's still plenty to do in this jewel-like resort park.

Named for the Duke of Cumberland in 1750 by Kentucky explorer Dr. Thomas Walker, the river found itself in a storm of controversy in the late 1920s, when a power dam was proposed for placement above the falls. Delaware politician T. Coleman DuPont, who had fond memories of summers here, stepped in to resolve the conflict by offering to buy the whole area, including the falls, and donate it to the state. Suspicious that DuPont had interest in the local utility company, the legislature took three years to accept the offer. Though DuPont had already died, his heirs made good on the offer, and Cumberland Falls State Park was dedicated on Aug. 21, 1931. The ubiquitous CCC built the DuPont Lodge and 15 cabins in 1933. The lodge burned in 1940, but was rebuilt the following year.

What to See and Do

If you're arriving from Corbin, stop off first at the **DuPont Lodge** for brochures and trail maps. But if you can't wait to see the falls, just continue the short distance on to the parking lot

and walk the paved path out past the coffee shop and gift shop and onto the rock slabs. The sight of pounding froth, the light mist on your skin, and the rush in your ears will keep you absorbed for a long time. A waist-high cable prevents you from straying too close to this force of nature, which is tempting. To see the moonbow (at night), look just downstream from the

Rafters in spray of Cumberland Falls

base of the falls—the bow begins here, rising up about 50 feet and curving slightly downstream. Your brochure will tell you when the phenomenon occurs.

For a good walk, continue downstream as far as you like on the **Moonbow Trail**—it's 10.7 miles to the mouth of Laurel River, but the trail continues (as Sheltowee Trace) north the entire length of the Daniel Boone National Forest. To make a 7-mile loop, in less than 2 miles cut right and up from the river on the **Cumberland River Trail**. After crossing Ky. 90, you follow the road east for 25 yards, then head back into the woods and down an old logging road to the river—take the trail downstream about 2 miles back to the parking lot. The **Eagle Falls Trail** on the other side of the river, about 3 miles round-trip, offers fine views of Cumberland Falls and 44-foot Eagle Falls.

To get an even better feel for the river, take a guided rafting trip (May-Oct.; fee), or arrange for canoe or kayak rentals with a local outfitter. There are Class III rapids below the falls, and Class I and II above. For further cooling off, take a dip in the Olympic-size pool (fee for visitors). Then tuck into some hearty country cooking in the **DuPont Lodge** dining room.

Camping and Lodging

The park has 50 tent and RV sites (April-Oct.), with shower facilities. Available on a first-come, first-served basis. Camping fee. There are also 10 cottages and 52 lodge units; call 606-528-4121 to reserve.

❏ *Cumberland Falls State Resort Park, 7351 Hwy. 90, Corbin, Kentucky 40701*

Natural Bridge

2 miles south of Slade on Ky. 11

● 2,100 acres ● 606-663-2214 or 800-325-1710 ● Year-round ● Sandstone arch ● Skylift ● Hiking ● Nature center ● Lodge ● Lake, swimming pool

Natural Bridge

Less than an hour from Lexington, this popular park showcases several of the many sandstone arches, rock shelters, and other impressive geological features found in the area. Existing for at least 100,000 years, Natural Bridge was originally a rock shelter with a solid back wall. As water, wind, joint fractures, and gravity broke away the back wall bit by bit, the rim of the rock house was left standing, thereby creating the arch. One of the more massive arches in the area, Natural Bridge has a mean width of 24 feet. There are over 100 arches found within a 5-mile radius, many formed in entirely different ways.

Early Indians discovered the area around 8,000 to 10,000 years ago, and began taking up residence in the rock shelters and carving figures into the walls. Explorers heading east from the Bluegrass arrived here in the mid-1700s, but the steep valleys and narrow ridges made settlement difficult.

Railroads put in by lumber companies were bringing tourists here by the turn of the century, with Hoedown Island serving Natural Bridge. In 1926 the Louisville & Nashville Railroad deeded the land to Kentucky, and the state park came into being.

What to See and Do

Start out at the **Activities Center,** the lower floor of which has a Nature Center with worthwhile exhibits on the area's flora and fauna. After your orientation, you can pick up a map of the park's nine trails and head out to **Natural Bridge.**

Blazed in the 1890s by the Lexington & Eastern Railroad, the **Original Trail** is your easiest bet—a 0.5-mile stroll up through a forest of rhododendron, hemlock, yellow poplar, and white pine. A natural fracture on the other side of the bridge allows access to the top. For a more challenging and scenic walk up, take the .75-mile **Balanced Rock Trail,** which starts with a series of limestone steps and goes up past a cave. If you walk through the cave, you'll emerge on the Original Trail. Otherwise, continue up and around to Balanced Rock, a tremendous sandstone boulder that appears perched on a cliff. You shortly arrive at a wooden shelter at the top of the arch.

A more leisurely walk up is available on the 1.75-mile **Rock Garden Trail.** For a four-hour hike, you can take the Balanced Rock Trail up to Natural Bridge, then take **Hood's Branch Trail** 4 miles around to the **Skylift** parking lot. Ride the lift *(mid-April–mid-Oct.; fee)* back down to Natural Bridge and take Rock Garden Trail back to the lodge or Activities Center. If you can work in **Laurel Ridge Trail,** only three-fourths of a mile, you'll be rewarded with wonderful views of Natural Bridge and Middle Fork canyon. Just north of the Mountain Parkway, the 26,000-acre **Red River Gorge Geological Area** *(606-663-2852)* has some 36 miles of additional trails leading to impressive rock formations.

You can rent paddle boats *(Mem. Day–Labor Day)* for the small but pleasant pond, and putter around **Hoedown Island,** where weekly square dances take place on an outdoor patio during the summer. Other recreational venues include a swimming pool *(fee for non-guests)* and a miniature golf course.

Camping and Lodging

The park has 82 tent and RV sites, with showers; and 12 primitive tent sites. All sites open March through November, on a first-come, first-served basis. Camping fee. Hemlock Lodge has 35 units; call 606-663-2214 or 800-325-1710 to reserve.

❏ *Natural Bridge State Resort Park, 2135 Natural Bridge Rd., Slade, Kentucky 40376*

Silver in Them Thar Hills

Generations of treasure seekers have been lured into the eastern Kentucky mountains by tales of an adventurer named John Swift, who allegedly found a Shawnee silver mine in the 1760s. In England to raise funds for a large expedition, Swift was jailed for his colonial sympathies during the Revolution. He later returned, a blind old man, and with his journal descriptions—which match with details in the Natural Bridge area—led believers on a search. They never found the silver, but just before his death Swift encouraged them, "Don't ever stop a lookin', boys. It's there and it'll make you and Kentucky rich." They didn't stop looking, and the unfortunate result was the destruction of many aboriginal sites.

159

Carter Caves

8 miles northeast of Olive Hill on Ky. 182

● 2,000 acres ● 606-286-4411 ● Year-round ● 20 caverns
● Natural bridges ● Hiking ● Golf, tennis, swimming,
fishing (license required) ● Fieldstone lodge

A hilly country carved by the narrow, meandering Tygart's Creek, Carter County is pitted with caves and graced by arches and other natural features produced by thousands of years' erosion of limestone layers that underlie a hard sandstone cap. Open to tourists since the 1880s, the commercial caves changed hands a number of times until private donors deeded the land to the state in 1946.

First of all, drive to the Welcome Center and make cave tour arrangements (*fee*). Considered the park's most scenic, **Cascade Cave** (75-minute tour) is the largest of the 200 caves in the county. Noteworthy are the spacious rooms, fantastic formations, and 30-foot waterfall. The **X Cave** (45 minutes), named for its crossing passageways, also contains a number of large decorations, and historic **Saltpetre Cave** (1 hour) was a noted source of gunpowder material during the War of 1812. You can explore **Laurel Cave** on your own if you get a permit at the Welcome Center. Thousands of endangered Indiana bats hibernate in **Bat Cave** during the winter; tours are offered June through August only.

From the Welcome Center, a 0.5-mile loop trail takes you to **Natural Bridge**—the 180-foot-long tunnel through the hill is strong enough to support a paved highway. It's also a good idea to take as much of the 3.25-mile **Red Trail** as you're up for. Coursing around the main part of the park, this gentle trail passes many geological highlights, including **Fern Bridge**—a sandstone arch 90 feet high and 120 feet wide—and **Smokey Bridge,** the state's largest natural bridge at 90 feet by 220 feet. The .75-mile **Cascade Trail** passes such striking features as Cascade Natural Bridge, Box Canyon, and the Wind Tunnel.

Long and narrow **Smokey Valley Lake** offers 40 acres for fishing and paddle boating (*dock open Mem. Day–Labor Day*). If you're a lodge or cottage guest, you can swim for free at the lodge pool; otherwise, use the community pool (*fee*). You can also float down Tygart's Creek on a guided canoe trip (*summer; fee*).

Camping and Lodging

The park has 89 tent and RV sites (some open in winter), with showers. Available on a first-come, first-served basis. Camping fee. There are also 15 cottages and 28 lodge units; call 800-325-0059 for reservations.

❏ CARTER CAVES STATE RESORT PARK, ROUTE 5, BOX 1120, OLIVE HILL, KENTUCKY 41164

John James Audubon

On US 41N, in Henderson

● 692 acres ● 502-826-2247 ● Year-round ● No pets in nature preserve
● Art museum ● Nature Center
● Hiking ● Golfing, swimming

The great naturalist and artist John James Audubon (1785-1851) lived with his wife and children in this small Ohio River town from 1810 to 1819. Located on the Mississippi flyway, Henderson held irresistible appeal to the young artist, his devoted wife noting, "I have a rival in every bird." After going bankrupt, Audubon spent the rest of his life traveling the land from Florida to Labrador, meticulously and obsessively painting birds and other animals in their natural settings. His masterpiece, *The Birds of America* was published in 1838. The park was developed in the 1930s to house a collection of Audubon's journals, paintings, clothing, and other memorabilia.

161

Beech-maple forest

Modeled after a French Norman inn, the **John James Audubon Memorial Museum** boasts four roomy galleries that chronicle Audubon's life and work with the world's largest collection of his memorabilia and one of the largest collections of his artwork. In the attached **Nature Center,** you can use binoculars in the observation room to stare at birds out in the garden and pond, hop in a giant bird nest, and enjoy other hands-on activities, plus join in naturalist-led nature talks and walks.

Several short trails totaling about 5.5 miles traipse about the nature preserve and to the wildlife lake; over 20 species of warblers visit here every spring. To make a circuit of 3.3 miles, walk out from the Nature Center on Warbler Road until it joins with the Back Country Trail. Then take the Wilderness Lake and Coffee Tree Trails back to the Nature Center.

While here, rent some clubs and hit the nine-hole golf course. Then enjoy a swim in the recreational lake (*Mem. Day–Labor Day*), or rent a paddle boat.

Camping and Lodging

There are 69 tent sites, with showers. First come, first served. Camping fee. Also, 6 cottages; contact the park to reserve.

❑ *John James Audubon S.P., P.O. Box 576, Henderson, KY 42420*

Minnesota

Itasca
Forestville/Mystery Cave
Tettegouche
Soudan Underground Mine
Blue Mounds

Michigan

Mackinac Island
Porcupine Mountains
Fort Wilkins
P.J. Hoffmaster
Hartwick Pines

163

Wisconsin

Devil's Lake
Peninsula
Rock Island
Copper Falls

Illinois

Giant City
Fort Massac
Starved Rock
Mississippi Palisades
Ferne Clyffe

Indiana

Brown County
Spring Mill
Falls of the Ohio
Indiana Dunes

Ohio

Hocking Hills
Hueston Woods
Kelleys Island
Maumee Bay

Grand Hotel, Mackinac Island, Michigan

Hocking Hills

12 miles west from Logan and US 33 on Ohio 664, in Hocking Hills

● 2,331 acres ● 614-385-6841 ● Year-round ● Waterfalls, caves, and hollows ● Hiking, swimming, fishing (license required)

164

Old Man's Cave

Richard Rowe so loved the sandstone overhangs along the creeks of the Hocking Hills that he moved into one, or under one, which became known as Old Man's Cave. Almost two centuries later, the recesses of the twisting gorge where Rowe lived (and is buried) still tempt those seeking refuge in the forest primeval.

Water cutting through the blackhand sandstone of these hills created a cluster of cool canyon streams that drop through potholes and waterfalls, beribboned with hanging ferns and long-armed hemlocks. Trails rise from their side to top soaring cliffs and then tunnel beneath overhangs. The park is actually comprised of six separate areas, each with a distinctive feature described by its name: Rock House, Cantwell Cliffs, Cedar Falls, Conkles Hollow, Ash Cave, and, of course, Old Man's Cave. Although the total park size is only 2,331 acres, the units fit into a larger patchwork of state forest and natural areas that compose over 10,000 acres, linked by trails and roads.

Glaciers never flattened these hills, but they crept close enough to narrow and choke the canyon outlets, leading roaming Wyandotte hunters to name a local river *Hockhocking*, or "bottle river." By the mid-19th century, non-Indian settlers had discovered the area's beauty; at one point, there was even a hotel with a ballroom near Rock House. During the Depression the Civilian Conservation Corps laid out trails, hewing steps and handholds into the sandstone, building stone bridges, and even tunneling through obstacles in the gorges.

Dress warmly for the damp, cool climate of the gorges, and spot the red-backed salamanders in the rock crevasses as you wander among the giant hemlocks, birches, and yews.

What to See and Do

Hikes in Hocking Hills are neither difficult nor overly long, but if you only have time for a few, include **Ash Cave** and **Old Man's Cave.** The first trail, about 2 miles long, leads to a huge recess cave beneath a towering ledge. The cave's mouth yawns 90 feet tall and its rear wall lies 100 feet deep. Large ash piles were found inside, along with flints, pottery bits, and corn cobs—presumably left by a prehistoric barbecue.

You can hike all or part of the trails that run up and down the gorge around Old Man's Cave, from **Upper Falls** and **Devil's Bathtub** at the north end to the **Lower Falls, Rowe's Cave,** and the **Sphinx Head** to the south. The eastern rim trail has some splendid overlooks, but it's worth hiking down into the gorge to feel the sheltering embrace of the tree-shrouded canyon and appreciate the handiwork of the CCC in the arched stone bridges and recessed rock stairs. The **Visitor Center** at the trailhead has exhibits on the hill's geology and human inhabitants.

If you have more time, tackle **Conkles Hollow,** a deep canyon with tall trees and spring wildflowers. The rim trail, dangerous in slick conditions, leads to an overlook above the falls.

Rock House, an extraordinary cave halfway up a 150-foot cliff, has a 25-foot-high ceiling

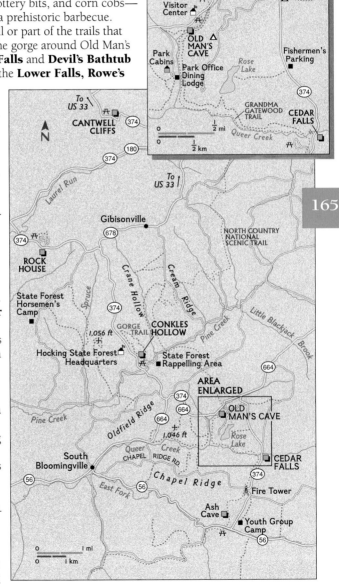

Cedar Falls

and a corridor 200 feet long, with pointed arches at each end. Erosion has widened cracks in the sandstone to form windows, and columns support the roof—all the work of water and wind. If you can, take a look at all six sections of the park. You may also want to check out the park facilities near Old Man's Cave, including campgrounds, cabins, a dining lodge, and a large, popular swimming pool.

Further Adventures

● In winter, the waterfalls that seem to spring from every rock on a wet spring day are replaced by hanging ice, turning gorges into crystal palaces. Ice at the **Ash Cave Waterfall** builds like a stalactite, eventually forming a column 90 feet high. Winter hikers are particularly cautioned to stay on trail. For over 30 years, park rangers have led an annual hike the third Saturday in January from Old Man's Cave to Ash Cave.

● Spring-fed **Rose Lake** offers ice fishing in winter and, in summer, serves up rainbow, golden, and brown trout (often fished out by midsummer), as well as bass and catfish.

● The ambitious **Grandma Gatewood Trail** cuts through state forest land to link three Hocking Hill areas: Old Man's Cave, Cedar Falls, and Ash Cave. The 6-mile route is part of the North Country National Scenic Trail, which will run over 4,000 miles from New York to North Dakota when completed.

● Surrounding the park, 9,238-acre **Hocking State Forest** (614-593-3341) provides some additional activities, such as 40 miles of horse trails, with a horse camp located near Rock House. The forest also hosts a popular mile-long rock-climbing area near Conkles Hollow, where climbers test themselves on 100-foot-high faces. Because the rock is sandstone, they anchor ropes to trees and top rope.

Camping and Lodging

The park has 172 tent and RV sites, with showers (about half available through winter), and two primitive walk-in camp areas (one for youth groups). Available on a first-come, first-served basis. Camping fee. There are also 40 two-bedroom modern cabins with fireplaces, available year-round; call 614-385-6841 to reserve.

❏ *HOCKING HILLS STATE PARK, 20160 S.R. 664, LOGAN, OHIO 43138*

166

Slump Blocks

The canyon walls in Hocking Hills expose layers of an ancient sea, eons of fine sand compacted by the enormous weight of water and sediments that settled or were washed down when the Appalachian Mountains rose to the east. Overhanging cliffs form when water cuts through harder layers and reaches the easily eroded softer sandstone. As streams take their twists and turns, they gouge recess caves into the cliff faces. Eventually, the weight of the overhang is too much, and it breaks off and falls. One of these big chunks of stone, called a "slump block," is in the middle of the Gorge Trail below the falls at Conkles Hollow.

Hueston Woods

45 miles west of Dayton, off Ohio 732

● 3,596 acres ● 513-523-6347 ● Year-round ● Fossils
● Nature preserve, Nature Center, interpretive programs
● Pioneer Farm Museum ● Golf ● Hiking, swimming,
fishing (license required), boating

The beech-maple forest that once stretched across Ohio
survives in this small enclave near the Indiana border. While
most of the region's once vast forest was being felled for farmland, soldier Matthew Hueston bought land along Four Mile
Creek in 1797 and kept the axes away. Today, the virgin forest
of the "Big Woods" is protected as a nature preserve along
Acton Lake's south shore.

Elsewhere around the lake the park is far from natural,
and caters to a wide range of recreational interests. There is a
golf course, a man-made lake with boat marina and rentals,
and a modern lodge and confer-
ence center with tennis courts
and two swimming pools.

Creature comforts like these
lure crowds, but they have not
overshadowed more traditional
park attractions. There are 10
miles of hiking trails, several fossil collection areas, and the Pioneer Farm Museum tucked
within the golf course. The
Nature Center has live animal
exhibits and naturalist programs,
and lovers of wildlife can visit the
nearby Raptor Rehabilitation
Education Project, a homeless
shelter for injured or orphaned
birds of prey.

What to See and Do

Pick up a map at the **Nature
Center** and walk into the 200-
acre **Big Woods,** where the cool
shade of beeches, oaks, and
maples shelters wildflowers and
wispy ferns on the moist forest
floor. Historians suggest the Hue-

Pioneer Farm Museum

ston family saved these trees so they could tap them for sugary
sap, and each March park naturalists set out with buckets to
do just that, boiling the sap in the lakeside sugar house. Across
the lake, mile-long **Cedar Falls Trail** is a favorite spring hike,

Raptor Rehab

In Ohio, when a fledgling hawk falls out of a nest, or a barred owl runs into a power line, the bird may soon be vacationing at a state park. At Hueston Woods, the Raptor Rehabilitation Education Project takes in battered birds from all over the state and nurses them back to health. Visitors can tour the cages and flight pen at the center for a close look at these injured birds of prey, from turkey vultures to golden eagles. Many can't make it back to the wild, and become permanent residents at Hueston Woods State Park.

when wildflowers blossom and the falls tumble down a series of shelves cut in shale and limestone.

The rocks of Hueston Woods are so riddled with marine fossils that visitors are free to dig up and pocket the remnants of whatever sea snails and octopuses they find. The tropical sea that covered the area 500 million years ago left buried in its sediments an enormous variety of ancient species. A booklet and map available at the Nature Center explains what bryozoans and trilobites are, and maps some of the better areas to collect.

The park has recently opened an area at the lake's west end to mountain biking (bicycles are not allowed on hiking trails), ranging from fairly relaxed loops to steeper, wilder trails. Bike rentals are available within the park. There's a fishing pier near the sugar house on the south shore, and anglers also troll the 625-acre lake with boats of 10 horsepower or less, trying to snag bass, bluegill, and catfish. In summer, an active small craft sailing contingent can be seen tacking back and forth, and canoes, pontoon boats, power boats, and sailboats can also be rented *(513-523-8859)*.

Camping and Lodging

The park has 490 tent or RV sites (75 open in winter), with showers. Available on a first-come, first-served basis. Camping fee. There are also three rent-a-camps, with equipment provided; a group camp; and a horse camp at the north end of the park (closed in winter). The park rents 59 cabins and offers a 94-room resort lodge, with a restaurant; for reservations, call 800-282-7275.

❏ HUESTON WOODS STATE PARK, RTE. 1, COLLEGE CORNER, OHIO 45003

Kelleys Island

Ferry from Marblehead

● **661 acres** ● **419-797-4530** ● **Year-round** ● **Glacial grooves** ● **Boating, fishing (license required), hiking, swimming beach**

Kelleys Island first became widely known for wine made here in the 1830s. The park, however, was established primarily to preserve the enormous grooves dug by glaciers moving across the island's surface over 20,000 years ago, among the largest glacial grooves in the world. In places the tracks are worn smooth as glass, as deep as 15 feet and 400 feet long.

The glaciers' path can be viewed from an observation point just north of the campground. Look closely for fossils of corals and shell animals. As spectacular as these grooves are, picnickers over a century ago reported glacial footprints longer and deeper—limestone quarrying later destroyed them.

A short bike ride across the 2,800-acre island leads to

Inscription Rock and petroglyphs created by Indian artists some 500 years ago. Now faded by erosion, the art was carefully copied in 1850 by Colonel Eastman, and his renderings decorate the informative signs at the site. The park also offers 5 miles of hiking trails, a swimming beach, and naturalists available to discuss the unique vegetation.

Camping

The park has 129 tent or RV sites, with showers available May through October; a group youth camp; and two rent-a-camp sites. First come, first served, but check occupancy sign at Marblehead ferry. Camping fee.

❑ *LAKE ERIE ISLANDS STATE PARK, 4049 E. MOORES DOCK RD. PORT CLINTON, OHIO 43452*

Maumee Bay

9 miles east of Toledo via Ohio 2, then north on North Curtice Rd.

Glacial grooves at Kelleys Island

169

● 1,400 acres ● 419-836-7758 ● Year-round ● Nature Center
● Wetlands and marshes ● Boating, golf, sledding

This is a remnant of the Great Black Swamp, the huge marsh wetlands that covered the plains south of Lake Erie after the glaciers receded and the lake shrank to its present shore. The swamp was drained and logged a century ago and much of it now is farmland, but preservation of the unique marsh-swamp habitat at **Maumee Bay** provides a home to slithery things as well as a huge variety of birds and plants.

Many visitors, however, are here for a round of golf on the "Scottish Links" course, for entertainment at the 3,000-seat amphitheater, perhaps a little walleye fishing (*license required*), or a day of swimming at the beach along the Lake Erie shore or at the inland lake, which also allows non-motorized boats.

Trautman Nature Center, between the golf course and Quilter Lodge, has park maps, a naturalist on duty, and exhibits on the area, as well as remote video monitors linked to the wetlands outside. A 2-mile boardwalk trail explores the wetlands to the east, with interpretive signs and an observation blind. In winter, sledders frequent **Big Hill,** west of the inland lake.

Camping

The park offers 256 tent or RV sites, with showers April through Oct. Available first come, first served. Camping fee. Quilter Lodge has 120 rooms, 20 cottages, and a restaurant; call 800-282-7275 for reservations.

❑ *MAUMEE BAY STATE PARK, 1400 PARK RD. #1, OREGON, OHIO 43618*

Mackinac Island

Ferry from St. Ignace or Mackinaw City, or fly into Mackinac Island Airport (906-643-7165)

● 1,800 acres ● 906-847-3328 or 517-373-4296 ● Year-round, Fort Mackinac mid-May through October ● No cars ● No camping ● Historic hotel ● Carriage rides ● Arch Rock ● Costumed interpreters ● Biking, hiking

Mackinac Island's peaceful shoreline

Hiking to the high point of the island above Fort Mackinac, it's hard to understand how the British maintained their concentration and aimed their cannons at the Americans below during a sneak attack on the fort during the War of 1812. The views from 320 feet above the lake are distractingly spectacular in all directions. Back in 1814, however, the island was coveted as a key strategic military post, guarding the Straits of Mackinac. The British quietly rowed ashore at the island's north end and marched under cover of darkness along Mackinac's spine. Today, it's the beauty of this Shangri-la most visitors hope to capture. Within the 2,200-acre island is the gem of Michigan's state parks.

Soldiers costumed in American uniforms now play music on the parade ground and load and fire the cannons, often with the help of youngsters in jeans and sneakers. Interpreters re-create military life in the 1880s, and if this is any indication, life at the outpost wasn't bad. Even then, Mackinac was a popular vacation spot, renowned for its beauty, its luxurious hotel, the absence of automobiles, and, swept clean by the lake breezes, a lack of irritating insects.

What to See and Do

Start at the **Visitor Center,** which sits by the boat slips just west of the marina, looking up at Fort Mackinac across **Marquette Park.** (There is also an information kiosk on Huron Street.) Here you can get maps and advice, and see an audiovisual program about the island.

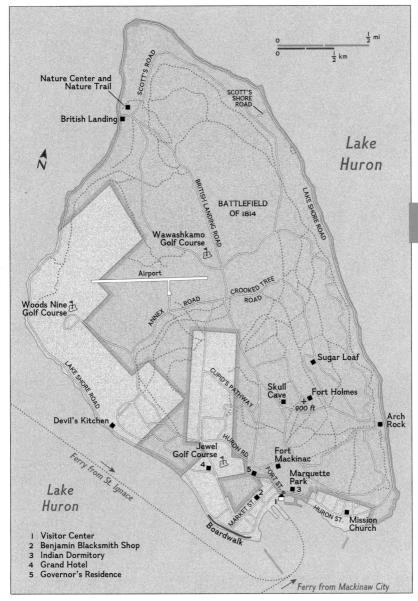

Nature Center and
Nature Trail

British Landing

SCOTT'S ROAD

SCOTT'S
SHORE
ROAD

Lake
Huron

N

BRITISH LANDING ROAD

BATTLEFIELD
OF 1814

LAKE SHORE ROAD

Wawashkamo
Golf Course

Airport

CROOKED TREE
ROAD

Woods Nine
Golf Course

ANNEX
ROAD

Sugar Loaf

CUPID'S PATHWAY

Skull
Cave

Fort Holmes

900 ft

LAKE SHORE ROAD

Arch
Rock

Devil's Kitchen

HURON RD.

Jewel
Golf Course

4

Fort
Mackinac

5

Marquette
Park
3

Ferry from St. Ignace

Lake
Huron

FORT ST.

2

MARKET ST.

1

HURON ST.   Mission
Church

Boardwalk

1 Visitor Center
2 Benjamin Blacksmith Shop
3 Indian Dormitory
4 Grand Hotel
5 Governor's Residence

Ferry from Mackinaw City

½ mi
0
0
½ km

Fort Mackinac

Before trekking up to the fort, you might want to visit some downtown attractions, from the **Benjamin Blacksmith Shop** on Market Street—note the scarifying tools for repairing horses' teeth—to the 1838 **Indian Dormitory** in Marquette Park, with displays about the Indians who once lived and traded on the island. There are also various buildings dating back to the 1820s, when the American fur trade was centered here. Continuing east along the lake, you pass 19th-century churches and some beautiful old hotels and summer houses.

The gleaming white ramparts of **Fort Mackinac** stand grandly 150 feet above the town, approached by a wide ramp up the hillside behind Marquette Park. There are 14 historic buildings within, from the barracks (which now houses a museum shop) to the officers' tea room, where you can drink English tea while taking in a view of the straits from the terrace. Music and musket fire by period-costumed guides take place in the vast parade grounds at the fort's center, and a comprehensive exhibit covers the area's history.

In today's mechanized age, the lack of autos on the island is one of its chief distinctions. Numerous island vendors rent bicycles of various capabilities, and this is how many folks tour, stopping along the routes for short hikes to particular features. You can also hire a carriage, or, if you like mini-marathons, run the 8.5-mile shore circuit. On the east shore, hardy souls climb the steep stairs to **Arch Rock,** while others take a less arduous route there by bicycle above the fort. You might see a sailboat on the lake framed in the arch, which spans 50 feet, while a seagull poses on top. **Sugar Loaf,** a limestone outcrop, is not far away.

About halfway around the island, on the northwest shore, is **British Landing,** where the British landed in 1814 and began their midnight march. Exhibits at the **Nature Center** describe the flora and fauna of the island, and explain how the climate is moderated by "lake effect." There is also a 0.5-mile trail with displays and plant identification signs.

From British Landing you can either continue along the sunny western shore or take the route of the invading soldiers up along the island's spine. The high road leads back to the south side of the island, where you can veer west by the Jewel Golf Course for a visit to the 1887 **Grand Hotel** (*800-33-GRAND. Mid-May–Oct.),* which keeps its Victorian

nose in the air by requiring that men wear jackets and ties and that women "not be attired in slacks" after 6 p.m. You can't miss seeing the 660-foot veranda as you approach the island by ferry, but if you want to stroll along it, you'll either have to rent a room or pay a fee . . . and dress correctly.

Further Adventures

Only about 500 people live on the island year-round, so it's a much quieter place when the fort and other living history sites reduce their hours after Labor Day. Other park facilities are open from mid-May to mid-October for a taste of fall color. Visitors can wander the island any time of the year, but getting there after the ferries stop in January is no easy feat. Locals snowmobile to the mainland on an ice bridge lined with discarded Christmas trees, but visitors may want to try the private planes and small commercial airline service that fly to the landing strip on the island. A few small hotels stay open for winter visitors, who can ride horse-drawn sleighs and ski on groomed cross-country trails.

In summer, stroll among the boats at the **Mackinac Island Marina,** east of the Visitor Center.

Nearby Sights

The history of Mackinac Island is closely linked to other events on the Straits of Mackinac, and the Mackinac State Historic Parks manages two related sites, **Colonial Michilimackinac** *(616-436-5563. Adm. fee)* and **Historic Mill Creek** *(616-436-7301. Adm. fee)*, which are both located across the straits on the northern shore of the Lower Peninsula, near Mackinaw City. Colonial Michilimackinac re-creates a fort occupied in the 18th century first by the French and then the British, who were vying for control of the regional fur trade. Within the reconstructed fort costumed interpreters dressed as British Redcoats show what life was like in a remote military outpost in the 1770s. Archaeologists have been working at this site since 1959, and visitors can enter a tunnel exhibit to look at such artifacts as religious medallions and porcelain.

East along the north shore is Mill Creek, where one water-powered sawmill supplied much of the lumber for building on Mackinac Island during the boom years of the fur trade. The site, rediscovered by amateur archaeologists with a metal detector in the 1970s, has an 18th-century reconstructed sawmill powered by a four-foot flutter wheel propelled by water—the saw moves up and down 100 times a minute. The park includes 625 acres of forest, nature trails, and a growing number of reconstructed buildings, based on findings in the archaeological digs.

❑ *Mackinac State Historic Parks, P.O. Box 370, Mackinac Island, MI 49757; Chamber of Commerce 906-847-6418 or 800-4-Lilacs*

Ancient Island

About 11,000 years ago, as the last of the great glaciers retreated to the north, Mackinac Island poked above the surface of Lake Algonquin, a huge body of water that included what are now Lakes Michigan and Huron. The high shelf at the center of today's island—about a half-mile long and a quarter-mile wide—is called the Ancient Island. Lake levels gradually fell as the glacier gouged a deeper trough to the north, until at one point Mackinac was not an island, but a highland peninsula jutting out from the Michigan mainland. Then the basins filled again, and Lake Nipissing rose to again submerge part of the island. A sharp geological eye can pick out six distinct terraces carved by erosion during the various ups and downs of the lake.

173

Porcupine Mountains

East entrance: 15 miles west of Ontonagon on Mich. 107. West entrance: 1 mile east of Wakefield, off Mich. 28

● 60,000 acres ● 906-885-5275 ● Year-round ● Entrance fee ● No mountain bikes, pack animals, or motorized vehicles in backcountry ● Waterfalls ● Lake of the Clouds ● Cross-country and downhill skiing ● White-water rafting ● Fishing (license required), hiking

174

Autumn color along the Carp River, Porcupine Mountains

Forget the small, huddled stands of tall pines found in pockets of virgin forest around the Midwest—if you want a real wilderness, the Porcupine Mountains are bristling with thousands of acres of forest never touched by the logger's ax, as well as remote lakes, wild trout streams, and panoramic views of Lake Superior, the wildest of the Great Lakes.

The "Porkies," named by Ojibwa Indians for the forested ridges resembling a porcupine's back, are the largest stand of old-growth forest between the Mississippi River and the Adirondacks. For wilderness-starved Midwesterners, the park offers 85 miles of trails, with towering hemlock, dozens of waterfalls, bald eagles and black bears, and overnight trailside shelters and cabins. While the vast majority of visitors make only a brief stop at the spectacular Lake of the Clouds escarpment, others who take a few days to trek the Mirror Lake Trail or the Lake Superior shoreline are richly rewarded.

Timber companies that had stripped much of Michigan

by the 1930s had their eyes on the Porkies, but, propelled by
a national conservation campaign (there was even consideration of a national park designation), Porcupine became a
state park in 1945. Over 35,000 acres of shaggy old-growth
forest forms the beating heart of the park, including some
maples with 3-foot-wide trunks. The park has a small population of black bears, and in recent years there have been
sightings of long-absent wolves and moose.

What to See and Do

Visitors who come only for a day follow an enjoyable, if
predictable, routine: A stop at the **Visitor Center** *(Mid-
May–mid-Oct.)* at the east entrance of the park for exhibits on
the park's geology, wildlife, and history; a drive to the **Lake of
the Clouds** escarpment for a sky-high view across the lake
of steep forested ridges and Government Peak; and a stop at
the sandy beach at **Union Bay** for a picnic and a dip.

For those with more time and sturdy hiking boots, trails
at the Lake of the Clouds escarpment head west before
dropping down to the Big Carp River, south to **Mirror
Lake,** or north to the lakeshore, where you can hike a section of the 16-mile **Lake Superior Trail.** Shelters and rustic cabins (no electricity) are spaced along the trails, and
the cabins at Mirror Lake, Lily Pond, and Lake of the
Clouds have boats for rent.

The west end of the park, less busy than the east, features
exciting white-water stretches along the **Presque Isle River.**

175

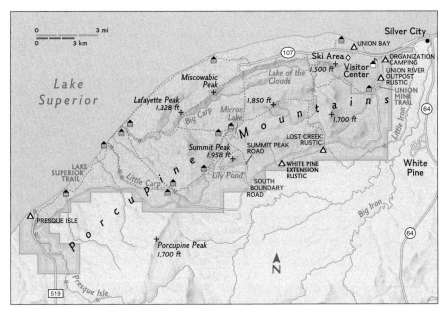

Black bear

Copper Fever

In the 1840s, when many Americans heard the siren call of mineral wealth from the western wilderness, the Porcupine Mountains attracted copper miners. All they ever found were some low-grade flecks in the basalt, but they dug 10 mines, looking for something better, inspired by the story of a huge copper mass sitting along the Ontonagon River just east of the mountains. First discovered by Alexander Henry in the 18th century, it was later rolled to the river mouth by entrepreneur Julius Eldred, and eventually ended up at the Smithsonian Institution in Washington, D.C. Luckily for the wilderness, the phenomenon never recurred.

Hikers can take a loop trail from the river's mouth a mile upstream past three waterfalls, across a bridge, and return on the other side of the river. Take a close, sobering look at the rapids before you drop your kayak in—this is not for the faint of paddle. In spring and fall, wading fishermen can run as thick as the steelhead and salmon returning to spawn.

Winter attracts skiers of both the downhill and Nordic variety. Those on skinny skis get 26 miles of groomed double tracks, and there is a downhill ski area near Union Bay. Three ski-in overnight cabins are for rent along the Nordic trail system, and snowmobiles are allowed on 32 miles of park roads.

Further Adventures

● The 16-mile **Lake Superior Trail** is the longest in the park, best done with a vehicle dropped at either end, unless you have enough time—at least five days—to loop inland from the lakeshore and return through the backcountry to your starting point. The trail moves in and out from the shore, crossing some steep ravines near the west end. A short hike inland along the Big Carp River brings you to **Shining Cloud Falls,** with a 22-foot drop, the highest in the park.

● The highest peak in the park, at 1,958 feet above sea level, is **Summit Peak,** and from the observation tower you can see the park in all directions. You can drive to within a half-mile of the peak on Summit Peak Road.

● History buffs will want to walk the 45-minute **Union Mine Trail,** a mile south of the Visitor Center. The stamp mill, blacksmith shop, and big machinery are gone, but the mine shafts are still visible, and markers tell the story of this unsuccessful attempt to hit copper pay dirt 150 years ago. Over 45 mines were sunk into the Porkies—10 of them fairly deeply—but the flaky copper in the basalt bedrock was too low-grade for success.

Camping and Lodging

The park has 187 tent or RV sites (May-Nov.), with shower facilities. Reservations advised in season; call 800-447-2757. Camping fee. There are also three rustic "outposts" with 23 campsites and 16 hike-in cabins available April through November (fee for cabins must be paid in advance); call 800-447-2757 for reservations. Three Adirondack shelters are available on a first-come, first-served basis. Backcountry campers must register, but may camp trailside.

❏ *Porcupine Mountains Wilderness State Park, 412 South Boundary Rd., Ontonagon, Michigan 49953*

Fort Wilkins

1 mile east of Copper Harbor on US 41

● 201 acres ● 906-289-4215 ● Year-round, buildings mid-May to mid-Oct. ● Lake Superior shore ● Costumed interpreters ● Historic lighthouse ● Fishing (license required), hiking

Soldiers were posted at Fort Wilkins to quell expected conflicts between Ojibwa Indians and the copper miners who came to Michigan's northernmost region, the Keweenaw Peninsula, in the 1840s. As it turned out, the only problems they had to deal with were their own—harsh winters, isolation, and loneliness. Today, costumed interpreters help visitors experience life in what was once an outpost on the frontier.

Get the lay of the park by hiking the 2-mile **nature trail** that begins near the east campground, skirts the park's perimeter, with views of both Lake Superior and Lake Fanny Hooe, and ends up at the historic fort, where most of the buildings are original. On the jutting peninsula enclosing the east side of Copper Harbor is **Copper Harbor Lighthouse** *(Adm. fee),* one of the oldest lighthouses on the lake, first constructed in 1849 and rebuilt in 1866. Taken out of service in 1933, the old light is now part of the park, visited by excursion boat from Copper Harbor. Inside the yellow brick station, period furnishings re-create the life of lighthouse keepers, and exhibits cover lighthouse history and shipwreck lore. A newer skeleton lighthouse stands nearby and still guides boats to the harbor.

Camping and Lodging

The park has 165 tent or RV sites (mid-May–mid-Oct.), with showers. Reservations advised; call park. Camping fee. There is also a small cabin; call 800-447-2757 for reservations.
❏ *Fort Wilkins State Park, P.O. Box 71, Copper Harbor, MI 49918*

P.J. Hoffmaster

10 miles south of Muskegon on I-96 and Pontaluma Rd.

● 1,183 acres ● 616-798-3573 ● Year-round ● Entrance fee ● No off-road vehicles ● Sand dunes ● Nature Center ● Swimming beach ● Hiking

Out the big window at the Gillette Visitor Center, a huge dune looms . . . and it's coming our way. Not to worry. Much too slowly for the eye to see, the dunes along the Lake Michigan shore are changing shape. Many park visitors come primarily to enjoy the swimming beach at the north end of the park, but there are opportunities for solitude hiking among

Dunes along Lake Michigan

178

Dune Dialect

A few choice terms in dune dialect so you can hold your own, like a foredune:

Blowout: Saucerlike dune depressions carved by wind, usually where vegetation has been destroyed.

Foredune: A dune running parallel to the shore, the first dune established.

Fulgerite: Fused grains of sand in the shape of a tube, caused by a lightning strike.

Marram grass: Grass species that builds dunes by trapping sand and stabilizing with its roots.

the mounds of sand that have been piled ashore here, anchored now where trees have taken root. The viewing platform atop the **Dune Climb Stairway** offers a magnificent vista of the blue lake and the dunes all around, a view increasingly rare along this coast as the park has become an island of natural beauty along a shore fringed by development.

Partly because they are young, and changing rapidly, the dunes along Lake Michigan have played a major role in scientists' understanding of plant succession—the way the family of plants and trees at a site evolves from the first seeds to take root to a climax plant community that may be quite different. When naturalists at Hoffmaster take groups for walks among the dunes, they take note of these ongoing changes—for instance, whether the decline of the trillium that once blanketed areas of the dunes is due to lower levels of water or the increase of browsing deer driven to the park as a refuge from surrounding development, or both.

What to See and Do

Stop first at the modern two-story **Gillette Visitor Center,** where a nine-projector slide show explains Lake Michigan's evolving shoreline, the largest expanse of freshwater dune shoreline in the world. Then take the 0.5-mile **trail** to the shore, noting as you descend between dunes how the sand blocks the wind and other sounds. Along this trail is the 165-step climb to the dune overlook platform, thoughtfully equipped with benches.

There are 10 miles of hiking trails winding along the entire 3 miles of shoreline and through the dunes, many clothed now by beech and maple forest. In summer, the soft sandy beach at the park's north end is popular for swimming and sunning.

In winter, the park opens 3 miles of cross-country skiing trails at the south end of the park. There is a shelter with a fireplace at the trailhead, but no equipment rental.

In order to protect the delicate ecology of the dunes, bicycles are allowed only on paved roads.

Camping

The park has 300 tent or RV sites, with showers. Reservations advised in season; call 800-447-2757. Camping fee.

❏ *P.J. Hoffmaster S.P., 6585 Lake Harbor Rd., Muskegon, MI 49441*

Hartwick Pines

3 miles north of Grayling on Mich. 93

● 9,672 acres ● 517-348-7068 ● Year-round ● Entrance fee ● Pine forest ● Logging camp museum ● Fishing (license required), hiking, cross-country skiing

From the clapboard farmhouses on the Great Plains to the railroad ties that crisscross the prairies, America's expansion in the early 19th century was largely built of white pine from Michigan's northern forest. One of the few stands of tall timber unfelled during the logging rampage forms the centerpiece of this park. The tallest pines in the 49-acre virgin forest, almost 150 feet tall, are estimated to be around 350 years old.

Start at the **Michigan Forest Center,** where exhibits explain the ecology of the forests and the economy of the great timber harvest, which reaped more millions than the California Gold Rush. From there, self-guided brochure in hand, take the **Virgin Pines Foot Trail** for an hour-long trek that shows you the variety of trees in the North Woods and leads to a **logging camp museum** *(May-Oct.)*. The steam-powered sawmill chugs back to life on several summer weekends.

Another 5 miles of hiking trails lead to **Hartwick Lake** and the **East Branch Au Sable River,** a good trout-fishing stream. On the park's west side, mountain-biking trails are open for cross-country skiing in winter.

Camping and Lodging

The park has 100 tent and RV sites, with showers; and a rustic cabin. Reservations advised in season; call 800-447-2757. Camping fee.

❏ *Hartwick Pines S.P., Rte. 3, Box 3840, Grayling, Michigan 49738*

Log-hauling wheels

Brown County

2 miles south of Nashville, via Ind. 135 and Ind. 46

● 15,696 acres ● 812-988-6406 ● Year-round ● Entrance fee, except weekdays in winter ● Scenic views ● Trail rides ● Covered bridge ● Swimming pool ● Historic inn ● Nature Center ● Hiking, fishing (license required), cross-country skiing

The old covered bridge at the north entrance to this venerable preserve aptly symbolizes the rural, old-timey atmosphere of the park and surrounding hills. This country has been called the "Little Smokies" for the mists that rise from its steep and wooded ravines, and there is an Appalachian ring to place names of the towns tucked into the hills, such as Beanblossom and Gnaw Bone. Along a particularly scenic network of ridges sits the largest state park in Indiana.

Once isolated by poor roads and densely forested hills, the region around Brown County State Park is now a tourist mecca with a concentration of craftspeople and artists. After a half-day in the galleries of nearby Nashville, travelers are often ready for a peaceful walk or picnic at one of the park's overlooks. In addition to its bridle and hiking trails, the park offers such comforts as a large swimming pool and the rustic Abe Martin Lodge. Many park facilities—including shelters, trails, and lookout towers—were the work of the Civilian Conservation Corps.

Old Brown County fence

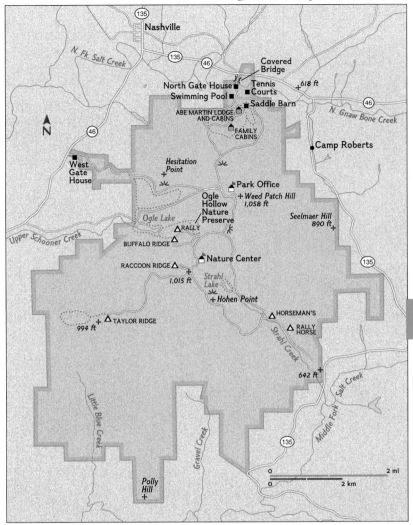

Fall colors in the Brown County hills are a rich mosaic of oranges, golds, and reds, out of which can sometimes be heard the gobble of wild turkeys. Spring, too, is a good time to visit, when forest highlights include white serviceberry buds, flowering dogwood, and redbuds in bloom. Deer are the most commonly spotted large animal—in fact, the park is overpopulated, since predators such as cougars were eliminated.

What to See and Do

If natural beauty ranks higher than services in your mind, use the park's west entrance, which almost immedi-

Grazing deer

182

ately brings you to a lookout tower and Hesitation Point, with views of canyons and hills so densely wooded they resemble a head of broccoli. Untouched by the glaciers that flattened much of the Great Lakes region, the ridges and valleys here were cut by streams through an ancient ocean bottom.

Or take the north entrance, crossing Salt Creek on a two-lane covered bridge that dates back to 1838. An Olympic-size swimming pool is just inside the entrance, along with tennis courts, a saddle barn, and an amphitheater. The **Abe Martin Lodge,** a Depression-era structure built with native stone and hand-hewn oak timbers from the park forests, awaits just up the road.

However you enter, head for **Weed Patch Hill,** the high ground at the center of the park and the location of the park headquarters, campgrounds, Nature Center, and interesting trails.

The **Nature Center** displays cross-cuts of park trees such as beech, locust, and elm, and mounted gray fox, great horned owls, and hawks. The timber rattler and copperhead snakes sometimes found in the glass case are alive—they are released in winter—and birdfeeders attract goldfinches, cardinals, and other birds to a viewing window. Interpretive programs such as walks, talks, and hikes are held daily from May through October, and weekends in winter. In addition, the Nature Center remains open all winter, when visitors come to ice fish at **Ogle Lake** or cross-country ski on ungroomed trails and closed roads.

From the Nature Center, hike down to **Strahl Lake,** or go the other direction, past the Buffalo Ridge Campground, to the **Ogle Hollow Nature Preserve.** This 41-acre area, with a mile-long, self-guided nature trail running through it, provides a rare view of what the forests of Indiana were like before farmers, loggers, and livestock did their damage. The steep, shady hillsides sustain a small population of yellow-wood trees, a delicate, gray-barked tree with wisteria flowers, rarely found north of the Ozarks.

Over 70 miles of bridle trails run through the roadless parts of the park's southern and eastern areas.

Camping and Lodging

The park has 429 tent or RV sites (150 open in winter, no showers), with showers; and a horse camp. Reservations for Memorial Day through October accepted by walk-ins and mail only, beginning March 1. Camping fee. Open year-round, Abe Martin Lodge offers 84 lodge rooms, 76 cabins, and a restaurant; call 812-988-4418 for reservations.

❏ *Brown County State Park, P.O. Box 608, Nashville, Indiana 47448*

Spring Mill

3 miles east of Mitchell on Ind. 60

● 1,319 acres ● 812-849-4129 ● Year-round ● Entrance fee
April through October ● Operating gristmill ● Pioneer village
● Caves ● Astronaut memorial ● Nature preserve ● Hiking,
fishing (license required), swimming, horseback riding

183

Historic village of Spring Mill

Back in 1814, the spring streams that still spout from openings in the cave-riddled limestone of southern Indiana attracted soldier Samuel Jackson, Jr., to build a crude water-powered mill. The site became the town of Spring Mill, and later owners built bigger mills to accommodate area farmers.

You can still buy a three-pound sack of cornmeal ground at Spring Mill, but the mood here today is more nostalgic than entrepreneurial. The village, abandoned in the late 19th century after the railroad chose a route to the north, has been restored to its period of early prosperity, around 1832. During the summer, craftspeople put on 19th-century clothes and pick up the old tools to re-create village life as it was over a century ago.

An eccentric Scot named George Donaldson had the foresight to recognize and protect the beauty and rarity of the forests and caves on his property around town. His reserve of virgin forest, now part of the park, offers a primordial kind of history, the type that couldn't be re-created if lumber companies had taken their cuts. The park also holds a memorial to astronaut Virgil I. Grissom, born in nearby Mitchell.

What to See and Do

This park's variety is a good match for visitors with wide-ranging curiosity and some time to try different adventures. Start at the **Visitor Center** near the park entrance for maps and information. Within the center, the **Grissom Memorial** has a small museum featuring the *Molly Brown*, a Gemini III space capsule, and exhibits on the life and work of astronaut "Gus" Grissom, who used to fish in the park as a boy. Grissom, the second American to fly in suborbital space, perished in the Apollo I launch pad fire in 1967.

The southeast corner of the park features the **Donaldson Woods Nature Preserve**, 67 acres of the kind of forest that once covered most of Indiana. Although a road skirts the edge of the preserve, it's more rewarding to walk through the huge tulip poplars and white oaks on **Trail 3**, looping from the Twin Caves parking lot around to Donaldson Cave and back to the Visitor Center. You can enter Donaldson Cave and walk a short way beside the rich blue stream that pours from it, or join a naturalist-led tour for a deeper journey.

In the northeast corner of the park is **Pioneer Village**, not far from where another stream emerging from Hamer Cave provides the water that drives the gristmill. The mill itself creaks and groans to life for ten minutes every hour from April through October, and within it you can purchase corn meal and the work of village artisans. Log houses of early residents are also open and decorated with period furnishings.

A **Nature Center** with displays on park history and a big wildlife observation window faces Spring Mill Lake, into which the cave streams drain. Boats are rented at the lake, electric motors only, and anglers fish for trout, bluegill, and bass.

Reserve a seat for the **Twin Caves** boat trips *(fee)* led by park personnel from April through October—a popular activity, so sign up early in the day. The trip takes about 20 minutes and goes 500 feet into one of the pitch-black caves. Eight to twelve people ride in each aluminum boat, with a guide to tell them about bats, crayfish, and blind cave fish. After heavy rains, when the volume of water in the cave rises, trips may be canceled.

From Memorial Day to Labor Day, trail rides on horseback *(fee)* are offered on the east side of the park at the saddle barn near the outdoor pool and showers. Evening hayrides *(812-849-4279 for reservations; fee)* from April through October also begin here.

Camping and Lodging

There are 223 tent or RV sites, some with showers; and a youth group tent area. Reservations advised weekends Mem. Day to Oct.; taken in person or by mail after March 1. Camping fee. Spring Mill Inn has 74 rooms; call 812-849-4081 to reserve.

❑ *Spring Mill State Park, P.O. Box 376, Mitchell, Indiana 47446*

Night of the Troglobites

In the dark recesses of the limestone caves at Spring Creek lives a pale scaley critter known as the Northern cave fish. When park visitors on boat trips into **Twin Caves** flash their lights in the water, these fish can't even blink—they don't have eyes. Animals that never leave the dark of the cave—called troglobites (cave dwellers)—include these blind cave fish as well as blind crayfish, their neighbors. While they are often smaller than distant cave-dwelling relatives with eyes (called trogophiles), scientists say the troglobites have acutely developed their other senses and do quite well in the dark.

Falls of the Ohio

1 mile west of US 31 and Jeffersonville on Riverside Drive

● 68 acres ● 812-280-9970 ● Year-round ● Fee for Interpretive Center ● No camping ● Fossil beds and cliffs ● Dam ● Birdwatching ● Kayaking, fishing (license required), hiking

Cardinal

185

If you find it farfetched that the hilly country of southeastern Indiana once lay beneath an ocean, watch the award-winning documentary shown in the Interpretive Center at Falls of the Ohio State Park—it takes you underwater for a look at a primitive sea like the one that was here more than 350 million years ago. Then walk along the Ohio River just below the long dam that crosses the river near Louisville, and look at the limestone rocks around you. You are walking through the Devonian Age, sometimes called the Age of Fishes, and the fossils seen everywhere are the corals, clams, and finned friends of that ancient ocean and time. There are so many unique fossils exposed in such numbers that it's hard to walk around without putting your sole on a gastropod or crinoid—snail- and plant-like creatures that were buried in ocean-bottom sediments eons ago.

Early explorers found it tough going when they reached this part of the Ohio, as the exposed bedrock formed cataract falls, blocking upstream travel and "grat[ing] harshly" on the bottoms of boats going downstream, as Walt Whitman put it after a bumpy ride. Because many travelers had to pull out and portage, it was a natural place for settlement. Gen. George Rogers Clark, who founded Louisville, Jeffersonville, and Clarksville, chose lands in the vicinity as his reward for service in the Revolutionary War.

In those early years no one realized the paleontological mother lode that lay in the tawny bottom of the river, though they certainly noticed the fossil beds when the water was low—particularly after a long dike was built in the early 1800s to divert some of the water around Goose Island. Today we know what an extraordinary find this is; yet visitors can still wander around informally, picking up the odd coral for a closer look (just don't take it out of the park!).

What to See and Do

The first thing you see as you drive into the park is the new **Interpretive Center,** its circular central hall banded with Indiana limestone and brick to look like the strata of the fossil beds below. In the lobby are full-size models of a woolly mammoth, fish, and early Native American inhabitants, who hunted near the falls. In addition, a laser video in the center's auditorium vividly re-creates the ancient tropical sea.

Go exploring on you own or, from May to October, join **fossil bed tours** (*Fee*) led by a park naturalist. Depending on water levels, you may be able to wander far out on the 220-acre bed, which is among the largest exposed Devonian beds in the world. From August to October, when water is lowest, a guided three-hour Saturday hike visits fossil-covered **Goose Island** (*By advance reservation only*) in the middle of the riverbed. The scouring effect of the river exposes new fossils every year.

Archaeological evidence indicates the Mississippian Indians enjoyed the area's rich wildlife, an abundance still evident today. The **Falls of the Ohio National Wildlife Conservation Area** set aside by the U.S. Army Corps of Engineers includes the islands in the river below McAlpine Dam, adjacent to the park. Birdwatchers will spot great blue herons and sandpipers, as well as migratory birds. Anglers cast lines from the shore or boats into the waters below the dam, fishing for bass, walleye, and catfish.

The .75-mile **Woodland Loop Trail,** just downriver from the Interpretive Center, gives hikers a look at diverse stream-side vegetation, from honey locust trees to the sunchokes that were staples in Indian diets. A longer hike along an old levee leads to the **George Rogers Clark homesite.**

Kayakers have a perpetual motion machine in the Falls of the Ohio: They put in below the Interpretive Center, ride an eddy back to the dam, then take off downstream for a mile before catching the eddy upriver again. Depending on the season, the water can be easy, or churned up to Class IV rapids.
☐ *FALLS OF THE OHIO S.P., P.O. BOX 1327, JEFFERSONVILLE, IN 47131*

Birdman of Indiana

While visitors to the Falls of the Ohio today come to see ancient life forms encrusted in riverbed outcroppings, painter and naturalist John James Audubon came in 1807 looking for living creatures. The artist, who spent three years sketching the birds at the falls, produced over 200 renderings, a large portion of his early work. Reproductions are on display at the Interpretive Center, where an observation window with birdfeeders attracts birds for today's artists.

186

Indiana Dunes

2 miles north of Chesterton on Ind. 49

● 2,182 acres ● 219-926-1952 ● Year-round ● Entrance fee, except weekdays Oct. to May ● Swimming beach ● Sand dunes ● Marshes ● Hiking, cross-country skiing

Nestled within the 14,000-acre **Indiana Dunes National Lakeshore,** this state park holds some of the prize scenery of a nonpareil lakeside landscape, including the highest dunes on the shore, dune "canyons" blown out by winds off Lake Michigan, and a popular swimming beach. There are live dunes that continue to move a few feet every year, and stabilized dunes anchored by an extraordinary range of plants and trees. The shoreline was threatened by encroaching industrial development early in the century, and its preservation became one

High dunes of Lake Michigan

of the country's earliest conservationist causes, leading to the state's purchase of the parklands in 1925.

187

Most summer visitors make a beeline to the popular half-mile swimming beach. Those with an interest in the dunes' extraordinary ecosystem, however, will want to drive to the **Nature Center,** where, after visiting exhibits about the process of dune creation and the diverse flora and fauna that thrive here, you can head off on a variety of trails.

In most areas, you must stay on trail to avoid disturbing the fragile ecology of the dunes, but in a few places you can take off your shoes and plunge down a sandhill. Regardless, the trail system offers a great variety of trail lengths, views, and biota. **Trail 8,** a 1.5-mile route beginning near the Nature Center, climbs through wildflowers to the top of **Mount Tom,** the highest dune on the lakeshore, standing 192 feet in a small cluster of dune peaks. Fine views and interesting dunes are found along **Trail 9,** which goes east from the Nature Center around the **Beach House Blowout,** a sand canyon dug by lake winds. Abundant and unusual spring flowers can be seen on trails through a marsh and forest just inland from the dunes.

In April and May, when silvery smelt swim in close to shore, people wade into the water with nets. On winter weekends with at least a 6-inch snow base, trails are open to cross-country skiers, with equipment rental available in the park.

Camping

The park has 286 tent or RV sites, with showers available mid-April to late October. Reservations for Mem. Day to Labor Day by mail or in person only, beginning March 1. Camping fee.
❏ *Indiana Dunes State Park, 1600 N. 25E, Chesterton, IN 46304*

Giant City

**12 miles south of Carbondale, off Ill. 13 onto
Giant City Rd., or east off US 51**

● 4,055 acres ● 618-457-4836 ● Year-round ● Stone fort
● Sandstone formations ● Observation platform ● Historic lodge ● Rare plants ● Horseback riding ● Hiking,
fishing (license required)

Names carved in the soft sandstone walls of Giant City
record sightseers even before the Civil War, not surprising
given the sights:
Slabs of sandstone
40 feet tall stand
like closely packed
buildings spaced by
narrow alleyways.
But these rocks certainly pre-date both
skyscrapers and the
Civil War—the
Makanda sandstone
is about 200 million
years old.

Along Stone Fort Nature Trail

In this park,
astonishing works of
nature stand out,
but there are also
notable works of
man. A stone fort
wall runs along a
bluff near the park's
northwest main
entrance, the work
of an ancient people
who somehow
maneuvered 200-
pound stones from
the creek below.
And, more recently,
the Civilian Conservation Corps built
the handsome Giant City Lodge using massive white oak
timbers and local sandstone.

Such achievements put some of the park's smaller
wonders in the shade . . . where they thrive. A forested
nature preserve protects rare plants and provides a retreat
for amateur botanists, birdwatchers, and people out for a
peaceful stroll.

What to See and Do

By way of the north entrance you have an immediate choice: a short hike up a steep slope to the **Stone Fort,** or a visit to the **Fern Rock Nature Preserve.** Make time to do both. The **Stone Fort Nature Trail,** a short, steep hike around a bluff with three unscalable sides, reaches a head-high wall guarding the one humanly possible approach, and evidently provided refuge from enemies for the native Lewis people, who inhabited this region between AD 400 and 900.

Flowering trillium

The 2-mile **Trillium Trail** through the nature preserve travels over bluff and through forest typical of the Shawnee Hills, but with the distinction of several rare flowers: Forbes' saxifrage, Grove bluegrass, and white-flowered mints among them. There are also colorful lichens and mosses on the rocky bluffs, and fissured rocks and caves. A self-guided brochure is available at the park office.

Whether or not you spend a night at **Giant City Lodge,** do stop in for a look. Similar to many buildings built during the Depression by the CCC, the lobby has a tall beam ceiling and native rock walls centered around a large fireplace; it manages to be monumental and intimate at the same time. Outside, climb the stairs to the 50-foot viewing platform on the bulbous water tower for a long view of the rolling, thickly forested hills. Not far away you can embark on various short trails, to Devil's Standtable, Giant City, and Indian Creek, and a handicapped-accessible trail to Post Oak.

From May through October, a trail circling through the park is open to riders who either bring their own horses or rent them from Giant City Stables *(618-529-4110).* **Little Grassy Lake,** bordering the park's east side, is actually part of the Crab Orchard National Wildlife Refuge, and many park visitors go there to swim or canoe. There are boat launching ramps for anglers interested in bass, bluegill, and crappie.

Just up the road from Giant City, you may spot a group of teens navigating across a wobbly rope ladder strung between two tall poles—one of several challenges offered by the **Touch of Nature Environmental Center** *(618-453-1121),* a 3,100-acre preserve adjacent to the park. Surrounding the park, refuge, and environmental center is the **Shawnee National Forest** *(618-253-7114).* Taken together, these various preserves provide wildlife, and humans, with lots of habitat variety.

Camping and Lodging

The park has 107 tent and RV sites, with showers; and 15 hike-in tent sites. Available first come, first served. Camping fee. There is also a horse camp (May-Oct.), and a youth group camp. Giant City Lodge has 34 rooms available February to mid-December; for reservations call 618-457-4921.

❏ *Giant City State Park, 336 S. Church Rd., Makanda, Illinois 62958*

189

Fort Massac

West side of Metropolis, off US 45

● 1,499 acres ● 618-524-4712 ● Year-round ● Ohio River
● Re-created fort ● Museum ● Boating

Fortifications at Fort Massac

190

The Ohio River that flows by Fort Massac hardly seems to warrant the unyielding timber stockade and blockhouses of this riverside fort, but back in the 18th century this was a key juncture in the struggle for North America. Today, you can safely visit the reconstructed fort and its interesting **museum** and walk through the blockhouses, and along scenic **Hickory Nut Ridge Trail** as it loops along the river.

Every October, a weekend encampment draws a huge crowd of latter-day frontiersmen and gawkers. People dress in period costume, a marching military band plays, and craftspeople make and sell their wares. Various events throughout the year involve demonstrations of old tools and weapons, often by costumed interpreters. A boat ramp is also available, and the fishing (*license required*) for catfish and bass is plentiful.

Camping

The park has 60 tent and RV sites, with showers mid-April to mid-Dec. Available first come, first served. Camping fee.

❑ FORT MASSAC STATE PARK, 1308 E. 5TH ST., METROPOLIS, IL 62960

Starved Rock

1 mile south of Utica on Ill. 178

● 2,630 acres ● 815-667-4726 ● Year-round ● Canyons
● Historic lodge ● Horseback riding ● Fishing (license required), boating, hiking

A good place to start a visit to Starved Rock is across the river at the **Illinois Waterway Visitor Center** (*815-667-4054*), an operating lock and dam on the north bank of the Illinois River. From here you get a good view of Starved Rock, a tall shelf of pale sandstone collared by woods that color up gorgeously in the fall. The park runs for 7 miles on the river's south shore, its bluffs cut by 18 canyons reaching down to the river. Having viewed it from afar, drive to the park and hike to the top of the sandstone butte after which it was named.

The sandstone here has been shaped into a number of

canyons and high overlooks, reached along 15 miles of trails that run along the south side of the river, snaking back into the canyons and climbing out onto the bluffs for dramatic views. The steep-sided canyons are ribboned with waterfalls during spring runoff (the bigger ones tumble year-round).

Starved Rock itself is big enough on top that the French built Fort St. Louis there in 1682 to oversee this key stretch of river rapids, hoping to protect their lucrative fur trade from British encroachment. Native peoples had been in the area for centuries before, and after the French military left, Starved Rock continued to be a meeting place for traders and various tribes. In the 1760s, when the Ottawa Chief Pontiac was slain by an Illiniwek at a council meeting, Pontiac's allies chased the assassin's outnumbered band up onto the bluff. There they held out, thwarted when they attempted to drop baskets on ropes to haul water from the river, succumbing eventually to starvation.

What to See and Do

The most crowded part of the park is at its center, home to a boat ramp, lodge, Visitor Center, and play areas. From there, trails run east along the river, riding the bluffs or skirting the riverside. Once you've put in a mile or so, hiking can be a peaceful and solitary adventure. Metal maps at the trailheads and color-coded markers keep you on track. You'll want to turn up one or more of the canyon trails, particularly when there's been rain or melting snow. Journey up **St. Louis Canyon,** where the steep walls suddenly open and you find yourself at the bottom of a high-sided rock bowl, with sandstone shelves and green tendrils. The sky above is framed by canyon rims like a blue arrowhead, its edges feathered by pine and cedar.

The **Starved Rock Lodge** was built in the 1930s by the Civilian Conservation Corps. Though modernized, the lodge retains much of its old rock-and-log charm, particularly in the high-beamed Great Room, centered around a huge stone fireplace. The large restaurant is popular, too. Notice the wood sculpture, including outdoor "chainsaw" wildlife carvings.

The **Illinois River** has catfish, bullhead, bass, wall-

191

Autumn at Starved Rock

eye, and crappie for anglers. A boat ramp at the park's far west end has canoes for rent from Memorial Day to Labor Day; stay clear of tricky currents near the dam just below Lover's Leap.

In winter, ice skating and sledding areas are open by the parking area. The **Visitor Center** itself, a small and time-worn building, has displays on flora and fauna and a model of the fort that once stood atop Starved Rock. There are guided hikes throughout the year and special annual events featuring canoeing, wildflower viewing, and autumn leaf-peeping. Nearby **Matthiessen State Park** *(815-667-4868)* offers horse camping and cross-country ski rentals.

Camping and Lodging

The park has 133 tent or RV sites, with shower facilities. Reservations by mail only. Camping fee. Starved Rock Lodge has 22 rooms; call 815-667-4211 for reservations.

❏ *Starved Rock State Park, P.O. Box 509, Utica, Illinois 61373*

Mississippi Palisades

3 miles north of Savanna on Ill. 84

● **2,550 acres** ● **815-273-2731** ● **Year-round** ● **Limestone cliffs** ● **Boating, hiking** ● **Fishing, hunting (license required for both)** ● **Birdwatching**

To get the awesome proportions of the Mississippi River right, to gauge both its powerful inscription on the landscape and its peaceful grace, you have to see it from on high; the towering Mississippi Palisades provide an excellent vantage. Thickly forested limestone cliffs open to magnificent overlooks near the juncture where the Apple River joins the Mississippi. Down below, across the highway, the park maintains a dock where boaters can put in on one of the finest wild stretches of what Mark Twain called a "monstrous big river."

Bald eagle

If your legs and lungs are in reasonably good working condition, hike the trails at the southern end of the park, which wind through dense forests—brightly colored in the fall—to the rims of bluffs above the Mississippi. Where the mile-long **Sentinel Trail** reaches the rim, a huge finger of dolomite points toward the sky, looking like you might push it loose with a good kick (you can't). These unprotected trails run right to the edges, so watch your footing. Southern end trails also visit **Indian Head Rock** and **Upton's Cave,** down by the highway, where a settler once hid from Indian hunters.

The northern end of the park offers easier hiking and camping areas. You'll see the white bark of paper birch and some of the huge gouges taken out of trees by pileated woodpeckers—you might even see the big bird itself. Early in the morning, flocks of wild turkeys sometimes gobble about.

Outside of an occasional passing barge or power boat, the big river that braids and twists below shows few marks of man, as it's protected as part of the **Upper Mississippi River National Fish and Wildlife Refuge** *(815-273-2732).* In January and February, keep an eye out for bald eagles fishing for channel catfish, perch, bass, and walleye. Boaters like the fishing here, and sometimes picnic or camp on the islands.

Camping

The park has 240 tent or RV sites, with shower facilities available May through October. Available first come, first served. Camping fee. There are also three primitive walk-in sites, a youth camp, and a horse camp.

❏ *Mississippi Palisades State Park, 16327-A Illinois Rte. 84 N, Savanna, Illinois 61074*

Ferne Clyffe

12 miles south of Marion, off Ill. 37

● 2,430 acres ● 618-995-2411 ● Year-round ● Waterfalls
● Caves ● Hiking ● Fishing (license required)

The hiss of falling water, the whisper of fern fronds, and the hollow echoes in large shelter caves are among the sounds you'll hear in this park. Among Ferne Clyffe's 15 trails, mile-long **Big Rocky Hollow Trail** travels to a thin 100-foot waterfall that drops from shelf to shelf in a tree-shrouded canyon before landing on moss- and lichen-decorated rocks. Another mile-long trail leads to **Hawks' Cave,** where a 100-foot ledge overhangs an echo chamber with a pulpitlike formation. Swimming and boating are prohibited on the 16-acre man-made **Ferne Clyffe Lake,** but anglers cast from its banks.

Camping

The park has 90 tent and RV sites, no showers; and 4 primitive hike-in camps. Available first come, first served. Camping fee. There is also a youth group camp and horse camp.

❏ *Ferne Clyffe State Park, P.O. Box 10, Goreville, Illinois 62939*

Devil's Lake

3 miles south of Baraboo, off US 12 and Wis. 123

● 8,864 acres ● 608-356-8301 ● Year-round ● Vehicle fee ● 500-foot bluffs ● Indian mounds ● Nature Center ● Rock climbing, fishing (license required), swimming beaches

A century ago, Victorian travelers arrived at Devil's Lake daily on one of several passenger trains that steamed along the lakeshore to elegant hotels, where formal dress was required for dinner and couples danced to big band music.

Today, bands of glacial till, not trumpets, attract visitors to the big lake, formed by retreating glaciers that cut off and rerouted the Wisconsin River 12,000 years ago. The hotel era ended in 1904, and few traces remain. Now the park is one of nine units in the Ice Age National Scientific Reserve, a clear indication of the park's commitment to putting the natural environment before creature comforts.

The park's popularity suggests that this suits modern visitors, who hike the tall bluffs around the lake to unique landmarks such as Balanced Rock and the Devil's Doorway, or boat on the 360-acre lake with fishing line dangling. The peaceable natural beauty here is all the more notable in contrast to the carnival atmosphere that has engulfed nearby Wisconsin Dells.

What to See and Do

Begin at the **Visitor Information Station** at the north end of the lake, where you can pick up maps, self-guiding tour brochures for various trails, and information on the park's animal-shaped mounds. Also check the schedule of naturalist programs. Close by is the **Nature Center,** where dioramas upstairs tell the geologic story behind the lake's formation, and exhibits downstairs describe the area's human history, including photographs from the posh resort era.

Trails run on both sides of the lake. The **West Bluff Trail,** 1.5 miles round-trip, offers magnificent vistas of the lake and the Baraboo Valley to the north. Examine closely the colorful—often purple—quartzite, the compacted sandstone that is the primary material of the bluffs. Self-guided tour brochure in hand, you can identify features left by upheaving mountains, a long-ago sea that buried the peaks in sediment, and the gradual erosion by rivers that uncovered the Baraboo Hills again.

The 1.5-mile **East Bluff Trail** is best begun from the lake's south end, a short drive from the Information Station on South Shore Road. The trail is a sometimes steep climb that takes you to potholes, grottoes, and such aptly named sights as Elephant Cave, Balanced Rock, and Devil's Doorway, where towering pillars of quartzite frame a large opening above the lake. Also along the East Bluff is a pygmy

---

Canyon Green

One place at Devil's Lake climbers can't play on the rocks is **Parfrey's Glen,** located in the eastern corner of the park. The delicate ravine's walls are mostly fragile sandstone and conglomerate, and visitors today must stay on the trails. In the past there were sawmills, gristmills, and flumes, and over a century of visitors who came to picnic amid the tumbling water, quartzite boulders, dense woods, ferns, and mosses. On a hot summer day the canyon is as much as 15 degrees cooler than the rest of the park, supporting vegetation normally unseen this far south, including the tangled roots of yellow birches. Parfrey's Glen can be reached with a short hike from a small parking area along County Road DL in the park's east corner, or a scenic and strenuous 4-mile journey from the lake along the Ice Age Trail.

forest of oak, hickory, and cedar stunted by thin soil and the elements. For a longer hike, travel part of the **Ice Age Trail,** which traces the glacier's historic edges from the southeast corner of Wisconsin to the northeast.

There are two swimming beaches, and concessionaires at **Devil's Lake** rent both fishing and snorkeling gear; only power boats with electric motors can be used. Though the trout don't reproduce in the lake—they are stocked—some big browns have been caught, as well as bass, walleye, northern pike, and panfish. Scuba divers and snorkelers enjoy 20-foot visibility at depths up to 45 feet. A mountain-biking trail shared with hikers loops along the east side of the lake.

The bluff's outcrops are about as mountainous as Wisconsin gets, and rock climbers find challenges here, often as a warm up for expeditions to western states. Quartzite is a good climbing rock because it's hard and withstands weathering; these rocks are 1.5 billion years old.

Climbing to Balanced Rock

In winter, 16 miles of cross-country ski trails are groomed for all skill levels. Ice fishing is popular, but snowmobiles are not allowed.

Camping

The park has 406 tent and RV sites, with shower facilities; 25 winter camping sites; and a group campsite. Reservations advised in season; call 608-356-6618. Camping fee.

❏ *DEVIL'S LAKE STATE PARK, S4975 PARK RD., BARABOO, WISCONSIN 53913*

Peninsula

Just north of Fish Creek on Wis. 42

● 3,776 acres ● 414-868-3258 ● Year-round ● Green Bay
views ● Cliffs and caves ● Eagle Bluff Lighthouse ● Summer
theater ● Beach ● Golf, hiking, biking (park pass required)

Like the New England coast, the image of Wisconsin's
Door County peninsula has evolved from a remote countryside of storm-whipped fishing villages to a vacationland of
quaint guest houses and art galleries. Peninsula State Park
embodies these contrasts, encompassing a vast acreage of
hardwood forest and cliff-edge scenery along Green Bay, as
well as an 18-hole golf course and summer theater.

Sunset over Green Bay

The park's raison d'être, though, is its Green Bay coast, best
seen from atop the peninsula's soaring bluffs. With a fresh
onshore breeze and gulls wheeling above, you can drive the
roads or walk the trails and look out at ships big and small. For
all its natural beauty, Peninsula's managers had attractions and
entertainment in mind from the park's beginning in 1909 (it was
only the second state park in Wisconsin). Golfers were putting
on sand greens in the 1920s, and the first superintendent
encouraged minstrel shows, a viewing tower, a ski jump, and a
small zoo. While the accent today is on nature, you can still
swing your nine-iron, and climb Eagle Tower for a terrific view.

What to See and Do

The 75-foot **Eagle Tower,** ostensibly built as a fire lookout, has from its beginning attracted hikers who climb the peninsula's highest bluffs and then want to climb another 110 steps to scan the horizon. Accessing the park through its north entrance, your first stop—unless you've reserved an early tee time *(414-854-5791)*—is likely to be the **Information Center** at Eagle Terrace. From there you can hike the steep 2-mile Eagle Trail along the shoreline and up on the bluffs to the tower.

The living quarters at **Eagle Bluff Lighthouse** have been restored to give visitors a sense of the lonely life of the lightkeeper's family. The stone light tower, automated in 1926, still orients ships entering the east passage into Green Bay.

Many prefer to take in the sights from their cars, driving **Shore Road** around the park's perimeter from Eagle Harbor to Nicolet Bay to Welcker's Point and on down to the south entrance near the village of Fish Creek—or the reverse. There are many vehicle pullouts. Bicyclists, who sometimes share the road, also have 1.3 miles of bike trails, some graveled, that crisscross the park. **Skyline Road** offers more panoramic views from an even higher vantage on the Niagara dolomite, the same tilted bedrock that forms Niagara Falls.

There is not a lot of beach along this shore, but on sunny summer days you'll find **Nicolet Bay** busy with swimmers and sunbathers. Canoes, sailboats, and sailboards are also rented here, with lessons available. On summer evenings, the popular **American Folklore Theatre** *(414-839-2329)* presents plays with regional themes six nights a week.

Green Bay is popular with people who like to fish, and it's made a strong comeback from the impact of pollution and overfishing earlier in the century. Coho salmon are prized, and other catches include trout (brown, rainbow, and lake), walleye, smallmouth bass, and perch. Not far from Nicolet Bay is **Horseshoe Island** (you can guess its shape), with a dock.

The **White Cedar Forest Natural Area,** in the park's southwest corner, is a damp, 53-acre preserve containing water-loving cedars, many of the park's beautiful wildflowers (including the rare Dwarf Lake iris), and herons, ducks, and a chorus of frogs. The separate **White Cedar Nature Center,** located off Bluff Road in the center of the park, describes the park's natural history, and a 0.5-mile nature trail brings it to life.

Camping

The park has 469 tent or RV sites, with showers, in four campgrounds; and one tent-only group camp. Most campsites can be reserved from May through October beginning on January 10 by mail or on March 1 by telephoning 414-868-3258. Camping fee.

❏ *Peninsula State Park, P.O. Box 218, Fish Creek, Wisconsin 54212*

Fish Boil

A Door County fish boil is a festive affair, and good eating, too. It features the whitefish, a plentiful Great Lakes fish with a blue collar reputation for feeding fishermen's families. At a traditional fish boil, a big iron kettle is placed over an open fire, and the whitefish is boiled with potatoes and onions. As the sun drops in the west, ladlefuls of butter are poured over the fish, with coleslaw on the side. Then, when you're about to expire from an excess of fish and festivity, someone sneaks up with the coup de grace: a fat slice of Door County cherry pie, which, of course, you are too polite to refuse.

Rock Island

Rock Island Ferry (414-847-2252) from Jackson Harbor, on Washington Island

● 905 acres ● 414-847-2235 (summer) or 414-854-2500 (winter) ● May through November ● No motorized vehicles ● Historic house ● Beach ● Hiking

This remote and undeveloped island so reminded inventor Chester Thordarson of his native Iceland that he bought the island in 1910 to preserve its beauty. A few of his distinguished buildings survive today. Long before Thordarson, however, the little island was a stopping point for Indian travelers and French explorers, including Jean Nicolet in 1634. Visitors who trek and camp around the island are particularly struck by the sounds of the lake and the gulls—with no motorized vehicles allowed, this kind of quiet is a rare experience.

198

Viking Hall

The ferry arrives on the southwest shore of the island, where visitors can enter the handsome stone **Viking Hall,** built by Thordarson as a boathouse and now on the National Register of Historic Places. Inside, take a look at photo displays and exhibits on the island's ecology. Naturalist-led programs leave from Viking Hall, and the sandy south shore beach is a friendly swimming spot in good weather.

Ten miles of trails crisscross the island, and make a 6-mile loop around its shoreline. On the tall bluffs at the island's northern end stands the **Potawatomi Lighthouse,** the first light station in Wisconsin, rebuilt in 1858 and still operating. These are dangerous waters, famous for shipwrecks. Steps below the lighthouse lead to the shore.

Camping

The park has 40 tent sites and two group sites. Reservations advised in summer; call 414-847-2235 (mid-April–mid-Nov.) or 414-854-2500 (mid-Nov.–mid-April). Camping fee.
❑ ROCK ISLAND S.P., P.O. BOX 118A, WASHINGTON ISLAND, WI 54246

Copper Falls

2 miles northeast of Mellen on Wis. 169

● 2,676 acres ● 715-274-5123 ● Year-round ● Ancient lava flows ● Waterfalls ● Canyons ● Hiking, birdwatching, fishing (license required)

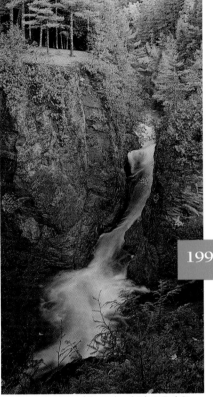

199

Junction of the Bad and Tyler's Fork Rivers

The falls of the Bad River and Tyler's Fork River cut a kind of geologic window through the layers of rock at Copper Falls. Sandstones and conglomerates, lava beds, sea-bottom sedimentary layers, and granite are exposed by the sagging of the Lake Superior Basin and the downcutting of the rivers. Lava beds resist erosion, and the result here is a series of spectacular waterfalls, including 20-foot **Copper Falls** and 30-foot **Brownstone Falls.**

The name of the park and falls is something of a misnomer: Though 19th-century miners dug shafts, the only copper present was left by glacial drift as the ice sheets retreated. The water's brown tint is due not to minerals, but leaching from cedar and tamarack bogs upstream.

It's a short 1.5-mile round-trip hike from the picnic area to Copper Falls, the Tyler's Fork Cascades, Devil's Gate, and Brownstone Falls, where the Bad River and Tyler's Fork combine and shoot through a series of rapids at Brownstone Falls. Hikers can continue downriver to the nearly completed **North Country National Scenic Trail,** which passes through the park on its way from upstate New York to North Dakota. Fishermen catch trout in the rivers, and hook pike and largemouth bass in **Loon Lake,** near the park's south entrance. It also has a swimming beach. Loons are one of over 200 species of birds sighted in the park, including songbirds such as wood thrush, red-eyed vireos, and warblers.

New mountain-biking trails are part of the recent improvements at the park, which also include a new **Visitor Center** near the south entrance. Some 6 miles of bike trails become part of a 14-mile network of cross-country skiing trails in winter.

Camping

The park has 56 tent or RV sites, with showers; two backpack camps; and one group camp. Reservations advised in season; call 715-274-5123. Camping fee.

❑ *COPPER FALLS STATE PARK, RRT 1, BOX 17AA, MELLEN, WI 54546*

Itasca

20 miles north of Park Rapids on Minn. 71

● 32,698 acres ● 218-266-2100 ● Year-round ● Vehicle permit fee ● Mississippi headwaters ● Virgin pine wilderness ● Naturalist-led boat tours ● Historic lodge ● Fishing (license required), biking, swimming ● Snowmobiling, cross-country skiing

Lake Itasca, source of the Mississippi River

Old Man River, the mighty Mississippi, begins its life rippling between stepping stones at the outlet of Lake Itasca. Explorers of North America had been guessing at the source of the big river for 300 years when Henry Rowe Schoolcraft, led by Ojibwe guide Ozaawindib (Yellow Head), found the headwaters in 1832. Though some dissenters still point to Elk Lake above Itasca's west arm, experts affirm Schoolcraft's claim that Lake Itasca is the uppermost collection basin where the river begins its 2,500-mile journey to the Gulf of Mexico.

In 1965 a 2,000-acre wilderness with a virgin stand of enormous white and red pine was set aside on the west side of the park, looped around by Wilderness Drive and threaded with hiking trails. Park facilities are concentrated along the lake's east arm. Self-guided or cassette-tape tours cover the wide variety of historic and natural landmarks in the park, and summer brings daily naturalist programs at various sites.

The loggers who changed the landscape of this region a century ago are long absent from the park, but nature continues to make alterations, sometimes with a little help. After a severe windstorm in 1995 took down a number of the big old trees, the park added the 0.5-mile Blowdown Trail off the Wilderness Drive. Scientists now set controlled forest fires, duplicating what once occurred naturally and helping to regenerate the pine forest.

What to See and Do

Enter the park through the north entrance and start your visit with a short walk to the **Mississippi Headwaters** at the lake outlet. The nearby **Headwaters History Center** describes the hydraulics of the great river system and the story

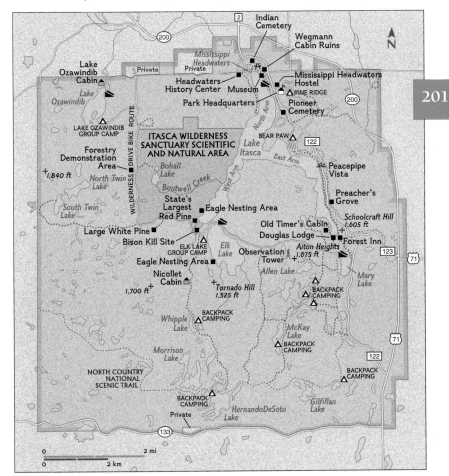

Name Game

The name "Itasca" comes from:

1. A legendary Indian girl whose tears for a lost lover began the Mississippi River;

2. A combination of the Latin words for "truth" and "head";

3. A water carrier in discoverer Henry Schoolcraft's favorite Verdi opera.

Answers:
1. A popular local tale, but untrue. 2. True. Schoolcraft combined Latin words "veritas" and "caput" to make the name. 3. False. Verdi hadn't written any operas in 1832.

of Lake Itasca's discovery. Pick up a copy of *Stepping Stones,* the park newspaper, for a map, descriptions of attractions, and a schedule of naturalist programs and other activities.

What you do next depends on your timetable—Itasca can easily occupy visitors for a week. If you don't have much time, take **Main Park Drive** south along the east shore (there is also a bicycle path), with stops at the Indian Cemetery, swimming beach, Pioneer Cemetery, and among the 275-year-old pines at Preacher's Grove. At the tip of the east arm stands **Douglas Lodge,** built in 1906 and offering rooms and meals. This is the starting point for self-guided walks along a nature trail and among historic buildings such as the log-and-stone **Forest Inn.** In addition, the **Chester Charles** (218-732-5318. *Mem. Day–Sept.; fare*) leaves from the Douglas Lake pier for a 90-minute ride around the lake while a guide tells the park's human and natural history and the loons, bald eagles, and other wildlife glide by.

To experience these woods as they were before settlers or tourists arrived, take the 11-mile **Wilderness Drive** (also a bicycle route) west from the Mississippi Headwaters and loop around the **Itasca Wilderness Sanctuary Scientific and Natural Area.** The 0.5-mile **Bohall Trail** passes through pine groves nearly 200 years old on its way to Bohall Lake. Orchid varieties also grow here, including the pink lady's slipper, the state flower. The 0.3-mile **Landmark Interpretive Trail** has a self-guiding leaflet that explains forest features such as spring ponds, porcupines, and windfalls. Beavers, which have come back since being hunted nearly to extinction around 1900, may be found along the 0.6-mile **Beaver Trail,** Allen Lake, and near Elk Lake (park naturalists will show the way).

Bicyclists can make a 17-mile loop that circumnavigates the park, encompassing the lake and the wilderness sanctuary. If you haven't brought your own, you can rent cycling gear in the park at Itasca Sports Rental (218-266-2150. *Summer only*), where they also offer canoes, pontoons, and motorboats. Fishing tackle and bait are sold for anglers after crappie, northerns, walleyes, or bluegill.

Camping and Lodging

Itasca has 237 tent or RV sites, with showers; limited number of sites open in winter. Reservations advised in July and August; call 800-246-2267. Camping fee. There are also 11 backcountry sites and two group camps. Also within the park, Douglas Lodge offers 7 rooms and 16 cabins; Nicollet Court has 18 rooms; Bear Paw Campground has six cabins; and the 10-bedroom "Clubhouse," built in 1910, is rented to groups. All are open Memorial Day to early autumn; call 800-246-2267 to reserve. The Mississippi Headwaters Hostel is open year-round; call 218-266-3415 to reserve.
❑ *ITASCA STATE PARK, HC 05 BOX 4, LAKE ITASCA, MN 56460*

Forestville/ Mystery Cave

12 miles southeast of Spring Valley via Minn. 16

● 3,035 acres ● 507-352-5111 ● Year-round ● Vehicle
permit fee ● Largest cave in Minnesota ● Historic town
with interpreters ● Spring-fed trout streams ● Horseback
riding, cross-country skiing

In 1910, when they closed the dry goods store in the
little farm town of Forestville, the shelves were still stocked.
That, along with detailed account books, helps costumed
interpreters today to re-create life in this small Minnesota
farm town, circa 1899. The buildings of Historic Forestville,
a key feature in Forestville State Park, survive despite its
fairly brief history—the town's population peaked at 200 in
1868 but declined after railroad tracks were laid elsewhere—
thanks to the family of Thomas Meighen, who owned the
store and surrounding farmlands in the 1890s. His house
was one of the buildings still standing when his descendants
sold the property to the state.

In Meighen's time, locals were aware that a big portion of

the South Branch Root
River seemed to disap-
pear into the ground a
few miles west of town,
but they didn't know
where it went. The
answer, discovered by a
local in 1937, is Mystery
Cave, where serpentine
passages visit shimmer-
ing pools, spiky stalac-
tites, and distinctive
formations with names
such as Carrot Sticks
and Hills of Rome.

Historic Forestville

What to See and Do

There are three distinct attractions to enjoy at
Forestville: the restored past of Historic Forestville; the outdoor adventure of its forested river valley; and the geological
wonders of Mystery Cave. Start at the **park office** near the
west entrance, where you can get maps, schedules for interpretive programs, and good advice.

If history is at the top of your list, drive through the park
on County Rd. 12 to the parking areas just south of the old
steel bridge. Cross the 1899 bridge and travel back a century
to visit with chatty residents (played by contemporary historic

Blue Pool Bridge

Snow White's Seven Dwarfs, where are you when we need you? Creosote from an old bridge deep in Mystery Cave was leaking into the cave's delicate Blue Pool, and the Minnesota Conservation Corps worked from late 1995 to mid-1997 to replace it. Bucket by bucket, they hauled out old timber and contaminated dirt—carrying the material along narrow passageways, sliding it down a chute, and hauling it up a long stairway. It was a tight squeeze and slow work, but light-years faster than the process that formed the unique "raft cones" in the lake—a feature that will be easier to view from the new 140-foot bridge.

interpreters) in **Historic Forestville** (*507-765-2785. Mem. Day–Labor Day Tues.-Sun., Labor Day–Oct. weekends only*). Among the restored buildings are the dry goods store, the Meighen residence, farm buildings, and historic garden and crop areas. The park also has three blue-ribbon trout streams. Anglers can cast a line below the bridge or into nearby **Forestville Creek,** or hike along **Canfield Creek,** excellent for fall trout fishing, to **Big Spring,** which bubbles up near the park's south border.

From the old town, the parking area, or the park office, bridle and hiking trails lead along the river and up the woody ridges. Hiking is particularly rewarding in spring, when bluebells and other wildflowers bloom, wild turkeys chortle, and migrating warblers sing. Or in fall, when the hardwood forests of oak, basswood, aspen, and sugar maple put on a color show. Birdwatching is a year-round favorite activity—there are nesting orioles, American redstarts, indigo buntings, and migrating eagles among the 175 species spotted in the park. There are also 14 miles of designated bridle trails—riders must not venture off them—and a special horse camp.

Then drive 5 miles east, following signs along County Rds. 12 and 5, to **Mystery Cave.** You don't have to crawl to get underground among the stalactites, flowstones, and dangling bats. From mid-April through mid-October, guided tours (*fee*) sample a small portion of the passageways that run a total of 13 miles underground, making it the longest known cave in the state. Tours through the **Historic Entrance** enjoy upright posture along well-lit passages on cement and metal grid walkways, while naturalists talk about cave geology and the biology of bats. The somewhat longer and more rustic tour from the **Minnesota Caverns Entrance** 2 miles away requires visitors to carry their own lights. Either way, coat and gloves are a good idea in a cave where the temperature is 47°F year-round.

Camping

The park has 73 tent or RV sites, with shower facilities, and a separate horse camp for 80 horses. Reservations advised in season; call 800-246-2267. Camping fee.

❏ *Forestville State Park, Rte. 2, P.O. Box 128, Preston, MN 55965*

Tettegouche

5 miles northeast of Silver Bay on Minn. 61

● 9,346 acres ● 218-226-6365 ● Year-round ● Vehicle permit fee ● Palisades ● 60-foot waterfall ● Hiking, rock climbing, fishing (license required), cross-country skiing

A recent visitor to the top of towering Palisade Head arrived just in time to see a young man jump off the cliff above

Lake Superior. For a moment his guts were in his shoes—then he saw a thick rope snaking over the edge. This is a favorite spot for rock climbing, and the fellow was rappelling down the 200-foot anorthosite cliff.

This recently expanded park—it went from 4,700 to almost 9,000 acres in 1992, then to 9,346 acres in 1994—has two of the lakeshore's most prominent rock headlands, along with many other attractions, including backcountry cabins, blue-ribbon fishing streams, a 60-foot waterfall, and spectacular autumn color along mountain trails.

The cabins are a remnant of a fishing retreat built by Duluth businessmen in 1910 after logging companies cleared much of the original pine forest. Various owners protected the area through the years before turning it over to the state for a park in 1979.

Basalt cliffs on Lake Superior's North Shore

Today's visitors follow in the footsteps of the Duluth outdoorsmen, quite literally: This is a park for hikers, and its fishing lakes (as well as its cabins) are reached by walking the trails.

What to See and Do

Travelers up Minnesota's North Shore often stick close to Lake Superior, enthralled by the scenery that shows itself at every turn of Minn. 61. For those who can't bear to leave the lakeshore, Tettegouche offers spectacular and accessible cliff-top views at 214-foot **Palisade Head** (*Off Minn. 61*) and **Shovel Point** (*1.5-mile round-trip hike from park office*), both towering remnants of lava flows a billion years ago. The cliffs are favorites of the carabiner set, rock hounds who will tie off to a tree and bounce down the sheer faces. Keep a good grip on the children, as the edges are largely without guard rails or supervision. For those who don't like heights, there are trails down to pebbly lakeshore beaches.

If you have time, leave the car and hoof it inland—the rewards are ample. From the parking lot trailhead, it's less than a mile round-trip to **High Falls,** the tallest waterfall in the state.

A Superior Hike

The North Shore of Minnesota now has a hiking trail that backpackers compare to California's Pacific Crest Trail or the Inca Trail in Peru. From Duluth to the Canadian border, the **Superior Hiking Trail** runs the ridges above the west shore of the lake through Tettegouche, passing on footbridges, over tumbling streams, through aspen glades and evergreen forests, and along the flanks of the Sawtooth Mountains. There are still a few unopened gaps in the trail, but the footloose footslogger may prefer to tackle the trail in sections, given its length and variety. There is always the vast blue lake nearby, a view that makes this wilderness trail unique. A guide to the Superior Hiking Trail is available from the Superior Hiking Trail Association (P.O. Box 4, Two Harbors, MN 55616. 218-834-2700. Fee).

Just above the falls, a suspension footbridge crossing the Baptism River is part of the **Superior Hiking Trail** running from Duluth to Canada. There are 23 miles of hiking trails winding up and down the Sawtooth Mountains from view to view, including a 3.5-mile hike from the parking lot trailhead to **Mic Mac Lake.**

To the southwest, **Palisade Valley** includes steep-walled **Bean** and **Bear Lakes,** with trout fishing. Hikers find the forest changing from birch-aspen near the lakes to maple, birch, and spruce inland, making for colorful autumns.

In winter, visitors make their way on skis and snowshoes along the park's 17 miles of groomed ski trails. There are also 12 miles of snowmobile trails, connecting with a larger trail network in adjacent **Superior National Forest** (218-666-5251).

Camping and Lodging

The park has 28 tent or RV sites, with showers (some open in winter); 6 walk-in sites; and 13 cart-in sites. Tettegouche Camp has four cabins and a group lodge. Reservations advised mid-June through September; call 800-246-2267. Camping fee.

❑ TETTEGOUCHE STATE PARK, 474 HIGHWAY 61E, SILVER BAY, MN 55614

Soudan Underground Mine

25 miles north of Virginia on Minn. 69

● 1,300 acres ● 218-753-2245 ● Year-round ● Vehicle permit fee ● No camping ● Mineworks ● Hiking

Riding the rattling, shaking elevator "cage" half a mile down into the **Soudan Mine** (Mem. Day–Labor Day; adm. fee), visitors may want to remind themselves that a century ago this was one of the safest iron mines in the region, and miners begged to work here. The Soudan opened in 1884, the first mine to produce iron ore in Minnesota, now famous for its iron ranges. The Soudan and the forest around it were donated to the state by U.S. Steel after it shut down the mine in 1962.

Walk through the **Visitor Center,** then take a look at the massive cables and hoist wheels outside and in the engine house, drill shop, and headframe. Next, don a hard hat and make like a miner, on a 90-minute tour down the shaft to the work areas, where spirited interpreters explain how the job was done in 1892, the height of the mine's production.

The park also features 5 miles of fairly steep hiking trails along a ridge following the shore of **Vermilion Lake.** In winter, 3 miles of snowmobile trails are groomed.

❑ SOUDAN UNDERGROUND MINE S.P., P.O. BOX 335, SOUDAN, MN 55782

Blue Mounds

6 miles north of I-90 on Minn. 75

● 2,028 acres ● 507-283-4892 ● Year-round ● Vehicle permit fee ● "Blue" cliff ● Tallgrass prairie ● Bison herd ● Swimming, bird-watching, snowmobiling, rock climbing

Prickly pear cactus and Sioux quartzite amid prairie grasses

207

When the sun set on the prairies of 19th-century Minnesota, pioneers trekking west saw a blue haze in an outcrop of Sioux quartzite and named the prominent landmark Blue Mound. This park is one of the rare places where today's visitor can see what the travelers in covered wagons saw: blooming wildflowers, bison, and in late summer bluestem grasses taller than a pioneer.

Take the south entrance and stop at the **Interpretive Center** *(Summer only),* once the home of Plains novelist Frederick Mannfred. Here you can pick up maps and learn about the Plains ecosystem. (The west entrance ranger station, open year-round, also has maps.) For wildflowers and a spectacular view, hike the **Upper Mound Trail,** which also crosses the Rock Alignment, a 1,250-foot line of rocks aligned in an east-west direction. Who built it and why is unknown, although sunrise and sunset line up with it on the first day of spring and fall. Also atop the Mound, the 0.7-mile **Bur Oak Trail** runs through wooded habitat friendly to birds and butterflies.

The mounds extend about 1.5 miles, rising as high as 80 feet from the prairie floor, with sheer faces on the east side that lure increasing numbers of rock climbers to the park. Near the north entrance are 230-acre winter and summer enclosures for 40 bison, with an observation platform just south of the road, and a mowed trail around the perimeter of the enclosure. The auction of excess bison in mid-October is an annual event.

In winter, snowmobilers use the 7 miles of groomed trails.

Camping

The park has 73 tent and RV sites, with showers; and 14 walk-in sites. Reservations advised in season; call 800-246-2267. Camping fee.

◻ BLUE MOUNDS S.P., R.R. 1, BOX 52, LUVERNE, MN 56156

North Dakota

Cross Ranch
Fort Abraham Lincoln
Lake Metigoshe
Icelandic

South Dakota

Custer
Fort Sisseton
Newton Hills

Nebraska

Fort Robinson
Lake McConaughy
Arbor Lodge

Kansas

Lake Scott
Prairie Dog
Clinton
Elk City

Missouri

Prairie
Ha Ha Tonka
Montauk
Meramec

Iowa

Backbone
Ledges
Maquoketa Caves
Stone

Map labels:

CANADA
U.S.
LAKE METIGOSHE
ICELANDIC
N. DAK.
CROSS RANCH
Bismarck
FORT ABRAHAM LINCOLN
Grand Forks
Fargo
FT. SISSETON
S. DAK.
Rapid City
Pierre
Missouri River
CUSTER
FORT ROBINSON
NEWTON HILLS
STONE
BACKBONE
MAQUOKETA CAVES
IOWA
NEBRASKA
Sioux City
LEDGES
Des Moines
LAKE McCONAUGHY
Omaha
Lincoln
ARBOR LODGE
Platte
PRAIRIE DOG
MO.
Mississippi
Topeka
Kansas City
St. Louis
CLINTON
Jefferson City
MERAMEC
LAKE SCOTT
KANSAS
HA HA TONKA
Wichita
PRAIRIE
ELK CITY
MONTAUK

0   100 mi
0   200 km

Custer State Park, South Dakota

Cross Ranch

15 miles south of Washburn on west bank of Missouri River, off N. Dak. 200A

● 589 acres ● 701-794-3731 ● Year-round ● Vehicle fee
● River-bottom ecology ● Hiking

Cottonwoods and prairie above Missouri River

The great Missouri River once flowed unchecked through North Dakota for some 360 miles, before dams turned most of the river's course within the state into lakes. One of the few remaining wild sections of the Missouri runs adjacent to this state park and the abutting 6,000-acre preserve owned by the Nature Conservancy. Together they protect a portion of this vanishing environment—the river-bottom ecology.

Cross Ranch's floodplain nurtures a lovely cottonwood forest—for now, at least. In order to regenerate, cottonwoods require occasional flooding and scouring of the landscape. With the construction of the Garrison Dam upriver, the Missouri here has largely been tamed, and periodic floods no longer wash through to create habitat for the thirsty cottonwood seedlings. Not a long-living tree in the best of circumstances, the cottonwoods are gradually being replaced by ash, box elder, and oak.

What to See and Do

Begin at the **Visitor Center,** where informative displays

discuss the river's effect on the countryside, forest succession, and changing river channels. There are also presentations on the early Indians, ranchers, trappers, and riverboaters, as well as the endangered and extinct wildlife of the area.

From here, hike out through the river-bottom forest along the Missouri, where over 15 miles of trails offer a peaceful and scenic education of this vanishing river environment. The paths double as cross-country skiing trails during the winter months, with some 10 miles groomed.

If time is limited, the 2.6-mile **Matah Trail** circles the campground and takes in a riverside stretch beneath towering cottonwoods. For those with more time, the **Matah, Cottonwood,** and **Bison Trails** lead 3.5 miles to the **Levis Trail,** which explores an accreted island, attached to the shore after Garrison Dam was built and the river course changed. The park's backcountry camping sites are located here. This 2.3-mile trail wanders along the boundary of the Nature Conservancy's **Cross Ranch Nature Preserve** (701-794-8741), where you may spot deer, coyote, or perhaps even a secretive bobcat. Keep an eye out for the bald eagles that hunt over the river in spring and fall, and two endangered birds—the piping plover and least tern—nesting on the sandbars in the river. During summer, the Nature Conservancy offers a self-guided nature trail, which can be done in different sections, one a .75-mile trip, the other about 2 miles.

Camping and Lodging

There are 42 tent and RV sites and 23 tent-only sites, with showers, as well as 5 backcountry sites. Mid-May–mid-Sept. Camping reservations beginning in April by calling 800-807-4723. Camping fee. There is also a cabin; call park to reserve it at 701-794-3731.

❏ *CROSS RANCH STATE PARK, HC-2 BOX 152, SANGER, NORTH DAKOTA 58567*

Fort Mandan

On Oct. 24, 1804, the Lewis and Clark Expedition camped across the river from what is now Cross Ranch State Park. From their Fort Mandan camp, Capt. William Clark described the area much as you still see it: "The land is low and beautiful, and covered with oak and cottonwood, but has been too recently hunted to afford much game." The party spent the ensuing very cold winter nearby, almost certainly returning to the Cross Ranch area to hunt. Today a reconstruction of **Fort Mandan** *(701-462-8129. Closed Mon.)* stands in Washburn, a few miles north of the park. The site of the original fort is believed to lie beneath the Missouri River.

Fort Abraham Lincoln

4 miles south of Mandan on N. Dak. 1806

● **1,006 acres** ● **701-663-9571** ● **Year-round** ● **Entrance fee** ● **Indian village** ● **Custer home**

Earthen lodge, On-A-Slant village

Visitors to this state park are faced with an interesting juxtaposition—the history of the Native Americans who lived here before white settlement, and the efforts of the U.S. Army to subdue their descendants.

Prior to European settlement, there were 27 Plains Indian tribes. Of those, ten were settled agricultural people, not the nomadic hunters of cowboy tradition. About AD 900, the groups that later formed the Mandan tribe arrived in the Dakotas. By the 1600s, several villages had been established near the Heart and Missouri Rivers, including On-A-Slant, an agricultural settlement occupied from the 1570s to the late 1700s. In 1781 smallpox hit the village, and the Mandan abandoned the site and moved about 70 miles north on the Missouri River. In 1834 smallpox struck again, wiping out three-quarters of the remaining tribe. Portions of On-A-Slant village, including several large earthen lodges, have been reconstructed within the park.

Fort Abraham Lincoln was built in 1872 and, beginning in 1873, served as the home base of Lt. Col. George Armstrong Custer and the 7th Cavalry. As such, it was a primary staging area for the Indian Wars. In 1875 the Interior Department ordered all Indians to report to reservations by Jan. 31, 1876. By February 1, many had not reported, and the job of enforcing the order was turned over to the military. In May 1876 Custer left Fort Lincoln to bring in the laggards. He and more than 225 other soldiers under his immediate command were killed June 25 in a skirmish at the Little Bighorn in Montana.

To appreciate the importance of this park, first visit the fine **Visitor Center.** It provides excellent displays on the tribes, villages, and local customs, as well as exhibits about Custer and the cavalry history of the fort. A walk just up the hill leads to the reconstructed village of **On-A-Slant.** Here a self-guided interpretive trail gives you a feel for the Mandan way of life, from the cool interior of the lodges to the agricultural crops and techniques employed by the tribe.

North of the Visitor Center lies the main fort area, or **Cavalry Post,** dominated by the reconstructed Victorian home of George and Libbie Custer. Guides in period dress lead tours (*April-Oct., by appt. rest of year*).

Camping

The park has 57 tent and RV sites and 38 primitive sites. April-Oct. For reservations call North Dakota's centralized reservation system at 800-807-4723. Camping fee.

❑ FORT ABRAHAM LINCOLN S.P., RTE. 2, BOX 139, MANDAN, ND 58554

213

Lake Metigoshe

15 miles north of Bottineau on N. Dak. 43

- ● 1,554 acres ● 701-263-4651
- ● Year-round ● Vehicle fee
- ● Waterskiing, swimming, boating ● Hiking, cross-country skiing, snowmobiling

Hard by the Canadian border in north-central North Dakota, Lake Metigoshe is one of North Dakota's most popular year-round vacation spots. The Chippewa called the lake *Metigoshe Washegum*, meaning "clear lake surrounded by oaks." The hills in the park are still thick with timber.

The Chippewa also named the Turtle Mountains,

Lake Metigoshe

in which the park is located. The thick woods of these low, rolling hills, dotted with intensely blue-black lakes, provide excellent cover for a great variety of wildlife. Keep an eye out for the area's marquee mammal, the large and clumsy-looking moose, as well as the occasional bear and even, though rarely, a wolf wandering down from Canada.

What to See and Do

Visitors looking to explore this state park should take the time to hike the **Old Oak Trail,** North Dakota's first National Recreation Trail. It takes about two hours to hike the full 3 miles, or you can bite off smaller chunks. A self-guided brochure *(available at trailhead)* explains marked sites along the trail and provides excellent background to the history, wildlife, ecology, and geology of this glacier-formed region. In addition, the park offers worthwhile naturalist programs and guided hikes. Contact the park office for more information on the various topics presented and the specific schedules.

For the most part, visitors come to **Lake Metigoshe** for water sports—boating, waterskiing, Jet skiing, and swimming. There are boat launch facilities and a terraced swimming beach. Motorized water recreation drives most of the fishermen off the lake in the summer.

If you have more time, rent a canoe and explore **School Section Lake,** where motorized boating is prohibited. For the very hearty, an ambitious inter-lake trip involving some portaging is available between School Section and nearby **Lake Erimosh**.

North Dakota is famous for its bitter winter weather, and most people wouldn't dream of visiting this state in the cold months, when "forty below keeps the riffraff out" becomes a popular local saying. But Lake Metigoshe State Park shines in these conditions, serving as a jumping-off point for the 250 miles of groomed snowmobile trails that cover the Turtle Mountains. One—taking about three hours round-trip—travels to the nearby **International Peace Garden** on the U.S.–Canada border.

In winter, the lake grows a coat of ice thick enough to support a colony of ice-fishing sheds and the trucks used to transport and access them. The park offers excellent cross-country skiing as well.

Camping

Lake Metigoshe offers 130 tent and RV sites, with showers; some sites have water and electricity. Reservations available by calling North Dakota's centralized reservation system at 800-807-4723. Camping fee.

❑ *LAKE METIGOSHE STATE PARK, #2 LAKE METIGOSHE STATE PARK, BOTTINEAU, NORTH DAKOTA 58318*

Métis

The land from Lake Metigoshe east to Lake Superior and north to Lake Winnipeg once comprised an improbable quasi-country, the rebellious province of the Métis. The Métis were descendants of Indian (mostly Chippewa) and French trappers in the 18th and 19th centuries. Indians in the area described them as "half man, half cart," after their constant companion, the wooden Red River cart with which they hauled trade goods. The wheels of the carts couldn't be greased because dust would cement them to the axle. The grinding wood made an interminable shriek, usually described as "hellish." In the latter half of the 19th century, Métis leader Louis Riel attempted to form a Métis country on lands in western Canada. The revolt was eventually put down and Riel hanged in 1885 by the Regina government.

214

Icelandic

**5 miles west of
Cavalier on N. Dak. 5**

- 912 acres ● 701-265-4561
- Year-round ● Vehicle fee
- Prairie natural area
- Pioneer heritage museum

Moose

This state park combines the natural history of North Dakota with the cultural heritage of the early immigrants who settled the area. The park also preserves some of the region's vanishing natural areas. When the glaciers in this region melted at the end of the last ice age, about 12,800 years ago, they left behind vast lakes. Glacial Lake Agassiz was the largest, stretching 350,000 square miles from Hudson Bay to North Dakota's southeastern corner. Lakes Winnipeg, Winnepegosa, Manitoba, and Lake of the Woods are remnants of this glacial lake, and the Red River Valley in North Dakota and Minnesota is its former bed. Today, nearly every acre of this fertile valley has been conquered for agriculture, but at Icelandic you can still see remnants of the primeval landscape. Located along what was the ancient lake shoreline, the park is underlain by 60 feet of sand in what is known as a sandgrass prairie.

Begin your visit in the modern **Pioneer Heritage Center,** where a museum showcases the history of the early settlers of North Dakota. A short walk outside takes you to the **Gunlogson Homestead** (*May-Sept.*), an 1882 two-story frame building, and three other preserved settlement-period structures. The beautifully restored **Akra Community Hall** provides an echo of the community life, revolving around church, school, and communal dinners.

A short walk north lies the second heart of this park, the 94-acre **Gunlogson Nature Preserve.** Located along the Tongue River, the preserve provides a look at an undisturbed Red River Valley ecosystem. A self-guided nature trail beginning at the homestead passes through lowland forests and marshes along several springs and a peat bog.

Down the road, **Lake Renwick** offers swimming, fishing (*license required*), and boating. If you choose to visit in winter, you can try ice fishing for a real North Dakota experience.

Camping

There are 169 tent and RV sites, with showers; plus primitive camping. Call 800-807-4723 to reserve. Camping fee.

❏ Icelandic State Park, 13751 Hwy. 5, Cavalier, North Dakota 58220

215

Custom

4 miles east of Custer on US 16A

● 73,000 acres ● 605-255-4515 ● Year-round ● Entrance fee ● Needles Highway closes in winter ● Bison herd ● Rock climbing, mountain biking, fishing (license required), horseback riding

Cathedral Spires, viewed from Little Devils Tower

216

To see how many stars there really are in the sky, visit South Dakota's Custer State Park. Here crystal-clear night skies show thousands of glittering diamonds from Orion to the Pleiades in a profusion not often observed in this electrically-lit nation. But the stars above Custer are just a sidelight to the natural treasures below.

This state park is located in the Black Hills, a geologic wonder of cracked limestone caves, dark forests, and craggy mountains. Known as *Paha Sapa* and sacred to the Lakota, the Black Hills are a combination of Olympian home of the gods, mecca of vision quests, and center of the world. It is hard to visit the area without sensing this mystery and spirit.

The hills are named for their dark appearance from a distance, a shade created by their thick covering of ponderosa pine. Geologically, they comprise an elliptically domed area about 125 miles long and 65 miles wide, stretching from western South Dakota into eastern Wyoming. The many caves in the area's cracked layers were created when the central crystalline portion uplifted through the limestone.

The Black Hills have become a major year-round destination, famous for its sublime natural wonders, including Custer State Park, Wind Cave, and Jewel Cave, as well as its man-made roadside attractions such as Mount Rushmore, the Crazy Horse Monument, and Reptile Gardens.

Custer State Park presents its visitors with classic, relatively undisturbed Black Hills scenery and activities accessible by car, foot, bicycle, or horseback. Travel to the park's northern end to view steep, craggy rock faces and mountainsides black with ponderosa pine. Or check out the southern portion, a landscape of open plains and rolling, bare-topped hills that shine green with new grass in spring and gleam a dormant red and brown in winter. Most of the park's famed bison herd roam these grasslands.

The park, originally established in 1913 as a game preserve, played a major role in the preservation of the American bison, which had been hunted nearly to extinction.

In 1988, the year of Yellowstone National Park's catastrophic fires, nearly 17,000 acres of Black Hills forest within Custer also burned. The fire's legacy is still visible throughout the park. But the positive role fire plays in ecosystems is evident in the many new, grassy meadows that provide habitat and food for a diversity of animals.

217

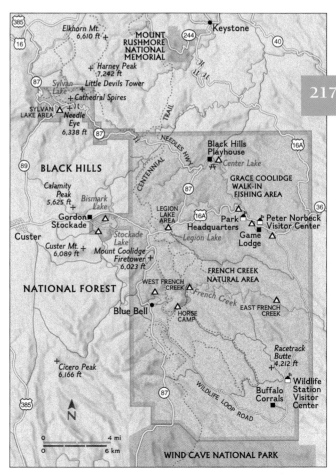

What to See and Do

A visit to Custer starts at the **Peter Norbeck Visitor Center,** which showcases the park through the four seasons, offers a "touch-and-feel table," and provides other valuable information about the area's history, geology, and wildlife. Be sure to visit the park's literal and figurative scenic high point,

Grace Coolidge Creek

the **Needles Highway** (*Closed in winter*). The 14-mile drive winds through sharp, needle-like granite rock formations to the popular **Sylvan Lake Area,** near Needles Eye, Harney Peak, and Cathedral Spires. Trailheads for several hikes may be found along this beautiful drive, including the 1-mile **Sylvan Lake Shore Trail;** the **Cathedral Spires Trail,** which spans about 6 miles of the park's mountainous country; and the **Sunday Gulch Trail,** a 2.8-mile loop.

You can also travel part of the **Centennial Trail,** which extends 111 miles from Bear Butte State Park near Sturgis to Wind Cave National Park.

Back down at the Visitor Center, pick up the 18-mile **Wildlife Loop Road** for a leisurely tour of the park's other main drawing card, its herd of 1,400 bison. About 10 miles south along the winding, well-maintained road lie the **Buffalo Corrals,** where you can sometimes find a few bison waiting for veterinary work or some other bison care. But most of them will be out grazing on the plains somewhere along this drive. Although they look slow, dumb, and placid while munching grass in the prairie, a mature bison bull can stand 6 feet high at the shoulders, weigh a ton, and turn with astounding agility while sprinting at speeds of up to 30 miles per hour. (Stay clear!)

Every year in late September or early October, cowboys round up the park's bison herd, bringing them into the corrals. Five hundred are sold at auction and the remainder released back into the park after branding and vaccination.

The sale of the culled bison, held on the third Saturday of November, attracts a large crowd.

Also loitering on the rolling plains is a herd of burros. Perhaps envious of the bison's status as the park's main mammal, the burros attempt to take center stage by asserting personality. You are almost certain to run into a "burro jam," when enchanted visitors stop along the road to feed these charming, outgoing quadrupeds. They may even stick their heads into your car searching for a snack.

Farther along the Wildlife Loop lies a prairie-dog town. The animals are important to the diet of many western predators, especially birds of prey. Their burrows are easy to find— they look like tiny black volcanoes. You may also notice many other animals along this road, including pronghorn, deer, elk, and bighorn sheep. Your chances of seeing these megafauna increase if you travel in the early morning and at dusk.

Near Legion Lake, almost back at the Visitor Center, is another important stop: **Badger Hole,** named for South Dakota's first poet laureate, Badger Clark. Clark lived alone in the small cabin here from 1927 until his death in 1957. You can visit his cabin and hike a short nature trail in the area.

Swainson's hawk

Further Adventures

● If you have more time, hike up **Harney Peak,** just outside of Custer's borders within the **Black Hills National Forest** *(605-673-2251)*. At 7,242 feet, it is the highest point in South Dakota. The park maintains four trails, all leaving from the park's Sylvan Lake Area. Ranging from moderate to strenuous, the hikes are among the park's most popular. Plan on four to five hours to make the 5 to 6.5 miles round-trip.

● A second worthwhile effort is a hike through all or part of the **French Creek Natural Area,** a 12-mile-long stretch of relatively undisturbed canyon country alongside the creek of the same name. There are no formal trails, but you can follow the creek through a steep-walled and timbered canyon. Hikers must cross French Creek several times, so be prepared to wade.

Camping and Lodging

Custer offers 7 developed campgrounds with 293 tent and RV sites and 30 tent-only sites, with shower facilities available May-September. The park also has 2 backcountry areas and a 27-site horse camp. Primitive camping year-round. Reservations recommended for all sites, but required for backcountry sites; call 800-710-2267. Camping fee. There are also 82 rooms in four lodges (May-October), and 107 cabins, some open year-round; call 800-658-3530 for reservations.

❑ *Custer State Park, HC-83 Box 70, Custer, South Dakota 57730*

219

East Comes West

In 1874 Lt. Col. George Armstrong Custer led his famous Black Hills expedition into what is now the park bearing his name. Prospectors with Custer discovered gold along French Creek, bringing a rush of settlers to the area and triggering the Indian Wars that eventually led to Custer's defeat and death. The park's second, somewhat lesser, brush with national renown came in 1927, when President Calvin Coolidge, vacationing here at the State Game Lodge, gave reporters a note with his famous statement, "I do not choose to run again for President of the United States." He sent for his staff and ran the country from the lodge for the summer.

Fort Sisseton

22 miles north of Webster via S. Dak. 25

● 125 acres ● 605-448-5701 ● Year-round ● Entrance fee

Fort Sisseton State Historic Park comprises a collection of military buildings dating from its days as a military post between 1864 and 1889. The park is located in the northern realm of the beautiful Coteau des Prairies, a plateau reaching an elevation of 2,000 feet.

The fort's construction in 1864 was prompted by the Minnesota Indian Uprising of 1862. Fourteen of the more than 45 original structures were restored in the 1930s by the Works Progress Administration. In 1866 Fort Sisseton chief scout Sam Brown had to intercept his own incorrect message about an "Indian war party," which turned out to be peaceful Lakota carrying word of a new treaty. To prevent bloodshed, Brown set out on horseback for the fort in a blinding snowstorm from a camp 150 miles to the north. He arrived by morning, in time to correct his error, but exhausted, frostbitten, and unable to stand. He never took a natural step again.

The **Visitor Center** (*Mem. Day–Labor Day*) has excellent displays about life in the fort, and an entire barracks has been re-created in period style. Interpretive signs drawing on the diary of Andrew Jackson Fisk guide you about. Fisk joined the Second Minnesota Cavalry at age 14, and became the camp quartermaster by 16.

The first weekend in June, the fort hosts a historical festival, complete with an encampment, muzzle-loader shooting contests, drill parades, fiddlers, and other frontier entertainments.

Camping

The park has 10 tent and RV sites and 3 tepee sites, without showers. Available first come, first served. Camping fee.

❏ FORT SISSETON STATE HISTORIC PARK, c/o ROY LAKE STATE PARK, 11545 NORTHSIDE DR., LAKE CITY, SOUTH DAKOTA 57247

Cannon in front of fort hospital

Newton Hills

6 miles south of Canton on 482nd Ave.

Red-winged blackbird

● 948 acres ● 605-987-2263 ● Year-round ● Entrance fee ● Hiking, swimming, fishing (license required) ● Cross-country skiing

For the visitor heading across the corn- and wheatfield country of South Dakota and Iowa, timbered Newton Hills pops up ahead in sharp relief, the legacy of glaciers from the last ice age. This state park preserves native countryside on the southern edge of the Coteau des Prairies. Extending along the eastern border of South Dakota, this plateau marks the western edge of the geographical province known as the Central Lowlands. To the west begin the true Great Plains, extending out to the Rockies.

Inside the park thrives a native upland forest, primarily oak, but laced with other hardwoods. To get a flavor of the park in a short time, hike the **Woodland Trail,** a .75-mile loop that travels along the Sergeant Creek drainage, then up a hill to a peaceful niche of beautiful old oaks, interspersed with small openings of preserved native prairie. An excellent place for birdwatching, Newton Hills has recorded over 200 species, including the peregrine falcon.

If you have time for another hike, consider the 0.5-mile **Coteau Trail,** an interpretive loop along the edge of the woods, where markers identify the various types of vegetation. Then travel to the southern edge of the park, where **Lake Lakota** offers swimming and fishing. If you are here in August, check out the Sioux River Folk Festival.

Camping and Lodging

Newton Hills has 122 tent and RV sites, with showers available April-Nov. Camping fee. Two cabins are also available year-round. Reservations advised in season; call 800-710-2267.

❏ *Newton Hills State Park, 28771 482nd Ave., Canton, SD 57013*

221

Fort Robinson

3 miles west of Crawford on US 20

● 22,000 acres ● 308-665-2900 ● Year-round ● Vehicle fee
● Red Cloud Agency ● Bison herd ● Hiking, mountain
biking, horseback riding

222

Horse-drawn Tour Train

Fort Robinson, the largest of Nebraska's state parks, nestles beneath the stark rugged bluffs of the White River. Its main attraction is its military history, from its role in 1873 as an Indian agency to its use as a German prisoner-of-war camp during World War II. The park complex takes in the original site of the Red Cloud Agency, established as a reservation for the Sioux under Chief Red Cloud.

Fort Robinson and the agency were among the most important staging areas for the 19th-century Indian Wars in the West, as the U.S. Army tried to entice the entire Sioux tribe to join Red Cloud on the reservation. Many Sioux refused, remaining on the plains with Crazy Horse, and later joining the Cheyenne to defeat Lt. Col. George Armstrong Custer at the 1876 Battle of the Little Bighorn. When Crazy Horse eventually surrendered in 1877, he was taken to Fort Robinson and imprisoned in the guardhouse. This is also where a soldier fatally stabbed him.

Beyond the fort complex, the park's 22,000 acres include an extensive plains environment, complete with bison herd.

What to See and Do

The activities available at Fort Robinson can keep you busy for a week. A good way to get an overview is to ride the **Tour Train** (*Mem. Day–Labor Day; fare*). There are also natural and historical tours available from the **Activity Center** inside Sutler's Store.

First on the list should be the fort's historic sites. The large 1887 **parade grounds** extend away from the main entrance, flanked by the **Adobe Officers' Quarters,** also dating from 1887. The restorations here show how officers of the period lived. The **Fort Robinson Museum** (*Oct.-April Mon.-Fri.*) interprets military life at the fort from the Indian Wars to World War II. The displays are colorful and informative, although like those at most fort museums they focus on the victor's side of the story. A second museum at the fort, the **Trailside Museum,** presents a comprehensive look at the geology and paleontology of Nebraska and includes a complete Columbian mammoth skeleton. The museum hosts a "knap-in" in late August, which demonstrates the ancient techniques of arrowhead and projectile point crafting, using the pressure flaking technique employed since prehistoric times.

After firmly grounding yourself in the fort's place in history, drive 1.5 miles from the main fort complex to the area that actually served as the Red Cloud Agency and the World War II prisoner-of-war camp. Once you've explored these facilities, take the 6-mile **Smiley Canyon Scenic Drive,** which dips and dives through classic broken cattle country. A bison herd frequents the pastures here.

If you have the time and the seat for it, an excellent way to see the park landscape is on horseback. Trail rides of varying length and difficulty are available at the stables on the fort grounds (*Mem. Day–Labor Day; fee*). Or travel by foot or mountain bike along the park's 30 miles of trails.

Camping and Lodging

Fort Robinson has 75 tent and RV sites, and additional tent-only sites, with shower facilities offered April to mid-November. Primitive camping available year-round. First come, first served. Camping fee.

The park also has a 23-room lodge; 32 cabins; and Comanche Hall, which houses 60 people and is open April to mid-November. Lodging is available by advance reservation; call the park at 308-665-2900.

❏ *FORT ROBINSON STATE PARK, P.O. BOX 392, CRAWFORD, NE 69339-0392*

Inside Fort Robinson

Cheyenne Outbreak

On Sept. 9, 1878, 300 Northern Cheyenne left their Oklahoma reservation to return to their native lands around the White River. A band of 149 led by Dull Knife were eventually captured and taken to Fort Robinson, where the commanding officer tried to starve them into submission. A group of the younger warriors escaped on Jan. 9, 1879, and managed to scale the bluffs nearby. They remained at large, without horses, for nearly two weeks, outmaneuvering the cavalry. After the soldiers found them, the warriors refused to surrender. In the ensuing fight, 64 Cheyenne and 11 soldiers were killed.

223

Lake McConaughy

9 miles northwest of Ogallala on Neb. 61

● 35,700 acres ● 308-284-3542 ● Year-round ● Vehicle fee ● Swimming, fishing (license required), boating, windsurfing

Lake McConaughy forms the core of this state recreation area, offering visitors white-sand beaches along much of its 105 miles of shoreline on the North Platte River. The North Platte and Platte Rivers—the Platte forming where the North Platte joins the South Platte—were major landmarks during the development of western America. The broad, flat river valley provided explorers and settlers with a fertile highway through what had become known as the Great American Desert.

Pioneers also followed the North Platte River to South Pass, a natural gateway through the Rockies. The first overland mail service, the telegraph, the Pony Express, and the transcontinental railroad all followed the Platte River.

Among the first things visitors do on entering the park is to take in the 3.5-mile-long, 162-feet-high **Kingsley Dam,** one of the largest earthen dams in the world. **Lake Ogallala,** the small lake below the dam, offers a bald eagle viewing area with heated blinds. In relative comfort, you can watch the eagles that congregate and feed here from mid-December until early spring.

But the main attraction of Lake McConaughy is as its name suggests: summertime water activities at Nebraska's largest lake. Your visit here will probably center in and near the water—fishing, swimming, boating, windsurfing, or simply sunning on the glistening sand. If you try your hand at some of the world-class fishing the lake offers, you may surface one of the dozen or so species of sport fish found here. Anglers have drawn state record-setting fish, including striper, rainbow trout, walleye, and tiger muskie from "Big Mac." In addition, extensive marshes at the lake's western end shelter a variety of birds, including sandhill cranes and Canada geese.

You may also wish to visit **Ash Hollow State Historical Park** (US 26. 308-778-5651. Mid-May–Labor Day; adm. fee), near the lake's west end. Exhibits here chronicle the area's Native American and pioneer history.

Camping

The park has 200 tent and RV sites, with showers; and 2,400 undesignated primitive sites. Camping also permitted on the beach. Available on a first-come, first-served basis. Camping fee.

❑ *Lake McConaughy State Recreation Area, 1500 Hwy. 61N, Ogallala, Nebraska 69153-5930*

Arbor Lodge

2300 W. 2nd Ave., Nebraska City

● 72 acres ● 402-873-7222 ● March through December ● Entrance fee ● No camping ● Historic house

Arbor Lodge

Arbor Lodge is the birthplace of Arbor Day, begun in 1872 at the instigation of newspaperman Julius Sterling Morton. The mansion grew from a relatively modest four-room frame house built in 1855—at the time reputedly the only frame house between the Mississippi River and the Rocky Mountains—when Morton and his wife, Caroline, arrived to take over the *Nebraska City News*. The property was a barren, 160-acre homestead, so Julius and Caroline planted trees to mimic the greenery of their native Michigan. In 1872, as president of the State Board of Agriculture, Morton formalized his enthusiasm for tree planting by introducing a resolution calling for the celebration of Arbor Day on April 22 (which also happened to be his birthday). Over a million trees were planted in Nebraska on that first Arbor Day. The idea spread, and now nearly every U.S. state celebrates the holiday.

Morton served two terms as a territorial representative, a term as secretary and acting territorial governor, and finally as secretary of agriculture in the second Grover Cleveland administration. He died in 1902. Meanwhile, the lodge's four major expansions were finally completed in 1905 by the Mortons' oldest son, Joy, founder of the Morton Salt Company. He donated the mansion and property to Nebraska in 1923.

The first and obvious stop is the 52-room neocolonial **Arbor Lodge,** with its terraced garden. Much of the Victorian and Empire furniture is original to the house. An ornate Tiffany skylight sparkles in the sun parlor, and the carriage house contains a large display of horse-drawn vehicles.

Then visit the 72-acre **arboretum,** with its more than 260 varieties of trees and shrubs. Walk along the 0.5-mile path beneath descendants of the trees planted by the Mortons, then visit a dense grove of white pine, a log cabin memorializing the original settlers, and a bronze casting of Julius Morton.

❑ *Arbor Lodge State Historical Park, P.O. Box 15, Nebraska City, NE 68410*

225

Backbone

2 miles south of Strawberry Point, off Iowa 410

● 1,780 acres ● 319-924-2527 ● Year-round ● Roads within park close in winter ● Hiking, swimming, boating, fishing (license required), rock climbing, winter sports

This state park preserves one of the largest forested areas in Iowa—a state in which large forested areas are rare. The park's centerpiece is The Backbone, a high rocky ridge of dolomite that early inhabitants named after the devil's backbone. Its precipitous sides rise 80 to 100 feet above the Maquoketa River.

The dolomite, sometimes called magnesian limestone, was deposited by a shallow tropical sea that covered Iowa some 430 million years ago. Dating from those times, The Backbone is studded with the fossils of extinct corals, occasionally measuring up to 20 inches in diameter.

Iowa's oldest state park, Backbone was established in

Backbone trout stream

1919 and has remained largely free of logging. As a result, 80 percent of the park is forested, dominated in the upland areas by white and red oak, and along the river bottoms by walnut, box elder, cottonwood, and other species typical of the environment. These trees provide excellent habitat for migratory songbirds and game birds such as wild turkey and grouse.

The Maquoketa River runs through the park, and its sandy bottom draws people to wade, ride inner tubes, and play that popular Iowa sport, in-stream volleyball.

What to See and Do

First, visit the park's signature formation, **The Backbone.** Circumnavigate its .25-mile length via a trail roughly a mile round-trip, watching for the Devil's Staircase, Big Oven, Little Oven, Rock Chimney, and other interesting shapes of stone. Below you on either side of the formation, the landscape drops away sharply to the Maquoketa River, offering spectacular panoramas.

If you have more time and energy, take a reliable flashlight to **Backbone Cave,** near the park's north entrance. This undeveloped cave slashes about 300 feet into the rock. There are no passages, just a single corridor through the rock, so there is no danger of getting lost. But be prepared to get dirty. A few stalactites and stalagmites remain, although most have long since been broken off and carried away as souvenirs.

If you have an interest in Depression-era history, take the time to explore the exhibits at Backbone's **Civilian Conservation Corps (CCC) Museum** (*Weekends Mem. Day–Labor Day*). Many buildings in this park—as in parks across the country—were built by the CCC in the 1930s. The corps also planted trees, built retaining walls, and installed telephone lines, among many other things. The museum commemorates their work in Iowa with artifacts and over 1,500 uncatalogued photographs.

The park's extensive rock formations have proven a popular draw for rock climbers, even though few of the faces reach even a hundred feet. Climbers scramble up **Razor's Edge** (40 feet) and **Slot Machine** (80 feet), among other formations, and rappel down. Backbone also contains 15 miles of hiking trails. The **East Lake** and **West Lake Trails** are open to mountain bikes.

Camping and Lodging

Backbone has 127 tent and RV sites, with shower facilities. Available on a first-come, first-served basis. Camping fee. There are also 18 cabins; for reservations call 319-933-6809.

❏ *BACKBONE STATE PARK, 1347 129TH ST., DUNDEE, IOWA 52038*

Backbone Stone

The Silurian dolomite bedrock exposed in The Backbone Formation is among the most resistant bedrock strata found in Iowa. This tough formation created the face not only of Iowa, but of other prominent landforms in the U.S. In east-central Iowa, the Mississippi River bumps up against the dolomite, causing the river to trend eastward in the "nose" of the state between Dubuque and Davenport. The long sweep of this same bedrock forms the escarpments on the shores of Lakes Michigan and Huron, and the Niagara escarpment at Niagara Falls.

227

Ledges

4 miles south of Boone, off Iowa 17

● **1,200 acres** ● **515-432-1852** ● **Year-round** ● **Hiking**
● **Birdwatching**

The broken valley of the Des Moines River cradles Ledges State Park in an unusual Iowa landscape. Gold and gray sandstone bluffs form a sharp valley, dug out over the millennia by the normally inoffensive Pease Creek. This narrowing stretches for about a mile along the creek, edged by sandstone bluffs rising to heights of 75 feet above the valley floor. The fragile sandstone was deposited by a swift running river beginning about 300 million years ago.

The park showcases intriguing "concretion" formations—big chunks of sandstone that are more firmly cemented by the water than the surrounding rock, much like an oyster produces a pearl. The resulting large rocky gargoyles extend straight out from the valley's side walls and hover over the creek bed. These formations eventually weaken and fall off the rock face—one broke off during the flood of 1993—and leave shallow indented caves in the wall. You can see several concretions and evolving caves in the park.

The park also features two restored sections of prairie, tiny remnants of the shortgrass and tallgrass prairies that once dominated a quarter of the lower 48 states. The site at the top of the canyon near the campground was planted in 1950 as the first native prairie restoration ever attempted in Iowa. The adjacent site was reclaimed in 1987.

Ledges' prairies are dominated by four grass types—sideoats grama, Indian grass, little bluestem, and big bluestem. Big bluestem is sometimes called turkeyfoot because its blooming buds resemble a turkey's foot. Black-eyed Susans, purple cornflowers, blazing stars, and other wildflowers color the prairie in late spring and early summer.

The park's prairie and surrounding forest provide a favored habitat to over 200 species of songbirds, promising good birdwatching.

What to See and Do

Your tour of the canyon carved through the sandstone is an experience that changes with the seasons. Spring brings wildflowers to the prairies, and in summer the valley provides a shady respite from the heat. Children especially enjoy playing in the pools near where the road fords shallow Pease Creek. You can drive this road as it meanders down the center of the clearing, across several shallow fords. But your experience here will be greatly enhanced if you choose to walk some of the park's 17 miles of hiking trails, many of which run along the valley rim. In autumn the leaves of the oak-hickory forest crown the ridge in breathtaking color.

Try out the **Lost Lake Nature Trail,** leading to **Sentinel** and **Solstice Rocks.** Here you stand 60 feet above the Des Moines River, looking out for miles in either direc-

229

Davis Creek

tion. Ledges has a rich history of habitation by the Mesquakie (Fox), and Solstice Rock is believed to be an observatory put in place by some agile tribe astronomer. The rock, which resembles the profile of an eagle's head, still has a red "eye" stained in berry dye. On the summer solstice, sunlight pours through a hole drilled in the rock, illuminating a small cavern behind it.

Remember that the sandstone is highly susceptible to erosion, so climbing on the bluffs is prohibited.

Camping

The park offers 54 tent sites and 40 RV sites, with shower facilities open mid-April to mid-October. Available on a first-come, first-served basis. Camping fee.

❑ *Ledges State Park, 1519 250th St., Madrid, Iowa 50156*

Maquoketa Caves

7 miles northwest of Maquoketa, off Iowa 428

● 323 acres ● 319-652-5833 ● Year-round ● Karst topography ● Cave exploration ● Hiking

This state park offers a primer to the karst processes that formed the 13 caves, sinkholes, and natural bridge along Raccoon Creek. Karst describes topography created when groundwater dissolves carbonate bedrock. The park also features rock caves formed when large blocks of stone slide down the face of rock walls, closing off areas behind.

Start at the brand new **Visitor Center** *(Mem. Day–Oct. Fri.-Sun.)*, which opened in 1997 in the former Sagers Museum. It features displays on the park's natural features, history, and archaeology.

Then head for the caves. Cave explorers should bring flashlights, very old clothes, and be prepared to get muddy. If you only have time to visit one—and want to stay relatively clean while doing so—choose **Dancehall,** the park's largest cave. Inside its upper entrance, just a short walk from the road, a paved and lighted walk explores its 1,100-foot length.

Located near Dancehall's upper entrance is another park attraction, **Natural Bridge,** a vast half-moon of craggy gray rock, overhung with ferns and clinging green finery. Eons ago, this was the entrance to Dancehall Cave, before the intervening sections collapsed.

Natural Bridge

If you have more time, an adventurous spirit, and a reliable flashlight, the other caves supply exotic experiences in the Iowa underground. Seven of the caves can be seen mostly standing up; six others require crawling. The trail system linking the caves totals about 6 miles, but the longest walk to any cave is only a half mile. Visitor Center staff can provide advice about which adventure is best suited for your group. In winter, water drips into some of the caves and freezes into icy columns, creating temporary imitations of the stalagmites and stalactites formed by mineral deposits.

Camping

The park has 28 tent and RV sites, with showers available mid-April to mid-October. Available on a first-come, first-served basis. Camping fee.

❏ *Maquoketa Caves State Park, 10970 98th St., Maquoketa, Iowa 52060*

Icicle, Maquoketa Caves

Stone

Off Iowa 12, in Sioux City

● 1,069 acres ● 712-255-4698 ● Year-round ● Loess Hills
● Hiking, biking, horseback riding

This state park is located within the geologically unique Loess Hills that stretch from the Iowa–Missouri border through seven counties to Sioux City. In the last glacial period, glaciers crushed quartz silt into a fine powder. This rock flour was then carried downstream by summer snowmelt; when the river flow dried up, the broad floodplains were left covered with powdery sediments. Some 12,500 to 150,000 years ago, prairie winds then deposited these sediments in what is now Iowa.

All of Iowa is covered with this fertile soil to a depth of several feet, but the Loess Hills were created because the Missouri River here ran perpendicular to the prevailing winds, creating deposits more than 60 feet deep, and sometimes as deep as 200 feet. Loess (pronounced "luss") landforms of this magnitude are duplicated in only one other place in the world—along the Yellow River in the Kansu province of China.

The **Loess Ridge Nature Center** within Stone State Park offers a fine introduction to prairie ecology and wildlife, including some small aquariums of Iowa fish species, dioramas of bluff vegetation, and a walk-through display of what it's like under the loess. Two miles of hiking trails around the center provide an up-close look at the grassland and bur oak woods that make up this park.

Then see the expanse of nature the Visitor Center prepared you for by driving the 3-mile **Stone Park Loop,** a narrow road offering vistas of the region and examples of upland forest habitat. This route is but a section of the **Loess Hills Scenic Byway,** 220 miles of designated roads through western Iowa.

Camping

The park has 32 tent and RV sites, with showers. Available on a first-come, first-served basis. Camping fee.

❏ *Stone State Park, 5001 Talbot Rd., Sioux City, Iowa 51103*

231

Prairie

17 miles west of Lamar on US 160, in Liberal

● 3,542 acres ● 417-843-6711 ● Prairie ecosystems
● Wildlife ● Hiking

Sunset on the prairie

Tallgrass prairie once covered a swath of land stretching from central Nebraska to central Ohio, reaching as far north as Manitoba, Canada, and as far south as Texas. With the conquest of agriculture in the 19th century, the prairie disappeared bit by bit, until it all but vanished. An island of tallgrass amid a sea of cultivation, Prairie State Park is the largest remnant prairie in Missouri, where more than 500 different plants and grasses can still be found.

Diaries of pioneers traveling west through the prairies often spoke of their covered wagons as ships in a sea of grass, noting a rocky cliff seen after many days amid the grasses as a sighting of "land." A little of that feeling can be recaptured in this park, where grasses often reach 6 to 8 feet in height. The park also has bison and elk herds. These animals can be dangerous. When you arrive, be sure to find out what areas are safe for hiking.

Prior to European settlement, fires swept through these prairies periodically, started either by lightning strikes or by

Native American tribes. A healthy prairie requires fire. Without it, woody plants—trees and shrubs—gain footholds and choke out the grasses. Prairie State Park burns one-third of its land each year, varying the season.

The park is home to a variety of wildlife, including several species listed as threatened or endangered—among them the northern harrier, grasshopper sparrow, and sedge wren. In addition, birds of prey abound; they sail through the skies, scanning the grasses below for a meal, or simply tumbling through the air in what appears to be an avian version of play.

What to See and Do

Begin at the modern **Visitor Center,** where dioramas and displays explain the prairie ecosystem as well as the cultural and social history of the area, including the early residents, the Osage, and their predecessors. Pay attention to the posted signs that announce where the bison and elk are grazing that day. To see these massive beasts, drive slowly along the dirt roads in the indicated section of the park. A major attraction, for those lucky enough to be here in the spring, is the new crop of pumpkin-colored bison calves. Note: Only guided or interpretive hikes are permitted through areas in which there are bison. Check with the Visitor Center staff for details about naturalist-led programs, including wildflower walks, bird-identification workshops, and pioneer living presentations.

Eight miles of trails traverse the park, providing an introduction to the colorful prairie plant-life and the opportunity—for the quiet and patient—of spotting wildlife. Try the mile-long **Coyote Trail,** the **Drover's Trail** (2.5 miles), and the **Gayfeather Trail** (1.5 miles). In addition, you can hike through the **Tzi-Sho Natural Area,** which presents an excellent opportunity to compare the prairie and agricultural landscapes.

Camping

Camping in the park is limited to two small, primitive group camps and a backpacking camp in the East Drywood Natural Area. For reservations, call the park or 800-334-6946. Camping Fee.

❏ *Prairie State Park, P.O. Box 97, Liberal, Missouri 64762*

> ### Prairie Seas
>
> When Napoleon marched on Moscow in 1812, he had only to move his army 1,500 miles. The army of emigrants crossing the American West between 1840 and 1860 often went 2,500 miles, much of it through tallgrass prairie. Children who wandered away from pioneer wagons were "drowned" in the tall prairie grasses. A parent had to stand on the back of a horse to have any hope of sighting the youngster.

233

Prairie chicken

Ha Ha Tonka

4 miles west of Camdenton, off US 54

● 2,993 acres ● 573-346-2986 ● Year-round ● No camping
● Castle ruins ● Hiking ● Karst topography

High on a bluff above the Lake of the Ozarks, the tall, white stone skeleton of a fire-ruined, 60-room mansion stands as a lonely reminder of an earlier age. Missouri's Ha Ha Tonka State Park preserves the remains of this grandiose turn-of-the-century project, along with some of the finest karst topography nature has assembled in a single Midwestern place.

In the heart of the park stands the remains of the Snyder mansion, a castle with a commanding view of the valley below and the rolling Ozarks all around. The mansion was begun in 1905 by Kansas City businessman Robert Snyder, who had purchased 5,400 acres in the Ozarks as a vacation getaway. But a year after beginning construction, Snyder was killed in an automobile accident, and the partially built residence remained untouched for more than 15 years.

In 1922 Snyder's sons finished the work, and their families used the beautiful place as a vacation retreat. Over time, the families came less and less often, and eventually leased it out as a hotel. In 1942 sparks from a fireplace ignited the roof and the building, along with the nearby carriage house, was gutted. The stark exterior walls, all that remain, now stand sentinel over the lake.

Ha Ha Tonka possesses another legacy of the past—caves, natural bridges, and sinkholes formed over thousands of years. Missouri is known for its plethora of caves, but rarely does one site possess Ha Ha Tonka's diversity of karst topography. The park's formations are the collapsed remains of a once extensive cave system. Whispering Dell sinkhole, for example, is 150 feet deep, one of a series of caverns whose roof collapsed. Its cool microclimate supports relict plant communities usually found at colder latitudes.

What to See and Do

There aren't very many castle ruins in America, and when you have the chance to admire the remains of one as grand as Ha Ha Tonka, it's best to put it at the top of your visiting list. The skeletal remains of the **mansion** are a very short walk along a trail from the main parking lot, and there are two overlooks from which to see the striking views of the Naingua Arm of the lake below and the Ozark hills beyond.

Next, visit the large **natural bridge** soaring more than 100 feet above the cavern floor. Just down the hill from the mansion ruins, the bridge was the original road access to the mansion. If you have time, hike from the nearby parking lot along the **Dell Rim Trail** to the **Spring Trail,** leading down to a huge spring. A portion of the trail drops 200 feet, down 300 steps. At the base of the canyon, the spring issues 48 million gallons of water a day. The walk is strenuous. You can also reach the spring by driving to a parking area beside the lake and hiking in about a half mile.

Finally, **River Cave,** near park headquarters, is home to a growing population of gray bats and the blind grotto salamander. To protect the habitat, the cave may be explored by permit only. Check with the park office for information.

❏ *Ha Ha Tonka State Park, Rte. 1, Box 113M, Camdenton, MO 65020*

235

Ruins of Snyder mansion

Montauk

21 miles southwest of Salem on Mo. 119

● **1,356 acres ● 573-548-2201 ● Year-round ● Fishing (license required), hiking**

At the headwaters of the Current River, Montauk is a paradise for anglers. Here Pigeon Creek combines with the 40 million gallons of water spewing forth daily from the seven Montauk springs to provide blue-ribbon trout waters. During the 19th century, Montauk's considerable water power was put into the service of industry. Settlers built four different grain mills here. One, dating from 1896, still stands and is open for tours in summer.

The fast-flowing waters that once powered the mills provide an excellent habitat for rainbow trout, and this has made Montauk a popular sporting spot with anglers. Several trout derbies are held here each year. During the official trout season, from March through October, trout are stocked daily. In winter, when bald eagles hunt the streams and springs, catch-and-release fishing is allowed.

Montauk is managed as a fishing park, so this is the place to get a close-up look at some trout—preferably at the end of your fishing line. Fishing equipment can be rented in the park, if you didn't bring yours. A portion of the stream is dedicated to fly-fishing and other sections allow artificial lures and bait; some areas are catch-and-release only.

Montauk's location at the headwaters of the **Current River** has also made it a popular jumping-off point for canoeists. Although canoeing is not permitted within the park, just below it the Current is designated as part of the **Ozark National Scenic Riverways** (573-323-4236), managed by the National Park Service. Canoe rentals are available from concessionaires at sites along the riverway. A half-day float along the fastest section of the river will take you from Inman Hollow to Cedargrove. Paddling down the Current, you'll see undercut banks, numerous springs, and high bluffs with vast square boulders tumbled like the dice of giants at their bases.

Birdwatchers, photographers, and nature lovers can also enjoy the park's scenic wonders. One designated hiking trail offers many opportunities to explore flora and fauna, and a designated natural area, also within the park, showcases a splendid mature pine-and-hardwood upland forest.

Camping and Lodging

The park has 156 tent and RV sites, with showers. Some may be reserved by calling 573-548-2201. Camping fee. Cabins and a motel are also available; call 573-548-2434 for reservations.

❑ MONTAUK STATE PARK, c/o MISSOURI DEPARTMENT OF NATURAL RESOURCES, P.O. BOX 176, JEFFERSON CITY, MISSOURI 65102

Meramec

50 miles southwest of St. Louis, off I-44

● 6,896 acres ● 573-468-6072 ● Year-round ● 42 caves
● Cave tours ● Hiking, canoeing, swimming

Towering bluffs, gaping cave entrances, and massive over-hanging trees furnish a picturesque backdrop for the alluring Meramec River. Within these clean spring-fed waters thrive Missouri's greatest variety of aquatic life, including more than a hundred species of fish. Several miles of this river flow through Meramec State Park's rugged Ozark landscape. Located within an hour's drive of St. Louis, Meramec is one of Missouri's most popular parks, especially as a cool respite from summer heat.

First, stop at the park's **Visitor Center,** which offers an introduction to the area through displays focusing on the river environment and the development of cave geology. A 3,500-gallon aquarium showcases the river's inhabitants.

If you have the opportunity, take the 90-minute guided

237

Canoeing the Meramec River

tour of **Fisher Cave** *(April-Oct.; fee),* the largest and some say most beautiful of the park's 42 caves. Using hand-held lanterns for lighting, the tours provide a sense of adventure. Fisher shows you a wide variety of the subterranean environment's features, from massive columns 30 feet tall to intricate calcite deposits.

Hiking and backpacking the 16 miles of park trails can lead to rocky glades laced with wildflowers, serene corners of quiet solitude, and lush forests carpeted with ferns or ablaze in fall color. But in summer, most people spend their time drifting down the calm water in canoes, rafts, or inner tubes. Rent them *(573-468-6519),* or bring your own.

Camping and Lodging

The park has 210 tent and RV sites, with showers. Some can be reserved by calling 573-468-6072. Camping fee. There are also 20 cabins and 22 motel rooms; call 573-468-6519 for reservations.

❏ *Meramec State Park, 2800 South Hwy. 185, Sullivan, Missouri 63080*

Lake Scott

15 miles north of Scott City, off US 83

● 1,020 acres ● 316-872-2061 ● Year-round ● Vehicle fee
● Pueblo ruins ● Hiking, swimming, fishing (license required)

238

Blooming yucca

Driving along the sweeping flat plains of agricultural Kansas, you could pass within a few hundred yards of a sunken canyon oasis without knowing it. But within Lake Scott State Park, rocky bluffs and walled canyons line Ladder Creek, leading north to the Smoky Hill River. The park sits in a long, narrow bowl, surrounded by high, rocky hills, stony outcrops, and classic bluffs reminiscent of a Hopalong Cassidy movie.

In late summer, when the wheat on the Kansas plains has been cut and the browned stalks give the terrain a dusty look, drop over the canyon rim into the cool green of this park. Here, with the yucca blooming ivory lies 100-acre Lake Scott. Park and lake are encircled by steep, orange-walled canyons with such picturesque names as Horsethief—

Canyon, Timber Canyon, and Suicide Cliff, the latter frequented by climbers and rappelers. According to popular folklore, its name arose from the cliff's supposed use as a bison jump for the Apache, or because a lovesick Indian suitor jumped to his death here. Although romantic, both theories are unsubstantiated.

What to See and Do

The site's most remarkable feature is **El Cuartelejo Pueblo ruins,** the unlikely home of a band of 17th-century Taos Indians, and believed to be the northernmost pueblo in North America. The ruins were discovered in 1889, and reconstruction began in 1970. The foundation has been laid out as it would have been originally. Note the lack of doorways, indicating that entrance was gained via ladders from the roof. This park was the site of a number of Indian camps, and a museum currently under construction in the nearby town of Scott City plans interpretive displays of the artifacts found in the park.

For those with an interest in bugs—or perhaps just the very, very rare—the .25-mile-long **Big Springs Nature Trail** near the park's main entrance passes natural rock steps over which spring water flows. These steps are home to the Scott riffle beetle, an endangered species that evolved only here at Big Springs. Its entire habitat is limited to this area.

For Kansans, the chief attraction of the park is simply the presence of a lake in the water-starved western portion of their state. **Lake Scott** offers excellent fishing for bass, crappie, and channel catfish. A trout-stocked pond below Barrel Springs is a favorite fishing spot for children, and a swimming beach provides another happy option.

Just outside the park's main entrance is another, somewhat larger, wildlife attraction, where two side-by-side fenced pastures hold one herd each of elk and bison. The animals are privately owned, but graze on park land for the pleasure of visitors. Also outside the park boundary lies the site of the **Battle of Punished Woman's Fork,** where in 1878 the Northern Cheyenne, including Dull Knife and Little Wolf, fought the U.S. Cavalry in the last Indian battle in Kansas.

Camping

The park offers 60 tent and RV sites and 140 primitive sites, with shower facilities available mid-April to mid-Oct. First come, first served. Camping fee.

❏ *LAKE SCOTT STATE PARK, 520 W. SCOTT LAKE DR., SCOTT CITY, KS 67871*

El Cuartelejo

In the early 1660s, a group of Taos Indians fled Spanish rule in present-day New Mexico to the area now preserved as Lake Scott State Park. Here they built the pueblo that has become known as El Cuartelejo, meaning old barracks or buildings. Although Spanish expeditions made forays into the area, the Taos inhabited the site—free of Spanish rule—until about 1730, when raids by the Comanche, Ute, and Pawnee forced them to return southward.

239

Prairie dogs on alert

Prairie Dog

4 miles west of Norton on US 36

- **1,150 acres** ● **913-877-2953**
- **Year-round** ● **Vehicle fee**
- **Fishing (license required)**
- **Prairie-dog town**

A 1,500-pound statue carved from Indiana limestone greets visitors to this northwest Kansas park. Its subject: the once ubiquitous wild rodent of the Plains, the black-tailed prairie dog.

Prairie dogs have been poisoned nearly out of existence in portions of the West, and, when this park was established in 1967, there were no prairie dogs in residence. The park was named not for the little fellows, but for **Prairie Dog Creek,** which flows through the park, filling the adjacent 2,000-acre Keith Sebelius Reservoir.

Early attempts by park managers to introduce prairie dogs to their namesake park failed, but in 1982 a pair arrived from somewhere and took up residence. The community has flourished since, growing from the original two to a population of three to four hundred.

You can visit the park's prairie-dog town, which covers 38 acres. You'll likely be greeted by an alert sentry, sitting at the entrance to its hole and emitting a high-pitched barking squeak when you approach. This watchdog-like barking, which warns fellow prairie dogs to retire quickly to their holes, is how this little rodent came to be known as a "dog."

Your second stop should be the **adobe homestead** *(Staffed seasonally or by appt.; call park for information),* down the paved road to the east of the prairie-dog colony. Built in the 1890s, this is the oldest surviving adobe structure in the state that is open to the public. The interior walls provide graphic demonstration of the adobe mud-and-straw construction.

Western Kansas has very few large bodies of water, and the **Keith Sebelius Reservoir** draws visitors from all over, especially for the fishing. Since 1992, high-water years have filled the reservoir beyond its original capacity—as evidenced by the skeletons of large drowned trees pointing skyward in mid-lake—creating the kind of habitat that grows record fish.

Camping

The park offers 42 tent and RV sites (10 may be reserved), and 5 primitive campgrounds with a total of 120 sites. Showers available mid-April through October. Call park at 913-877-2953 for reservations. Camping fee.

❑ *Prairie Dog State Park, P.O. Box 431, Norton, Kansas 67654*

240

Clinton

4 miles west of Lawrence, off US 40

● 1,455 acres ● 913-842-8562 ● Year-round ● Vehicle fee
● Swimming, boating, fishing (license required), biking

The popularity of Clinton State Park stems from 7,000-acre **Clinton Reservoir.** The lake is devoted primarily to water sports and provides excellent angling. In addition, wooded trails along the lakeshore have special appeal for mountain bikers—the challenging trails have caused more than a few cyclists to carry, rather than ride, their bikes out of the woods.

The park is overseeing the restoration of the 19th-century **Barber School,** which was constructed of rubble stone, an unusual building material for the period. Thomas Barber was an abolitionist and a martyr during the "Bloody Kansas" pre-Civil War era. The park also has plans to restore some 40 acres of native prairie adjoining the school to its Civil War period appearance.

Camping

The park has 400 tent and RV sites (15 may be reserved), with showers available mid-April to mid-October. Call park at 913-842-8562 for reservations. Camping fee.

❑ *Clinton Office, RR1, 798 N. 1415 Rd., Lawrence, Kansas 66049*

Elk City

5 miles west of Independence on US 75/160

● 857 acres ● 316-331-6295 ● Year-round ● Vehicle fee
● Hiking, fishing (license required), boating, swimming

Rimmed by 250-foot-high bluffs, this park challenges the usual perception of Kansas as a flat plains state. The park is situated within the **Osage Questas**—alternating beds of shale and limestone deposited more than 250 years ago when a shallow sea covered the area. These have eroded into a series of tilted hills, steep on one side and sloped on the other and covered with hickory and oak trees that are particularly beautiful in fall. The park lies at the juncture of woodlands and bluestem prairie.

Sunflowers,
Kansas state flower

Paved roads and several trails of varying steepness lead to overlooks offering views of reservoir, prairie, and woodlands. Nearby, **Elk City Reservoir** attracts waterfowl and visitors to fish, boat, Jet ski, and swim.

Camping

The park has 95 tent and RV sites and 65 primitive sites, with shower facilities available mid-April through October. First come, first served. Camping fee.

❑ *Elk City Unit Office, P.O. Box 945, Independence, Kansas 67301*

Oklahoma

Beavers Bend
Quartz Mountain
Black Mesa
Osage Hills

Arkansas

Petit Jean
Devil's Den
Village Creek
Crater of Diamonds
Lake Chicot

243

Texas

Big Bend Ranch
Enchanted Rock
Brazos Bend
Caddo Lake

Louisiana

Lake Fausse Pointe
Chicot
Poverty Point
Lake Bistineau

Rio Grande, U.S.–Mexican border

Beavers Bend

10 miles north of Broken Bow, off US 259

● 3,482 acres ● 405-494-6300 ● Year-round ● Rugged Ouachita Mountain terrain ● Mountain Fork River ● Broken Bow Reservoir ● Nature Center ● Hiking, nature trails

Paddlers on Mountain Fork River

The entrance road at Beavers Bend winds sinuously along a ridge top before dropping down to the Mountain Fork River—a journey of only 3 miles that nonetheless serves as a preview of this region, nicknamed the "Little Smokies." The Ouachita Mountains of eastern Oklahoma and western Arkansas were formed some 400 million years ago by tremendous tectonic forces that squeezed and folded the earth, resulting in today's sometimes tortuous terrain of long, east-west ridges separated by steep-sided valleys and ravines. It's a rugged yet intimate landscape, seen best up close—from a hiking trail through open, pine woodland, or a canoe on a clear, rocky river.

Mountain Fork was dammed in 1969 to create 14,000-acre Broken Bow Reservoir; the park includes areas on the reservoir—lodge, campsites, and Cedar Creek Golf Course (405-494-6456. *Greens fee*)—and on the river. The two areas are connected by road and by the 24-mile David Boren Hiking Trail. Beavers Bend lies within what was once Choctaw territory. Its name comes not from the aquatic mammal, but from Choctaw citizen John T. Beavers.

What to See and Do

If you'd like to learn a bit about the history of forestry, stop by the **park office** and the **Forest Heritage and Education Center** (405-494-6497), which chronicles trees and their uses, from the age of dinosaurs through the modern timber industry. While here, pick up a park map and trail guide.

At the **Beavers Bend Nature Center** you can learn about park programs on subjects from snakes to birds of prey to nature-related crafts. A naturalist may let you hold a king snake, and you can see specimens of local venomous species behind glass. Several live hawks and owls are usually on display here; some are awaiting rehabilitation, while others, too badly hurt to be released, are kept for educational purposes.

Walk down to the **Mountain Fork River** and admire the bluff on the opposite bank. In winter you may see a bald eagle perched in a streamside tree and ducks or double-crested cormorants paddling on the water. Bald cypress and sycamore line the river, while scrubby cedar and oak cling to the cliff.

Beavers Bend provides several reasonably short trails, all worth exploring. The **Cedar Bluff Nature Trail,** a fairly strenuous, 1-mile loop, repays your effort with a splendid overlook above the river; the easier 1-mile **Dogwood Nature Trail** stays near the river for much of its length, wending through mixed woodland; the 1.1-mile **Forest Heritage Trail,** beginning at the park office, features interpretive signs on Ouachita forest ecology. To avoid confusion, note that the hiking trail is blazed white, while the nature trails are blue on white.

Appealing as the park's trails and forest are, most visitors focus on the beautiful Mountain Fork. Swimming, canoeing, and paddleboating are popular in summer; anglers wade its shallows throughout the year, testing their skill against trout. You may discover, though, that the best activity is no activity at all: Just find a flat rock at a secluded spot, lie back, and enjoy the sound of bird song, the smell of pine, and the grand scenery of one of the prettiest places in Oklahoma.

Camping and Lodging

The park has 50 tent and 110 RV sites, with shower facilities, and 47 cabins. For limited reservations call the park. Camping fee. There are also 40 lodge rooms. For reservations call 405-494-6179.

☐ *Beavers Bend Resort S.P., P.O. Box 10, Broken Bow, OK 74728*

Scenic Route

Sixty miles north of Beavers Bend, you'll find one of the region's most spectacular drives: the **Talimena Scenic Byway** in the Ouachita National Forest (501-321-5202). Called Hwy. 1 in Oklahoma and Hwy. 88 in Arkansas, it runs for 54 miles from Talihina in the former state to Mena in the latter. Following the high ridges of the Ouachita Mountains, Talimena offers all-encompassing vistas of heavily wooded hills and valleys. **Queen Wilhelmina State Park Lodge** (501-394-2863), 5 miles across the Arkansas state line, is a fine choice fora meal or overnight lodging.

Quartz Mountain

17 miles north of Altus via US 283 and Okla. 44

● 4,284 acres ● 405-563-2238 ● Year-round ● Rugged granite hills ● Lake Altus-Lugert ● Diverse flora and fauna ● Hiking, birdwatching

On a clear day you may be as far away as 35 miles when you first see the red granite dome of Quartz Mountain on the horizon, rising from the southwestern plains. As imposing as it and other Wichita Mountain peaks are, you're actually seeing only part of them: Millions of years of weathering have covered their bases with eroded rock to a depth of many thousands of feet, leaving only their tops showing above ground.

246

Lake Altus-Lugert from Quartz Mountain

Quartz Mountain is a strikingly attractive place, its rugged, boulder-strewn slopes in sharp contrast with the blue of Lake Altus-Lugert. This juxtaposition of rock and water, mountain and plains, produces great diversity in the park's wildlife and vegetation—which also shows the influence of its location in the country's midsection. You could, for instance, see an Eastern collared lizard sliding past a pecan or an Eastern redbud here, where, ecologically speaking, North meets South.

What to See and Do

Stop first at the **park office,** where exhibits introduce

Quartz Mountain's natural history. The area's granite, you'll learn, came to the surface as magma more than 500 million years ago; a shallow sea covered it in sedimentary limestone (long since eroded away), and later it was uplifted far higher than its present worn-down elevation. Kids will enjoy the touch table, where they can handle feathers, cattails, rocks, and—if they're brave enough—animal bones and skulls.

The short **Wichita Interpretive Trail** leads from the office to Campground B, paralleling an intermittent stream. Its muddy banks often reveal tracks of wild turkey, white-tailed deer, raccoons, and even bobcats, which come down from the mountain to drink, but are seen by only the luckiest visitors.

The park's 0.5-mile **New Horizon Trail** begins at a parking lot a short distance beyond the office. It heads rather steeply up Quartz Mountain to a lookout point about three-fourths of the way to the top; you're free to continue all the way up, and to pick your own route back down if you don't want to retrace your steps. Be aware that rocky hillsides are a favored habitat of rattlesnakes; watch where you step and put your hands. Another fearsome-looking—but in this case harmless—reptile found here is the horned lizard, armed with sharp spines over its body. You may see this little "horned toad" sunning itself in sandy and rocky areas on hot days; it skitters away with surprising speed when you come too close.

Wildflower-lovers should note that long-haired phlox, a species endemic to the Wichitas, can be seen at Quartz Mountain in spring. The park's annual May Wildflower Festival is a great time to observe some of the 80 varieties that grow here, including coreopsis, larkspur, prickly pear cactus, and the beautiful Indian blanket or firewheel, a sunflower relative with red-and-yellow flowers.

In winter **Lake Altus-Lugert** can host a dozen or more bald eagles; ask a naturalist about the best viewing locations. Another species seen on the lake in spring and fall, to the surprise of some visitors, is the white pelican; although many people think of them as seabirds, the birds migrate through the park on their way to and from their breeding grounds in the northwestern United States and Canada.

Quartz Mountain also offers various additional outdoor activities, ranging from paddleboats *(405-563-2465)* on the **North Fork Red River** to the Quartz Mountain Golf Course *(405-563-2520)* to a designated off-road vehicle area *(April-Sept.)* on the north shore of the lake.

Camping

The park has 50 tent and 120 RV sites (some open year-round), with showers. For limited reservations call the park. Camping fee. There are also 8 cottages; call 405-563-2424 to reserve. The lodge is currently under renovation.

❏ *Quartz Mountain State Park, Rte. 1, Lone Wolf, OK 73655*

On the Wild Side

About 40 miles east of Quartz Mountain State Park, **Wichita Mountains Wildlife Refuge** *(405-429-3222)* holds a historic place in the national refuge system. Designated a national forest reserve in 1901 by proclamation of President William McKinley, it provides today's visitors the chance to see bison, elk, white-tailed deer, and Texas longhorn cattle up close along its 15-mile-long scenic drive. With nearly 60,000 acres of varied habitat, Wichita Mountains is well worth a side trip for anyone visiting southwestern Oklahoma.

Black Mesa

27 miles northwest of Boise City, off Rte. 325

- 349 acres, plus 1,460 acres in nearby nature preserve
- 405-426-2222 ● Year-round ● Highest point in Oklahoma
- Flora, fauna, geology

For many travelers Black Mesa State Park is only a stopping-off point on the way to **Black Mesa** itself, about 15 miles northwest. While the park offers pleasant camping near **Lake Carl Etling,** the nature preserve's combination of geological features, wildlife, and vegetation make it one of Oklahoma's top natural history destinations. The flat-topped mesa is a remnant of an ancient lava flow that hardened into erosion-resistant basalt. Because of its height and its location in the tip of Oklahoma's Panhandle, Black Mesa is more akin to the Rocky Mountain region than to the rest of the state.

Stop at the **park office** for maps and travel advice, then continue west on Rte. 325 to a paved road heading north. Follow signs to a parking lot at **Black Mesa Nature Preserve,** where a 4-mile trail leads up a short, rocky slope dotted with juniper and scrub oak. Allow at least four hours for the round-trip to the summit (more if you stop to birdwatch or take photos); be sure to carry sun protection and water.

Rock Window

On top of the mesa, more than 600 feet above the surrounding plains, you'll find a granite monument marking the highest spot in Oklahoma: 4,973 feet above sea level.

Black-billed magpies and pinyon jays are among the western birds found at Black Mesa, and you may see mule deer or pronghorn as well.

Take time to enjoy the park's impressive views and unique environment, but keep an eye out for occasional thunderstorms, which can bring dangerous lightning.

Camping

There are 30 tent and 29 RV sites, some with showers. Available first come, first served. Camping fee.

❏ *BLACK MESA STATE PARK AND NATURE PRESERVE, HCR-1 BOX 8, KENTON, OKLAHOMA 73946*

Osage Hills

11 miles west of Bartlesville, off US 60

● **1,199 acres ● 918-336-5635 ● Year-round ● Rolling, wooded hills ● Scenic creek, bluffs ● Hiking**

Lake Look-Out

249

In his 1835 book called *A Tour on the Prairies,* Washington Irving wrote that traversing Oklahoma's Cross Timbers region was "like struggling through forests of cast iron." These north-south belts of woodland, stretching from Texas to Kansas, once grew so thickly and continuously that they presented a serious challenge to pioneers headed west. You'll find a modern-day sampling of this environment at Osage Hills State Park—but, unlike Irving, you're likely to find a visit far more a pleasure than a struggle.

Trails wind through hills covered primarily in post and blackjack oak. Stop at the **park office** for a map, then drive through the campground to a road leading north, where an observation tower provides a good overview of the area.

Return through the campground and turn south to the **Sand Creek Loop Trail** leading to the bluffs along **Sand Creek.** Another popular path, the **Waterfalls Trail** leads from the parking lot at the public swimming pool to a series of small cascades. You'll likely see white-tailed deer and wild turkey along park roads or paths; under park protection, both species have become accustomed to their human neighbors.

Osage Hills lies at the edge of what was once a great sea of tallgrass prairie, covering 140 million Midwestern acres. Don't miss a chance to see a 37,000-acre expanse of this endangered habitat at the Nature Conservancy's **Tallgrass Prairie Preserve** *(918-287-4803),* north of nearby Pawhuska. Bison still roam and prairie chickens still dance here, just as they did when Washington Irving visited a century and a half ago.

Camping and Lodging

There are 27 tent and 20 RV sites, with showers. Available first come, first served. Camping fee. The park also has 8 furnished cabins. To reserve call 918-336-4141.

❑ *Osage Hills State Park, HC 73, Box 84, Pawhuska, OK 74056*

Petit Jean

20 miles west of Morrilton via Ark. 9 and Ark. 154

● **2,658 acres** ● **501-727-5441** ● **Year-round** ● **Adm. fee**
● **Cedar Falls** ● **Mountaintop panoramas** ● **Indian
bluff shelters** ● **Hiking, swimming, boating, fishing
(license required)**

Arkansas River Valley from rocky outcropping

Petit Jean Mountain rises some 800 feet above the
Arkansas River, its long silhouette like a rampart looming
over the flat valley floor. Even back in prehistoric times,
however, the mountain has been a place more inviting than
forbidding. Native Americans used its shallow bluff caves as
shelters, and early settlers found in its breezy elevation some
relief from sweltering summer temperatures in the lowlands.

In 1819 explorer and naturalist Thomas Nuttall wrote
that "the hills of the Petit John appear conspicuous and picturesque," an observation that countless travelers have since
echoed. Petit Jean's striking scenery, as well as the broad vistas from its perimeter cliffs, made it a natural choice when
Arkansas' first state parklands were acquired in 1923. Over
the years it has remained a favorite getaway spot for hiking,

picnicking, camping, and weekend getaways.

Ark. 154 offers fine views as it winds up the mountainside—but it's wise to keep your eyes on the often tortuous road. A turnoff at the summit leads to **Petit Jean's grave** (see sidebar),where you can take all the time you like to enjoy the panorama of river valley and hills

Back on the highway, you'll soon pass **Lake Bailey,** a 170-acre impoundment on Cedar Creek, where anglers try their luck with bream, bass, and catfish, and the young in spirit scoot across the water on paddleboats.

What to See and Do

Get an introduction to Petit Jean's natural history at the park **Visitor Center,** where you'll find exhibits on the area's flora, fauna, and geology. You can also pick up a schedule of interpreter-led hikes and special programs.

From here it's only a short drive to what is probably (and deservedly) the most popular spot on the mountain: **Cedar Falls,** a lovely waterfall nestled in a heavily-wooded, steep-sided gorge. During dry summers the falls can slow to a trickle, but after rainy spells in spring and autumn, Cedar Creek cascades over a rock ledge and plunges spectacularly 95 feet to a pool encircled by vertical bluffs. It's one of Arkansas' most famous (and most photographed) sights, and no one should visit the park without taking it in.

The easy **Cedar Falls Overlook Trail** leads from a parking lot off Ark. 154 to a viewpoint above the falls.

Those who are able, though, should hike the more challenging **Cedar Falls Trail** to the pool below. The trailhead is located behind **Mather Lodge**—named for Stephen Mather, head of the National Park Service at the time of Petit Jean's founding—which perches on the edge of a bluff just west of the turnoff to the overlook. (If it's near mealtime, be sure to stop in at the lodge dining room, which is famed for its fabulous view of Cedar Creek Canyon.) The 2.25-mile round-trip hike requires a steep descent to Cedar Creek before turning upstream to the falls. The way back out is, of course, exactly equal in steepness—but can seem far more strenuous, especially on a hot summer afternoon. Stops along the way provide welcome opportunities to appreciate the forest, wildflowers, and birds.

Typically for this part of the state, the woodland here is dominated by oak, hickory, and shortleaf pine, with maple, pawpaw, and dogwood among the many other accompanying species. Spring flowers, which begin their annual show as early as late February, include bloodroot, toothwort, mayapple, Solomon's seal, rue anemone, and trout lily. Later in the year varied daisies, asters, and milkweeds brighten the park's open fields and roadsides.

Legend of Petit Jean

Several Arkansas localities possess French names, but none has such a fanciful origin as Petit Jean's. According to one legend that reads like a movie script, a young Frenchwoman disguised herself as a man—"Little John"—to accompany her boyfriend on an expedition to America. Not until after she became ill and died was her secret exposed. Petit Jean's supposed grave lies at a suitably romantic overlook on the eastern edge of the mountain; the view is well worth a visit—even if you take the story with a grain or two of salt.

Natural Bridge

Further Adventures

If you have more time the **Seven Hollows Trail,** a 4.5-mile loop, is one of Arkansas' most rewarding short hikes. Fascinating rock formations are the main attraction along here: **Natural Bridge,** for example, is a choice location for "we were there" snapshots; and the caves you see beside the trail were once used as shelters by early Indians.

The varied habitats along the way make for excellent birdwatching, especially when song is at its peak in the late spring. A walk just after dawn (when birds are most active, and most people are not) will likely bring sightings of such common species as Carolina chickadee, tufted titmouse, red-bellied woodpecker, pine warbler, and the brilliant-red summer tanager. Luckier finds might include a big, noisy pileated woodpecker, with its crimson crest, or a yellow-billed cuckoo, whose "cow-cow-cow" call is much more often heard than the singer itself is seen.

Red Bluff Drive, on the opposite side of Cedar Creek Canyon from Mather Lodge, leads to scenic overlooks and to the **Rock House Cave Trail.** Native Americans once lived in the shallow grotto at the end of this path. It's easy to imagine the tall, dome-shaped cave here as a comfortable retreat from winter rains and summer sun.

Camping and Lodging

The park has 127 tent and RV sites, with showers. Reservations are accepted for 24 sites only; call the park. Camping fee. There are also 32 cabins and 24 rooms at Mather Lodge. Reserve early; especially during the fall foliage season; call 501-727-5431 or 800-264-2462.

Nearby Sights

The **Museum of Automobiles** (*501-727-5427. Adm. fee),* on the mountain just east of the park, displays a fine collection of antique cars. Fourteen miles west of the park, **Holla Bend National Wildlife Refuge** (*501-229-4300)* is one of Arkansas' best locations for viewing wildlife. Turkey, deer, bobcat, hawks, and a variety of songbirds are present all year; winter brings flocks of ducks and geese, as well as an impressive number of bald eagles. Reach the refuge by driving west on Ark. 154, and then turning north on Ark. 155.

❏ *Petit Jean State Park, 1285 Petit Jean Mountain Rd., Morrilton, Arkansas 72110*

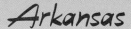

Devil's Den

13 miles west of Winslow on Ark. 74

- ● 2,047 acres ● 501-761-3325 ● Year-round ● Geological formations ● Mountain stream ● Interpretive trails
- ● Backpacking, biking, horseback riding

In the hundreds of millions of years since the Ozark mountains of northwestern Arkansas were uplifted from an ancient sea, creeks and rivers have deeply dissected the soft, underlying sandstone and limestone, forming steep-sided valleys of striking beauty. Lying at the bottom of one of these "hollers" (as the old-time locals call them), Devil's Den State Park offers visitors a microcosm of the Ozarks's rugged terrain, dense hardwood forest, and crystalline rivers.

What to See and Do

You'll experience this eroded, synclinal landscape (basically, a tilting or folding of rock layers) as you wind down Ark. 74 into the park, arriving, after many switchbacks, at **Lee Creek,** the stream traveling through the park. Before you begin your explorations, stop at the **Visitor Center** to pick up trail brochures and to talk to the interpretive staff about guided walks and programs. If you're interested in learning about park flora, follow signs to camping area E and the .25-mile **Woody Plant Trail,** where signs identify native trees and shrubs.

Next, return to the Visitor Center and the start of the 1.5-mile **Devil's Den Trail,** the park's most popular

253

Rocky stream in autumn woods

hike. With a flashlight to guide your way, you can walk several hundred feet into **Devil's Den,** the cave that gave the park its name; a little beyond is **Devil's Ice Box.** Both are "fracture" caves, formed by slippage of sandstone blocks. Air entering the Ice Box higher up the hillside is cooled in summer (or warmed in winter) by contact with below-ground rocks that remain at a constant 55-60°F. Local legend asserts that outlaws used these caves as hideouts in the 19th century, causing law-abiding folks to shun the area.

Ferns and wildflowers, and near-constant bird song, make the Devil's Den Trail a naturalist's delight in spring. Watch along the way for sassafras, an aromatic shrub or small tree once used by country people to make tea; look for its mitten-shaped leaves (some with two "thumbs"). Watch, too, for birds such as the beautiful orange-and-black American redstart and the drab, greenish red-eyed vireo. The latter, abundant throughout the Ozarks, sings even in the heat of summer afternoons when other birds are silent.

For more geological exploration drive to camping area A and walk the 1-mile **Lee Creek Trail.** The first half of the loop winds through a typical Ozark woodland, with occasional openings into old fields; the second part follows the stream bed of Lee Creek. Examine the rocks here for fossils of sea creatures, including coral and crinoids (relatives of sea stars). Take time, too, to look into the creek itself, where you may spot a crayfish or a tiny, colorful darter.

In addition to typical campsites, Devil's Den offers a walk-in, tents-only area for those who prefer a more quiet, peaceful setting. The park's most popular accommodations, though, are its rock-and-log cabins, built in the 1930s by the Civilian Conservation Corps; updated to modern standards, these historic structures offer an appealing blend of comfort and rusticity.

Further Adventures

To experience the Ozarks more intimately, walk the park's 15-mile **Butterfield Hiking Trail,** which offers fine scenic views as it loops south of the park. The truly energetic could make the journey in a long day, but it's much better to take it more slowly and camp overnight at one of the designated sites along the way. (The park has backpacking equipment for rent.) You'll likely be alone for hours at a time as you hike, giving a hint of what the land was like when the only footprints here were those of Osage Indians.

Camping and Lodging

The park has 97 tent and RV sites, with shower facilities. Available first come, first served. Camping fee. There are also 13 cabins, with kitchen and fireplace. Reserve cabins well in advance; call 800-264-2417.

❏ *Devil's Den State Park, 11333 W. Ark. Hwy. 74, West Fork, AR 72774*

Butterfield Trail

The Butterfield Hiking Trail at Devil's Den is named for the celebrated Butterfield Overland Mail stage line, which began carrying mail between St. Louis and San Francisco in 1858. Part of the trail traces a section of the historic route that connected mail stops in nearby Fayetteville and Fort Smith. The Butterfield line's life span was as short as its mission was ambitious: The Civil War in 1861 put an end to its cross-country journeys.

Village Creek

13 miles north of Forrest City on Ark. 284

● 7,000 acres ● 501-238-9406 ● Year-round ● Varied wildlife and vegetation ● Unusual geology ● Hiking, swimming, fishing (license required)

Driving across the farmland of eastern Arkansas, most of it flat and featureless as a tabletop, you suddenly come upon a long ridge rising 200 feet above the surrounding terrain. Quite obviously, something extraordinary happened here. You can't help but wonder: What on earth built this?

Geologists say that the precursor of the Mississippi River once flowed west of its current course, while the predecessor of today's Ohio flowed where the Mississippi runs today. As these prehistoric rivers meandered across the landscape, a thin strip of high ground between them was left relatively untouched. Later, during a dry climatic period, windblown soil piled up against the elevated land, raising it even higher. The result is today's 150-mile-long **Crowleys Ridge,** a region so different from the rest of Arkansas that biologists classify it as a separate natural division.

255

Swinging bridge on Lake Dunn trail

Set like a gem in a lushly forested valley on the ridge's eastern slope lies Village Creek—Arkansas' largest state park and, for naturalists, one of its most rewarding.

What to See and Do

Stop at the **Visitor Center** for fine exhibits on local geology and history. You'll learn, for instance, that the higher, drier ground of Crowleys Ridge made it a natural choice for towns, such as Forrest City and Wynne, and that the first improved road between Memphis and Little Rock, authorized by Congress in 1821, passes through the park.

Just steps away are two trails offering an introduction to Crowleys Ridge ecology: The easy **Arboretum Trail** identifies many of the park's trees, including sugar maple, beech, and butternut, all uncommon in most of Arkansas, and the magnificent tulip tree, a type of magnolia that grows naturally

Fossil Finds

Although a layer of loess—fine soil left by the wind—tops the crest of Crowleys Ridge, its lower layers are made up of sediments left by an ancient sea that once covered the region. It receded about 50 million years ago. Digging in the clay soil at the base of the ridge often turns up sharks' teeth and other marine fossils—reminders that, sometime in the distant past, the land here would have been beachfront property.

nowhere else west of the Mississippi. Other species found here include white oak, sweetgum, red oak, basswood, black hickory, white ash, and swamp chestnut oak.

Cross the road to the **Big Ben Nature Trail,** a pretty, 0.5-mile walk that runs alongside **Village Creek.** ("Big Ben" was a huge beech tree, named for settler Benjamin Crowley. The venerable giant blew down several years ago, but its name lives on in the trail designation.) Here you'll get a close look at the wind-deposited soil, called loess, that caps Crowleys Ridge, sometimes to a depth of 50 feet. Fine as powder, it erodes easily when the protective forest cover is removed.

If you'd like to walk in the footsteps of early pioneers and enjoy a fine nature hike, drive the short distance to **Lake Austell** and take the **Military Road Trail,** a 2.25-mile loop that follows part of the historic Old Military Road. In places, the path has been worn into the soft soil over the past 150 years by countless footsteps, hoofprints, and wagon wheels.

If you're feeling energetic, you can continue east, where the Military Road Trail turns back; follow the path across a swinging bridge and hike all the way to **Lake Dunn,** nearly 3 miles north, before retracing your steps.

To cool off after all this walking, take advantage of the swimming areas at both park lakes. (The beach at Lake Dunn is for registered campers only.) Picnic sites are available near Lake Austell; the marina at Lake Dunn offers boat rentals, if you'd like to try your luck fishing for bass, bream, or catfish.

Camping and Lodging

The park has 104 tent and RV sites, with showers. For limited reservations, call the park. Camping fee. There are also 10 cabins, with kitchen and fireplace. Call 800-264-2467 for reservations.

❏ *Village Creek State Park, 201 CR 754, Wynne, Arkansas 72396*

Crater of Diamonds

2 miles southeast of Murfreesboro on Ark. 301

● 888 acres ● 870-285-3113 ● Year-round
● Diamond-hunting

Rough diamonds

When a park experience is described as rewarding, the meaning is not usually so literal as at this little-known spot in southwestern Arkansas. The gems here are real, unearthed by an ancient volcanic eruption and exposed by millions of years of erosion.

For a small fee, you can join others scouring a 36.5-acre field of kimberlite soil and keep any diamonds you find. Whoppers, such as the Uncle Sam (40.23 carats) and the Star of Murfreesboro (34.25

carats), are about as likely as a lottery win—but with more than 750 diamonds discovered in an average year, the odds are not bad that you'll come away with a sparkling souvenir. (Semiprecious stones, such as jasper, quartz, garnet, peridot, agate, and amethyst make pretty consolation prizes.)

Check with a park ranger for tips on diamond-hunting and look over the display samples before you start your search. You may see hopeful prospectors using everything from dowsing rods to "magic" glasses, but—as with many things in life—the best tools are persistence, patience, and hard work. And, of course, luck.

Camping

The park has 60 RV sites, 12 with tent pads, with showers. For reservations call the park. Camping fee.

❑ *Crater of Diamonds S.P., Rte. 1, Box 364, Murfreesboro, AR 71958*

Lake Chicot

8 miles northeast of Lake Village on Ark. 144

● **132 acres** ● **501-265-5480** ● **Year-round** ● **Scenic lake** ● **Birdwatching, fishing (license required)** ● **Barge tours**

257

Pier fishing on Lake Chicot

This small park in the flat Mississippi River alluvial plain lies at the northern tip of picturesque **Lake Chicot;** at 20 miles long, it is America's largest, natural oxbow lake. With its countless bald cypress trees, it is an evocative vision of the Deep South.

Rent a boat from the park marina to explore the lake, or to try your luck fishing for catfish, bass, bream, or crappie. In late spring or fall, join one of the park's celebrated barge tours *(501-265-5480. April-June, Aug.-Sept.; fare)*, which provide close views of hundreds of egrets and herons. The endangered wood stork, a rare wanderer to Arkansas, is seen regularly here; in winter, bald eagles perch in lakeside cypress. Ask at the **Visitor Center** about a driving tour atop the nearby **Mississippi** and **Arkansas River levees.** An unconventional route, it offers excellent wildlife viewing.

Camping and Lodging

The park has 127 tent and RV sites, with showers. For limited reservations call the park. Camping fee. There are also 14 cabins. Call 800-264-2430 to reserve.

❑ *Lake Chicot State Park, 2542 Hwy. 257, Lake Village, AR 71652*

Lake Fausse Pointe

18 miles southeast of St. Martinville via La. 86, La. 679, and La. 3083; and the West Atchafalaya Protection Levee Rd.

● 6,127 acres ● 318-229-4764 ● Year-round ● Vehicle fee
● Atchafalaya Swamp ● Canoeing trails ● Hiking

Sunset on Lake Fausse

Home of bald eagles, alligators, and otters, the Atchafalaya River easily deserves a place among the country's finest and wildest natural areas. The Atchafalaya (from a Native American word meaning "long river") stretches 120 miles northward from the Gulf of Mexico; its floodplain, more than 20 miles wide in places, comprises the largest river-bottom swamp in America. Few roads cross this wetland wilderness, and access to the interior is hard for outsiders without a boat and a guide to point the way through trackless waterways.

Lying just outside Atchafalaya's western levee, Lake Fausse Pointe offers a sampling of the swamp environment with the conveniences of a modern state park. Visualize the scene by imagining yourself enjoying a cool drink on a cabin porch while an alligator glides across the bayou below.

What to See and Do

The most challenging part of a trip to Lake Fausse Pointe

is simply getting there—but it is marked. You'll change direction and roads several times as you wind through the sugarcane fields east of St. Martinville, before turning south (parallel to the levee) on the final 7-mile stretch to the park.

Although Lake Fausse Pointe encompasses extensive swamp and wetland, its developed land area is compact. Bottomland woods line the park roads and water is never far away. Local wildlife ranges from the tiny ruby-throated hummingbird to white-tailed deer and gators, and includes herons, egrets, armadillos, squirrels, and nutria—a South American rodent introduced into Louisiana around the turn of the century as a potential fur resource.

Cross the footbridge over **Old Bird Island Chute** to reach the park's hiking trails. Two paths, called **Trail A** and **Trail B,** totaling nearly 2.5 miles, loop through vine-tangled woods of bald cypress, oak, willow, sycamore, and sugarberry. The trailside can be alive with birds any time of year: The warblers, flycatchers, vireos, and buntings that breed here in spring are replaced in winter by finches and sparrows. Trail B passes an observation platform, from where, depending on the season, you may see waterfowl, gulls, terns, or wading birds. Listen for the rattle of a belted kingfisher, or the scream of a red-shouldered hawk.

The forests and waterways of south Louisiana provide habitat for many kinds of reptiles—including, of course, snakes, the cause of much needless worry for some visitors. The reptiles you're most likely to see, though, are turtles: Variously called map turtles, painted turtles, cooters, and sliders, all can often be seen basking in the sun to warm their cold-blooded bodies.

Two canoe trails, one of which is marked, lead through a canal system on the lake's east side; exploring these routes is the park's best opportunity to experience the Atchafalaya ecosystem. Stick close to home by paddling the quiet Old Bird Island Chute, or venture farther away to see huge bald cypress trees around **Sandy Cove** (*Boat rentals at the dock. 318-229-6333. Fee*). Seek advice before heading out on your own.

Camping and Lodging

The park has 50 tent and RV sites, with showers. Camping fee. There are also 8 cabins. Reservations optional; call the park.

❏ *Lake Fausse Pointe State Park, 5400 Levee Rd., St. Martinville, Louisiana 70582*

Cajun Country

Lake Fausse Pointe lies in the heart of Cajun country, the home of French-speaking Acadians, who were forced out of present-day Nova Scotia and New Brunswick by the British in the 1750s. Nearby Lafayette likes to call itself "the Cajun Capital;"its **Acadian Cultural Center** (*501 Fischer Rd. 318-232-0789. Adm. fee*) and the adjoining living history village of **Vermilionville** (*1600 Surrey St. 318-233-4077 or 800-992-2968. Adm. fee*) are excellent places to discover that there's more to Cajun culture than spicy food and great dance music.

259

Alligators

Chicot

7 miles north of Ville Platte on La. 3042

● 6,400 acres ● 318-363-2403 ● Year-round ● Vehicle fee
● Hiking, fishing (license required)

An appealingly varied forest surrounds 2,000-acre **Lake Chicot,** where the pine woods of northwestern Louisiana begin giving way to the swampy lowlands of the south. The lake is popular with local folks fishing for largemouth bass and crappie (called *sac-à-lait,* or "milk sack," by Cajuns). If you're not an angler, you'll enjoy hiking along the picturesque lakeshore, or exploring the adjacent arboretum.

For a quick introduction to the park's environment, first drive the 4-mile road between the south and north landings. The route winds through rolling terrain covered in pine, oak, sweetgum, palmetto, and magnolia, dotted throughout with the straight gray trunks of beech. Stop at the north landing, where a long fishing pier makes a good lookout point. Winter is the best time to see waterfowl on the bald cypress-ringed lake, and you may spot a bald eagle perched in a tall tree nearby.

The **Walkers Branch Hiking Trail** circles the lake, passing areas designated for primitive camping. Short sections of the trail allow you to get away from cars and picnickers without having to carry backpacking gear.

Be sure to visit the nearby **Louisiana State Arboretum** *(319-363-6289),* located off La. 3042, a mile north of the main park entrance. The 2.5 miles of trails here, traversing ridges and ravines amid lush woodland, are among the prettiest in Louisiana. The type of beech-magnolia forest found in the arboretum and the park was once widespread across the South; today, mature examples such as this are as exceptional and as treasured as they are beautiful.

Camping and Lodging

There are 208 tent and RV sites, with showers; 27 cabins; and 3 lodges. For reservations call 888-677-2442. Camping fee.
❏ *CHICOT STATE PARK, RTE. 3, BOX 494, VILLE PLATTE, LOUISIANA 70586*

Poverty Point

16 miles north of Delhi via La. 17, 134, and 577

● 402 acres ● 318-926-5492 ● Year-round ● Adm. fee
● No camping ● World heritage archaeological site
● Museum ● Seasonal tram tours ● Self-guided trail

About the time Solomon was writing the Proverbs and tending to his 700 wives, a thriving community existed on the edge of a waterway in what is now northeastern Louisiana. Expansive and orderly in design, Poverty Point seems to have been the region's dominant economic hub. The community carried on trade and extended its influence over a wide area; it built mammoth earthworks and erected grand ceremonial mounds—one of them in the form of a flying bird, nearly 100 feet high and more than 700 feet long.

Archaeologists call this place Poverty Point, a name that also has come to identify the principal culture of the lower Mississippi Valley, from about 1500 to 500 BC. The importance of this ancient town, about 20 miles west of the Mississippi River and surrounded by agricultural land, can be judged from its designation as a world heritage archaeologi-

261

Tree-studded Mound A

cal site. Today's Poverty Point State Commemorative Area rewards visitors with tantalizing glimpses of a long-vanished civilization, which left traces as haunting as a carved stone effigy, as substantial as the ground beneath your feet.

What to See and Do

Your experience at Poverty Point will probably begin before you even know it: As La. 577 approaches the park's **Visitor Center,** the road cuts across a series of low ridges so long and uniform in appearance that they seem at first to be naturally occurring geological features. In reality, though, you're crossing six concentric, semicircular earthworks stretching, from one extremity to the other, nearly three-quarters of a mile. Believed to have served as foundations for houses, these ridges originally stood 6 to 10 feet high, and their construction required a highly organized

Name Game

What's in a name? Not much, really, at Poverty Point. Early settlers struggling to survive on America's frontier often gave their homesteads jokingly ironic epithets, such as "No Hope" or "Hard Times Farm." In the mid-19th century, a plantation on Bayou Macon was known as Poverty Point, and this traditional designation was eventually applied to the archaeological site. The cheerless name has nothing to do with the prehistoric inhabitants of the area, who, as far as we know, were a very prosperous and happy people.

effort involving millions of hours of labor.

Poverty Point's Visitor Center is located in the 37-acre opening that was once the town's central plaza, alongside **Bayou Macon** (pronounced "mason"). A short film shown here explains the importance of the site and reviews its history. After watching it, take time to study the exhibits in the adjoining room, where some of the huge number of artifacts found in the area are displayed. Among them are beautiful little owls carved from red jasper; graceful plummets, which were probably used as weights for fishing nets; gorgets and beads; projectile points; and, especially, artificial cooking stones of fire-hardened silt that were heated and placed into earth ovens with food for cooking. These stones are identified so closely with the site and its culture that archaeologists call them "Poverty Point objects."

Climb the observation tower for a view of the surrounding earthworks and of massive **Mound A,** to the west. Shaped like a bird with its wings outstretched, this mound contains 300,000 cubic yards of earth and was built—probably for ceremonial purposes—one basket of dirt at a time, with material excavated from nearby "borrow pits."

From Easter to Labor Day, Poverty Point operates tram tours, which cross the ridges and visit Mound A (you'll be allowed time to climb to the top) and **Mound B,** a smaller construction that has revealed evidence of a cremation fire.

An alternative to the tram is a self-guided, 2.6-mile walking trail that winds alongside Bayou Macon, through the ridges, and back to the Visitor Center. (Wear comfortable shoes if you plan to hike this trail, which can be wet in winter and spring.)

As you can imagine, many mysteries remain about a place so far removed from our own time. Archaeological research continues here; if you come in summer, you may well get to watch scientists at work trying to resolve some of the countless questions still unanswered about Poverty Point and its industrious inhabitants.

❏ POVERTY POINT STATE COMMEMORATIVE AREA, P.O. BOX 276, EPPS, LOUISIANA 71237

Lake Bistineau

9 miles south of Doyline on La. 163

● 750 acres ● 318-745-3503 or 888-677-2478 ● Year-round
● Vehicle fee ● 17,000-acre lake ● Boating, fishing
(license required)

Stand on the shore of **Lake Bistineau,** a large, shallow reservoir 30 miles east of Shreveport, and you find yourself at the meeting of two worlds: On one side is a swampy expanse of bald cypress and water tupelo, of wood ducks and cat-fish, muskrats and mud turtles. On the other is a segment of the great pine forest that stretches from the Atlantic to Texas. This conjunction makes this state park a place of diverse beauty— and an excellent base from which to explore the lake.

The entrance road to **Park Area 1,** where the office and cabins are located, passes through a forest predominated by loblolly pine, some of which have gained impressive size. Opportunities for dry-land recreation are limited at Bistineau, so check at the park office about renting a boat—by far the best way to enjoy a visit here.

Low-flying great egret

263

You don't have to go far to begin your discoveries. The shoreline near the park is a picturesque scene of bald cypress, their swollen trunks and protruding "knees" draped with Spanish moss. In spring and summer, you may see a brilliant golden-yellow prothonotary warbler, a spar-row-size bird that's something of a specialty of southern swamps. Pairs often nest in tree cavities over water. In fall, the needles of the bald cypress turn reddish-brown, for this species is a deciduous conifer—that is, a cone-bearing tree, like pine and spruce, that loses its leaves annually, like an oak or a maple.

When you visit Bistineau, consider renting one of the cabins, attractively set on the lakeshore. Staying here, you'll have only to look out the window to appreciate this uniquely attractive park.

Camping and Lodging

There are 67 tent and RV sites, with showers. Camping fee. Also, 14 cabins. For reservations call 888-677-2478.

❏ *Lake Bistineau State Park, P.O. Box 589, Doyline, LA 71023*

Big Bend Ranch

8 miles southeast of Presidio on Rte. 170

● 287,000 acres ● 915-229-3416 ● Year-round ● Adm. fee ● Rugged wilderness ● Desert wildlife ● Barton Warnock Environmental Education Center ● Rafting, hiking, backpacking

Rio Grande, Canyon Colorado

The Chihuahuan Desert stretches across an immense expanse of northern Mexico and the southwestern United States. To some, the terrain it encompasses is lonely and forbidding. To others, the wild lands here offer a renewing respite from civilization's demands.

Big Bend Ranch State Park sprawls northward from the Rio Grande, just west of Big Bend National Park. Its 420 square miles are composed mostly of desert grassland. The river acts as a long, narrow oasis, providing habitat for an incomparable variety of plants and animals (mountain lions still roam the rocky slopes, and golden eagles cruise the canyons) that otherwise would be absent from this parched land.

Little development has taken place since the park, once a cattle ranch, was acquired by the state in 1988: Rte. 170 parallels the river, one gravel road penetrates the park's northern section, and a few hiking trails venture into the rugged backcountry, but access to most of the area is difficult.

What to See and Do

Your adventure begins as you drive south from Presidio on Rte. 170. Known as *El Camino del Rio*, or the **River Road,** it surely ranks among the most breathtakingly scenic drives in America. With the Rio Grande on one side and the Bofecillos Mountains on the other, the route twists and curls, climbs, and descends for 50 miles of ever-changing views of a landscape shaped by ancient seas, continental collision, scarring volcanoes, and eroding rivers. Enjoy the surroundings, but drive with caution; be especially careful at the road's many low-water crossings, and don't enter water that looks deep or fast-flowing and muddy.

En route to the park (just 8 miles from

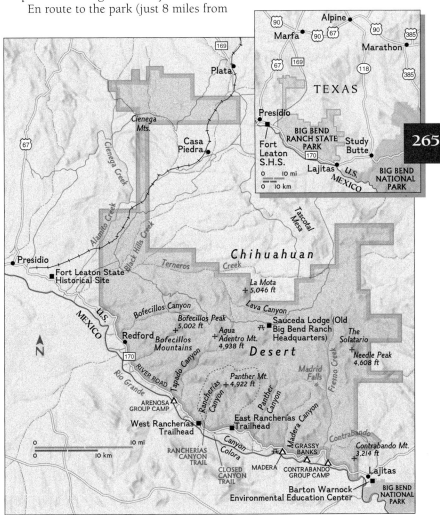

River Running

River rafting and canoeing are popular activities at Big Bend Ranch, which borders the Rio Grande's majestic Canyon Colorado. With a permit, you can take your own craft downriver, but most travelers go through one of the outfitters in Lajitas or Terlingua; the park office can provide contacts. These companies can also organize a trip through Big Bend National Park's awesome Santa Elena, Mariscal, and Boquillas Canyons—one of the most spectacular river journeys on earth.

266

Indian pictograph

Presidio), you'll pass **Fort Leaton State Historical Site** *(915-229-3613. Adm. fee),* one of two places where you can pay fees and obtain information about Big Bend Ranch. If this is your first visit, though, continue on to the **Barton Warnock Environmental Education Center** *(915-424-3327. Adm. fee),* at the other side of the park in Lajitas, for your introduction to the area's ecology. Walk through the 2.5-acre botanical garden, which displays such typical regional plants as the lechuguilla, an agave that botanists call the Chihuahuan Desert's chief "indicator"—that is, a species that grows naturally nowhere else.

Ask center personnel about current park trail and road conditions, and about naturalist-led **bus tours** *(512-389-8900. Reservations required; fee)* of the backcountry, offered on the first (from Fort Leaton) and third (from the Warnock Center) Saturdays of each month.

Retrace your route for 20 miles to the trailhead for **Closed Canyon,** a short hike off Rte. 170. Here a tributary has carved a narrow, steep-sided gorge in welded tuff: rock that originated as fine volcanic ash. Not only is this an easy walk, but the high canyon sides keep much of it in shade—an important consideration in this sun-drenched climate.

Follow Rte. 170 northwest again toward Presidio; a few miles past the park's western border, turn right onto a gravel road, which runs for more than 30 miles into the mountains. *(Large motorhomes may have difficulty on this road.)* Look and listen for desert birds, or at dusk, the eerie howling of coyotes. Mule deer and javelina (small piglike creatures) are seen often, but it's a lucky traveler indeed who catches even a glimpse of their predator, the mountain lion.

The road leads to **Sauceda,** where lodging is available in the old ranch headquarters buildings. Beyond Sauceda, you'll find splendid views of the imposing mountain complex called the **Solitario,** and a lookout point into Fresno Canyon.

Further Adventures

For hardy hikers, the **Rancherías Canyon Trail,** north of the River Road, leads up a canyon past ancient lava flows to a waterfall. Although the entire out-and-back distance is 9.6 miles, beautiful canyonland begins after just 2 miles or so, making shorter walks highly rewarding. The same trailhead serves the **Rancherías Loop Trail,** a 19-mile, two- or three-day wilderness trek that should be undertaken only by experienced backpackers.

Camping and Lodging

The park has 13 primitive campgrounds. Available first come, first served. Camping fee. Dormitory accommodations (30 bunk beds) in Sauceda fill up quickly; for reservations call 915-229-3416.

❑ *Big Bend Ranch State Park, P.O. Box 1180, Presidio, Texas 79845*

Enchanted Rock

17 miles north of Fredericksburg on Rte. 965

- 1,643 acres
- 915-247-3903
- Year-round
- Adm. fee
- Visitor limits
- No vehicular camping ● Pink-granite formations
- Rock climbing

Eroded granite formations

267

The rugged countryside west of Austin, fondly called "Hill Country" by Texans, encompasses a variety of attractions, from scenic rivers to historic towns. For sheer visual impact, though, nothing can match the high dome of pink granite at the center of Enchanted Rock State Natural Area. Rising more than 425 feet above the surrounding terrain and covering some 640 acres with rock, it seems out of earthly scale, as if it had been transported from another world. Which, in effect, it was.

Enchanted Rock is a batholith ("rock from the deep")—a huge mass of molten material that rose from within the earth and solidified as it neared the surface. In the billion years since its formation, the weaker overlying rock has eroded away, exposing its crown. The visible portion of Enchanted Rock is only a small fraction of the entire mass, which underlies almost 90 square miles of central Texas.

The descriptive name "enchanted" is said to have been passed down from Indians, who may have attributed the loud sounds of temperature-related rock expansion and contraction to spirits. Archaeological evidence shows that Native Americans lived near the rock from at least 8,000 years ago until European settlement displaced them in the mid-19th century.

What to See and Do

The foremost activity at Enchanted Rock is quite plainly to get to the top. While the **Summit Trail** is well-marked and requires no technical skill, an elevation gain of 425 feet in just over half a mile makes it more than a casual stroll. Still, almost anyone can do it—especially with frequent breaks along the way to enjoy the views.

Before you begin, stop at the **headquarters** to see displays on local geology. Enchanted Rock is part of Texas' Central Mineral Region, an area known for its geological diversity; an appreciation for what's below ground will enhance your experience here. You can also pick up information on archaeology, birdlife, or rock climbing.

Among the plants along the Summit Trail are mesquite, several types of oak, black hickory, prickly pear cactus, elm, hackberry, and Texas persimmon, a smaller relative of the common persimmon found in the East. Bluebonnet and Indian paintbrush are seen in spring. Park animals, like the plants, constitute an intriguing blend of eastern and western species: You may see both foxes and rock squirrels at Enchanted Rock, just as you'll find both pecan and catclaw acacia.

As you climb higher onto the rock itself, look for the small depressions known as **vernal pools,** a remarkable ecological feature of the park. Vegetation in these ephemeral basins slowly progresses from lichens to grasses to live oaks, creating islands of life in a sea of bare granite. Tiny invertebrates called fairy shrimp inhabit this fragile environment, enduring drought as eggs, which hatch when rain refills the pools.

You'll discover a splendid panorama of the Hill Country at Enchanted Rock's broad summit. The high points surrounding you, similar to but smaller than the one you're standing on, represent other outcrops of the same mammoth granite batholith. Plan on taking plenty of time here to enjoy the views—and to celebrate your success at reaching the top.

After you've made your way back down, walk the 4-mile **Loop Trail,** which circles Enchanted Rock and provides a good look at the park's varied habitats, including oak woodland, mesquite grassland, and the floodplain of Sandy Creek. The trail leads to three designated primitive-camping areas.

Rock climbing is popular on the mountain's steep, northwest-facing cliffs, but it's not for the inexperienced. Climbers must check in at headquarters for rules before beginning; no pitons, bolts, or other devices that might damage the rock are permitted. Ask, too, about exploring the 1,000-foot-long **Enchanted Rock Fissure,** which runs beneath huge sections of fallen granite. This can be an exciting adventure, but you must have sturdy footwear, carry a flashlight, and be mindful of your physical limitations.

To protect the environment, the park limits the number of daily visitors; call in advance on weekends and holidays.

Camping

The park has 46 walk-in and 60 primitive tent sites, with shower facilities. Call 512-389-8900 to reserve. Camping fee.

❑ *ENCHANTED ROCK STATE NATURAL AREA, 16710 RANCH RD. 965, FREDERICKSBURG, TEXAS 78624*

Little Germany

Fredericksburg, just south of Enchanted Rock, is one of the best-known ethnic communities in Texas. Founded by a German immigrants' society in 1846, it retains a strong Old World flavor, from its Fachwerk ("half-timbered") buildings to bakeries specializing in German-style breads and pastries. The **Pioneer Museum Complex** (*309 W. Main St. 210-997-2835. Adm. fee*) and the **Vereins Kirche** ("people's church") **Museum** (*Center of Markt Platz. 210-997-7832, Adm. fee*) vividly recount local history.

268

Brazos Bend

20 miles south of Richmond on Texas 762

● 4,897 acres ● 409-553-5101 ● Year-round
● Adm. fee ● Excellent wildlife viewing ● Hiking and
biking trails

269

Field of spider lilies

Named for its location on a broad curve of the Brazos
River, Brazos Bend is one of Texas' prettiest and most popular
parks. The greatest rewards await those who thrill to the insis-
tent hoot of a great horned owl at dusk, the cold gaze of an
alligator, or the graceful ballet of an egret searching for prey.

Much of the park is bottomland-hardwood forest of
almost tropical lushness. Wispy strands of Spanish moss hang
from the gnarled limbs of live oak; cottonwood and sycamore
line the banks of the Brazos and the lakes that dot the flat
floodplain. Marshes draw waterfowl, wading birds, otters, and
nutria, while upland prairie sparkles with wildflowers.

What to See and Do

Although you'll be tempted to get out of your car and
begin exploring the park's trails immediately, your first stop
will depend on whether it's the weekend, when the **Habitats
& Niches** Visitor Center is open. If so, continue past the
entrance for 2.6 miles to the building on your left, where

you'll learn about Brazos Bend's three ecological zones (forest, wetland, and prairie), and about the park's most popular resident, the American alligator.

The **Creekfield Lake Nature Trail** continues your orientation. The paved, 0.5-mile loop can be explored with an audiotape tour (*ask at Visitor Center or park headquarters*).

Next, return to the parking lot at **40-Acre Lake**, near the park entrance, where a fishing pier makes an excellent viewing platform. Depending on the time of year, you may see ducks, herons, egrets, coots, or grebes. Wood ducks, which many consider America's most beautiful waterfowl, are among 70 or so birds that nest in the park.

Before you walk the 1.2-mile trail that circles the lake, read (and heed) posted warnings about safety around alligators. Seeing these big reptiles is always a thrill, but don't be fooled by their sluggish demeanor: Gators can move with shocking speed when they want to. Never feed an alligator, and absolutely do not approach a nest or a female with young.

Along the trail you may also see white-tailed deer, yellow-crowned night heron, swamp rabbit (closely related to the cottontail), or one of the several kinds of snakes found here. On the far side of the lake, climb the observation tower for a view over extensive wetlands, where patient watching will reveal a variety of wading birds. A side trail leads to **Elm Lake;** following this route, circling Elm Lake, and returning to the 40-Acre Lake parking lot comprises a 4.1-mile hike, nearly guaranteed to reveal a variety of wildlife.

If you have more time, explore the trails that lead from **Hale Lake** down to the Brazos River. Intersecting loops make possible hikes of from less than a mile to several miles. The 2-mile **Red Buckeye Trail,** which loops down to **Big Creek,** takes its name from a shrub whose bright-red blossoms brighten the woods in spring.

On Saturday nights, the **George Observatory** (*409-553-3400*), operated by the Houston Museum of Natural Science and located at Creekfield Lake near the Visitor Center, offers public viewing through its 36-inch **telescope** (*Tickets sold on a first-come, first-served basis; fee*) and a variety of smaller instruments.

Camping

Brazos Bend has 77 tent and RV sites, with showers. Reservations advised; call 512-389-8900. Camping fee.

❏ *Brazos Bend State Park, 21901 FM 762, Needville, Texas 77461*

Armadillo Land

While at Brazos Bend, you may well come upon a nine-banded armadillo snuffling through the underbrush for beetles and other food. Though its armor plating makes it look something like a reptile, this intriguing and harmless little animal is a mammal; females give birth in spring to four, genetically identical young—all always of the same sex. Since the armadillo has poor eyesight, if you approach quietly from downwind, you often can come quite close to it as it goes about its business.

270

Angler on Elm Lake

Caddo Lake

15 miles northeast of Marshall via Tex. 43 and Tex. 2198

- 8,253 acres ● 903-679-3351
- Year-round ● Entrance fee
- Picturesque lake ● Nature and
hiking trails ● Canoeing

Bald cypresses in autumn

271

Heading east from Caddo Lake State Park, a motivated crow could be in Louisiana in just a few minutes: The state line is only 8 miles away, as that renowned arbiter of distance flies. This proximity is reflected in the park's environment, for the swampy bottomland here is far more like some Mississippi Delta bayou than like the pine woods and prairies of most of eastern Texas.

For the adventurous visitor, canoeing ranks as the most rewarding activity at this attractive park on the shore of **Big Cypress Bayou.** Gliding silently beneath moss-draped bald cypress, feeling the solitude, getting close-up looks at a barred owl or an alligator . . . Enjoy it all with this word of warning: Once you've left the immediate vicinity of the park and paddled downstream, take care not to get lost in the maze of channels on 32,000-acre **Caddo Lake.** (Before it was dammed early in this century, Caddo was the largest natural lake in Texas, and one of the largest in the South.)

You can rent canoes at a small store *(903-679-3743. March-Nov.; fee)* on **Saw Mill Pond.** Get advice here about the safest way to explore the area, and buy a map of the lake's "boat roads." If you don't trust your navigational skills, you can take a guided tour on a pontoon barge.

Don't neglect the park's nature and hiking trails, which link to form a loop of more than 3 miles. The paths meander over ridges and down into ravines, through a mixed forest of oak, sweetgum, hickory, elm, and pine. Birdwatching can be excellent here. At dawn in late April and early May, the woods ring with the songs and calls of dozens of species, from the impressive red-shouldered hawk to diminutive warblers.

Camping and Lodging

Caddo Lake has 20 tent and 28 RV sites, with shower facilities. Reservations advised in season; call the park. Camping fee. There are also 8 screened shelters and 9 cabins. For reservations call 512-389-8900.

❏ *CADDO LAKE STATE PARK, RTE. 2, BOX 15, KARNACK, TEXAS 75661*

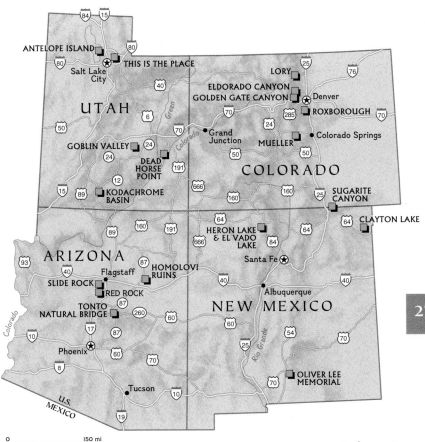

0 ——————— 150 mi
0 ——————— 300 km

Utah

Antelope Island
This Is The Place
Dead Horse Point
Goblin Valley
Kodachrome Basin

Arizona

Slide Rock
Red Rock
Tonto Natural Bridge
Homolovi Ruins

Colorado

Mueller
Roxborough
Golden Gate Canyon
Eldorado Canyon
Lory

New Mexico

Sugarite Canyon
Clayton Lake
Heron Lake and
  El Vado Lake
Oliver Lee Memorial

Goblin formation, Goblin Valley State Park, Utah

Mueller

3.5 miles south of Divide on Colo. 67

● 12,103 acres ● 719-687-2366 ● Year-round ● Entrance
fee ● Panoramic views of the Rockies ● Fourmile Creek
Canyon ● Hiking, mountain biking, horseback riding
● Wildlife watching ● Cross-country skiing

Near Outlook Ridge

Managed primarily to preserve its extensive wildlife population, Mueller State Park has retained much of the natural
character of the Rocky Mountain ecology. Punctuated by
granite outcrops, timbered hills and open grasslands give way
to the rugged terrain of Fourmile Canyon, shaped by Fourmile Creek. Throughout the park, overlooks take in this
spectacular setting, along with offering long views of the surrounding Sawatch and Sangre de Cristo mountain ranges.

Among the park's diversity of wildlife is a herd of 250
elk. If you visit Mueller when the elk calve in spring, you
can see the youngsters by hiking to **Elk Meadow,** about a
1.5-mile trip (one way) from the Elk Meadow trailhead. In
fall, bulls in rut bellow across the landscape. About 75
bighorn sheep reside near Dome Rock, and a larger herd
overwinters here. Other denizens include mule deer, rabbits,
mountain lions, and black bears.

Once the hunting grounds of Ute Indians, the region

was settled by pioneers in the 1860s. In the 1950s, the Mueller family owned a cattle ranch here, and later designated their property a game preserve. The site's importance as a bighorn habitat enticed the Nature Conservancy to buy the land in the 1970s, and in turn made it available to the state.

What to See and Do

Your first stop should be the **Big View area,** site of the new **Visitor Center.** From the parking area, look out on the 300-degree panorama of distant valleys and mountains. An open gazebo has plaques identifying the prominent features, including 14,110-foot **Pikes Peak.** The Visitor Center provides a park overview and describes its importance as a wildlife habitat.

The developed areas of the park are concentrated on only 400 acres; the best way to visit the remaining 11,703 acres is on foot, mountain bike, or horseback, along the nearly 85 miles of trails. If you're on a short visit, the 0.8-mile **Wapiti Self-Guided Nature Trail** *(Trailhead at Rock Pond)* offers a quick primer on the region's diverse ecosystems. The 1.8-mile **Outlook Ridge Trail** *(From Outlook Ridge trailhead)* winds past several panoramic overlooks including Raven Ridge, where you can look down into the beginning of the canyon formed by Fourmile Creek. The trail continues on to Lost Pond in the shade of aspen and conifer.

For a longer hike, consider the 9.6-mile route to **Dome Rock,** a popular trek into Fourmile Canyon. At one point you pass the remains of Jack Cabin Lodge, built in the early 1900s to show cattle to prospective buyers. Farther ahead, you come to Dome Rock, rising 800 feet above the canyon floor. The trail fords Fourmile Creek nine times, so be prepared to get your feet wet.

Camping

The park has 132 tent or RV sites, including 21 walk-in tent sites, with showers mid-May through October. Some sites open through winter. Reservations advised mid-May through September; call 303-470-1144 or 800-678-2267. Camping fee.

Nearby Sights

Don't miss the mostly unpaved, 19-mile drive up nearby **Pikes Peak** *(719-684-9383. Toll),* which ascends 6,310 feet through forest and wildflower-sprinkled meadows to tundra—the highest vertical rise of any Colorado mountain that you can drive. The historic gold rush towns of **Cripple Creek and Victor** *(Visitor information 719-689-2169 or 800-526-8777),* bustling with mine tours, gold panning, restored saloons, and gambling, lie 15 miles south of the park via Colo. 67.

❑ *Mueller State Park and Wildlife Area, P.O. Box 49, Divide, CO 80814*

Mountain Lion Encounters

Puma, cougar, ghost cat, mountain lion—by any name these big cats flourish in such wildlife-rich landscapes as Mueller State Park, where they have an array of elk and deer to choose from for dinner. Numbering some 3,000 in Colorado, mountain lions are powerful but secretive; human attacks are extremely rare, and usually come from inexperienced adolescents. If you meet a mountain lion, stay calm and try to back away. If the lion behaves aggressively, throw stones, branches, or anything else handy. Stand up straight, wave your arms, and make a lot of noise. Most mountain lions will be deterred.

275

Roxborough

Just south of Littleton, off Colo. 121

● 2,245 acres ● 303-973-3959 ● Year-round ● Entrance fee
● No pets ● No camping ● Red-rock formations
● Unusual mix of wildlife and plant life ● Hiking

You enter Roxborough State Park through a cleft canyon that looks like it was cleaved by a giant ax—providing a taste of the beautiful terrain that lies beyond this rocky gate. A cathedral of steeply tilted layers of red sandstone, with craggy fingers pointing skyward, Roxborough embraces more than 1.2 billion years of geologic history.

The park's showpiece is the Fountain Formation, a ridge made of debris eroded from the ancestral Rockies about 300 million years ago; the formation's striking red color is caused by small amounts of iron oxide minerals. The Lyons Formation, which overlies the Fountain Formation, is composed of beach sands deposited about 250 million years ago, after the ancestral Rockies were eroded away.

On the park's eastern edge, the Dakota Formation forms a long ridge, known locally as the Dakota Hogback for its resemblance to a hog's spine. The tan sandstones and gray mudstones of the Dakota Formation were deposited along a swampy coastal area during the age of the dinosaurs, about 125 to 100 million years ago. Paleontologists have found footprints and bones of several dinosaur species along the Dakota Hogback. Examples of these prints are on display in the Visitor Center.

The park lies in a transitional zone, where plains rolling in from the east meet the Front Range of the Rocky Mountains, sustaining a rich mix of plants and wildlife: Seven different plant communities are found here, ranging from riparian to prairie to a forest of ponderosa pine and Douglas-fir atop Carpenter Peak. It's not unusual to spot yucca and prickly pear thriving just steps away from wild roses and aspen. Wildlife includes deer, coyote, bobcat, and the occasional bear and elk. Golden eagles and prairie falcons nest along the ridges.

The park's unusual topology and hydrology encourage the growth of aspens at elevations a thousand feet lower than their usual range. Gambel oak, usually a shrub-size species, grows to a height of 40 feet in some park locations.

What to See and Do

First stop by the **George O'Malley Visitor Center** to examine the displays on park geology and wildlife, plus pick up maps and brochures. If you're only going to do one hike, take the **Fountain Valley Trail** (*Trailhead at Visitor Center*), a 2.2-mile loop through the Fountain and Lyons rock formations,

---

Tales of the Past

Until the early 1900s, Roxborough was known as Washington Park, for a sandstone formation that allegedly resembles the profile of the first president. In 1902 Henry Persse, then the owner of the property, changed the name to Roxborough, after the Persse family estate in Ireland. The 1903 Persse House now found along the Fountain Valley Trail was the first installment of a grand plan by Henry Persse to turn Roxborough into a major tourist destination resort, much like the Broadmoor in Colorado Springs, complete with golf course and luxury amenities. Unfortunately, one day Henry chased his windblown hat into a Denver street, stepped in front of an oncoming streetcar, and was killed. This effectively scotched his development plans.

Red-rock Fountain Formation

past the stone Persse House. Short detours to Fountain Valley and Lyons Overlooks provide panoramas of the entire Fountain Formation ridge. Another excellent hike is the easy 1.4-mile **Willow Creek Loop** *(Trailhead at Visitor Center)*. Strolling along the gentle creek beneath cottonwoods and willows, listen for the cheerful tunes of canyon wrens and spotted towhees.

For a more difficult hike, take the 6.4-mile, out-and-back trek to 7,200-foot **Carpenter Peak** *(Trailhead at Visitor Center)*, which includes an elevation gain of 1,000 feet—explaining the spectacular 360-degree view from atop. Along the way, look for signs of mountain lions and black bears. The very ambitious can continue from here along the famous 470-mile-long **Colorado Trail.**

❑ *Roxborough S.P., 4751 N. Roxborough Dr., Littleton, CO 80125*

Golden Gate Canyon

14 miles W of Golden on Golden Gate Canyon Rd.

● 14,400 acres ● 303-582-3707 ● Year-round ● Entrance fee
● Hiking, mountain biking, horseback riding

278

Just a half-hour's drive from Denver, Golden Gate Canyon shows you a classic, unspoiled Rocky Mountain environment, flanked by a rugged canyon. Gentle hiking trails explore lichen-covered granite outcrops, sunny meadows dotted with butterflies, lodgepole pine forests, and the arroyos of intermittent streams.

Roaming these lands is a representative sampling of Rockies wildlife, including mule deer, cottontail rabbit, coyote, beaver, and elk. Encounters with mountain lions and black bears are rare, but backcountry users are advised about possible meetings with these animals.

About a half million people flock to Golden Gate Canyon

Hillside meadow

annually, mostly on summer weekends. If you can hike the timbered trails during the week or in the off-season, you will have the park much to yourself, even during the busy summer.

What to See and Do

Stop first at the **Visitor Center** for an orientation to this large park, and to take in the exhibits about the ecology, wildlife, and history. Outside, the handicapped-accessible **Wilbur and Nellie Larkin Memorial Nature Trail** winds around a pond filled with rainbow trout.

From here, head immediately to the park's northwest corner to **Panorama Point.** As its name promises, this overlook offers a spectacular view of the soaring granite peaks of the Rocky Mountain Front Range, topped in eternal snows. A plaque at the overlook helps you pick out Longs Peak, Mount Evans, and Indian Peaks, and the views invite you to linger.

Next, it's best to get out of the car and into your hiking boots. The park features 35 miles of hiking trails, and you can't go wrong with any of them. Remember that you are more than a mile and a half above sea level, so it might be best to start out easy. The park recommends that you carry your own water; water from park streams should be treated and purified before drinking.

If you don't have much time and would like a relatively short, easy, and interesting hike, take the 1.8-mile **Horseshoe Trail,** beginning just down the road from the Visitor Center. You ascend through a forested drainage to grassy Frazer Meadow, in the shadow of craggy Tremont Mountain. A few switchbacks through steeper parts along the way make you feel like a Rocky Mountain hiking veteran. Dotted with harebells and brown-eyed Susans, Frazer Meadow entertains a variety of butterflies, including tiger swallowtail and the increasingly rare clodius parnassian. Here, too, you can view the remains of the Frazer homestead.

If you have more time, try the **Mountain Lion Trail** in the eastern portion of the park, a 6.7-mile loop to Windy Peak and a spectacular view of the plains to the east. City Lights Ridge along this trail looks out on Denver's lights (at night) and skyline on the plains below.

For those who want more of an adventure, the park's most difficult trail is the 2.8-mile (one-way) **Black Bear Trail,** which begins from Ralston Roost picnic area and trailhead near the Visitor Center and ascends to Frazer Meadow.

Camping

Golden Gate Canyon has 106 tent and RV sites (May-Oct.), with showers, and 35 tent-only sites (year-round). There are also 27 backcountry sites, including 4 Appalachian-style wood huts. Reservations advised in season; call 303-470-1144 or 800-678-2267. Camping fee. Backcountry sites are issued on a first-come, first-served basis at the Visitor Center.

❏ *Golden Gate Canyon State Park, 3873 Hwy. 46, Golden, CO 80403*

Rich History

First visited by Native Americans seeking game and berries, then by trappers looking for beaver in the early 19th century, the Golden Gate Canyon area first boomed with the gold discovery of 1859. No gold was ever found in the park itself; timber proved the treasure here, which built the gold camps of nearby Central City and Black Hawk. Golden Gate Canyon Road, which now brings visitors to the park, originally was a toll road for shipping gold out of and supplies into the gold fields. Eventually, when the gold petered out, ranching homesteads cropped up and the area became semi-quiet—that is, except for its flourishing moonshine and bootleg operations during Prohibition.

Eldorado Canyon

Just west of Eldorado Springs via Colo. 170

● 885 acres in two units ● 303-494-3943 ● Year-round
● Entrance fee ● No camping ● Wild canyon ● Rock climbing, hiking, mountain biking

The core of Eldorado Canyon State Park is a spectacular, narrow canyon rising 800 vertical feet from South Boulder Creek. Speckled with vivid multicolored lichen, its sunlit red rock seems to glitter, recalling the fabled city of El Dorado—"the Gilded One."

Long a shelter for Native Americans, Eldorado Canyon became a popular resort destination at the turn of the century for its scenery and artesian warm springs. Dwight and Mamie Eisenhower honeymooned here in 1916. One of the highlights of a visit in those days was the high-wire act of Ivy Baldwin, who walked a 400-foot-long wire strung 500 feet above the canyon floor. The canyon was preserved as a state park in 1978.

Mountain lion

280

Eldorado Canyon is a well-known rock-climbing site, with over 500 designated climbing routes. **Bastille Crack** is perhaps the region's most popular 5.8 climb (a climber's degree of difficulty, with 5.14 currently being the hardest), and the **Naked Edge,** at 5.11, was for a time considered the world's most difficult free climb. Even if you don't climb, watching the climbers attack the walls is entertainment in itself.

Begin your visit at the **Visitor Center,** where exhibits detail the canyon's natural history. Then, if time is short, at the very least hike the 1.4-mile round-trip **Fowler Trail** (*Trailhead 0.5 mile east of Visitor Center*), which follows a contour of the canyon, offering spectacular views of the plains beyond; on the canyon's opposite side you can see climbers advancing up Redgarden Wall. The trail is wheelchair accessible as far as the park boundary.

If you have more time, take the moderately steep, 3.4-mile round-trip **Rattlesnake Gulch Trail** (*From Fowler Trailhead*) for views of the canyon and plains, up to the Crags Hotel ruin. The hotel, part of the original resort property, burned down in 1912. The trail leads a little farther to an overlook of the Continental Divide, 1,200 breathtaking feet above the trailhead.

The **Crescent Meadows** portion of the park—featuring hiking and mountain-biking trails that wind through high, rolling meadows—is detached from the main canyon section and is most easily reached by car. However, there is a hiking connection via the **Eldorado Canyon Trail,** a difficult 9-mile out-and-back trek that gains over 1,000 feet in elevation in under 5 miles. Ask for directions at the Visitor Center.

❏ *Eldorado Canyon State Park, P.O. Box B, Eldorado Springs, Colorado 80025*

Lory

7 miles northwest of Fort Collins via US 287

● **2,479 acres** ● **970-493-1623** ● **Year-round** ● **Entrance fee** ● **Hiking, mountain biking, horseback riding,** ● **Wildlife watching**

Charles A. Lory State Park sits in the Rocky Mountain foothills outside Fort Collins, where the grassy plains to the east make an abrupt transition to a lower montane forest of ponderosa pine, Douglas-fir, and aspen. The park fills a long valley that tips toward Horsetooth Reservoir, whose shimmering blue waters peek through low, red-rock canyon walls. Onetime ranchland, this wild landscape was purchased by the state in 1967 and named for Dr. Charles A. Lory, president of Colorado State University from 1909 to 1940.

Lory's chief attraction is its 30 miles of hiking trails. The park's marquee trail is the 1.7-mile trip up **Arthur's Rock.** Beginning at the end of the park road in a narrow granite canyon, the moderate-to-difficult trail then switchbacks up the granite outcrop named for an early settler. From here, you find a panoramic view of the plains to the east, taking in most of Fort Collins and Loveland below.

If you are short on time but still want a flavor of the park, take the **Well Gulch Nature Trail,** an easy, 1.5-mile self-guided tour of the area's vegetation and ecology. It ends at the Timber Trail, providing the option of continuing on through thick forest.

The **Waterfall Trail,** located just inside the park entrance, offers a short (only one-tenth of a mile), pleasant stroll beside a series of small waterfalls (*spring and early summer*). In May wildflowers such as harebell and penstemon flourish along the way, and wetland vegetation thrives in summertime.

Camping

There are 6 backcountry sites; permits are required and are available at the park entrance on a first-come, first-served basis. Camping fee.

❏ *Charles A. Lory State Park, 708 Lodgepole Dr., Bellvue, CO 80512*

Sugarite Canyon

11.5 miles east of Raton via N. Mex. 72 and N. Mex. 526

● 3,420 acres ● 505-445-5607 ● Year-round ● 1,200-foot-deep canyon ● Wildflowers ● Boating, hiking, fishing (license required) ● Cross-country skiing, ice skating

One of New Mexico's prettiest parks, Sugarite Canyon abuts Colorado in mountainous high country where abundant water creates an unusually lush mix of ecosystems: stands of fir and aspen on north-facing slopes; riparian grasslands on the meadowlike canyon floor; scrub oak and ponderosa pine on sunnier, drier south slopes—much of these terrains colorfully stippled by exuberant wildflower blooms in spring and summer.

The 1,200-foot-deep canyon was once hunted by the Ute and Apache, who came for its wild turkey (still abundant), deer, and beaver. From 1910 to 1941, mining sustained the Sugarite Coal Camp, swelling its population to a peak of 1,000, and bequeathing to the park an evocative collection of tumble-down stone buildings and foundations.

What to See and Do

Take N. Mex. 72 east and north from Raton, bearing left after 4.8 miles onto N. Mex. 526. You'll soon reach the **Visitor Center,** where superb exhibits present Sugarite's natural and human history and showcase its plant and animal life.

The historical accounts deepen your appreciation of the polyglot culture that briefly flourished in the coal-mining camp whose ruins adjoin. Take the 1-mile **Coal Camp Trail** from the Visitor Center along rattling Chicorico Creek, which bisects the park and carries runoff from the two lakes to the north. Crossing it, you'll find what remains of the camp, populated mainly by laborers from the Far East and Europe. The path soon forks: The Coal Camp Trail continues to an abandoned mine, then loops back to the parking area.

Back in your car, continue north along the Chicorico past tiny **Lake Alice,** whose serenity is preserved by a boating restriction. Gasoline motors are banned on larger **Lake Maloya,** farther north. Both lakes are stocked with rainbow trout, and Lake Maloya has a fishing pier specially designed for flycasters in wheelchairs.

About a mile north of Lake Maloya, a turnoff leads to **Soda Pocket Campground,** where 25 sites stretch over a half-mile of oaks, ponderosa pines, and meadows, with pleasing views of volcanic cones and hills to the south. Take time to walk the easy .25-mile **Vista Grande Nature Trail,** which loops away from the campground's southwest corner. Self-

---

Pittsburgh of New Mexico

Raton—Spanish for mouse—was a sleepy stopover on the Santa Fe Trail until 1879, when the new Atchison, Topeka & Santa Fe Railroad established a repair station there. Within a year the town claimed 3,000 citizens. Proximity to rails made for easy shipment of traditional building materials rare in the Southwest. Raton soon boasted so many Eastern-style buildings that boosters proclaimed it the "Pittsburgh of New Mexico." Leaner decades followed, saving Raton's antique architecture from the demolition ball. The result is a downtown historic district of unusual authenticity.

282

guiding pamphlets keyed to numbered markers reveal why Sugarite has such a diversity of wildlife—including cougar, bear, and elk. The trail ends on a knoll where you can sit down on a bench and savor a grand view of the canyon. It's a bit arduous, but the nearby .25-mile **Little Horse Mesa Trail** to the 8,300-foot-high caprock of Little Horse Mesa ends with 360-degree vistas extending north into Colorado.

If you can stay at least a day, consider the moderately strenuous **Ponderosa Ridge/ Opportunity Trail,** a 6-mile circle that leaves Soda Pocket's north end and passes through a succession of environments to panoramic canyon views from 8,400 feet, the park's highest viewpoint. (In winter, the Opportunity Trail segment of the loop, which begins at Lake Maloya, is an excellent route for cross-country skiing and snowshoeing.)

Elk

Camping
There are 41 tent and RV sites, with nearby showers. Reservations advised in season; call 888-667-2757. Camping fee.
❑ *Sugarite Canyon State Park, NCR 63, P.O. Box 386, Raton, NM 87740*

Clayton Lake

12 miles northwest of Clayton via N. Mex. 370 and N. Mex. 455

● **570 acres** ● **505-374-8808** ● **Year-round** ● **Dinosaur tracks**
● **Rock garden** ● **Nature trail** ● **Fishing (license required)**
● **Birdwatching**

A remarkably well-preserved dinosaur trackway with over 500 footprints left in mud some 100 million years ago (one of the most extensive in North America) distinguish this out-of-the-way fishing spot and migratory bird refuge. Set on the mile-

Dinosaur tracks

284

high western edge of the Great Plains among rolling grasslands, volcanic rocks, and sandstone bluffs, the park embraces a 170-acre lake noted for trout, catfish, bass, and walleye fishing from April through October. (New Mexico's record walleye, a giant of 16 pounds and 9 ounces, was hooked here in 1989.) A dam across Seneca Creek started the reservoir in 1955, creating a stopover for mallards, Canada geese, pintails, teals, and other waterfowl. Protective hillsides provide a windbreak, and sandy swimming beaches notch the lake's rocky shoreline.

Heading toward the park from Clayton, the two-lane road wiggles through terrain that's scenic in a wide-open-spaces way, evoking the isolation 19th-century travelers must have felt as they traversed these lonely grasslands on the Santa Fe Trail's Cimarron Cutoff. (The alternative route forked south from Kansas through the Oklahoma panhandle, trading greater risk of Indian attack for a route speedier than the main trail's axle-busting wagon path over Raton Pass.)

Inside the entrance gate, bear right past the park office to the parking lot beside the boat launching ramp. (Sailboats, canoes, and fishing scows are permitted, but motorized craft are restricted to trolling speeds.) Walk the half-mile trail across the dam to the **Dinosaur Pavilion interpretive center.** An adjoining boardwalk affords a close look at the tracks, impressions from the Mesozoic era, the age of the dinosaurs. The best times for viewing the tracks are early morning and late afternoon on sunny days, when shadows darken their depressions. The fearsome footprints are preserved in stone that was once the muddy shoreline of a primordial seaway running north from the Gulf of Mexico to what is now Canada. At least eight species planted their three-toed feet here. Some were plant-eaters, some preyed on their cousins, and at least one, the birdlike, leather-winged pterodactyl, looked down on the scuffle from aloft.

Camping

The park has 35 tent sites, with showers. Reservations advised in season; call 888-667-2757. Camping fee.

❏ *Clayton Lake State Park, Star Route, Seneca, New Mexico 88437*

Heron Lake
and El Vado Lake

Heron Lake: 5 miles southwest of Los Ojos via US 84 and N. Mex. 95. El Vado Lake: 21 miles southwest of Tierra Amarilla via N. Mex. 531 and N. Mex. 112

● 10,012 acres (Heron Lake) and 4,948 acres (El Vado Lake) ● 505-588-7470 (Heron Lake) and 505-588-7247 (El Vado Lake) ● Year-round ● Two scenic lakes ● Hiking ● Swimming, sailing, boating, windsurfing, fishing (license required), Jet skiing ● Birdwatching

A scenic day hike links the adjoining lakes of Heron and El Vado in northern New Mexico's forested mountain country, each surrounded by its own state park. On Heron Lake, a "no-wake" speed limit makes the 5,900-acre reservoir especially popular with flycasters, sailors, windsurfers, swimmers, and campers who value tranquility. There are no speed limits on 3,200-acre El Vado Lake, where motorboaters, water-skiers, and Jet skiers roil the water from spring through autumn. Come winter, cross-country skiers, snowshoers, and dogsledders mush into the parks' snowbound timberlands.

Both lakes serve as important wintering grounds for bald eagles, which you may see perched on snags along the water's edge or floating by overhead. Preying on other birds, snakes, small animals, and fish, these majestic predators boast a wingspan up to 8 feet. Other birds to watch for: red-tailed hawks, white-throated swifts, ospreys, common mergansers, and Western flycatchers.

What to See and Do

Primitive backcountry roads and the Rio Chama canyon make it difficult to access one park directly from the other. It's quicker and easier to backtrack to US 84 and loop around.

If you prefer peace and a wider selection of campsites, make **Heron Lake** your destination. Southbound from Los Ojos on N. Mex. 95, watch for signs indicating the turnoff into **Willow Creek Recreation Area,** the reservoir's prime camping spot. There is a paved boat ramp here, and another just past the dam near the Ridge Rock campground. If you brought a boat, you'll find that both lakes have serpentine shorelines with many sheltered coves, where trout and salmon fishing is good. On Heron, windsurfers usually first check the breezes off the Island View, Brushy Point, and Salmon Run camping areas east of the dam.

You can rent a canoe or boat in Rutheron from JR's Rental

You Say You Hate Camping?

You say you had a miserable camping experience years ago? It's time to try it again. Improved equipment has greatly reduced the labor associated with outdoor adventure. Forget the unwieldy canvas tents and heavy sleeping bags you shivered in at camp. Today's tents set up as easily as folding tables, and modern sleeping bags are as toasty as comforters. Forget leaky air mattresses that seldom made it through the night; new-fangled sleeping pads inflate themselves. And for the ultimate luxury, fill a plastic-bag "solar shower" with water, leave it in the sun, and count on a hot shower at night.

285

Heron Lake's south shore

(505-588-7274), located at the rustic Stone House Lodge near **El Vado Lake**'s north end off N. Mex. 95. Built in 1935 by the Santa Fe Elks Club, the lodge is now privately operated, and a pleasant place to dine. In winter it's a bustling base camp for parties of cross-country skiers.

El Vado Lake's waterskiing season lasts from May through September, with skiers generally favoring the lake's northeastern arm. Conventional wisdom among flycasters is that the odds are best at the dam and just below it, where the Rio Chama runs free again. (A 4-pound, 6-ounce Coho salmon reeled in here in 1972 still holds the state record for the species.)

If you're in good shape (remember that Heron stands at 7,186-feet elevation) and have a day, walk the 5.5-mile **Rio Chama Trail** from the southwest corner of Heron Lake to El Vado Lake. Rated highly by naturalists, the trail explores the river canyon—crossing the Rio Chama on a suspended bridge—then winds overland past lofty viewpoints and meadows where quaking aspen flutter in the breeze. The trail is fairly strenuous, with occasionally slippery footing across rocky terrain. Sturdy hiking shoes are a must.

Camping

Heron Lake has 111 tent and 139 RV sites (some with hook-ups), with showers. Another 250 primitive sites are situated west of the spillway. At El Vado Lake there are 70 tent and 20 RV sites, with showers. Reservations advised in season; contact both parks at 888-667-2757. Camping fee.

❏ EL VADO LAKE STATE PARK, P.O. BOX 29, TIERRA AMARILLA, NM 87575; HERON LAKE STATE PARK, P.O. BOX 159, LOS OJOS, NM 87551

Oliver Lee Memorial

12 miles south of Alamogordo via US 54, then 5 miles east on Dog Canyon Rd. (County Rd. A16)

● 180 acres ● 505-437-8284 ● Year-round ● Desert canyon oasis ● Hiking ● Birdwatching ● Nature trail

A west-trending cut in the massive 35-mile-long Sacramento Mountain Escarpment, Dog Canyon—Cañon del Perro—alerts the instinct at first sight: From the Tularosa Basin's sweep of yucca, mesquite, and prickly pear cactus, you sense a natural stronghold. Entering the canyon, you find an attenuated oasis between steep cliffs, watered by seeps and springs, and a rocky stairway into the piney Sacramento and Guadalupe Mountain uplands 3,000 feet above.

A hiking trail traces a route already in use some 4,000 years ago by New Mexico's original desert people, following the creek up past wild orchids and ferns to grassy benchlands, where willow, cottonwood, and ash flourish. Birds and wildlife thrive here, once an impregnable Apache enclave. Oliver Lee is made all the more inviting by this verdant center, highly unusual in this generally parched region.

287

Start your visit at **Park Headquarters** beside the canyon mouth, where a .25-mile **nature trail** showcases native plants. Exhibits inside explain the chasm's geology, identify its abundant wildlife, and sketch its most significant historical events, which include decisive battles between Mescalero Apache and the U.S. Cavalry. Archaeological artifacts date from prehistoric human settlement through the late 19th-century homesteading era.

Wear sturdy shoes, take water, and plan on devoting a half-day to walk the strenuous 4.2-mile **Dog Canyon National Recreational Trail,** which climbs from Park Headquarters (elevation 4,400 feet) to the escarpment's 7,550-foot-high rim. But even the first half-mile brings rewards, climbing 500 feet to the grassy First Bench, a pleasant place to picnic.

Inquire about weekend tours of the reconstructed **ranch house** of Oliver Lee, a controversial cattle baron and state lawmaker who made the canyon his headquarters in 1893, and figured large in New Mexico affairs until his death in 1941.

Camping

The park has 44 tent and RV sites, with showers. Reservations advised in season; call 888-667-2757. Camping fee.

❏ *OLIVER LEE MEMORIAL S.P., 409 DOG CANYON RD., ALAMOGORDO, NM 88310*

Roadrunner, New Mexico's state bird

Slide Rock

7 miles north of Sedona, off US 89A

● 43 acres ● 520-282-3034 ● Year-round ● Parking fee
● No pets ● No camping ● Red-rock canyon ● Natural
water slide ● Apple orchard ● Nature walks ● Trout fishing
(license required), hiking, birdwatching

People who urge you to visit Sedona often cite the scenic drive through the piney corridor of 12-mile-long **Oak Creek Canyon** as the primary reason. US 89A follows the stream's 2,000-foot-deep cut into the Colorado Plateau's rock shelf, skirting sheer-sided white, yellow, and red sandstone and limestone cliffs representing some three million years of erosion. About halfway through the gorge, the highway passes **Slide Rock,** one of Arizona's most popular natural playgrounds, best known for a 70-foot-long water chute

Sliding down Slide Rock

worn by eons of water coursing over sandstone. Come autumn at Slide Rock, nearby Hospital Canyon's dense groves of Douglas-fir, Gambel oak, bigtooth maple, sycamore, and Arizona walnut burst into vivid colors with the cymbal-clashing bombast of an orchestra.

Traffic through Oak Creek Canyon is often heavy from spring through fall, making it difficult to savor the wooded beauty and vertical drama of the enclosing cliffs. Leave your car at Slide Rock, take your camera (and a pair of old jeans and shoes if you want to try the chilly water and the not-very-smooth slide), and walk the .75-mile trail to **Hospital Canyon** behind the park. (On October Sundays at 1 p.m., ranger-guided Canyon Colors walks tour the hidden transept.)

Early 20th-century homesteader Frank Pendley's legacy to Slide Rock is an **apple orchard,** still producing over a dozen varieties harvested in autumn and sold at the park's snack bar. History tours of his idyllic farm are given on Saturdays spring through fall.

Throughout the year **Oak Creek** creates a natural refuge noisily abounding with birdlife, the variety of which is especially apparent to those with binoculars and a field guide. Arrive early on Sunday mornings from April through November for ranger-guided bird walks, which leave the Visitor Center area at 8 a.m. During the summer, check for other organized activities, including the Friday morning Natural History Walkabout.

The park is a day-use area only; however, there are several campgrounds in the surrounding **Coconino National Forest** (520-282-4119).

❑ SLIDE ROCK STATE PARK, P.O. BOX 10358, SEDONA, ARIZONA 86339

Red Rock

4 miles west of Sedona, off US 89A via Lower Red Rock Loop Rd.

- ● 286 acres ● 520-282-6907 ● Entrance fee ● No pets
- ● No camping ● Nature Preserve ● Native plant garden
- ● Hiking ● Wildlife viewing, birdwatching

After a visit to Red Rock, an Oak Creek Canyon recreation spot only 12 miles from Slide Rock, you might call it an outdoor living museum, or think of it as one big interpretive nature trail. Biologists classify it as a diverse riparian habitat, rich as Eden in plant- and wildlife, and once a hunting ground of the Sinagua, Hohokom, and Yavapai peoples. Park literature dubs Red Rock a center for environmental education. In fact it is all of these, in a setting that begs to have its picture taken.

Ancient Gardening

Planting seeds in holes dug with sticks, the Southwest's early farming tribes grew varieties of corn, beans, squash, sunflowers, gourds, amaranth, and devils claw. They used sunflower oil for cooking, and hollow gourds for bowls, scoops, cups, canteens, and other containers. Amaranth seeds mixed with other seeds thickened stews and soups, and were ground for flour. Black devils claw fibers were woven into baskets for decoration. When boiled, they produced a deep black dye.

For a look at what the garden of a seasonal encampment at **Red Rock** probably looked like, visit the park's Native Plant Garden, sowed with native seeds using traditional methods.

289

As its name implies, the park is framed by sheer cliffs of rust-red Hermit Formation sandstone that distinguishes the Sedona region, the product of iron oxide-rich silt deposited some 270 million years ago at the bottom of a primordial sea.

290

Oak Creek Canyon

The park has ten nature trails, each exploring a distinctive life zone. Ranger-guided nature walks leave from the Visitor Center every morning at 10.

For a self-guided walking tour amounting to a sampler of Red Rock's diverse environments, take the 0.5-mile **Smoke Trail.** You wander past Bonpland willow and Arizona alder, ascending from one life zone to another. Drier, higher zones bring netleaf hackberry, whose leaves and branches local tribes boiled to produce red and brown dyes. Then comes the region's trademark red-earth, dusky-green pinyon-juniper and scrub oak habitat. Rock faces near the trail's end bear petroglyphs, art probably the work of Sinagua people, who, it's believed, camped here seasonally to hunt, fish, and perhaps farm between AD 600 and 1200.

If your visit falls on a Saturday, call ahead to ask about the ranger-guided hike to **Eagle's Nest overlook,** Red Rock's loftiest vantage point, and arguably its most impressive view.

Red Rock is a day-use area only; however, nearby campgrounds in the **Coconino National Forest** (520-282-4119) offer similar terrain.

❑ RED ROCK STATE PARK, 4050 RED ROCK LOOP RD., SEDONA, ARIZONA 86336

Tonto Natural Bridge

13 miles northwest of Payson, off Ariz. 87

● 160 acres ● 520-476-4202 ● Year-round ● Parking fee
● No camping ● Natural rock bridge ● Nature trails
● Swimming, wading ● Historic building

Whether or not it truly is the world's largest natural travertine span, Tonto Natural Bridge's massive arch over a 400-foot-long tunnel cut by spring-fed Pine Creek could hardly be more impressive. Nor could the park's setting, in a small, steep, forested valley notched by the stream's narrow canyon, create a more appealing, hidden-away-from-the-world feeling.

The Tonto Apache had used the site as a seasonal farming and hunting camp for nearly four centuries when, in 1877, a nomadic Scottish gold prospector named Gowan escaped attacking warriors by darting into the dark passage and hiding on a ledge inside. Venturing out three days later, he found the all-but-inaccessible valley, with its dripping grotto, grassy meadows, and cool forest so inviting that he returned in 1882 to file a homestead claim. In 1898 kinfolk named Goodfellow emigrated from Scotland to join him. Their pack burros could barely negotiate the narrow, 3-mile-long trail into the valley; most of their possessions had to be lowered down the 500-foot slope with rope. (The steep entrance road bars trailers or motorhomes over 16 feet.)

The bridge's fame spread, attracting visitors, and by 1908 the Goodfellow clan had carved out a cliff-hanging entrance road and built a guest lodge on the meadow below. In 1927 new owners replaced the original inn with a larger, handsomely airy hostel now serving as a small museum, displaying antiques and Gowan-Goodfellow family heirlooms; it's listed on the National Register of Historic Places.

What to See and Do

A day-use area only, the park is probably the most appealing public picnic spot in central Arizona's forested high country. (The elevation here is about 4,500 feet.) Leave your car in a parking area and walk to the renovated inn for a glimpse of the genteel styles of old-time "guest ranching" and an historical overview. (The lodge may be

Bridge-building the Natural Way

Tonto Natural Bridge is actually a part of the floor of the valley that surrounds it. Long ago, spring water high in concentrations of calcium carbonate laid down the bowl's flat travertine floor, across which primordial Pine Creek flowed. Some creek water seeped down through the rock, eventually opening up a small subterranean fissure. Erosion continued below as more travertine was deposited above, eventually channeling the stream's entire flow beneath the slowly thickening bridge. Geologists trace the beginning of the phenomenon back 1.7 billion years.

291

Gambel's quail

toured by reservation; call ahead.) If possible, include an alfresco lunch on the meadow flanking the inn.

Park trails are short, but steep and rough in places. Don sturdy shoes before you embark on the 0.5-mile **Gowan Loop Trail,** which winds down from the roof of the bridge into **Pine Creek Canyon,** where an observation deck permits a dramatic view upstream through the passage, yawning 150 feet at its widest. From creekside you're looking up nearly 200 feet to the top of the bridge. You may explore the drippy tunnel, but rangers advise using caution, as the passage is dim and the footing slippery.

The 300-foot-long **Waterfall Trail** from the picnic area adjoining the lodge stops short of the stream beside a small cascade and a cave similar to the one inside the tunnel where Gowan hid. For a leafy creekbank idyll, walk the 0.5-mile **Pine Creek Trail** beginning southeast of the lodge parking lot. You'll quickly descend into a cool, dim, and peaceful fairyland of overhanging ferns and trickling springs.

The park is a day-use facility only. The nearby Houston Mesa Campground in **Tonto National Forest** (*Near junction of Ariz. 87 and Rte. 199*) has 75 tent and RV sites. For reservations and information call 520-474-7900 or 800-280-2267. Camping fee.

❏ TONTO NATURAL BRIDGE STATE PARK, P.O. BOX 1245, PAYSON, AZ 85547

Homolovi Ruins

5 miles northeast of Winslow via I-40 and Ariz. 87

● 4,500 acres ● 520-289-4106 ● Year-round ● Ancient Indian ruins ● Guided archaeological tours ● Hiking, wildlife viewing

Four major ruins on Arizona's nearly treeless high desert grassland at Homolovi (Ho-MO-low-vee) composed an important farming and trading settlement built by the Hisat'sinom, ancestors of the Hopi people, who lived here from about AD 1200 to 1400.

The settlement's name means "place of the little hills" or "where the hills come down toward the river" (in this case, the Little Colorado River). Since excavation began in 1896, archaeologists have identified over 340 sites including pit houses, kivas, campsites, places of agricultural activity, petroglyphs, and "lithic scatters" of hand-worked stone and potsherds.

At an elevation of 4,850 feet, the park is open year-round, but winter often brings treacherous highway

---

292

Where State Parks Come From

Typically, the idea forms among ordinary citizens fearing the loss of a cherished resource. In the case of **Homolovi,** Hopi tribal members and non-Indian locals believed the depredations of private pot-hunters—one used a back-hoe to speed his looting—threatened to destroy the site's archaeological record. Most of the land was already state-owned; what was needed were funds to develop it. A governor's interest in Hopi culture led to official support, and in 1993 Homolovi became Arizona's first "archaeological" state park.

conditions to surrounding mountains. If possible, plan your visit for June or July, when archaeologists work key sites while you watch over their dusty shoulders. Selected findings from each summer's work are displayed during Archaeology Day on the last Saturday in July.

Introduce yourself to Homolovi at the **Visitor Center,** where exhibits chronicle the site's history, and display significant artifacts recovered here.

Then tour the two main ruins, **Homolovi I and II,** by following self-guided trails posted with interpretive information developed in cooperation with the Hopi. At wheelchair-accessible **Homolovi II,** a collapsed pueblo believed to have enclosed a thousand chambers, five rooms and a rectangular ceremonial kiva chamber have been excavated and stabilized to provide an authentic, if fragmentary, picture of the adobe trading and cotton-growing center, which peaked in population between 1340 and 1380. Catastrophic flooding is believed to have caused Homolovi's abandonment, driving its people north to Hopi Mesas.

293

Half- and one-day workshops *(fee),* some offering college credit, are offered throughout the year. Subjects range from storytelling, traditional seed planting, gardening, and harvesting presented by Hopi elders, to ranger-led birdwatching and wildlife viewing field trips.

Camping

The park has 53 tent and RV campsites, with shower facilities May through September. Available

Pueblo ruins

on a first-come, first-served basis. Camping fee.

❏ *Homolovi Ruins State Park, HC 63, Box 5, Winslow, Arizona 86047*

Antelope Island

35 miles north of Salt Lake City, off Utah 127

● 28,022 acres ● 801-773-2941 ● Year-round ● Entrance fee ● Buffalo ranch ● Scenic loop drive ● Saltwater bathing ● Boating, birdwatching, hiking, biking, horseback riding ● Wildlife viewing

Playa patterns, left by receding lake waters

294

The biggest of the Great Salt Lake's ten isles, with an area roughly twice that of Manhattan Island, Utah's largest state park rises nearly 2,400 feet above the saline sea, its treeless tan rumple of rocky ridges, hilly grasslands, and flat sagebrush prairie tethered to the mainland by a 7.2-mile causeway. Visitor activities are largely confined to a 2,000-acre area at the island's northern reach, traversed by paved and gravel roads and trails. For urbanites escaping the Ogden–Salt Lake City sprawl, the 8-mile paved scenic loop through the park is a popular day trip. The lake's extreme salinity (six to eight times that of the sea) makes for unusually buoyant floating.

Members of the Great Salt Lake band of Utah's prehistoric Fremont people living in the Wasatch foothills probably hunted the island's mule deer, waterfowl, and game birds. Described in the 1820s by trapper Jim Bridger and French explorer Étienne Provot, it went unnamed by newcomers until the 1840s, when low water permitted frontiersman John C. Frémont and his guide, Kit Carson, to spur horses across what is usually briny shallows. Spotting pronghorn antelope (reintroduced to the island a few years ago), they christened it accordingly.

They might have called it Bobcat Island, or Coyote Island, for these creatures also roam its north-south trending ridgelines and slopes, along with myriad other small creatures. Though not native to the isle, American bison were introduced in 1893, and about 600 graze here. In March 1997 a small herd of bighorn sheep was placed on the island.

Ranching began in 1848, when Mormon pioneers drove cattle out to the island and settler Fielding Garr claimed a knoll overlooking the southeastern shore and built an adobe ranch house. The following year he led his wife and six children across the threshold, creating a monument to Utah's strong family tradition. Occupied until about a decade ago, the stolid residence became the state's oldest continually inhabited pioneer-built house.

What to See and Do

From I-15, take the Syracuse exit west to the 7.2-mile Davis County Causeway, which has extra-wide bike lanes for pedaling or roller-blading from the "mainland." (If you don't have a bicycle, but have the inclination, check phone listings for bike rental concessionaires in the Clearfield/Syracuse area east of the causeway.)

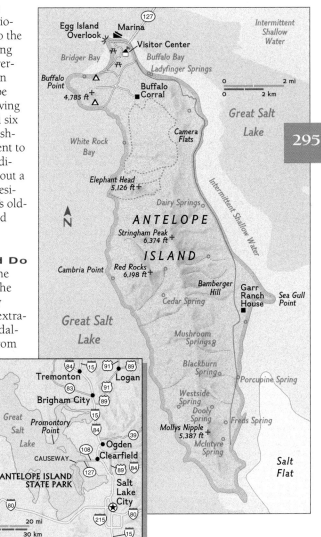

295

In recent years on selected weekends, parts of the island's more mountainous, ecologically fragile southern reach have been opened to visitors. Plans call for increased access and an enlarged trail system, including paving the road as far as the Fielding Garr ranch house. Currently, about 20 miles of trails cross over into the limited-use area, permitting hikers, horseback riders, and bicyclists to venture south.

The causeway road passes the **marina** and follows the island's northern shoreline. Watch for signs to the **Visitor Center,** which has an excellent little historical and natural history museum. Here you'll find maps of the park's system of roads and trails, current information about access to the island's southern reach—usually off-limits—and, from March to October, privately operated weekend tours of the **Garr Ranch House,** located 11 miles south of the Visitor Center. (In 1998 the ranch house is scheduled to be opened on a daily basis.)

Continue on to **Egg Island Overlook,** where an easy .25-mile trail leads to a promontory with a view of **Egg Island,** a seagull and migratory bird rookery in Bridger Bay. Picnic tables here make the overlook an appealing place to linger and scout the long white beach fronting Bridger Bay. (It's not sand you'll see, but tiny rock pellets called oolites, deposited by brine shrimp and encrusted with calcium carbonate crystals to form their distinctive oval shape.)

Coming off the hill, you'll pass a succession of picnic areas along the Bridger Bay strand, Antelope's most popular swimming and sunbathing spot. A spur road leads to Bridger Bay Campground. From here, a 3-mile trail winds south along the lakeshore to a group camping ground at **White Rock Bay.**

Be sure to drive up to **Buffalo Point Overlook,** where the specialty of the café there is broiled buffalo burgers. You can burn off some of the calories by walking the short but steep .25-mile trail up to 4,785-foot-high **Buffalo Point,** a lookout with a 360-degree panorama.

Most of the park's bison range freely in the island's southern section, keeping their distance from visitors. About 20 of the shaggy brown beasts are kept ready for close-ups in the **Buffalo Corral,** where they graze with a ponderous dignity.

Camping

The park has 2 campgrounds, one at Bridger Bay with 13 primitive tent and RV sites, and the other on White Rock Bay with 5 large group sites. Advance reservations are recommended through the park. Camping fee.

❑ ANTELOPE ISLAND STATE PARK, 4528 WEST 1700 SOUTH, SYRACUSE, UTAH 84075

Still Untamed

Though Great Salt Lake averages only 14 feet deep (its greatest known depth is 40 feet), fluctuating water levels have played havoc with park access. The lake's surface normally stands at 4,200 feet and covers an area roughly 75 by 30 miles, about 1,500 square miles of brine. In 1983, however, record Wasatch Range runoff flooded the causeway, closing Antelope Island for a decade. (Levels peaked 12 feet above normal in 1987, claiming an additional 1,000 square miles of shoreline.) A massive pumping program diverted water to an adjoining evaporation basin, and all's well again—for now.

This Is The Place

2601 Sunnyside Ave., Salt Lake City

● 400 acres ● 801-584-8391 ● Year-round ● Entrance fee
● No camping ● Old Deseret Village (April to early Oct.;
adm. fee) ● This Is The Place Monument ● Interpretive
exhibits ● Museum ● Biking, wildlife viewing, cross-
country skiing

According to the lore of the Church of Jesus Christ of Latter-day Saints, here in 1847 Brigham Young proclaimed the Salt
Lake Basin the promised haven from religious persecution. The
park is named for words attributed to the church leader as he
gazed west from the 4,900-foot-high overlook fronting Emigration Canyon, the end of the 1,400-mile Mormon Pioneer
National Historical Trail from Nauvoo, Illinois. An imposing
monument commemorates the colonists' trek, and its tableau
of bronze statuary honors Utah's native Paiute, Goshute,
Shoshone, and Ute people; Spanish explorers; and "mountain
men," shaggy scouts of the Westward Movement.

Young envisioned a Mormon State of Deseret reaching to
the Pacific. Its first sproutings included the pioneer-era
buildings moved from around the Salt Lake Valley and preserved here at Old Deseret Village, re-creating a settlement
typical of Utah's mid-19th-century newcomers.

297

First take in the **Visitor Center,** where exhibits provide an
historical overview of the long trek from
Illinois, and a film describes the village and
its agricultural and community life.

Then wander among the adobe
houses, shops, schools, churches, and
outbuildings of **Old Deseret Village,**
and chat up its citizens, living history
docents in period dress and pursuing the
tasks of daily life in Utah's pre-railroad
days. (In summer, Young's peaked-roof
farmhouse is open for tours.)

If time permits, take a stroll into
Emigration Canyon along a footpath
tracing the final 4.2-miles of the **Mor-
mon Pioneer National Historical
Trail.** Or try the **Bonneville Shoreline
Trail,** eventually scheduled to run 90
miles along ancient Lake Bonneville.
The current portion goes from the park
past the University of Utah toward the
foothills of the Wasatch Range
❏ *This Is The Place State Park, 2601 Sunnyside*
Ave., Salt Lake City, Utah 84108-1453

This Is The Place Monument

Dead Horse Point

31 miles from Moab via Utah 191 and Utah 313

● 5,362 acres ● 801-259-2614 ● Year-round ● Entrance fee
● Interpretive museum ● Hiking

Dead Horse Point

Carved mainly by the Colorado and Green Rivers, the vast, labyrinthine wilderness of southeast Utah's canyonlands is so impressive to the appreciative, so provocative to the curious, and so enticing to the adventurous that it's no wonder the panoramas from 5,900-foot-high Dead Horse Point are often praised as the most spectacular of any Beehive State park. Add a scenic drive from Moab through sand and sagebrush canyons, past cliffs and spires of liver-hued Kayenta sandstone, and you have one of Utah's most memorable day trips—ending with long views sweeping some 50 miles south across Canyonlands National Park to a horizon steepled by the Henry, La Sal, and Abajo Mountains. Easy walking trails along the mesa flirt with the edge of the 2,000-foot-deep gorge, leading to a half-dozen overlooks of some of the Southwest's least-accessible public land.

Wranglers once corralled wild mustangs on the long, narrow rimrock promontory for which the park is named: Local lore holds that culls, or "broomtails," left there unfenced failed to move to nearby water-filled slickrock potholes, and died of thirst. Nothing else here conjures dark thoughts, however—the scenery is simply too grand.

If your time is limited, drive to Dead Horse Point, leave your car, and walk to **Dead Horse Point Overlook,** the park's signature panorama. You can savor the experience of this exhilarating overlook by parking at the **Visitor Center,** letting its historical and geological exhibits deepen your appreciation of what you're about to witness, then strolling the 1.5-mile **Main Trail,** skirting the mesa's southeast precipice to the 90-foot-wide "neck" of the promontory (where the wranglers placed their fence). From here stroll the half mile to the Dead Horse Point Overlook and the Observation Shelter in the day-use area, whose picnic tables are arguably the best-situated in Canyonlands.

From here, the main trail loops back along the mesa's western edge to the **Meander Overlook.** Less well-marked and with trickier footing, this footpath looks down on an exceptionally complex landscape—spires, pinnacles, buttes, and convoluted benchlands and wriggly canyons notorious for disorienting wilderness hikers. Keep walking north and you'll come to the **Rim Overlook,** and then the **Big Horn Overlook,** each claiming a unique section of the Canyon-lands panorama. Along the way you'll encounter shallow slickrock concavities called potholes, some of them perma-nent reservoirs supporting tiny fairy shrimp and tadpoles.

Check at the Visitor Center for ranger-led activities, particularly evening talks offered from late spring through early autumn.

Camping

The park has 21 tent and RV sites. Reservations advised in season; call 800-322-3770. Camping fee.

❏ *Dead Horse Point State Park, P.O. Box 609, Moab, Utah 84532*

Goblin Valley

46 miles southeast of Green River, off Utah 24

● **3,654 acres** ● **801-564-3633** ● **Year-round** ● **Vehicle fee**
● **Hiking** ● **Amateur archaeology**

Its wind and water-worn formations make some people laugh. Others shake their heads in wonder at the profusion of spires, balanced boulders, and pedestals, for few places in Utah exhibit the appealingly mixed-up topography of Goblin Valley, an out-of-step cut-up at the remote south end of the geologic chorus line known as the San Rafael Reef. Massive subterranean upheavals pushed up the reef's jagged ridge, a great rock spine running north from the park to I-70. Goblin Valley's bowl, however, is an ancient sea bottom whose layers of silt, mud, and sand formed this region's rusty red-brown, gray-green, and dark brown bands of sedimentary rock. Softer in some places than others, it erodes unevenly—after cloud-bursts you'll see runoff the color of chocolate milk streaming between the "goblins"—reshaping before your eyes the vast basin of improbable shapes adults liken to sculptures and young children treat as cartoon creatures come to life.

Remote to begin with, these sun-baked badlands, cliffs, and myriad eroded oddities, surrounded by imposing buttes,

Floating Canyonlands

The Green River's gorge holds magnifi-cent, ever-changing rock formations. Outfit-ters in Moab rent fully-equipped canoes at modest prices, drop you off near Canyon-lands' northern bound-ary, and pick you up 3 to 6 days and some 60 placid river miles south at The Conflu-ence, where the olive-drab stream joins the Colorado. In between are ancient Indian ruins and petroglyphs, and The Maze, a vast puzzle of dry canyons. And silence so pure you'll hear things you might not have heard before, like the feathery whistle of bird wings and the beating of your wonderstruck heart.

Call 'Em as You See 'Em

In the early 1900s, when cowboys were still fetching stray cattle from what is now called Goblin Valley, the sandy basin had no name. A Green River ferry operator scouting roads through it in the late 1920s proposed Mushroom Valley. The fanciful shapes of the fairytale landscape inspired the whimsy of locals and visitors alike, who dubbed them Utah's "Parade of the Elephants," a "Dance of the Dolls" where "Skulls in the Sky" grinned among "hoodoos, stone babies, toadstools, ghosts, knobs, gnomes"—and, of course, "goblins."

impart to hikers, campers, and day-tripping strollers a delightful sense of escape and discovery.

If you visit in summer, be prepared for blistering heat. The park is nearly treeless, its campground generally unshaded, and the stone formations radiate warmth long after midday.

What to See and Do

As you enter the park, look for the covered **Observation Shelter** overlooking Goblin Valley. There's interesting geologic information here that corresponds to the unusual shapes before you, and a useful brochure of park trail routes that will help you choose a walk. Short, easy footpaths wander away from here, down to the **Goblins,** which range in height from around 10 feet to 20 times that.

Two trails offer rewarding half-day hikes. The 1.5-mile **Carmel Canyon Loop** leaves from the Observation Parking Lot, drops into a canyon, and wanders among cliffs and badlands of red siltstone and sandstone in the direction of **Molly's Castle,** a towering, magnificent butte of greenish-gray Curtis Formation sediments.

The **Curtis Bench Trail** from the campground is a bit longer at 2 miles, and though its landscapes are similar to the Carmel Canyon trail, some consider its rumpled up-and-down route a more entertaining stroll. One spur leads into Goblin Valley; another winds up to a view of the north-south trending **Henry Mountains,** rising above 11,000 feet some 30 miles south, and a panorama of the **San Rafael Plain.**

Only hardy desert plant species, which have learned to survive firey temperatures and constantly blowing sand, grow in the park's harsh environment. Along your hikes, look for Mormon tea, Russian thistle, tumbleweed, and various cactuses. Higher elevations sustain juniper and pinyon pine. You probably won't see any resident wildlife during the day; the skunks, porcupines, chuckwalla lizards, kangaroo rats, kit foxes, coyotes, and bobcats usually wait for the cooler evening temperatures to venture into the open.

Camping

The park has 21 tent and RV sites, with showers. Reservations advised in season; call 800-322-3770. Camping fee.

❏ *Goblin Valley State Park, P.O. Box 637, Green River, Utah 84525*

Goblin Valley moonscape

Kodachrome Basin

8 miles southeast of Cannonville via Utah 12 and Cottonwood Canyon Rd.

● 2,241 acres ● 801-679-8562 ● Year-round ● Entrance fee
● Unusual geology ● Hiking
● Stagecoach and guided
horseback rides ● General
store ● Photography

A pleasing sense of remoteness and desert solitude attracts campers and hikers to 5,800-foot-high Kodachrome Basin's peculiar geology, a meringue of red-rock spires that changes its hues as the sun moves across Utah's arid "color country." Geologists speculate that the park's 67 ruddy towers formed when sedimentary calcite and feldspar filled extinct geysers' throats, then remained after softer surrounding sandstone eroded away like massive molds, leaving the chimneys. (The tallest rises 156 feet.)

Thunderstorm over Kodachrome Basin

301

Struck by the park's photogenic character and vivid palette, National Geographic Society visitors in 1948 suggested it be named in honor of the pioneering color film.

If your itinerary doesn't permit an overnight amid juniper and red-rock spires, be sure to treat yourself to a walk on at least one of the park's trails. (Take your camera. A park trail map, available at the **Visitor Center,** is a must.) The 0.5-mile **Nature Trail** leaves the campground for a tour of desert plants and Kodachrome's trademark formations. The self-guided **Panorama Trail** is an easy 3-mile loop, with several side trails leading to unusual formations, including the graceful Ballerina Slipper spire, wide-brimmed pedestals in Hat Shop, and the intriguing Secret Pass, a narrow corridor squeezed between high red-rock walls. The main trail continues on to a short, steep spur ending on **Panorama Point,** an overlook with lovely sweeping views of the multihued landscape.

Camping

The park has 27 tent and RV sites, with shower facilities. Reservations advised; call 800-322-3700. Camping fee.

❏ *Kodachrome Basin State Park, P.O. Box 238, Cannonville, Utah 84718*

Montana

Flathead Lake
Bannack
Chief Plenty Coups
Makoshika

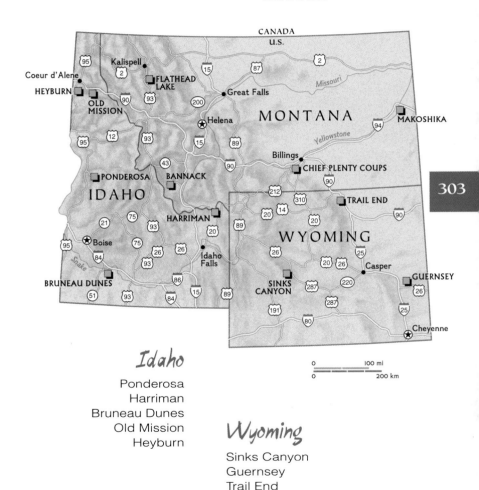

Idaho

Ponderosa
Harriman
Bruneau Dunes
Old Mission
Heyburn

Wyoming

Sinks Canyon
Guernsey
Trail End

Savoring the solitude of Sinks Canyon State Park, Wyoming

Flathead Lake

Between Kalispell and Polson via US 93 and Mont. 35

● 2,607 acres ● 406-752-5501 ● Year-round ● Day-use fee
● West's largest natural freshwater lake ● Hiking ● Abundant wildlife ● Boating, swimming, fishing (license required)

304

Mountain-ringed Flathead Lake

Flathead Lake—the largest natural freshwater lake west of the Mississippi—stretches for 28 shining miles along the steep, darkly wooded base of northwest Montana's awesome Mission Range. Among the bays, coves, points, and peninsulas that make up the lake's irregular shoreline, Flathead Lake State Park lies scattered in six separate units that offer a representative sample of the area's varying terrain, vistas, and wildlife.

Clean, deep, irresistible on a hot August day, Flathead is one of just a handful of large Rocky Mountain lakes warm enough for swimming most of the summer. Push off from shore and, as you float along on your back, a bald eagle or an osprey may glide out over the water, plunge for a trout, then return with its catch to a roost in the pines. Large sailboats angle silently across the bays, and thundering speedboats make a racket throughout the day.

The lake was formed during the last ice age, when large glaciers scoured much of the surrounding terrain. As the glaciers retreated, they left behind an enormous block of ice at the foot of the Mission Range. Mud, sand, stones, and

gravel were washed down from the highlands and filled in around the block. When the ice melted, it left the depression now occupied by Flathead Lake.

The bulk of the state park consists of one large unit, Wild Horse Island, an enticing, largely undeveloped place where bighorn sheep, deer, coyotes, and a few wild horses live amid knobby upland prairies and mature Douglas-fir and ponderosa pine forests. Accessible only by private boat, the island rises roughly 800 feet from the water and offers grandstand vistas of the lake, the Missions, and two other mountain ranges.

The rest of the park units are compact, shaded tracts just big enough for a campground, picnic area, boat ramp, beach, and perhaps some casual walking trails. Along the west shore, Big Arm lies beneath a canopy of ponderosa pine and offers a narrow, pebbly beach frequented by Canada geese. It also makes a convenient launching point for Wild Horse Island, which stands 3 miles offshore. Farther north, the larch-fir forest at West Shore ends abruptly along a set of glacially carved cliffs facing the Mission and Swan Ranges. It's a particularly appealing spot at sunset, with the breadth of the lake in shadow and the mountains bathed in yellow light.

Three more units dot the eastern shore. The southernmost, Finley Point lies along a narrow peninsula shaped a bit

305

Map labels:

To Kalispell and park headquarters, 9 miles
93 · 82 · 83
Somers
Kalispell Bay
Flathead
Swan
Bigfork
209
Conrad Point
FLATHEAD LAKE STATE PARK, WAYFARERS
Point Caroline
N
Blacktail Mountain 6,757 ft
Lakeside
35
M i s s i o n
93
Angel Point
Woods Bay
Kerr Mountain 6,121 ft
FLATHEAD LAKE STATE PARK, WEST SHORE
S a l i s h   M o u n t a i n s
Goose Bay
Flathead
To Lake Mary Ronan State Park
Rollins
Skags Lake · Bow Lake
Shelter Island · Cedar Island
Painted Rocks
L a k e
FLATHEAD LAKE STATE PARK, YELLOW BAY
M o u n t a i n s
Black Lake
Dayton
Cromwell Island
FLATHEAD LAKE STATE PARK, WILD HORSE ISLAND
Deepest point in lake 340 ft
Elmo
Big Arm Bay
Melita I.
Wildhorse I.
Bird Island
FLATHEAD LAKE STATE PARK, BIG ARM
Big Arm
Wymore Lake
Bull Island
Skidoo Bay
5,176 ft
Jette Lake
Kings Point
FLATHEAD LAKE STATE PARK, FINLEY POINT
35
Loon Lake
93
Polson Bay
Bird Point
East Bay
0   4 mi
0   4 km
Flathead
Polson
93

Blackfoot boy

Messing With Mother Nature

During the 1980s, an attempt to increase the average size of kokanee salmon led to the dramatic collapse of kokanee populations throughout the Flathead drainage. Taking a tip from Canadian biologists, who had fattened up kokanee in British Columbia's Kootenay Lakes, Montana's Department of Fish, Wildlife, and Parks introduced as a food source a half-inch crustacean called the opossum shrimp. Unfortunately, the shrimp competed directly for the kokanee's main food source, zooplankton. Worse, they failed to serve as prey because they settled to the bottom of the lake at night, when the fish rose to feed. In Canada, the approach worked because lakebed springs forced the shrimp to spend the night near the surface.

like a fishhook. Though the campground caters to RV owners with large boats, the point offers good views of the lake and a string of islands that stretch across the mouth of Polson Bay like stepping stones. Sweet cherry orchards abound near Yellow Bay, a tiny park unit tucked into the shoreline beside a small creek and a broad gravel beach. Finally, Wayfarers lies within a mature evergreen forest near the town of Big Fork and offers lovely vistas of the gently rolling Salish Mountains across the lake. It has a good beach, but strong swimmers may prefer the low cliffs and rocks that also line the shore.

What to See and Do

Though it requires some planning and can take up most of a day, a trip to **Wild Horse Island** combines some of the best experiences Flathead Lake has to offer: a nautical jaunt, an invigorating hike, plenty of opportunities for spotting wildlife, stirring vistas of mountain and lake, secluded swimming holes, peace and quiet.

The park publishes a pamphlet (available from campground hosts) that includes a topographical map and logistical advice. There are neither bathrooms nor drinking water on the island, so go prepared. If you don't have a boat, you can rent one at any of the private marinas that dot Big Arm Bay.

Once equipped and afloat, plot a course for **Little Skeeko Bay** on the island's northwest side, where a loop trail climbs into the highlands. There are four other landings, and you're free to roam virtually anywhere on the island as long as you keep clear of several dozen private cottages.

For a more casual outing—a picnic, a swim, some birdwatching or fishing—head for any of the other park units. Along the way, you might pick up a sack of sweet cherries at one of the orchards, or a bottle of sparkling wine at the **Mission Mountain Winery** (406-849-5524. May-Oct.) in Dayton.

One caution about swimming in Flathead Lake: The "swimmer's itch" parasite is common in shallow water, so it's important to towel off immediately or take a shower.

Excursion vessels ply the waters from Polson, Somers, and Big Fork. Most are large, motorized craft, but the Big Fork outfit, Questa Sailing Charters (406-837-5569), glides across the lake in a restored 1929 Q-class sloop.

Camping

The park's Big Arm unit (406-849-5255 in summer) has 30 RV sites and 6 tent sites, with showers; plus group sites (406-751-4577). The West Shore unit (406-752-5501) has 26 RV sites; Finley Point (406-887-2715) has 16 RV sites, each with accompanying boat slip; Yellow Bay (406-752-5501) has 6 sites, including 4 walk-in tent sites, with showers; and Wayfarers (406-752-5501) has 30 tent and RV sites. Reservations advised in season. Camping fee.

Nearby Sights

● In late summer, you can pick huckleberries—a tiny, intensely flavored type of blueberry—at **Lake Mary Ronan State Park** (*7 miles NW of Dayton. 406-752-5501*), which lies in the Salish Mountains. It's a pleasant spot, shaded by Douglas-fir and larch, and the lake offers good fishing for trout and bass.

● The southern half of Flathead Lake as well as much of the land extending nearly to Missoula lies within the **Flathead Indian Reservation.** For a view of the area through Native American eyes, visit **The People's Center** (*53253 Mont. 93 W, N of Pablo. 406-675-0160 or 800-883-5344. Adm. fee*), which examines the lives of the Kootenai and Salish people, past and present.

● Farther south, at the **National Bison Range** (*35 miles S of Polson, near Moiese. 406-644-2211*), a herd of 300 to 400 bison amble among rolling palouse prairie grasslands that face the most spectacular section of the Mission Range. A 19-mile loop gravel road (no trailers) winds through the refuge and climbs 2,000 feet to panoramic vistas. The drive offers excellent chances for seeing not only bison but also elk, deer, pronghorn, bighorn sheep, and many different birds.

● For a pleasant day in the high country, head for the **Jewel Basin Hiking Area** (*NE of Flathead Lake. 406-387-5234. Maps available in Big Fork and at area ranger stations*), a 15,000-acre tract set aside in the Swan Range for the exclusive use of foot travelers. The network of relatively short trails explores forests, alpine lakes, streams, snowfields, and wildflower meadows.

❏ FLATHEAD LAKE S.P., 490 N. MERIDIAN RD., KALISPELL, MONTANA 59901

Flathead country

Bannack

25 miles SW of Dillon via I-15 and Mont. 278

● 1,156 acres ● 406-834-3413 ● Year-round, with some buildings closed October through April ● Vehicle adm. fee ● Gold rush ghost town

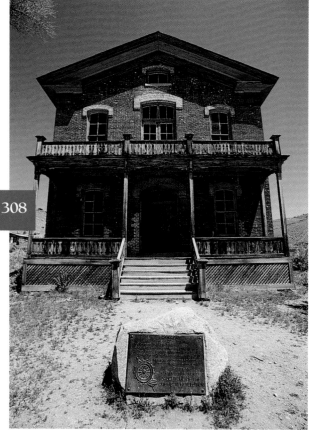
Hotel Meade

Gold is the story of Bannack—gold in the ground, but mostly gold in the dreams of people drawn to this quiet corner of Montana. In 1862 a group of Colorado prospectors made the first significant gold discovery in Montana when they sank their shovels into the bed of Grasshopper Creek. Within a year, a new town of over 3,000 people mushroomed into existence. In 1864 Bannack was declared the first capital of the newly designated Montana Territory, and seemed to be headed for bigger things. But the fortunes of gold towns are by nature ephemeral. Bigger discoveries soon drew attention elsewhere. The fabulous placer strike at Alder Gulch gave rise to Virginia City. To the north, a vast copper lode built the brick mansions of Butte, while gold from Last Chance Gulch supported Helena and its claim as the permanent state capital.

Meanwhile, Bannack survived for nearly a century, and produced millions of dollars in gold by various techniques. The hand-operated pans and sluices of the original miners gave way to hydraulic jets and great dredges that scoured the gravel to bedrock. Other efforts focused on quartz veins; miles of tunnels were blasted beneath the hills, providing ore to stamp mills that pounded out the gold. Built in 1919, the Apex Mill still stands, though its hammers ceased their thunder in 1976.

Today, with its more than 50 original buildings, Bannack reveals much about life in a frontier mining town. The bawdy houses, saloons, and tumbledown shacks were built in a time when the sheriff himself led a gang of murderous road agents called The Innocents, and citizens formed a vigilance committee to stamp them out. Bannack also reveals the gentler side of human nature—the desire to establish home, church, school, and community.

What to See and Do

Exhibits at the **Visitor Center** describe Bannack's role in the Montana gold rush. Sign up for a tour or strike off at your own pace with a self-guiding brochure. Highlights include the red-brick **Hotel Meade,** originally the courthouse and for many years the social center. Next door, **Skinner's Saloon** was home base for Henry Plummer's gang of road agents (see sidebar this page). Some of them, including their leader, were hanged on the outskirts of town, where a reconstructed gallows now stands. The first electric dredge in North America, the **Fielding L. Graves** floated in a pond of its own making; its generator was powered by water brought 30 miles in a hand-dug ditch. Some of the buildings are empty, but others—notably the second-story **Masonic Temple** and school below it—have been restored and retain some original furnishings.

What is a ghost town without ghosts? It is said that crying babies can be heard in **Amede Bessette's house,** where a number of infants died of diptheria around the turn of the century; and that the Hotel Meade houses the apparition of a young girl who died in Grasshopper Creek.

Camping

Bannack has 2 campgrounds with 24 primitive tent and RV sites. First come, first served. Camping fee.

Nearby Sights

Two undeveloped sites along the Beaverhead River commemorate the passing of Meriwether Lewis and William Clark on their famous expedition to the Pacific Ocean. Fourteen miles south of Twin Bridges along Mont. 41, **Beaverhead Rock** was a landmark recognized by Sacagawea, the Shoshone woman who was a member of the party. Seeing the rock, she knew the expedition was close to her people's summer hunting camps; and indeed, she soon located her brother, Chief Cameawhait.

Not far upstream, Captain Clark scrambled to the top of a limestone outcrop above the river to take compass bearings and sketch a map of the valley. The spot, now called **Clark's Lookout Historic Site,** stands a mile south of Dillon on old US 191. It's a good place to imagine how the country looked in 1805.

☐ *Bannack State Park, 4200 Bannack Rd., Dillon, Montana 59725*

Ladies Man, Highwayman, Lawman

When Henry Plummer drifted into Bannack in 1862, he was already an outlaw. Smooth-talking, gray-eyed, and mean, he had left a trail of broken hearts and dead men in mining camps from California to Idaho. But he was no miner. He wanted gold without digging, so he organized a gang of highwaymen. Bannack's Sheriff Crawford challenged him and shot him in a gun duel; but it was Crawford, intimidated by Plummer's gang, who fled the scene. The wounded Plummer got himself elected sheriff, and the fox was in control of the henhouse. While pretending to protect gold shipments, he orchestrated robberies, and did well by himself until Jan. 10, 1864, when members of the Montana Vigilante Committee overrode his silver star, and hanged him with two of his deputies.

309

Chief Plenty Coups

35 miles south of Billings, 1 mile west of Pryor

● 195 acres ● 406-252-1289 ● May through September,
by appt. in off-season ● Vehicle adm. fee ● No camping
● Historic buildings ● Museum

Porcupine

Born in 1848, Alech-chea-hoos (Plenty Coups) was the
last head chief of the Crow Tribe. A dedicated peacemaker, he
strove to help his people through the difficult transition from
nomadic freedom to government-imposed confinement on a
reservation. In the 1880s, he built a log house and store
beside a sacred medicine spring to set an example for his people of a new, more settled way of life. Before his death in
1932, he donated his property to the United States as "a park
for all people." Although the federal government wasn't able
to accept the gift, Montana eventually did. The chief's homestead became a state park in 1965.

Go first to the **Chief Plenty Coups Museum,** which tells
the story of Plenty Coups. His life bridged two centuries, two
cultures, and a broad sweep of history. It began as a traditional Crow boyhood and grew in scope to include friend-
ships with such men as Theodore Roosevelt. Primarily,
however, the museum focuses on the culture and history of
his people, the Apsaalooke, or Crow.

Outside, stroll around the house and store. Visit the **medicine spring,** a spiritual place shaded by cottonwood, where
people leave offerings, sample the water, and whisper prayers.
Walk on to the grave of Plenty Coups and ponder the stormy
confluence of cultures that he tried to understand.

If you visit at the right time, don't miss the Crow Fair *(406-
638-2601),* held annually in August at Crow Agency. This cultural celebration is a major Native American powwow, a vibrant
display of color, traditional dress, dancing, drumming, and
other events. For a glimpse into prehistory, visit **Pictograph
Cave State Park** *(7 miles SE of Billings via I-90. 406-247-2970).*
A self-guided interpretive trail leads along the base of an over-
hanging sandstone cliff covered with prehistoric rock paintings.
❏ CHIEF PLENTY COUPS STATE PARK, BOX 100A, PRYOR, MONTANA 59066

Makoshika

Just east of Glendive on Snyder Ave.

● 8,832 acres ● 406-365-6256 ● Year-round ● Adm. fee
● Scenic badlands ● Fossils ● Hiking

The Makoshika badlands reveal a significant transition in
the earth's history. Its buff-colored sediments were laid down

65 million years ago, when eastern Montana lay flat and swampy on the edge of a shallow sea. Tyrannosaurs, triceratops, and other dinosaurs roamed the coastal plain, but this was near the end of their era. They would fall and new species would rise in their place, only to be buried in turn. At Makoshika, the lower levels contain heavy dinosaur bones; in the upper levels, the delicate skeletons of early mammals.

Makoshika's scenic drive climbs to the rim of a pine-studded mesa, where viewpoints overlook the badland canyons. The **Visitor Center,** near the park entrance, is at the bottom of Cains Coulee. Stop there for a look at fossils, prehistoric stone tools, and the enormous skull of a triceratops; and to pick up a park road guide.

Don't pass up **Cap Rocks Nature Trail,** which leads for a half-mile through a sculpture garden of erosional features. Mud, stone, and weather combine to create wonderfully eccentric forms called rain pillars, baked potatoes, toadstools, and popcorn. There are sinkholes, a natural bridge, and a black seam of coal. Be careful: In wet weather exposed clay is more slippery than ice.

311

Continue past Radio Hill Junction, where an unimproved road turns off to **Artists Vista** and **Sand Creek Overlook.** In wet weather this road quickly becomes impassable; if in doubt, stay on the all-weather main road, which leads to more views of the badlands.

Badlands rock formations

For a boots-on experience, try the **Kinney Coulee Trail.** From the trailhead along the drive, the marked but rugged trail descends 300 feet to the base of the badlands. There is always the chance of finding a fossil. The triceratops skull at the Visitor Center was discovered when a park worker nearly sat on the brow tine sticking out of the dirt. If you do find something interesting, leave it alone and notify a park employee.

Camping

The park has 16 tent and RV sites, plus additional primitive tent sites. Reservations advised in season; call the park at 406-365-6256. Camping fee.

❏ *Makoshika State Park, P.O. Box 1242, Glendive, Montana 59330*

Sinks Canyon

6 miles southwest of Lander on Wyo. 131

● 600 acres ● 307-332-6333 ● Year-round ● Scenic canyon with disappearing river ● Hiking, wildlife viewing, fishing (license required)

The Sinks, fed by glacier melt

312

High in the Wind River Range, the Middle Fork Popo Agie River begins among glaciers, naked rock, and alpine meadows. It is a lovely river, but only one of many similar streams pouring out of these well-watered mountains. What sets this one apart is an unexpected trick. Having entered a narrow canyon on the east side of the range, the river turns suddenly to the right and dives noisily into a yawning cavern called The Sinks. Half a mile away, it quietly returns to the surface in a deep green pool called The Rise.

It seems obvious that The Sinks and The Rise would be connected, yet it took years and several attempts to prove the case. Even now the underground picture remains a matter of conjecture. Tracer dye poured into the river above The Sinks turns up in The Rise as expected, but it takes two hours to get there, and the water comes out warmer than it went in. There is also more water coming out than entering, suggesting additional underground sources and a complicated network of passages—perhaps a large subterranean reservoir.

Even without its centerpiece geologic stunt, Sinks Canyon would make a worthy state park. Stretched out for more than 2 miles along the river, it lies sheltered beneath high buff-colored walls of sandstone and limestone. Its sunny, south-facing side has elements of a desert environment, with juniper, limber pine, and sagebrush. The shady, north-facing slope, being cooler and wetter, supports Douglas-fir, cottonwood, aspen, and willow. These, together with the riparian zone, provide a wide range of wildlife habitat. Elk, moose, deer, and bighorn sheep live in the canyon's narrow confines, along with mink and muskrats, rainbow and cutthroat trout, prairie rattlers, and 94 species of birds.

What to See and Do

Start at the **Visitor Center** *(Mem. Day–Labor Day),* but before you go inside, walk the short distance to **The Sinks.** At its normal summer level, the river is much smaller than the cavern, and it's hard not to feel a little spooky shiver as you stand watching the water disappear into that yawning darkness. From there, go back to the Visitor Center. Its excellent displays interpret the underground story in addition to the natural history of the area.

Next stop is **The Rise,** located a half-mile drive down the canyon. A high platform provides a good view of the pool. Huge rainbow and brown trout drift like happy whales in the spring water. No fishing is allowed in this stretch of the river, but food pellets are available for tossing, and the trout eagerly take them.

In spring, the river overflows The Sinks and fills an overflow channel. You can see this along the .25-mile **Visitor Center Trail,** and learn about native vegetation in the process. For a longer self-guided walk (just under a mile), head for the **Popo Agie Nature Trail** near the upper campground. A booklet describes many aspects of the canyon's natural history. Treks of greater length begin with the **Middle Fork Trail,** which begins at Bruces Camp parking lot, just outside the park, and leads into the Popo Agie Wilderness and beyond. Just 1.5 miles up the trail, **Popo Agie Falls** marks the head of the canyon.

Throughout the park, watch for bighorn sheep. The canyon should be an ideal wintering ground for them; its south-facing slope stays relatively warm and free of snow, while the rocks and lack of forest provide the sort of open, rugged country in which they feel secure. However, sheep have not had an easy time here. The original population died out many years ago. In the 1980s, a new herd of 54 animals was brought here from the north end of the Wind River Range. Yet they have not thrived, and currently number only about a dozen animals. One problem is their failure to discover migration routes to summer grazing in the high mountains. As a result, they stay year-round on range that cannot provide sufficient forage.

Contributing to their decline are the recent increase in human contact and an outbreak of pneumonia, which killed a third of the population in 1992.

Higher and Deeper

The road that climbs Sinks Canyon provides an excellent tour of Wind River Range geology. From Lander to Switchback Overlook is nearly 4,000 vertical feet of different rock layers. Because the mountains were formed by uplifting of a block of old granite tilting through younger sediments that now dip basinward on the flanks of the range, climbing the canyon takes you deeper into older rocks as you climb in altitude. The trip begins with brilliant red Triassic shale and sandstone, yielding to Tensleep sandstone at the canyon entrance. The Sinks are formed in Madison limestone, while farther up-canyon, the road switchbacks dizzyingly through Devonian and Cambrian sediments before emerging at the overlook among Precambrian granite and spectacular views of the range.

Camping

Sinks Canyon has 30 tent and RV sites in two campgrounds. May–mid-October, with limited sites open through winter. Available on a first-come, first-served basis. Camping fee.

Nearby Sights

● Above The Sinks, Wyo. 131 gives way to a seasonal forest road that climbs to the head of the canyon and wanders through rolling country of forest and meadow, past several alpine lakes, campgrounds, and trailheads to Wyo. 28

Overlooking Sinks Canyon

near **South Pass,** an important landmark in Western history. Here, emigrants on the Oregon, California, and Mormon Trails crossed the Continental Divide. Despite the considerable difficulties still facing them, they must have been encouraged to know they had topped the ridgeline of the continent.

● In 1867 prospectors found gold near South Pass. The discovery set off a gold rush that, at its peak, involved thousands of miners, a dozen stamp mills, two stage lines, and the usual assortment of saloons, hotels, promoters, lawyers, and grocers. The only thing lacking was enough gold to support expectations, and by 1875 fewer than 100 people clung to diminished hopes. Despite several attempts at revival, including one energetic fraud, South Pass never hit the big time. Today, the **South Pass City State Historic Site** *(42 miles S via Wyo. 131 and US 28. 307-332-3684. Mid-May–Sept.; adm. fee)* protects 27 original, restored, or reconstructed buildings crammed with artifacts. Check in at the Visitor Center, a former store and warehouse, before exploring the buildings and history of South Pass Avenue.

● Ask park staff about other historical landmarks in the area, including **Pony Express stations,** visible ruts of the **Oregon Trail,** further mining relics, and **Willie's Handcart Site,** where Mormon emigrants pulling handcarts to Salt Lake City were caught—and many killed—by early winter storms in October 1856.

❑ *Sinks Canyon State Park, 3079 Sinks Canyon Rd., Rte. 63, Lander, Wyoming 82520*

Guernsey

1.5 miles north of Guernsey, off Wyo. 26

● 8,602 acres ● 307-836-2334 ● Year-round ● Entrance fee spring through fall ● Historic buildings ● Oregon Trail ● Hiking, swimming, boating

Located near the main route of the Oregon Trail, Guernsey State Park takes in a pleasant, serpentine canyon rimmed with sandstone cliffs and shaded by stands of ponderosa pine and juniper. The North Platte River, impounded as a reservoir here, laps placidly at the base of the cliffs and offers an inviting respite from the heat of the Wyoming plains.

During the 1930s, the Civilian Conservation Corps built trails, roads, bridges, and rustic buildings throughout the park. Much of the CCC's work survives, including the lovely stone-and-timber Visitor Center overlooking the reservoir.

Starting in the 1840s, waves of Oregon Trail emigrants traveled this way as they followed the North Platte River through southeastern Wyoming. Just a few miles south of the park, they left two vivid records of their passage—deep wagon ruts carved across a stony bluff, and hundreds of names etched onto the face of Register Cliff.

What to See and Do

The park's **Visitor Center** is worth a stop just to admire the handiwork of the CCC and to gaze across the rock-rimmed canyon. Exhibits touch on Native American culture, but focus more on 1880s cattle ranching and the activities of the CCC.

A Lighter Yoke to Bear

When traffic along the **Oregon Trail** was at its height in the 1840s and '50s, emigrants jettisoned an astounding variety of high-quality trash between Fort Laramie and modern Glenrock. The route was strewn with bar-iron and steel, anvils, bellows, crow-bars, drills, augers, gold-washers, chisels, axes, trunks, grindstones, plows, ovens, cook stoves, kegs, barrels, clothing, books, and food. Why did those with overloaded wagons wait until this point to reduce their burden? With the mountains looming ahead, the trail became steeper—and the trash piles rose.

The 1.5-mile **Evergreen Glade Nature Trail** departs from the Visitor Center and wanders among grassy rolling hills dotted with ponderosa pine, juniper, and cedar. Plaques and a self-guiding brochure help identify various wildflowers, trees, and animals.

To get to the **Oregon Trail ruts,** drive south on Wyo. 26 through the town of Guernsey and follow the signs across the North Platte River. From the well-marked parking area, a short trail climbs to the top of a ridge of sandstone, where you'll find unmistakable wagon ruts cut

Commanding officer's restored office, Fort Laramie

deeply into the rock. Forced by a topographical bottleneck to come this way, hundreds of thousands of emigrants guided their creaking loads over this beautiful prairie highland. Their wagon wheels soon cut through the thin soil and eventually left ruts in the stone as deep as 5 feet.

Many of the emigrants who struggled over this ridge spent the previous evening just a few miles downriver scratching their names into **Register Cliff,** a 60-foot bluff of tan sandstone. Visible names date back to the 1840s and '50s, but legions of modern vandals have desecrated the site by adding their own names.

Camping

The park has 142 tent and RV sites in 7 separate campgrounds. May-Sept., with a limited number open through winter. Available first come, first served. Camping fee.

Nearby Sights

It would be a shame to come this close and not visit **Fort Laramie National Historic Site** (*13 miles E of*

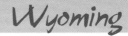

Guernsey on US 26. 307-837-2221), one of the West's finest living history museums with more than a dozen fully restored military buildings and a large cast of costumed guides. Founded in 1834 by fur-trappers, it became an important stopover on the Oregon Trail and a major military outpost. ❏ *GUERNSEY STATE PARK, P.O. BOX 429, GUERNSEY, WYOMING 82214*

Trail End

400 Clarendon Ave., Sheridan

● 3.5 acres ● 307-674-4589 ● April to mid-Dec. ● No camping ● Restored 1913 mansion ● Carriage house ● Landscaped grounds

A posh, 1913 Flemish Revival mansion, **Trail End** overlooks Sheridan from spacious, formally landscaped grounds offering fine views of the Bighorn Mountains. Built for John B. Kendrick—cattle baron, Wyoming governor, and three-term U.S. Senator—the 21-room house portrays turn-of-the-century Wyoming life at the top of the heap. The polished mahogany, Italian marble fireplaces, stained-glass windows, and hand-painted ceilings all speak of a life far removed from the sweat, dust, and bone-crushing toil that built the Kendrick fortune. The mansion stands beside a matching carriage house and a reconstructed homesteader's cabin that has been moved to the site.

As you approach Trail End's red tile roofs, balconies, and neoclassic porticos, it's interesting to note that Kendrick started out as a Texas orphan who drifted north as a common cowpoke. He began building a 200,000-acre cattle ranch that sprawled across northern Wyoming and southern Montana, and in 1891 married into a wealthy ranch family.

Guided tours of the mansion are available by appointment, but most visitors simply wander through at their own pace. While in the drawing room, you might pause over the Kurdistani rug, which served as a touchstone for decorating much of the home's interior. Virtually all of the furnishings you see throughout the house—from beds and bureaus to dolls and golf clubs—belonged to the Kendricks.

Outside, get a taste of how average Wyoming homesteaders lived during the 1880s by visiting the 1879 **Mandel Cabin,** a simple log house that doubled as the Sheridan area's first post office.

Finish up with a stroll through the mansion's shaded grounds, which include a sunken rose garden, lawn tennis court, and apple orchard. ❏ *TRAIL END STATE HISTORIC SITE, 400 CLARENDON AVE., SHERIDAN, WYOMING 82801*

317

Ponderosa

1 mile northeast of McCall, follow signs

● 1,450 acres ● 208-634-2164 ● Year-round ● Vehicle fee
● Old-growth forest ● High cliffs ● Lake ● Boating, fishing
(license required) ● Biking, hiking, cross-country skiing

Payette River, near Banks

High in the gently rolling mountains of west-central Idaho, Ponderosa State Park occupies a narrow, wooded peninsula that stretches across the crystalline waters of Payette Lake. This relatively small finger of land rises through groves of immense fir, larch, ponderosa and lodgepole pine to an airy bluff of basalt lava overlooking the lake. Here and there, grassy meadows, bug-rich marshes, and even vestpocket sagebrush flats press back the trees and provide an abundance of habitats for wildlife. Mule deer nibble shrubs along the forest edge. Coyotes, hawks, and owls hunt for mice and other rodents in the meadows, while beavers, muskrats, salamanders, and frogs muck about in the spongy ooze of the marshes.

Footpaths and bike trails skirt the shoreline, climb the bluffs, and loop through forest, marshes, and meadows. Most are suitable for casual strolls or, during winter, for cross-country skiing. There is a paved, .25-mile path along the lakeshore that is wheelchair accessible.

You'll find three small beaches on the peninsula, but the most inviting tract of warm sand lies across the water at Ponderosa's North Beach Area. There, the North Fork Payette River lazily enters the lake after meandering through a forest of mature evergreens and gliding past a marsh full of ducks and songbirds.

What to See and Do

First of all, stop at the **Visitor Center** to pick up a park map and to review the schedule of ranger-led activities *(mid-June–Labor Day)*. These include guided nature walks, campfire chats, and special programs for children that cover geology, plants, animals, local history, and archaeology. Sometimes, a naturalist from the nearby Snowdon Wildlife Sanctuary drops by with a fox, a hawk, an owl, or some other injured animal the sanctuary has rehabilitated.

For a quick overview of the park, drive the length of the peninsula (about 3 miles) and follow the short footpaths to **Osprey Cliff Overlook** and the **Narrows Overlook,** where a terrific vista of Payette Lake opens from the top of the lava cliffs. The rock here was deposited as part of the Columbia Plateau, a vast accumulation of lava that spread over much of the Northwest about 16 million years ago. Later, glaciers covered this area, smoothing the mountains and scooping out the lakebed to a maximum depth of 304 feet.

On the return trip, take some time to watch for ducks and other waterfowl dabbling on **Lily Marsh,** or park in the shade by the picnic area and take a quick dip in **Payette Lake.** The water, enticingly clear, is bracing but swimmable most of the summer.

To admire the most impressive examples of the park's namesake tree, the ponderosa pine, stroll through the campground. Some of the trees tower 150 feet high and were seedlings when the Spanish Armada set sail for England.

Next, slather on some bug repellent and follow the 1.4-mile **Meadow Marsh Trail** through the forest around Meadow Marsh, a spongy wetland gradually evolving into a meadow. You'll find the trailhead at a parking area just north of the Visitor Center. A pamphlet (available at the Visitor Center) identifies various shrubs and trees throughout the park and points out likely areas for spotting animals and rare wildflowers.

Designated mountain-biking trails cover most of the park's important landscapes and extend from Meadow Marsh to Osprey Cliff Overlook. By combining the trails

Ponderosa Pines

Area vegetation has evolved with frequent fires that create scattered, old-growth ponderosa pines widely spaced in pleasant open groves, where little more than prairie grass and wildflowers form the understory. This is not true at Ponderosa State Park, where a century of fire suppression and no logging have permitted the growth of a rather lush understory and shade-tolerant evergreens such as grand firs.

River otter

with stretches of the main park road, bikers can stitch together several casual loop tours of the peninsula. If you don't have a bike, you can rent one in McCall.

If time permits, drive around the lake to the **North Beach Area** and spread your towel on the large sand beach that faces due south and offers fine views of the entire lake. From the parking area, an interpretive boardwalk wanders over the marsh to the beach.

One of the most inviting ways to visit the North Beach Area is to float to it on the **North Fork Payette River,** a gentle stream appropriate for novice paddlers. As it switchbacks through forest and marsh, the river offers good chances for seeing deer, moose, ducks, herons, beavers, otters, and other animals. For a leisurely half-day trip, start a few miles north of the lake at the Fisher Creek bridge. Local outfitters rent canoes and provide shuttle service.

During the winter, the park grooms 10 miles of cross-country skiing trails that loop through rolling forested hills and climb to some of the ridgetops overlooking Payette Lake.

Camping

Ponderosa has 138 tent and RV sites (mid-May–mid-Oct.), with shower facilities. Reservations advised Memorial Day to Labor Day; call park at 208-634-2164. There are also 20 primitive tent sites at the North Beach unit. Camping fee.

Nearby Sights

In McCall, an old timber and resort town, you can tour the **McCall Smokejumper Base** (Mission St. 208-634-0390), where skydiving firefighters train for their mission of suppressing remote forest fires. Also in town, you can wander through the **McCall Summer Chinook Fish Hatchery** (300 Mather Rd. 208-634-2690), where thousands of small summer chinook salmon teem in narrow raceways and larger rainbow trout pump their gills in a nearby pond.

❏ PONDEROSA STATE PARK, P.O. BOX A, MCCALL, IDAHO 83638

Harriman

18 miles north of Ashton on US 20/91

● 4,700 acres ● 208-558-7368 ● Year-round ● Entrance
fee ● No pets ● No camping ● Historic buildings ● Wildlife
viewing ● Fishing (license required) ● Hiking, mountain
biking, cross-country skiing

Perched on the edge of the rugged Yellowstone Plateau
and surrounded by mountainous terrain, Harriman is a peaceful landscape with a shockingly violent past. Roughly 1.3 million years ago a huge volcanic eruption blew everything sky
high—even the underlying rock—leaving behind a collapsed
volcanic crater, or caldera, some 20 miles across. What was
then a steaming gaseous ruin is now a watery haven for
wildlife, a placid terrain of meadows, marshes, lakes, and
streams. Most of the caldera rim has eroded into insignificance.
The only visible remnant is a line of forested hills to the northwest, but these are enough to give a sense of scale. Skirting
their eastern corner, the trout-filled Henrys Fork slips gently
through lodgepole pine forest into the park meadows before
plunging into a canyon and over two impressive waterfalls.

At the park's center stand 27 original buildings of the
Railroad Ranch, founded in 1902 as a working cattle company

321

Along Henrys Fork

Grand Catastrophe

The volcanic explosion that created Harriman's landscape was one in a long chain of such eruptions that moved across southern Idaho over a period of some 17 million years. The eruptions seem to have moved from Oregon to Yellowstone, but in fact the continent has done the moving, sliding across the top of a stationary hot spot that periodically blows up. Almost 2 million years ago, it was the Huckleberry Ridge Caldera on Yellowstone's southwest corner. The most recent, the Yellowstone Caldera took out the center of the park 600,000 years ago. In a matter of hours it spewed hundreds of cubic miles of molten rock. In comparison, the famous eruptions of Krakatoa and Pompeii fade to insignificance. The hot spot still broods beneath Yellowstone. Geologists predict it will erupt again, in what we must hope is the very distant future.

and retreat for wealthy Eastern families, notably the Harrimans (of the Union Pacific Railroad) and Guggenheims. In 1977 the land was donated by its owners to Idaho. Together with adjoining national forest land, the park is the heart of approximately 16,000-acre Harriman Wildlife Refuge.

What to See and Do

Begin at the **Visitor Center** in the Jones House, which features history and wildlife displays. From here, join a guided tour or set off on your own through historic ranch buildings. Cottages for owners and their guests are set on a low rise overlooking the Henrys Fork and, in the distance, the distinctive crags of the Teton Range. The **Harriman Cottage** is kept in its 1970s condition, as it was when the family turned it over to the state. Other structures belong to the working ranch.

The Harrimans came here for wildlife and the natural setting, and these remain the best features of the park. You might do nothing more than sit by the ranch buildings and scan the river meadows for trumpeter swans, sandhill cranes, moose, or elk. Beyond that, 20 miles of trails are open to hiking, mountain biking, and horseback riding. First choice is the mile-long **Ranch Loop,** which visits Silver Lake and the Henrys Fork, as well as the historic buildings. Fly-fishermen will head straight for the meadow trails for access to some of the best fly-fishing water in the West (flies only, catch-and-release). A rewarding longer hike is the 4.5-mile **Golden Lake Loop,** which, if connected to the **Ridge Loop** (5.5 more miles and 400 vertical feet of climbing), takes in the whole range of park habitats.

On winter weekends, the Visitor Center's warming house is open for cross-country skiers. Being mostly spring water, the river almost never freezes, making this an important wintering area for trumpeter swans, bald eagles, and other wildlife.

Lodging

There is no campground, but groups can reserve a log dorm facility. Call the park at 208-558-7368. Several national forest campgrounds are located nearby.

Nearby Sights

● Follow the Henrys Fork downstream to Mesa Falls Scenic Area (*14 miles S of Harriman on Idaho 47*), where boardwalks lead to excellent views of two impressive waterfalls.

● Henrys Fork originates with a small stream flowing out of Henrys Lake, but most of its water comes from **Big Springs** (*4.5 miles E of Mack's Inn*), whose crystalline water forms a small pond filled with protected fish: cutthroat, brook, and rainbow trout; coho and kokanee salmon. No fishing, but you can stand on footbridges and watch them forage among gently waving aquatic plants.

❑ *HARRIMAN STATE PARK, HC 66 BOX 500, ISLAND PARK, ID 83429*

Bruneau Dunes

20 miles south of Mountain Home via Idaho 51 and Idaho 78

● 4,800 acres ● 208-366-7919 ● Year-round ● Entrance fee ● Dune field ● Lake, marsh, and desert ● Swimming, hiking, fishing (license required)

Rippled Bruneau Dunes

323

Bruneau Dunes is the sort of place children might build if they could design their own landscape. With mountains of clean, sifted sand rising above a cluster of lakes and marshes, there are bluegills to catch, lizards to chase, and clear water for swimming. The dunes are an unearthly terrain where the lead-footed sensation of going up combines with the thrill of leaping or rolling back down. For those who make the hike, a wind-carved crater sets into the crest of the dunes. If you slide to its bottom and lie on your back, all you see is a circle of sky.

The dunes have been here for some 15,000 years, thanks to an abandoned meander of the Bonneville Flood called Eagle Cove, which serves as a trap for wind-blown sand. Because countervailing winds blow just about equally from the northwest and the southeast, the dunes remain essentially stationary. Covering some 600 acres, this is a relatively small dune field, but it boasts the highest single-structured dune in North America —470 feet high. The lakes clustered at its base are a much more recent development, having appeared after 1950 as a result of flood irrigation in the surrounding Snake River Plain. The water table came up, and the lakes rose among the dunes as if ordered by a Hollywood movie producer. The result is a happy coincidence of dunes, prairie, desert, lake, marsh, and a rich variety of flora and fauna, all in one compact area.

What to See and Do

Start at the **Visitor Center.** Among its natural history displays are fossils collected from the sediments of prehistoric lakes within a few miles of the park. They call to mind an era when camels, giant ground sloths, saber-tooth tigers, and mammoths wandered the area. The mammoth femur, turtle shells, and 6-foot minnow are highlights. So are tales of the great flood that scoured the Snake River Valley during the last ice age, when Lake Bonneville, which covered 20,000 square miles of Utah, broke free and released a vast, sudden deluge.

Bruneau's little lake is more peaceful, and attracts swimmers, boaters, picnickers, and birdwatchers. Dune hikers can choose from several routes. Start at the boat launch and climb the western ramp to the dune, or pick up the trail at the picnic area and approach from the east.

For a more ambitious walk that takes in most of the park's varied landscape, consider the **Sand Dunes Hiking Trail,** a 5-mile loop that begins and ends at the Visitor Center. Be careful; it can be a hot trek in summer. Much of the trail is in desert country, where jackrabbits run from coyotes, and lizards zip beneath rocks as you approach. After climbing the high dunes, the path descends to the lakeshore and circles around to the picnic area, an optional ending point.

Camping

There are 48 tent and RV sites, with showers. Reservations advised in season; call the park at 208-366-7919. Camping fee.

Nearby Sights

● In the immediate area, **C.J. Strike Reservoir** (*Idaho 78. 208-845-2324*) is a popular fishing lake and an important wintering ground for waterbirds. If the high desert sounds appealing, drive southeast from the town of Bruneau on Hot Springs Road for 20 miles (12 of which are unpaved) to a viewpoint overlooking the spectacular Bruneau River Canyon. A map is available at the park.

● History adds interest to the landscape at **Three Island Crossing State Park** (*1 mile W of Glenns Ferry. 208-366-2394*). At this point on their long journey, Oregon-bound emigrants had a difficult choice. Should they continue along the harder, drier southern route, or brave a river crossing to reach the easier northern trail? Visitor Center displays and interpretive programs recount the dramatic story. Each year in August, the park hosts a re-enactment of the hazardous crossing.

❏ *BRUNEAU DUNES S.P., HC 85 BOX 41, MOUNTAIN HOME, IDAHO 83647*

Wind Shapes

Sand dunes reflect the winds that built them. A single grain moves up the windward, gentler side of the dune, and tumbles into the calm space on the steep lee side. Where prevailing winds blow in one direction, dunes form crescents called barchans, their horns pointing downwind. In exposed desert landscapes, barchans themselves are in constant motion, migrating smoothly downwind. However, if the winds are variable, dune shapes become more complicated. The sinuous crest of Bruneau's main dune is caused by opposing winds that push it first one way, then the other. The big dune, in turn, alters wind patterns in the immediate vicinity, as reflected by the fields of smaller dunes on either side.

324

Old Mission

24 miles east of Coeur d'Alene on I-90

- 100 acres ● 208-682-3814 ● Year-round
- Vehicle fee ● No camping ● 1850 church

Old Mission, Cataldo

Anchoring this small park, the ivory-colored **Old Mission** was built in 1850 by Coeur d'Alene Indians and Catholic missionaries. Using the simplest of tools, they erected the elegant timber-frame marvel of rustic ingenuity overlooking the Coeur d'Alene River. The Coeur d'Alene worshipped in its sanctuary until 1877, when the tribe was forced onto a reservation. It is the oldest building in Idaho.

Start at the **Visitor Center** (*March–mid-Nov.*), where a slide show traces the history of the Coeur d'Alene and explains how the Jesuits and Indians built the church. Then visit the colonnaded church to admire the handcarved altar, the chandeliers fashioned from tin cans, and the sky-blue ceiling painted with berry juice. Next door, visit the restored **Parish House.**

❏ OLD MISSION STATE PARK, P.O. BOX 30, CATALDO, IDAHO 83810

325

Heyburn

42 miles south of Coeur d'Alene on US 95, then 5 miles east on Idaho 5

- 7,835 acres ● 208-686-1308 ● Year-round ● Deep forest
- Marshes ● Canoeing, hiking, mountain biking

Located at the marshy southern end of **Coeur d'Alene Lake,** Heyburn combines the serenity of deep, old-growth forest with the bird-busy clamor of extensive wetlands that harbor ducks, songbirds, muskrats, herons, frogs, and salamandars. Footpaths trace the shoreline, explore portions of the marsh, and climb through lush cedar-and-hemlock forest to open stands of immense ponderosa pine overlooking the lake.

Drop by the **Visitor Center** for a primer on the culture of the Coeur d'Alene tribe, area history, and the park's wildlife. Then head for **Plummer Creek Marsh,** where you can birdwatch, or paddle your canoe (rentals available) among the bulrushes. If a deep-forest hike appeals, consider the **Indian Cliffs Trail,** a 3-mile loop offering excellent views of St. Joe River.

Camping

The park has 66 tent sites and 67 RV sites (April-Nov.), with showers. Available first come, first served. Camping fee.

❏ HEYBURN STATE PARK, RTE. 1, P.O. BOX 139, PLUMMER, IDAHO 83851

Alaska Chugach
Denali
Wood-Tikchik
Totem Bight

Washington
Deception Pass
Moran
Fort Canby
Riverside

Oregon
Fort Stevens
Silver Falls
Sunset Bay
Farewell Bend

Denali, or Mount McKinley, Denali State Park, Alaska

Fort Stevens

10 miles west of Astoria via US 101 and Fort Stevens Hwy.

● 3,763 acres ● 503-861-1671 ● Year-round ● Vehicle permit fee ● Military museum ● Historic artillery emplacements ● Peter Iredale shipwreck ● Hiking, biking ● Beach

Japanese Invasion

On the evening of June 21, 1942, an intruder slipped across the Columbia River bar along with the returning fishing fleet. The Japanese submarine surfaced just past 11 p.m., and 30 minutes later its deck gun opened fire on Fort Stevens. Of 17 shots, most landed on the beach or in a swamp. The worst damage occurred when a shell blew up the backstop of a baseball diamond. The men of Fort Stevens were ordered to hold their fire, since the sub was out of range. However, recent studies have indicated that, indeed, the sub was probably within reach after all.

Although the continental United States hasn't been attacked by a foreign adversary since the early years of the republic, the nation's military has been prepared. From the Civil War until shortly after World War II, Fort Stevens helped defend our borders; along with Forts Canby and Columbia in Washington, the artillery of Fort Stevens guarded the mouth of the Columbia River.

Besides, strictly speaking, the U.S. *has* been attacked since 1812, and right here at Fort Stevens. In 1942 a Japanese submarine shelled the fort, making it the only military installation in the lower 48 states to be fired upon since the War of 1812 (see sidebar this page).

Though the big guns are gone, the massive concrete bunkers remain atop the bluffs. Logically enough, the emplacements command a sweeping view of the Columbia's mouth, which visitors today can enjoy without the added burden of scanning for enemy warships. The park also includes natural areas, such as a long beach that extends to the extreme northwestern tip of Oregon.

What to See and Do

It's fitting to begin your tour at the **Military Museum** (*503-861-2000. Adm. fee*), which also serves as a Visitor Center. The museum exhibits weapons, uniforms, photos, and other artifacts from the installation's 100-plus years as an active fort, along with much illuminating information. For example, you can learn why the United States decided to build a fort way out here during the Civil War, when virtually all the action was taking place far to the east: The Union feared that the Confederacy would ally with Britain, and that both Confederate and British sea raiders would come sailing up the Columbia.

Before heading out the door, pick up a walking tour map and, during the summer, sign up for a guided tour of the fortifications in a two-ton Army truck.

Outside the museum you can explore the extensive network of gun emplacements. One is a restored earthworks artillery site that dates back to the Civil War, but most are massive concrete structures constructed at the turn of the century. In summer you also can visit an underground gun battery that served as a command center during World War II. From atop the batteries awaits an exhilarating panorama of the mouth of the Columbia River and the Oregon and Washington coasts.

Aside from the artillery batteries, only a few buildings remain at the fort. But if you use the walking tour map and your imagination, or take the guided tour, these few structures and the bits and pieces of foundations come together to create an accurate picture of Fort Stevens during its active days. The **Guardhouse,** built in 1908, still stands and can be visited on a limited schedule during the summer. Its main function was to corral disorderly soldiers on pay day. Other sites run the gamut from the mundane (laundry, bakery) to the flashy (buildings far from the heart of the post, where torpedoes and sea mines were stored and tested).

From the museum, a 0.5-mile trail leads to a wildlife-viewing platform above **Swash Lake,** where you might spot waterfowl, wading birds, or even a beaver. Another mile west through the trees and undergrowth will land you on the beach. Or you can head south half a mile to the campground and gain access to several other trails.

You can hike, bike, or drive down to the **_Peter Iredale,_** once a sleek British schooner. Part of the skeleton of this

1906 shipwreck still protrudes from the sandy beach at the southwest corner of the park. Heading north, you can go out **Clatsop Spit,** the northwestern-most point in Oregon. There's a wildlife-viewing bunker on Trestle Bay and a viewing platform on the

Visitors to Fort Stevens

ocean side from which you can watch ships crossing the dangerous Columbia River bar.

Camping

Fort Stevens offers 253 tent sites, 128 RV sites, 213 trailer spaces for RVs or tents (no hook-ups), and 9 yurts (circular domed tents with wood floors), all with showers. Reservations advised in season; call 800-452-5687. Camping fee.

❏ *Fort Stevens State Park, Ridge Rd., Hammond, Oregon 97121*

Silver Falls

26 miles east of Salem on Oreg. 214

● 8,706 acres ● 503-873-8681 ● Year-round ● Vehicle permit fee ● Waterfalls ● Historic lodge ● Wildflower gardens ● Hiking, biking, horseback riding ● Wildlife watching

South Falls

330

Waterfalls are one of nature's most charming extravagances: that graceful arc as gravity and the forward rush of the stream combine to curve the water down through the air; that fine mist that dampens your face and creates rainbows; that refreshing rush of water-cooled air; that surflike sound of water splashing on water. Flamboyant displays of one of life's essential ingredients, waterfalls simultaneously exhilarate and calm our souls. And 14 waterfalls—ten of which can be enjoyed by hiking a single trail—lie at the heart of Silver Falls State Park.

These 14 falls range in height from 27 feet to 178 feet, but numbers hardly capture their beauty. Festooned with ferns and surrounded by vine maples, Douglas-firs, and Western hemlocks, they tumble over old lava flows—left over from volcanic activity some 16 million years ago. In spring, violets and trilliums brighten the already bright sights, and in autumn, the vine maples burn with color, while winter ice frames the falls, forming silvery sculptures.

Something you won't see is a logger riding a canoe over the falls. Nor will you see old cars being pushed over the edge. These stunts went on in the 1920s, when one D.E. Geiser owned the property; he even charged a dime to look at the falls, when nothing else but water was spilling over them. The falls became a state park in 1948.

Although the Trail of Ten Falls serves as the park's centerpiece, Oregon's largest state park offers other attractions. Equestrians can explore the forested hills along 14 miles of bridle trails in the southern portion of the park. During spring and summer, the gardens surrounding the conference center bloom with columbines, fairy bells, kinnikinnic, and other wildflowers; plus a special garden features seven species of ferns. There's also a natural swimming pond that bulges out from the South Fork Silver Creek, near the main parking area.

What to See and Do

Heed the siren call of those waterfalls and head right for the main parking area, at the **South Falls Day Use Area.** Here, drop by the historic **Day Use Lodge** *(503-873-3495)*, built by the Civilian Conservation Corps in the 1930s, and take a look at the displays on the park's history, wildlife, and geology. A short walk brings you to a variety of viewpoints overlooking 177-foot-high **South Falls.**

From South Falls you can take the **Trail of Ten Falls** (a.k.a. Silver Creek Canyon Trail), which follows the South Fork Silver Creek to the north, swings east along the North Fork Silver Creek, then strikes out through the forest back to the South Falls area. The full, ten-falls loop is 7 miles long, but cutoffs allow less ambitious hikers round-trips of either 2 or 5 miles.

Hugging the creek, the trail winds a mile or so to **Lower South Falls,** where you stroll *behind* the curtain of cascading water, then curves over to the North Fork Silver Creek and **Lower North Falls.** Seven more cascades await as you continue up this creek branch. Don't forget to appreciate some of the sights beyond the falling water: lush hemlocks, wood violets, browsing deer, and a profusion of ferns. Along the way, also note the small caves in the lava formed by huge gas bubbles. People unable or unwilling to take the trail can view several of the falls from overlooks along Oreg. 214, or by taking short strolls off the road.

Camping

The park offers 51 tent sites and 54 RV sites, with showers. Reservations advised in season; call 800-452-5687. Camping fee. The Silver Falls Conference Center has 4 lodges and 10 cabins; call 800-452-5687 for reservations.

❏ *SILVER FALLS STATE PARK, 20024 SILVER FALLS HIGHWAY SE, SUBLIMITY, OREGON 97385*

Why the Falls Fall

The park's falls came to be because Yakima basalt is hard. This rock underlies much of the park, and it strongly resists erosion. But below the Yakima basalt lie layers of softer material, which erodes lower and lower beneath the pounding water while the basalt stands tall. The falls also migrate upstream when winter winds blow tumbling water back into cracks in the basalt cliffs, where it freezes, expands, and splits the rock.

331

Sunset Bay

**12 miles southwest of Coos Bay
on Cape Arago Hwy.**

Oregon's wild coast, at Sunset Bay

● 1,286 acres ● 541-888-3778
● Year-round ● Vehicle permit
fee ● Rocky coastline
● Sandy beach ● Seal and sea
lion colonies ● Historic garden ● Tide pooling, whale-
watching, hiking

Embraced by sandstone bluffs, half-moon **Sunset Bay** showcases the Oregon coast to perfection. Here you can hike atop 100-foot-high cliffs and watch burly Pacific waves burst against massive offshore rocks; lounge on a sandy beach backed by a verdant conifer forest; or poke through tide pools filled with sea anemones, tiny crabs, and purple sea urchins. Low tide exposes a good but overused tide-pooling area on the beach's north end.

Sunset Bay is one of three adjacent state parks overlooking the Pacific Ocean. You can drive from one to the next, or hike a 4-mile section of the **Oregon Coast Trail,** which strings the parks together. Passing through lush coastal forest, the narrow trail winds atop sandstone bluffs that yield fine ocean views.

Neighboring **Shore Acres State Park** (*541-888-3778. Vehicle permit fee*) invites you to walk along seaside cliffs; there's even an enclosed gazebo to watch the crashing surf of winter storms. But the heart of Shore Acres—the former estate of pioneer shipbuilder and lumberman Louis J. Simpson—lies a few hundred feet inland, amid the tulips, elegant roses, azaleas, and other seasonal flowers that fill the elaborate formal gardens.

Of the three state parks, **Cape Arago** (*541-888-3778. Vehicle permit fee*), located just south of Shore Acres, possesses the most dramatic bluff views, taking in Simpson Reef and Shell Island. From this high perch you can watch sea lions and elephant seals cavort offshore, plus gray whales migrating south from March to June. For a closer look, take the trail that leads down to a sandy beach.

Camping

Sunset Bay has 72 tent sites, 63 RV sites (some with hook-ups), and 4 yurts, all with showers. Reservations advised in season; call 800-452-5687. Camping fee.
❏ *Sunset Bay State Park, 10965 Cape Arago Hwy., Coos Bay, OR 97420*

Farewell Bend

25 miles northwest of Ontario, off I-84

● **70 acres** ● **541-869-2365** ● **Year-round** ● **Oregon Trail history** ● **Snake River fishing (license required)** ● **Pioneer- and Indian-style camping**

More than 150 years ago, pioneers used Farewell Bend as a rest stop to prepare for the final leg of the Oregon Trail. After following the Snake River for 320 miles, they left the river at this point to avoid the forbidding Hells Canyon area—hence, "Farewell Bend." If those pioneers were traveling through today, they still would recognize the rolling sagebrush-grasslands, harboring deer, pronghorn, partridge, chukar, and, during spring and summer, a profusion of high-desert wild-flowers. But they would also find a popular site for camping, hiking, and fishing. And the Snake River—since impounded into a reservoir—they wouldn't know at all.

To get your historical bearings, start at the kiosk, which imparts the basics about the Oregon Trail. Knowing that the pioneers began their trek in Missouri, thousands of grueling miles away, helps you comprehend the bone-weary fatigue that must have plagued them at this point in their journey.

Now drive north from the park on US 30, toward the little town of Huntington. After a mile or two, pull over and look for the **wagon wheel ruts** on either side of the road, made by bulky Conestoga wagons loaded with the lifelong possessions of pioneers. The ruts run for a couple of miles into Huntington.

About 2 miles from the park, you'll spot a small iron cross. It marks the site of an 1860 conflict between pioneers and Snake River Shoshone Indians, in which eight settlers were killed and two small children carried away.

Back at the park, appreciate the ease of your life as you fish, picnic, or hike the hills watching for wildlife. Come nightfall, you can taste a bit of the frontier experience by staying in one of the covered wagons or tepees.

Camping

The park has 93 tent and RV sites, with showers; 43 primitive tent sites; 4 walk-in tent sites; 2 group sites; 4 tepees; and 2 covered wagon campers. Reservations advised in season; call 800-452-5687. Camping fee.
❏ *Farewell Bend Recreation Area, Star Route, Huntington, OR 97907*

Deception Pass

North end of Whidbey Island and south end of Fidalgo Island, on Wash. 20

● 4,128 acres ● 360-675-2417 ● Year-round ● Beaches ● Forest and wetlands ● Interpretive Center ● Wildlife watching, hiking, swimming ● Boating, fishing (license required) ● Tide pooling

West Point and Deception Pass

Most people who daydream of island vacations envision tropical isles, but a visit to Deception Pass can make contenders of the islands off Washington's northern coast. Evergreens instead of palm trees, rocky shores instead of sugar-sand beaches—it's like comparing apples and oranges when both taste great. Small wonder that this is Washington's most popular state park, drawing nearly four million visitors a year.

The park straddles Fidalgo and Whidbey Islands—two of the largest of the dozens of islands that sprinkle the Strait of Juan de Fuca and Rosario Strait. The soaring bridge that connects the two islands is in itself a prime attraction, affording fine views of the islands, Rosario Strait, and the narrow channel below, which churns four times daily as tidal waters squeeze in and out. On either side of the bridge, visitors enjoy hiking trails, forested hills, bird-rich marshes, freshwater lakes, picturesque coves, striking oceanside bluffs, and even a few sandy beaches.

Capt. George Vancouver, the 18th-century British explorer, gave the park its name. In fact, he named it twice. In 1792,

Washington

when he first sailed through the area, he dubbed the inlet near today's bridge site "Port Gardner." He later discovered that the inlet wasn't an inlet, but a channel between the two islands; feeling deceived, he came up with "Deception Pass."

What to See and Do

Start at ground zero: **Deception Pass Bridge.** For the full, vertiginous effect, park in the lot at the south end, on Whidbey Island, and walk to the center of the 1,000-foot-long, 186-foot-high span. Gazing over the railing, most people step gingerly and parents clutch children's arms. You'll enjoy maximum spine tingles and knee weakness if the tide is running. Deception Pass is the only channel for many miles north and south, so a huge volume of water funnels through this narrow opening between Rosario Strait and Skagit Bay, at times resembling a white-water river.

Next, follow Wash. 20 south about a mile to the **park office,** where you can get maps and information. From the office, drive along the north shore of **Cranberry Lake** to **West Beach.** The park's longest sandy shore, West Beach is strewn with shells and driftwood, making it a favorite among beachcombers. It also features picnic sites, seasonal concessionaires, and, across the parking lot on the northern tip of

335

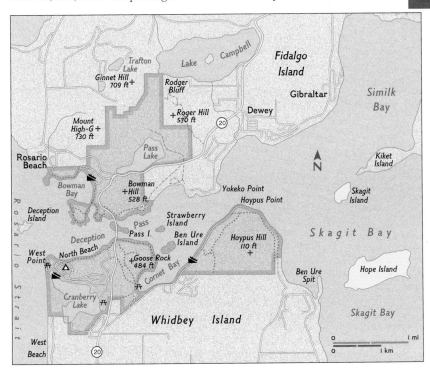

Maiden of Deception Pass

A Samish Indian story pole near the beginning of the Rosario Head Vista Point Trail tells the myth of Ko-Kwal-Alwoot, the maiden of Deception Pass. The sea spirit fell in love with this mortal Samish girl and asked for her hand in marriage. Her father refused, so the sea spirit, as spoiled immortals are wont to do, heaped famine and drought upon the Samish until he got his way. When Ko-Kwal-Alwoot entered the sea, her long hair floating in the current, she became immortal herself. Today her hair still can be seen waving in the water as the tide surges through Deception Pass, though some people think the hair looks a lot like seaweed.

Cranberry Lake, a cordoned-off swimming area. Here, too, is the trailhead for the 0.8-mile **Sand Dune Trail,** a paved loop through low beach dunes and along Cranberry Lake's western shore. Linger at the **Marshland Environmental Overlook** and scan the reeds and grasses for loons, thrushes, wrens, beavers, muskrats, and mink.

To explore the Fidalgo side of the park, drive over the bridge and take the turnoff to **Bowman Bay.** The handsome stone picnic shelters and restrooms you soon pass by, along with trails throughout the park, were built by the Civilian Conservation Corps in 1934-35. During the summer, a small but informative **Interpretive Center** displays artifacts and photographs of everyday life in the CCC camp.

The nearby **Bowman Bay/Rosario Beach Trail** heads north and west half a mile to Rosario Bay. Don't let the steep stretch near the trailhead discourage you; most of the trail is gentle. Passing through a varied forest, you occasionally glimpse the rocky bayshore. At trail's end, branch onto the .25-mile **Rosario Head Vista Point Trail,** looping out to Rosario Head Vista Point and back. From atop the 100-foot bluffs you'll have grand views of the straits and of the San Juans. If it's low tide, investigate the fecund tide pools along the way.

Further Adventures

● People with more time and stamina can try any of eight other trails. The longest is the 1.5-mile **Lighthouse Point Trail,** which begins at the lower parking lot at Bowman Bay and skirts a peninsula thrusting into the sea. Hikers savor sky-scraping groves of Douglas-fir and Western red cedar, a lively marsh, expansive ocean views, and a trek along the beach when the tide allows. (Note that it's dangerous and prohibited to enter the lighthouse.) Near the beginning, branch onto the 0.5-mile **Canoe Pass Vista Trail,** which provides a splendid view of Canoe Pass, as well as a look at numerous secluded coves.

● The steepest trail, which leads to the highest point in the park, is the **Goose Rock Summit Trail,** a 0.3-mile ascent yielding a vast panorama of the straits.

● A very different view of the straits awaits below sea level. Off Rosario Head, a designated underwater park gives scuba divers a look at life in these rich coastal waters. Visitors with the proper experience and gear—don't forget a thick wet suit—can get close-up and personal with sea cucumbers, ling cod, purple sea urchins, and perhaps a stingray.

Camping

Deception Pass has 246 tent and RV sites (no hook-ups), with showers; 5 walk-in sites; and 3 group camps. Reservations advised in season; call 800-452-5687. Camping fee.

❑ DECEPTION PASS STATE PARK, 5175 N. WASHINGTON, RTE. 20, OAK HARBOR, WASHINGTON 98277

Moran

6 miles southeast of Eastsound on Orcas Island, in the San Juan Islands

- 5,176 acres ● 360-376-2326 ● Year-round
- Mount Constitution ● Hiking, wildlife watching
- Boating, swimming, fishing (license required)

Start at the top. Drive (or hike, if you're feeling energetic) to the summit of **Mount Constitution;** at 2,407 feet, it's the highest mountain in the San Juan Islands. Ascend the historic **stone tower** and imbibe the 360-degree views of Orcas Island, the rest of the San Juans, Vancouver Island, the Gulf Islands, and the Washington and Canadian mainlands. Don't overlook the tower itself. Patterned after the 12th-century watchtowers of the Caucasus, it was built by Civilian Conservation Corps artisans in the 1930s.

Atop Mount Constitution, Orcas Island

The forests and lakes visible from the tower can be explored via some 30 miles of hiking trails. A flat, 4-mile path circles **Mountain Lake,** providing views of Mount Constitution and of bald eagles, ospreys, kingfishers, and other birds. Another flat trail rich with wildlife, the 2.5-mile **Cascade Loop** passes through a conifer forest. Watch for river otters, deer, muskrats, as well as an abundance of birds.

Camping

The park has 136 tent sites, with showers; and 15 primitive sites. Reservations required April through September; call 800-452-5687. Camping fee.

❏ *Moran State Park, Star Route, Box 22, Eastsound, WA 98245*

337

Fort Canby

2 miles southwest of Ilwaco off US 101, on Wash. 100

- 1,882 acres ● 360-642-3078 ● Year-round ● Lewis and Clark Interpretive Center ● Historic lighthouses
- Overlook of Columbia River mouth ● Benson Beach
- Hiking, surf fishing (license required), clamming

The "fort" part of Fort Canby State Park nearly has vanished, but the reason why a fort was built here remains: its strategic perch at the mouth of the Columbia River.

For millennia this junction of the continent's second-biggest river with the Pacific Ocean was a focal point for Native Americans. In more recent times, this crossroads drew the ships of 18th-century explorers, including Robert Gray, the American captain who in 1792 gave the river its name after

Cape Disappointment Light

338

Fort Columbia

A long cannon shot to the east of Fort Canby lies another historic military site, **Fort Columbia State Park** (360-777-8221. Interpretive Center open May-Sept. Wed.-Sun., grounds April-Sept.). Like Fort Canby, Fort Columbia was built to protect the entrance to the Columbia. Unlike Fort Canby, this site retains buildings, bunkers, and artillery from its active days. An Interpretive Center tells much about life at the fort, including old letters written by soldiers stationed here. One, penned in 1917 to "My dearest girl Rose," says in part: "...never until Uncle Sam called me from you did I fully realize what life would be like without you..." The lovesick G.I. goes on to propose.

making the first successful crossing of the treacherous Columbia River bar.

The mouth of the Columbia also served as the target for the first party to cross North America overland: the Lewis and Clark Expedition. The explorers first encountered the Pacific at this site, in 1805, inspiring Capt. William Clark to write in his journal: "men appear much satisfied with their trip beholding with astonishment the high waves dashing against the rock and this 'emence Ocian.'"

What to See and Do

Drive directly to the **Lewis and Clark Interpretive Center,** which stands on the bluffs high above the dramatic meeting of river and sea, and plan to stay an hour or two in order to savor its richly detailed exhibits. The bulk of the story of Meriwether Lewis and William Clark and their exploration of the West is told via a **"trail."** This winding corridor of artifacts and information follows the expedition from its May 14, 1804, beginnings in Missouri to its Nov. 15, 1805, arrival at a point near where you're standing. You'll learn that Thomas Jefferson officially labeled the expedition a "literary pursuit," concealing its commercial and territorial intentions from world powers; and that among their supplies were six kegs of brandy.

Take the time to read some of the journal entries. One describes a grizzly attack on six of the men. Four shot at the great bear, but it kept coming, driving them into a river and wading right in after them. It didn't stop until one man shot it in the head and killed it.

At the end of the Lewis and Clark path you'll emerge into a viewing room. Walk over to the huge windows and look upon the broad mouth of the mighty Columbia—as Lewis and Clark did nearly 200 years ago.

Exhibits in this part of the center also tell you that the

mouth of the Columbia is known as the "graveyard of the Pacific"; these treacherous waters have claimed nearly 2,000 vessels. That's the reason for the large **Coast Guard station** just below the Interpretive Center. It's also the reason for the **Cape Disappointment Lighthouse** *(Closed to visitors)*, which can be reached via a short trail from the Interpretive Center. Built in 1856, it's the oldest operating lighthouse on the West Coast.

Drive out to the **North Jetty** and you may see members of the Coast Guard doing lifeboat drills in the surf. From the jetty, stroll along **Benson Beach** or hike through the forested interior of the park along 4 miles of trails. Near the other end of the park you can visit the **North Head Lighthouse** *(360-642-3078. Daily June-Aug., weekends April-May and Sept.-Oct.; adm. fee)*, built in 1898.

Camping and Lodging

Fort Canby offers 250 tent and RV sites, with showers. Camping fee. Also available are 3 yurts, 3 cabins, and a summer house. Reservations advised in season; call 800-452-5687.

❏ *Fort Canby State Park, P.O. Box 488, Ilwaco, WA 98624*

Riverside

339

Northwest edge of Spokane, on Wash. 291

● 7,575 acres ● 509-456-3964 ● Year-round ● Spokane House Interpretive Center ● Riverside trails ● Wetlands

Riverside State Park consists of several units. The main parcel winds for several miles along a pretty, wooded stretch of the Spokane River. **Aubrey L. White Parkway** provides motorists with a scenic river overlook, taking in striking "bowl and pitcher" rock formations rising from the water. Hiking trails lead along the banks and up Deep Creek to a fossil bed.

A little farther north, at the confluence of the Little Spokane River, lies the **Spokane House Interpretive Center** *(509-466-4747. Mem. Day–Labor Day)*, which recalls the history of a fur-trading post built on that site in 1810. Just east of the center awaits the **Little Spokane Natural Area,** comprising about 1,300 acres of wetlands and woods. Much of the natural area is a freshwater marsh favored by wildlife, including a great blue heron rookery. Nearby is **Indian Rock Paintings,** a 1-acre parcel containing a large rock covered with Indian pictographs.

Camping

The park has 101 tent and RV sites (no hook-ups), with showers. Reservations advised in season; call 800-452-5687. Camping fee.

❏ *Riverside S.P., 4427 N. Aubrey L. White Pkwy., Spokane, WA 99205*

Chugach

Eagle River Nature Center: 26 miles east of Anchorage via Glenn Hwy. (Alas. 1) and Eagle River Rd.; Park Headquarters: 12 miles south of Anchorage via Seward Hwy. (Alas. 1)

● 495,204 acres ● 907-345-5014 ● Year-round ● Hiking, mountain biking, rock climbing, horseback riding ● Boating, fishing (license required) ● Wildlife viewing ● Whitewater rafting ● Historic railroad section house

What Central Park is to Manhattan, Chugach is to Anchorage: the place where locals relax, play with their kids, read a book under a tree, birdwatch, picnic, take a stroll (often a very long stroll), row a boat—even cross-country ski in winter—except that Anchorage's "backyard wilderness" is about 37 times the area of Manhattan, and its animals are not in a zoo.

Chugach also has several dozen glaciers and 70 peaks. Part of the northern terminus of the 300-mile-long Chugach Range, the dark, jagged mountains are the wreckage of ancient sea-bottom sediments lifted by colliding continental plates, then crushed by ice age glaciers so heavy the region rose in elevation as they melted. White dots on their rock faces might be climbers, but more likely they are Dall's sheep, some 2,000 of which live here along with hundreds of mountain goats, black bears, lynx, and moose. Fewer in number, but carrying formidable mythologies, are wolves and perhaps two dozen Alaskan brown bears—the fabled humpbacked grizzly—citizens of a park whose main Visitor Center is barely a half-hour drive from Anchorage.

Ice floes drifting in Turnagain Arm

Alaska

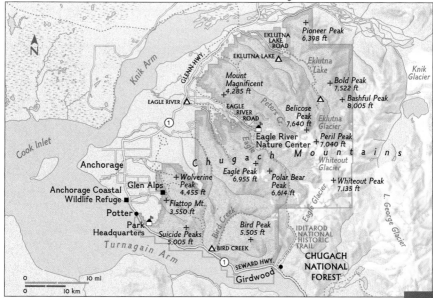

Map labels:

N

Knik Arm

EKLUTNA LAKE ROAD

EKLUTNA LAKE

+ Pioneer Peak 6,398 ft

Eklutna Lake

Knik Glacier

GLENN HWY.

Mount Magnificent 4,285 ft

△ EAGLE RIVER

EAGLE RIVER ROAD

Peters C.

+ Bold Peak 7,522 ft

+ Bashful Peak 8,005 ft

Belicose Peak 7,640 ft

Eklutna Glacier

Cook Inlet

Eagle River Nature Center

Peril Peak 7,040 ft

Chugach Mountains

Whiteout Glacier

Anchorage

Eagle Peak 6,955 ft

Polar Bear Peak 6,614 ft

+ Whiteout Peak 7,135 ft

Anchorage Coastal Wildlife Refuge ■

Glen Alps

+ Wolverine Peak 4,455 ft

Eagle Glacier

L. George Glacier

Potter

+ Flattop Mt. 3,550 ft

Bird Creek

Bird Peak 5,505 ft

Park Headquarters

Suicide Peaks 5,005 ft

△ BIRD CREEK

IDITAROD NATIONAL HISTORIC TRAIL

Turnagain Arm

SEWARD HWY.

CHUGACH NATIONAL FOREST

Girdwood

0   10 mi
0   10 km

What to See and Do

Chugach's proximity to the city makes for easy tours of wildlife and historical exhibits at both the Visitor Center and Nature Center, a trail walk or two, and a picnic in mountain forest or near the mudflats at the **Anchorage Coastal Wildlife Refuge** *(907-267-2556. Warning: At low tide the exposed mudflats act as quicksand)*, where shorebirds take to the air like exploding confetti. The park's proximity to urban areas has not compro-

mised its wild heart; the quality of wilderness here rivals that of remote Alaskan destinations beyond the reach of roads.

If you have only half a day, drive east from Anchorage on the Glenn Highway (Alas. 1), taking Eagle River Road from Milepost 19 to the **Eagle River Nature Center,** where interpretive exhibits survey park wildlife and geology. Pick up a copy of the park's visitor guide, entitled *Ridgelines,* which has maps and descriptions of driving and walking tours to fit all schedules, interests, and capabilities. Stroll the boardwalk along the glacier-fed **Eagle River,** which crosses a tundralike basin between timbered foothills rising steeply into the forbidding Chugach Mountains. For an introduction to Alaskan wilderness, walk the **Albert Loop Trail,** a nearly level 3-mile loop through mixed forest to the river, where silt-laden snowmelt rushes over braided gravel bars. Picnic tables in the **Eagle River Campground** offer an excellent place to relax a bit on your return.

Another half-day option is to take the Seward Highway south from Anchorage. Near Milepost 116, the reedy **Potter Marsh** wetlands hide limpid trout and salmon streams where migratory waterbirds nest. A boardwalk across the marsh is posted with interpretive information on the fish and wildlife beneath your feet. Continue south 1 mile to **Park Headquarters** at the **Potter Section House State Historic Site,** once an important Alaska Railroad worker camp. Picnic tables outside afford a sweeping view of **Turnagain Arm,** a fjord-like extension of Cook Inlet dug by ice age glaciers and swept by dangerous tides. (The Turnagain Arm Trail parallels the shoreline, highway, and railroad south from here for 9.4 miles.)

For an easy but rewarding quarter-mile walk to views across Anchorage and Cook Inlet to the Alaska Range 80 miles distant (North America's tallest peaks), backtrack toward Anchorage on Alas. 1, turning right (east) onto De Armoun Road. Continue east via Hillside, Upper Huffman, and Toilsome Roads to the head of the **Glen Alps Trailhead.** A wheelchair-accessible path leads to a sitting area and viewing deck.

If your schedule permits a day-long visit, and you have a mountain bike, pedal the 12.7-mile **Lakeside Trail** from **Eklutna Lake** to the **Eklutna Glacier.** (Access the lake from Glenn Highway, Eklutna Lake Road exit.) The trail skirts the lake, then follows vast gravel bars to a final mile-long walk over glacial detritus to the foot of the mammoth blue ice river. The easy trail climbs only 300 feet, but ends with a face-to-face meeting with the Alaskan wilds.

Camping

The park has 3 campgrounds with 147 tent and RV sites (May–Sept.), no showers. Reservations advised in season; contact the park. Camping fee.

❏ *CHUGACH STATE PARK HEADQUARTERS, POTTER SECTION HOUSE STATE HISTORIC SITE, HC 52 BOX 8899, INDIAN, ALASKA 99540*

Encounters with Ursidae

The principle for dealing with bears is brains versus brawn. If you spot one, backtrack. If it sees you, retreat slowly and diagonally. If it approaches, stop. If it charges (usually a bluff), don't run. (You can't outrun them.) Stand tall, wave your arms, and speak loudly in a deep voice. Charging bears usually veer off at the last moment. If attacked, play dead—curl up in a ball with your hands behind your neck. The bear might nudge you, but will typically stop attacking. If not, fight back ferociously: Aggressive bears are often young and can be intimidated.

Denali

132 miles north of Anchorage, on the George Parks Hwy. (Alas. 3)

● 324,240 acres ● 907-745-3975 ● Year-round, but facilities closed mid-Oct. to mid-May ● Mount McKinley viewpoints ● Backcountry hiking, white-water kayaking, fishing (license required)

In the sunset shadow of Mount McKinley and its mammoth, glacier-collared companions in the towering Alaska Range, the unsung neighbor of Denali National Park and Preserve is much less visited, yet, unlike its federal sister, traversed with an extensive trail system. Alaska's own Denali requires no backcountry permits and is designed for avid hikers and campers seeking deep solitude amid wilderness terrain rising from lowland river basins and glacier-gouged valleys to alpine tundra and barren peaks.

343

Fleet-footed Dall's sheep

The park is bisected by the braided gravel channels of the Chulitna River and an adjoining, 37-mile stretch of the George Parks Highway. River and road are paralleled on the east by the imposing Curry and Kesugi Ridges, their slopes etched by six trails ranging in length from a well-maintained and easy 1.2 miles to a difficult 36.2-mile trek requiring first-rate map-reading skills.

What to See and Do

If you're just driving through, stop at Milepost 135.2 along the George Parks Highway for what is considered the finest roadside view of the **Alaska Range.** There's an interpretive display here that explains the geology of the panorama and identifies the mountains, but you'll need no prompting to appreciate the mountains' grandeur. (Other viewpoints are located at Mileposts 147.1, 158.1, and 162.3.)

Park information is available at the **Visitor Contact Station,** adjoining the Alaska Veterans Memorial at Milepost 147.1. There are forested picnic sites at nearby **Byers Lake**

The High One

Long before William McKinley became 25th President of the U.S. in 1897, Athapaskan-speaking Alaska natives knew as Denali—"the high one"—the 20,320-foot mountain that would eventually commemorate him. High indeed: Driving from Anchorage you'll first see the eternally snow-mantled massif, North America's tallest peak, around Milepost 69.1, weather permitting—though you are still 95 miles from the mountain. And no wonder: McKinley towers 18,000 feet above the surrounding terrain, a vertical rise surpassing Mount Everest's.

Campground, a roadside haven at Milepost 147. If you have two hours and comfortable walking shoes, consider strolling the easy, well-maintained 4.8-mile **Byers Lake Loop Trail** from here around tree-ringed Byers Lake. There are picnic sites there as well, and two rental cabins. The lake's serenity is preserved by a ban against gasoline-powered boats.

If you're prepared to hike difficult terrain and have a day to spend at it, consider trekking a portion of the **Kesugi Ridge Trail,** which you can access from Byers Lake Campground, or from a roadside trailhead at Little Coal Creek at Milepost 163.9.

As you drive through the park, you'll skirt the churning gray flow of the **Chulitna River.** The milky soup is laden with "glacial flour," rock pulverized by glaciers rasping Alaska Range mountains to the west. From the Lower Troublesome Creek Campground Trailhead at Milepost 137.2, it's an easy, 1.2-mile stroll down to the river on the **Chulitna Confluence Trail.**

If you've come for extended backcountry sojourning, consider exploring the rugged Peters Hills in the park's western reach, where the absence of trails rewards hikers with a splendid isolation watched over by the south face of Mount McKinley.

Camping

The park has 4 campgrounds with 114 tent and RV sites. Backcountry camping permitted throughout the park. Available on a first-come, first-served basis. Camping fee. Byers Lake cabins available by reservation year-round; call the park or 907-269-8400.

❑ DENALI STATE PARK, DIVISION OF PARKS & OUTDOOR RECREATION, HC 32 BOX 6706, WASILLA, ALASKA 99654

Wood-Tikchik

350 miles west of Anchorage, access by plane

● 1,555,200 acres ● 907-269-8698 ● Year-round ● Wilderness camping ● Hiking, river running ● Hunting, fishing (license required for both)

A sampler of Alaskan terrain, the Delaware-size preserve is not only the nation's largest state park, but also its most remote. Wood-Tikchik takes its name from two separate systems of river-connected lakes within it. Deep, crystal-clear, and teeming with trout and other sport fish, the 12 lakes range in length from 7 to 45 miles, lapping gravel shores in marshy lowland tundra on the east and mirroring the dark spires of the Wood River Mountains in fjordlike arms on the west.

Heather tundra and spruce-birch forest green the park's lower elevations. Climbing, hikers pass through coniferous forest into alder-choked foothills, then alpine meadows giving way to treeless mountains of glacier-polished rock. They also find beavers, moose, bears, marmots, otters, foxes, wolverines, mink, and bald eagles in an utterly wild kingdom.

Daily airline service links Anchorage and Dillingham; however, the park's isolation makes it best suited for experienced campers well-equipped for self-reliant backcountry fishing and hiking sojourns. Access to the Wood River Lakes is possible by Jet boat from Dillingham or Aleknagik, 24 road miles north. Most visitors, however, fly in and out of these as well as the northerly Tikchik Lakes *(expect air taxis to charge at least $250 per hour)*. Ask park personnel to suggest destinations appropriate to your interests, abilities, equipment, as well as commercially available guide services.

Camping

The park is open to no-impact, "leave-no-trace" camping.
❑ *Wood-Tikchik S.P., P.O. Box 3022, Dillingham, AK 99576 (mid-May–Sept.); 3601 C St., ste. 1200, Anchorage, AK 99503 (Oct.–mid-May)*

Totem Bight

**12 miles north of Ketchikan
on North Tongass Highway**

● 11 acres ● 907-465-4563 ● Daily mid-May to mid-Sept.,
Mon. to Fri. rest of year ● No
camping ● Re-created Native
Alaskan totem art and architecture ● Interpretive trail

Native American culture found extraordinary expression among southeast Alaska's Tlingit and Haida people, whose skill as hunters and fishermen in the Inland Passage region created ample leisure time to refine the art of carving and painting totem poles. Among other reasons, the demise of native barter economies by the early 20th century led to the abandonment of villages, whose houses and totems fell into decay. A program of reconstruction using tribal artists and traditional methods and materials commenced in the 1930s. Its crowning achievement is Totem Bight, where a re-created 19th-century clan house and 14 totem poles are arranged along a self-guided **interpretive trail.**

Detail of reconstructed Clan House

Don't walk the forested trail without the keyed brochure —it's essential for appreciating the totems' storytelling symbolism, and understanding family life in the clan house.
❑ *Dept. of Natural Resources, Division of Parks & Outdoor Recreation, Southeast Area, 400 Willoughby Ave., 4th Fl., Juneau, AK 99801*

Far West

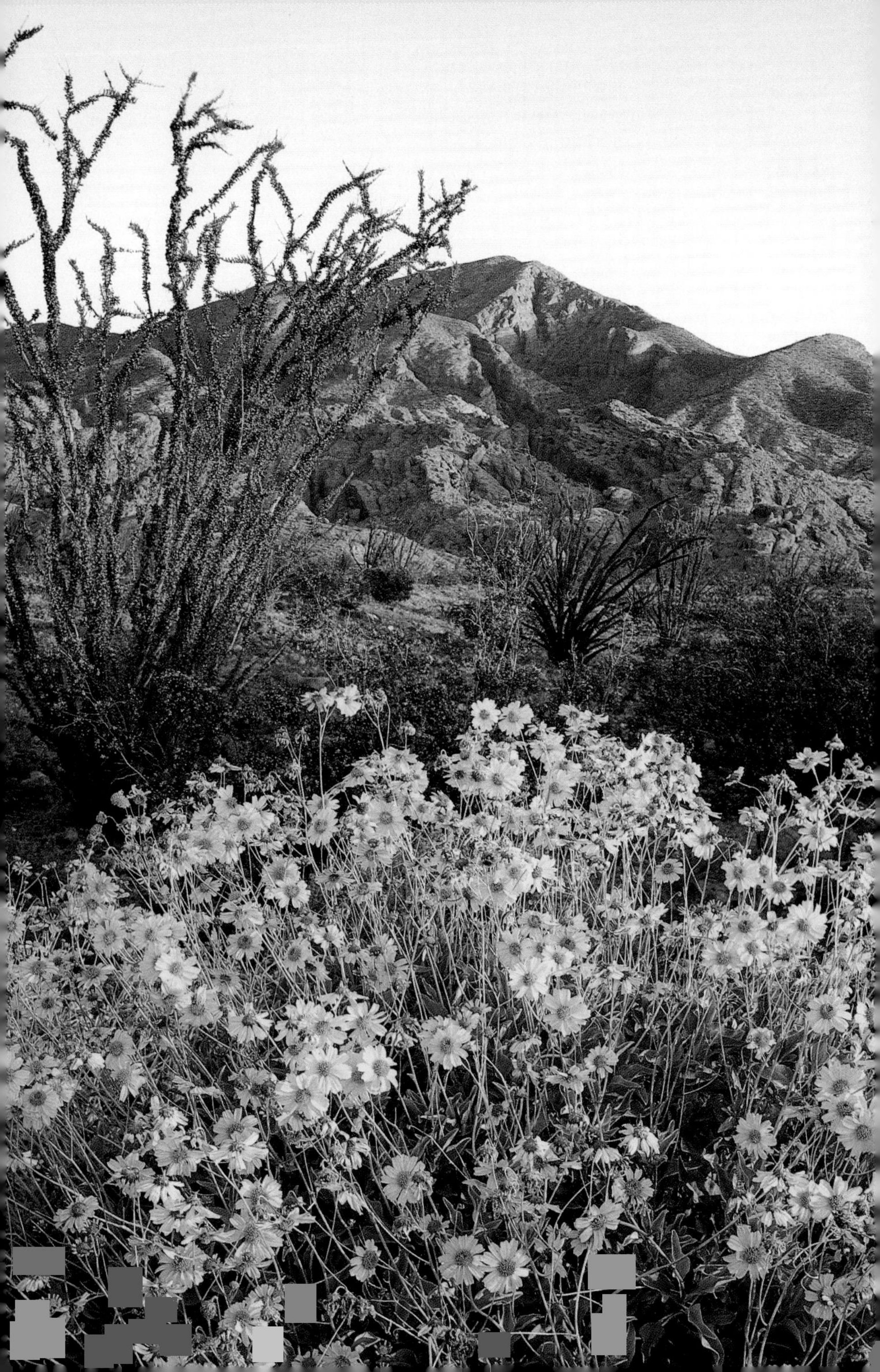

Nevada

Lake Tahoe Nevada
Valley of Fire
Cathedral Gorge
Berlin-Ichthyosaur

California

Anza-Borrego Desert
Humboldt Redwoods
Plumas-Eureka
Mount Tamalpais
Pfeiffer Big Sur
Año Nuevo

Hawaii

Na Pali Coast
Waimea Canyon and Kokee
Kealakekua
Iao Valley
Iolani Palace

Anza-Borrego Desert State Park, California

Lake Tahoe Nevada

15 miles west of Carson City on Nev. 28

Lake Tahoe

- 14,242 acres
- 702-831-0494
- Year-round
- Day-use fee
- Snows closes some trails in winter ● Lakeside beaches ● Mountain backcountry ● Fishing (license required), hiking, mountain biking, cross-country skiing

Nevada's most popular state park reaches toward the sky among the granite peaks and pine trees of the Carson Range, and also sprawls along the undeveloped northeastern shore of Lake Tahoe. From 6,225 feet at the lakeshore, the terrain rises to 9,214 feet at Snow Valley Peak, all in a distance of just 1.5 miles.

Tahoe, in the language of the Washo Indians who once spent summers fishing here, probably means "big water." The lake, filling a basin between the Sierra Nevada mountains and the Carson Range, measures 22 miles long, 12 miles wide, and 1,645 feet deep. It holds more than 39.8 trillion gallons of water and is clear enough in places to see to a depth of 65 feet. Its vibrant colors range through prismatic spectrums of blue and green.

After the 1850s, loggers came to Tahoe, then settlers. Tourism and summer house development began before the turn of the century and boomed after World War II. Today, the park has five visitor areas along Nev. 28 and US

50 that offer a range of resources, from white-sand beaches and swimming spots to 13,000 acres of wooded backcountry laced with trails and small lakes.

What to See and Do

Many travelers set off for the park from the casino hub of South Lake Tahoe. Leaving behind the temples of temptation, drive north on US 50 to the park's first section at **Cave Rock.** Here you'll take in gorgeous views of the lake, with the mighty Sierra Nevada as a backdrop. Cave Rock is a popular spot to launch boats and fish; it also has picnic sites and a small beach.

The entrance to the next section, **Spooner Lake,** is on Nev. 28 just north of the junction with US 50. Visitors can enjoy catch-and-release fishing for trout, as well as picnicking, mountain biking, and hiking. Along the lakeside nature trail, you'll likely see herons; if you're lucky, you

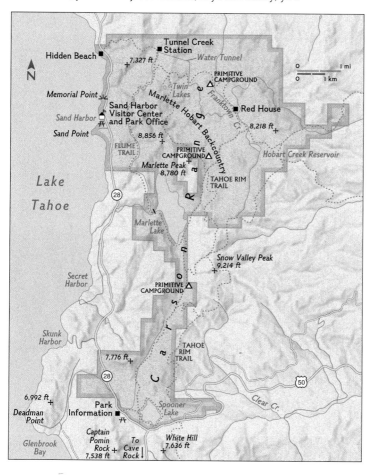

Black-tailed jackrabbit

Tahoe's Trees

During the latter part of the 19th century, Nevada's Comstock Lode and booming Virginia City created a ravenous market for mine timbers, building materials, and firewood. Most of the centuries-old pine trees around Lake Tahoe fell to the woodsman's ax. Thickets of fir trees replaced pine forests, but unfortunately, firs aren't well adapted to Tahoe's periodic droughts. Today, visitors see many large, dead, second-growth firs, weakened by drought and attacked by bark beetles.

350

may even spy an American bald eagle.

Spooner Lake is also a backcountry trailhead. The **North Canyon Trail** leads 5 miles to **Marlette Lake,** while a scenic trail follows the western shore. This connects with the historic **Flume Trail,** which mountain bikers rate among the top in the nation; the terrain is challenging, the views of Lake Tahoe unforgettable. North of Marlette Lake, above **Little Valley,** stands an old-growth forest, saved because 19th-century lumbermen found the trees too difficult to clear.

For an alternative route from Spooner Lake, hike the **Tahoe Rim Trail** along the crest of the Carson Range. From this angle, you see Lake Tahoe as it can't be viewed from water level. Look for glacier-gouged **Emerald Bay** on the far shore. Or gaze east at the Carson Valley, the Stillwater Range, and the Shoshone Mountains.

In winter, Spooner Lake maintains 60 miles of groomed cross-country ski trails (702-749-5349. Trail pass required; equipment rentals and ski lessons offered).

Back on Nev. 28, head north about 8 miles to **Sand Harbor,** where beaches edge a point of land marked by boulders and pines. The warm, sun-drenched sand is a welcome relief if you've waded into the lake, whose high temperature in midsummer is only 68°F. Snorkelers and scuba divers often plunge into the water north of the point, where conditions are calm; there's also a boat launch here. You can explore the point itself along the **Sand Point Nature Trail,** then have lunch in the shade of Jeffrey pines in a designated picnic area equipped with barbecue grills.

At the end of the 19th century, a Comstock mining mogul named Walter Hobart threw spectacular parties at his Sand Harbor summer home. Nowadays the community hosts a summer festival of music and Shakespeare at an outdoor theater (800-747-4697. Adm. fee) by the lake.

A mile north of Sand Harbor, you reach the park's final section, alongside Nev. 28. Stop first at **Memorial Point** overlook, which offers a broad view of Lake Tahoe (photographers take note); a trail here leads down to the rocky shoreline. Drive another mile toward Incline Village to a spot known mostly to locals, **Hidden Beach.** (Note: There's no parking here; leave your car along the highway and walk in.) The beach is popular with sunbathers (who aren't always wearing clothes).

Also in this area is the **Tunnel Creek Trailhead,** another way into the Carson Range backcountry. The trail climbs steeply to link with the Flume Trail, the Tahoe Rim Trail, and **Hobart Creek Reservoir.**

Camping

The park has 15 primitive tent sites. Available on a first-come, first-served basis. Camping fee.

❏ LAKE TAHOE NEVADA STATE PARK, P.O. BOX 8867, INCLINE, NV 89452

Valley of Fire

55 miles northeast of Las Vegas on Nev. 169

● **34,880 acres** ● **702-397-2088** ● **Year-round** ● **Adm. fee** ● **Summer temperatures reach well above 100°F** ● **Colorful rock formations** ● **Prehistoric rock art** ● **Petrified wood** ● **Hiking**

The Valley of Fire seems otherworldly, a surreal realm of stone formations with evocative names like Cobra Rock, Indian Marbles, and Grand Piano. Indeed, the area is named for a phenomenon of cosmic scale: In the morning and the evening, the low slanting sun touches the ancient red sandstone like a torch, setting it ablaze.

351

Here the past is laid bare. You have entered a basin of Aztec sandstone that formed during the age of dinosaurs (about 200 million years ago) from vast dunes of sand. In this stone, water carved canyons, spires, domes, and spiny ridges. Wind scoured the exposed walls of buttes and canyons, gouging them into odd textures and shapes, including arches and balancing rocks. Upon these sculptures, chemical reactions created tints across the entire warm spectrum: ruby, rosé wine, terra cotta, apricot, copper, gold.

Hiker on sandstone slickrock

On some rock walls, prehistoric Indians left petroglyphs depicting suns, lizards, eagles, mountain sheep, snakes, and other symbols of life in the desert. The park still offers a habitat for these creatures, as well as for the gila monster and desert tortoise, two rare reptiles that visitors must avoid disturbing. The Valley of Fire State Park, the oldest in Nevada, was established in 1935 to protect this fragile and beautiful desert environment.

What to See and Do

If you've driven east from Las Vegas on I-15 and Nev. 169, you'll enter the park through the west gate into a classic scene of the Wild West, where red rocks are set off by skies as blue as Navajo turquoise. In the jumbled stone formations you might see sphinxes, whales, or anything else your imagination can conjure out of all these oddities of rock. Just ahead, for instance, lie the **Beehives,** sandstone deposits that were shaped in a swirling pattern by the desert's relentless onslaught of heat, cold, rain, and wind.

Beyond the Beehives on the right, a **loop trail** leads to a deposit of petrified wood, solid evidence of a forest that thrived here 225 million years ago. You'll see some whole logs, but mostly fragments.

A spur road on the opposite side of Nev. 169 leads to **Atlatl Rock.** Here you climb iron stairs up a sheer wall of rock to see a panel of Indian petroglyphs. This register of ancient life was left by the valley's earliest visitors, the Ancestral Puebloans who, from around 300 B.C. to A.D. 1150, occupied the Lost City, located just east of the park along the floodplain of the Muddy River (see sidebar). These prehistoric people came to the Valley of Fire to hunt game and gather seeds.

The designs were carved through desert varnish, a dark coating created when leaching water draws minerals from the rock. Outstanding among the depictions is an atlatl, a notched wooden stick used by prehistoric hunters to throw darts faster and farther. You'll also see concentric circles and bounding mountain sheep. The designs' meanings are not known, but some may have had ceremonial signifi-

Atlatl Rock petroglyphs

cance or represented social clans.

Driving again on Nev. 169, stop at the **Visitor Center** to study fine exhibits on the valley's human and natural history. You'll learn that the dominant plants here are creosote bushes, and beavertail and cholla cactuses, all of which have adapted to living on sparse, irregular rainfall. Spring wildflowers include marigolds and desert mallow, which bloom along the park roads.

From the Visitor Center, a spur road leads to the **Petroglyph Canyon Trail,** a 0.5-mile, round-trip walk on the sandy floor of a canyon. On the vertical walls look for more prehistoric Indian rock art. In this canyon you'll also experience the park's immense silence; the only sounds are the crunching of your shoes in the sandy wash and your breath huffing into the empty skies.

The trail leads to **Mouse's Tank,** named for a renegade Paiute Indian of the 1890s, who reportedly murdered two prospectors and then fled to the Valley of Fire. This rugged spot offered a perfect hideout—but how could anyone live here without water? Mouse stumbled upon a natural water-collection basin, a depression in the rocks that could hold rainwater for months, known today as Mouse's Tank.

Continue along the spur road *(closed at sunset)* to **Rainbow Vista,** where you can look out over rock formations tinged in a dramatic splash of reds. Across from Rainbow Vista catch a roller-coaster of a gravel road to an overlook on **Fire Canyon,** a 600-foot-deep gorge. Also here is **Silica Dome,** whose whiteness contrasts starkly with the underlying red rock, separated by a line as straight as a yardstick.

Back on the spur road, continue north about 3 miles. You'll come to a closed dirt road used as a hiking and mountain-biking trail to **Duck Rock** (which looks vaguely like a duck, or perhaps a baseball hat). At road's end stand the **White Domes,** two formations of white silica melting together with red sandstone to create tints of pink and lavender.

Upon returning to Nev. 169 east, you pass the **Seven Sisters,** a gaggle of towering monoliths on the south side of the road. Ahead you'll see the stone cabins built by the Civilian Conservation Corps in the 1930s, later used to accommodate overnight travelers. Then comes the much-photographed **Elephant Rock,** reached via a short trail; the chunky rock indeed looks as wrinkled as an elephant's hide.

Camping

The park has 51 tent and RV sites, with showers. Available first come, first served. Camping fee.

❏ *VALLEY OF FIRE STATE PARK, P.O. BOX 515, OVERTON, NEVADA 89040*

Lost City

An exhibit in nearby Overton commemorates the vanished culture of the ancestral Puebloans, also known as the Anasazi ("Ancient Ones"), who hunted and gathered in the Valley of Fire. They lived in the Pueblo Grande de Nevada, an area where pithouses and pueblo apartments once were clustered in sites stretching over some 30 miles. The **Lost City Museum** *(721 Moapa Valley Blvd. 702-397-2193. Adm. fee)* stands on part of this old pueblo, now referred to as the Lost City. Exhibits include a replicated dwelling of wattle and daub, as well as tools, jewelry, and pots made before the Anasazi disappeared mysteriously around A.D. 1150.

Cathedral Gorge

2 miles northwest of Panaca on US 93

● 1,633 acres ● 702-728-4460
● Year-round ● Entrance fee
● Extreme summer and winter
temperatures ● Small gorge
● Clay formations ● Hiking

Bentonite cliffs and canyon

354

At first the park's main feature—bentonite clay formations—sounds like something only a geologist could love. But you soon adopt a geologist's appreciative eye.

Today you see the remnant of a Pliocene lake; if you were standing here three million years ago, you'd be buried under water and mud a thousand feet deep. Over time the lake drained and its sediments dried and hardened. The resulting siltstone and shale was eroded by the elements, leaving buff-colored canyons and cliffs.

After Mormon settlers founded nearby Panaca in 1864, ranchers used the chasm as a garbage dump. (You can still find old cans and glass bottles.) In the 1890s, a local woman, upon viewing the delicately eroded spires, was reminded of European cathedrals—thus the name Cathedral Gorge. Later, two Panaca teenagers built a series of ladders through the maze of canyons and crawlways. By the 1920s, families came to picnic, and open-air pageants were staged at the gorge. It became a state park in 1935.

The **Visitor Center** exhibits regional geology and wildlife, including jackrabbits, coyotes, packrats, lizards, and snakes.

A 0.5-mile loop trail links the campground and the **"caves,"** actually narrow canyon sections also accessible by car. A 4-mile trail leads from the campground through the remote **upper gorge** among ridgelike fins. The 1-mile **Miller Point Trail** passes between 100-foot-high walls.

Off US 93, 2 miles north of the main entrance, **Miller Point Overlook** offers views into two side canyons. A nature loop along the access road reveals the upper gorge.

Camping

The park has 22 tent and RV sites, with showers. Available first come, first served. Camping fee.

❑ CATHEDRAL GORGE STATE PARK, P.O. BOX 176, PANACA, NEVADA 89042

Berlin-Ichthyosaur

22 miles east of Gabbs, off Nev. 844

● 1,132 acres ● 702-964-2440 ● Year-round ● Marine fossils ● Ghost town ● Old mine ● Seasonal tours

For over a century, men have dug here on the western slope of the Shoshone Range seeking two things: precious metals and fossils. Not surprisingly, this park has two main attractions. The first is **Berlin,** a turn-of-the-century mining town set among pinyon pines and junipers; its mine produced about 850,000 dollars worth of silver, gold, and mercury, which supported a community of 250 people, including a doctor and a prostitute. The other attraction is a display of **fossil ichthyosaurs** (ICK-thee-oh-sores), ancient marine reptiles that swam in warm seas covering central Nevada perhaps 225 million years ago.

Stop at the **park office** at the town entrance for an informational brochure. From here a trail leads among a dozen wood-frame buildings, many containing artifacts from the early 1900s. You may also want to tour the **Diana Mine;** examine the walls for quartz deposits veined with real gold.

From Berlin head to the adjacent settlement of **Union,** or what's left of it: a ghost town with one adobe building and traces of a mill along an interpretive trail.

Then drive (or walk the 0.5-mile nature trail from the campground) to the **Fossil Shelter.** The A-frame structure stands above a deposit of fossil ichthyosaurs, or "fish lizards," which grew up to 50 feet long and had eyes as big as dinner plates. They gave birth to live young, making them unique among reptiles.

The site was first excavated in 1952 by a local woman using a broom and a pick. She alerted the University of California at Berkeley, which uncovered about 40 ichthyosaurs here, including the world's largest specimens.

The park also offers daily tours from Memorial Day to Labor Day, and thereafter on weekends to mid-November.

Camping

The park has 14 tent and RV sites, with showers. Reservations advised in season; call the park. Camping fee.

❏ *BERLIN-ICHTHYOSAUR S.P., HC 61 BOX 61200, AUSTIN, NV 89310*

Berlin mining camp

Anza-Borrego Desert

85 miles northeast of San Diego on Calif. 78

● 600,000 acres ● 619-767-5311 ● Year-round ● Entrance fee ● Summer temperatures exceed 100°F ● Desert flora and fauna ● Historic trails ● Indian rock art ● Hiking

New to the desert? At first you may be dismayed by the seeming emptiness of Anza-Borrego. The park sprawls across more than 900 square miles of rock and grit, and hundreds of washes and canyons. But soon the vast space, the pure light, and the silence flood your soul—healing antidotes to the noise of civilization.

The "empty" park turns out to contain many riches—oases of palm trees, bighorn sheep and other wildlife, and eroded badlands. Paradoxically much of the park's terrain was shaped by the one element of nature conspicuous by its absence: water. A desert cloudburst can deepen a canyon by a few feet in just a couple of hours.

Mammoth fossils were recently uncovered here, and humans have dwelled in this desert for more than 5,000 years. Native Americans left mysterious petroglyphs and pictographs on rock walls. The first outsiders to see the region were a party of Spanish settlers led by Juan Bautista de Anza in 1774.

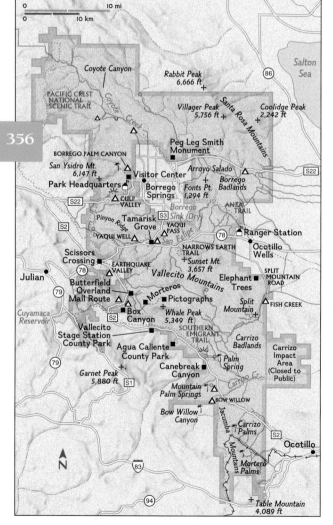

California

You can see traces of his overland route, as well as the later Southern Emigrant Trail that brought gold seekers and others to California. The park takes its name from explorer Anza, and from the Spanish word for lamb, *borrego,* referring to desert bighorn sheep.

What to See and Do

Approach the **Visitor Center** *(2 miles west of Borrego Springs on Palm Canyon Dr.)* by several scenic routes: Montezuma Valley Road (County Rd. S22) from the west, Borrego-Salton Seaway (County Rd. S22) from the east, or County Rd. S2 from the southeast.

The underground Visitor Center presents two slide programs and exhibits on the park's 60 species of mammals, 225 birds, and 60 reptiles and amphibians. In the gardens outside grow native shrubs and trees, and a pond contains endan-

Yaqui Flat

gered desert pupfish, holdovers from the Ice Age that can live in both fresh and salty water, at temperatures from near freezing to 108°F.

There's another pupfish pond at the **Borrego Palm Canyon** trailhead *(west end of Borrego Palm Canyon campground).* The first mile of this trail is a self-guided walk that introduces the park's notable features—alluvial fans, ocotillos, dry washes, Cahuilla *morteros* (holes in boulders where Indians ground seeds), and scurrying lizards. Another half-mile brings you to a grove of native California fan palms, whose trunks are sheathed in skirts of dead leaves that evoke Hawaiian hula dancers. Indians once ate the fruits and used the frond fibers for sandals and baskets.

To explore more of the park, head east on County Rd. S22. After a couple of miles you can turn north on Di Giorgio Road for a side trip to **Coyote Canyon.** *(The route is suitable only for hikers, horseback riders, and four-wheel-drive vehicles.)* You'll find here a stream, surprisingly lush vegetation, and part of the historic Anza Trail.

California fan palms

Ahead on County Rd. S22 stands a pile of rocks called the **Peg Leg Smith Monument,** honoring a colorful, 19th-century prospector who claimed to have found a gold mine—and then lost it in the rugged terrain. The old faker inspired an annual event called the Peg Leg Liar's Contest *(held on the Sat. closest to April 1)*; anyone is invited to tell a tale, as long as none of it is true. Behind the monument rises Coyote Mountain, whose metamorphic rocks hold deep-red garnets.

Continue to Font's Point Road for a side trip to view the gullies and ragged ridges of the **Borrego Badlands,** which were carved by countless thunderstorms. **Font's Point** itself is being eroded away by rain and faulting.

North of County Rd. S22 lies **Clark Dry Lake,** the desiccated basin of a lake that existed 20,000 years ago. Its clay bottom conceals the eggs of tadpole shrimp that hatch when flood waters penetrate the soil. Ahead rise the **Santa Rosa Mountains,** where rain has washed rocks and sand down from the slopes, forming classic alluvial fans. These ragged mountains are so young that they are still rising. The Santa Rosas lie along the San Jacinto Fault, one of California's most active fault zones.

To visit the center of the park, known as the **Yaqui Pass Triangle,** take County Rd. S3 south from Borrego Springs toward Calif. 78. Along here the **Mescal Bajada Overlook** shows off a *bajada* (ba-HA-da), a sloping plain created when a series of alluvial fans blend together at the base of desert mountains. Just ahead the **Cactus Loop Trail** leads you among hundreds of teddybear cholla, beavertail, and hedgehog cactuses.

At Calif. 78, turn east to the **Narrows Earth Trail,** where a short walk reveals how mighty mountains are reduced to grains of sand. In this small canyon you'll view a fault line and rocks 100 million years old. Look also for the chuparosa plant, whose red flowers draw hummingbirds.

If you have time, continue on Calif. 78 to Ocotillo Wells, then turn south on Split Mountain Road to the **Elephant Trees Nature Trail,**

Costa's Hummingbird

named for a small herd of chubby-trunked trees with wrinkly bark. Other vegetation includes smoke trees and barrel cactus, whose ribs expand like an accordion to hold water.

Another major park route is the old **Southern Emigrant Trail,** which you pick up where County Rd. S2 joins Calif. 78 at Scissors Crossing. Over this trail have passed Spanish explorers, frontier scout Kit Carson, and passengers on the Butterfield Overland Stage. After driving through Earthquake Valley, turn east on the marked dirt road for a side trip to the **Butterfield Overland Mail Route Historical Monument.** You'll come to **Foot and Walker Pass**—terrain so steep that stagecoach passengers had to get off and push the coach over the ridge. Here you can walk in wheel ruts dating from the 1850s. Farther along lies a short trail to Indian morteros and a rutted spur road leading to a 1-mile trail to Indian pictographs.

Back on County Rd. S2, proceed to **Box Canyon.** During the Mexican War in 1847, the Mormon Battalion conquered this dead-end canyon, using only axes and a pry bar to hack out a wagon trail. After that, thousands of soldiers, travelers, and gold-crazed emigrants poured across California on the two rough trails below you.

Continue to the **Vallecito Stage Station,** originally built in 1857 and authentically reconstructed. Ahead, take a side trip on the bumpy road to **Palm Spring,** where trails lead to oases shaded by California fan palms. Take a moment to rest here, as stagecoach travelers did more than 130 years ago.

One more route is the Montezuma Valley Road *(County Rd. S22 SW of Visitor Center);* turn north on the dirt road to the Culp Valley primitive camp area. A trail leads west of the campground about three-quarters of a mile to **Pena Spring,** whose waters lure deer, coyotes, and many birds, including quail. Another short, marked trail leads to a lookout on the **Borrego Valley** and the Santa Rosa Mountains. At 3,400 feet this spot offers a retreat from the hot desert floor.

Camping

The park has 142 tent/RV and 52 RV sites, some with showers; and 9 primitive camping areas. Reservations advised Feb. through April; call 800-444-7275. Camping fee.

☐ *Anza-Borrego Desert S.P., 200 Palm Canyon Dr., Borrego Springs, California 92004*

Desert Bloom

After a wet winter, it appears that a passing goddess has strewn blossoms across Anza-Borrego—creamy dune primroses, purple sand verbena, and bright red flowers on the twiggy ocotillo. Blooming season runs from late February into April, usually peaking in early March. Tip: Write a self-addressed postcard saying, "The flowers are blooming," stamp it, and mail it in an envelope to Anza-Borrego Desert State Park, 200 Palm Canyon Dr., Borrego Springs, CA 92004. The staff will mail back the card two weeks before the expected peak. *(For recorded wildflower information, call 619-767-4684.)*

359

Humboldt Redwoods

45 miles south of Eureka on US 101

● 52,000 acres ● 707-946-2409 ● Year-round ● Day-use fees for Women's Federation and Williams Groves ● Old-growth redwoods ● Hiking, biking, horseback riding ● Swimming, canoeing ● Summer interpretive programs

When early morning fog drapes the giant coast redwoods, you can almost peer into the past, when the ancestors of these magnificent trees flourished across the Northern Hemisphere. Climatic changes over time altered the lush, moist growing conditions, reducing the number of coast redwoods to a narrow strip running 450 miles from southern Oregon to central California. In the heart of this unique world lies Humboldt Redwoods State Park—52,000 glorious acres of redwoods, plus cool mountain streams, brilliant spring wildflowers, chaparral-clad hills, steep ridges, and prairies.

Take a moment to ponder the greatness of the redwood: So immense are they—many standing more than 300 feet tall—that they occupy three different climatic zones: semi-shade at their base, cool and moist at their midriff, and dry and windy at their crown. So high up is the canopy that such creatures as marbled murrelets and flying squirrels never even touch the ground.

These trees are so tolerant of fire, thanks to a thick bark and lack of resin, that only the greatest of conflagrations can bring them down.

360

Indeed, their scientific name, *Sequoia sempervirens,* roughly translates as "ever living." Appropriate, since many that you see today are 600 to 1,200 years old, and some are more than 2,000.

What these trees can't survive is the lumberman's ax. In the late 1800s and early 1900s, the lumber companies started bringing these giants down. Fearful that the trees would be lost forever, a group of concerned citizens in 1918 formed the Save-the-Redwoods League. In 1921 the league made its first purchase of redwoods in what would become the present state park. Since then, more than 100 memorial groves have been established here with the help of league funds. Humboldt has become California's third largest state park, and it continues to grow.

Coast redwoods

What to See and Do

Most of the state park can be seen along the 32-mile **Avenue of the Giants** *(Driving-tour guide available at the Phillipsville and Jordan Rd. entrances),* a curving, slow-moving route paralleling US 101. Winding along the **Eel River** through magnificent redwood groves, it passes turnouts, hiking trails, campgrounds, and picnic areas.

While the sunny southern and the dark, moody northern portions each have their charms, it's the central section that epitomizes the redwood experience. Begin at the **Visitor Center,** midway along the drive. Exhibits here detail life in the redwood forest, spotlighting such denizens as the mountain lion and black bear. Pick up brochures and maps here and watch the slide show, then be on your way.

The most popular hiking trail, starting about 4 miles north at **Founders Grove,** provides a short, interpretive foray into the forest of monarchs. Right off you're greeted by the 346-foot **Founders Tree,** believed to be as old as 1,600 years.

Delving deeper into the forest, you can't help but be amazed by the enormous girths of the ruddy barked tree trunks that tower above lush ferns and oxalis. Midway lies a veritable graveyard of fallen giants, the most venerable being the **Dyerville Giant.** Before toppling in a rainstorm some years back, this tree stood at least 362 feet tall—57 feet higher than the Statue of Liberty.

Ranking in spectacular scenery is nearby **Rockefeller Forest** (Along Bull Creek via Mattole Rd.)—the largest, undisturbed, contiguous tract of old-growth coast redwoods in existence. Just a half mile long, the **Rockefeller Forest Loop Trail** gives a sense of what the north coast looked like centuries ago. (And, the cathedral-like silence is overwhelming.)

For a longer hike, follow the **Bull Creek Flats Trail** through the forest to the **Big Tree Area,** where reside three world-class specimens, including the Giant Tree, which has replaced the Dyerville Giant as the champion redwood. The 8.8-mile round-trip trail returns to Rockefeller Forest on the opposite side of Bull Creek.

You can also reach the Big Tree Area by driving west on scenic Mattole Road, a narrow, winding route fringed with redwoods so close you can lean out the window and touch them.

Further Adventures

Laced with footpaths and fire roads, Humboldt's backcountry promises all kinds of adventures for backpackers, mountain bikers, and horseback riders alike. While the redwoods congregate along stream valleys, the backcountry mostly embraces prairies, sunny uplands, and steep ridges covered with madrone, chaparral, and Douglas-fir. Trails wind past pioneer cemeteries, homestead ruins, and old moonshine locations, dating back to the days of the area's first settlers.

If you're up to an overnight trek, you have a choice of five trail camps. All trails begin at Bull Creek Flats Road; distances from the trailheads aren't far, but the trails can be steep. The two closest camps are also the most appealing: At **Johnson Trail Camp,** you can stay in a rustic cabin used by tie hacks from the 1920s to 1950s. At the **Whiskey Flat Trail Camp**—named for a moonshine still operated here during Prohibition—you can pitch a tent beneath old-growth redwoods.

Camping

The park has 160 tent and 90 RV sites (most open late May–Sept., 57 tent/RV sites open through winter), with shower facilities. There are also two environmental (primitive) campgrounds, some open Mem. Day–Labor Day only; 5 trail camps (see above), which require permits from park headquarters; and a group camp. A horse camp can accommodate up to 75 people with horses. Reservations advised Mem. Day through Labor Day; call 800-444-7275. Camping fee.

❑ HUMBOLDT REDWOODS STATE PARK, P.O. BOX 100, WEOTT, CA 95571

"Coast" Redwoods

You won't find coast redwoods near the ocean—the salt air is too drying, and the ocean winds too rough for their shallow root systems. Instead, these magnificent giants prefer foggy stream courses that wind through inland canyons. One reason is that this location supplies life-giving water. A mature redwood can lose 500 gallons of moisture a day; thick fog helps condense this lost water into a rain-like drip, which is then recycled back into the redwood's environment. Secondly, the streams bring rich alluvial silts and gravels from farther upstream, compacting them in benches and flats—ideal places for nurturing big trees. So where are the biggest trees? Founders Grove and Rockefeller Forest, of course, where the air is the foggiest and the soil the richest.

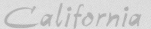

Plumas-Eureka

6 miles west of Graeagle on County Rd. A-14, off US 89

● 5,500 acres ● 916-836-2380 ● Year-round ● Eureka Peak
● Mountain lakes ● Restored mine buildings ● Old mining
equipment ● Hiking, fishing (license required)

Tucked away in a little-known corner of the Sierra
Nevada, Plumas-Eureka State Park embraces an unsung
realm of piney woods, glacier-gouged lakes, and jagged,
snowcapped mountains.

The place wasn't so anonymous more than a century
ago, when gold was discovered on Eureka Peak. In 1851
miners searching for a rumored "gold lake" climbed the massive mountain, where they stumbled across a quartz outcropping embedded with gold, silver, and lead. Soon after, the
Sierra Buttes Mining Company moved in, digging 65 miles of
tunnels; by the time operations ceased in the 1940s, they had
extracted some 8 million dollars worth of gold.

Hard-rock mining was tough work, but the miners managed to enjoy themselves during the long winters. Taking the
lead from early pioneer "Snowshoe" Thompson, who deliv-
ered the mail over the Sierra Nevada on skis, the miners
would strap on their own versions and race down the base of
Eureka Peak. Catching a lift on the mining tram, ordinarily
used to haul bucketfuls of ore down the slopes, they made
Plumas-Eureka one of the nation's first (if unofficial) ski areas.

363

Mohawk Stamp Mill

While Plumas-Eureka preserves the region's mining history, it's the park's location in the pristine **Lakes Basin** wilderness that makes it a supreme mountain escape, ideal for hiking, camping, fishing—and, of course, skiing.

What to See and Do

Spend some time at the **Visitor Center** in the heart of the park. It contains an excellent **museum** (*Adm. fee*), chock full of assorted mining memorabilia: homemade tools, a miniature model of a stamp mill, pioneer household items, and early skis, including those belonging to local legend "Snowshoe" Thompson.

Across the street you'll see structures built by the Plumas-Eureka Mine, now in various stages of restoration, including a five-story, 60-stamp mill, where most of the gold was processed. You can tour the **Moriarty House** (*June-Aug. on Sat.*), refurbished to reflect mining camp life in the 1890s.

Next, visit the nearby village of **Johnsville** (population 100 in summer). The rough-and-tumble buildings—some restored, others not—preserve the atmosphere of gold rush days. On the outskirts of town, a steep park road leads to the vicinity of the miners' makeshift ski area, now the site of the **Plumas-Eureka Ski Bowl** (*Mid-Dec.–mid-March Sat.-Sun.* 916-836-2317), popular with downhill skiers.

The trail that best showcases the region's natural beauty is the 3-mile, moderately tough **Eureka Peak Loop** around 7,447-foot Eureka Peak. From picturesque **Eureka Lake,** you climb through the piney domain of coyote, bobcat, porcupine, long-tailed weasel, mountain lion, and black bear to a magnificent panoramic view of the surrounding peaks, including Sierra Buttes.

If you're not up to this trek, consider walking the gentler, 3.5-mile round-trip **Grass Lake Trail** to one of the area's deep-blue, alpine lakes, nestled beneath Jeffrey pines and red firs. Find the trailhead at the ruins of Jamison Mine, near the camping area, and head out through the rocky landscape, past 40-foot **Jamison Falls,** to the picture-perfect lake.

Another popular hike, the 1.5-mile trail to **Madora Lake** explores a small, marshy pond alive with birdlife; watch for ducks, coots, geese, pileated woodpeckers, hummingbirds, and saw-whet owls. The trail begins just off County Rd. A-14, near the park entrance.

Camping

The park has 67 tent and RV sites (May–mid-Oct.), with shower facilities. Available on a first-come, first-served basis. Camping fee.

❏ *PLUMAS-EUREKA STATE PARK, 310 JOHNSVILLE RD., BLAIRSDEN, CA 96103*

Lake Country

Plumas-Eureka sits in the northern portion of the **Lakes Basin,** a pristine glacial landscape boasting three dozen lakes, trout streams, old-fashioned resorts, and plenty of mining history. Perhaps the best-kept secret is **Sardine Lake,** a blue-green jewel sparkling in the shadow of the jagged Sierra Buttes. Hike to the top of the buttes, where a 360-degree view takes in a good swath of the rugged Sierra. Then retreat to the rustic **Sardine Lake Lodge** (*Mid-May–mid-Oct. 916-862-1196. Reservations advised*), famed for its cuisine. Nearby **Gold Lake** was named after a Sierra lake reputedly filled with nuggets so big that pioneer children used them as marbles. No gold was ever found there, but the pine-fringed, trout-filled lake is a gem in its own right. Try the popular trail to lovely **Long Lake,** near the Lakes Basin campground.

364

Mount Tamalpais

10 miles north of San Francisco, off Calif. 1

- 6,300 acres ● 415-388-2070 ● Year-round ● Entrance fee
- Mountain wilderness ● Panoramic views ● Spring wild-
flowers ● Hiking, mountain biking, horseback riding,
- Mountain Theatre

Bolinas Ridge

Standing sentinel over Marin County, Mount Tamalpais is the dream-come-true of every nature lover. Trails wind through shady redwood groves and lupine-covered meadows, across sunny, chaparral hillsides, and up to the dramatic East Peak, where a heart-stopping view takes in the entire San Francisco bay area.

As mountains go, Mount Tam isn't so big—just 2,571 feet above sea level. But its slopes plunge to the San Francisco Bay on one side and to the Pacific Ocean on the other, making it seem mightier than it really is. The Coast Miwok Indians were among the first people to sense its mystique; they believed its peak was inhabited by evil spirits. Legend likens the mountain's silhouette to a sleeping maiden; with a little imagination, you can see her today.

In the 1890s, the local gentry rode a creaking train to the mountaintop, where they danced and dined at the Tamalpais Tavern (only the view platform remains). Back then, elk, grizzlies, bobcats, and mountain lions roamed the wilds, before the

Bike Fever

Back in the 1970s, daredevil cyclists would truck their balloon-tired, beach-cruiser bicycles to the top of Mount Tam, then whiz downhill. In order to climb back up the mountain, bike techies Joe Breeze, Gary Fisher, and Tom Ritchey fashioned multigear components that could better negotiate rapid changes in slope and terrain. The trend caught on: In 1981 the first mass-produced mountain bike, called the Stump Jumper, entered the marketplace. By 1990 some 15 million mountain bikes had hit the trails; and, that same year the number of mountain bikes sold surpassed that of road bikes. Today, mountain bikers flock to Mount Tam's **Old Railroad Grade,** a smooth and easy double-track trail that begins opposite the Pantoll Park Headquarters and follows the former railbed of the Mount Tamalpais Railroad. Those up for a more thrilling ride start atop East Peak.

mountain was designated a game refuge and their populations reduced. Mount Tam owes much to the Tamalpais Conservation Club, which as early as 1912 began fighting to save the land for hikers. In 1928, 692 acres were set aside for the fledgling state park. Today the park, Muir Woods National Monument, Golden Gate National Recreation Area, and Marin Municipal Water District collectively preserve the whole mountain.

What to See and Do

Head up Ridgecrest Blvd. (*off Panoramic Hwy.*) toward East Peak and hit the 0.5-mile **Plank Trail** to the fire tower, where you'll be dazzled by the 360-degree view of the shimmering bay, the miniature buildings of San Francisco, acres of chaparral-covered slopes, and the wide, blue Pacific. Like many people, you may be content to just sit on this magical mountaintop. However, you won't regret strolling along the easy, .75-mile **Verna Dunshea Trail,** which circles the peak.

Next, you're ready to explore the mountain itself, laced with 30 miles of park trails (offering access to an additional 200-plus miles of trails contained in adjoining Muir Woods and Golden Gate NRA). Stop by the **Pantoll Park Headquarters** and pick up a trail map.

Popular among families is the 3.5-mile **Matt Davis Trail,** which descends from park headquarters to the **Mountain Home Inn** (*415-381-9000. Reservations suggested for lunch or dinner*), since 1912 a hikers' rendezvous still offering cocktails, meals—and stunning sunsets.

The perennial favorite is the **Redwood Creek Trail,** a 2.5-mile loop through majestic redwood groves. Begin near the **Muir Woods park headquarters** (preferably in early morning or late afternoon to avoid the crowds), and become entranced by the ruddy barked giants that tower hundreds of feet above the lush, fern-carpeted earth.

Only the brave (and the fit) should undertake the spectacular 7.2-mile (one-way) **Dipsea Trail,** the scene of an excruciating footrace every August. Beginning in Mill Valley, just east of the park, with a steep ascent up 671 steps, the trail climbs up and over the mountain, crossing hills with names like Suicide and Cardiac. Finally you drop down through a temple of redwoods to **Stinson Beach,** popular with surfers and sunbathers.

After a day of hiking, sit back and enjoy a musical at the **Mountain Theatre** (*May-June. 415-383-0155. Adm. fee*), set in a natural bowl above the city and the bay. You can get there by shuttle bus or by hiking 2 miles through the woods.

Camping and Lodging

The park has 22 walk-in tent sites; 16 first come, first served. There are also 10 cabins and a horse camp with 12 sites. Reservations advised in season; call 800-444-7275. Camping fee.
❑ *MOUNT TAMALPAIS S.P., 801 PANORAMIC HWY., MILL VALLEY, CA 94941*

Pfeiffer Big Sur

30 miles south of Monterey on Calif. 1

- 800 acres ● 408-667-2315 ● Year-round ● Day-use fee
- Redwood groves ● Big Sur River ● Hiking, swimming
- Summer interpretive programs

Flowing through the rugged Santa Lucia Mountains on its way to the sea, the clear-running Big Sur River has carved a small, flat-bottomed valley—the site of Pfeiffer Big Sur State Park. Tiny by most park standards, Pfeiffer Big Sur contains a grand share of stunning scenery: Chaparral- and oak-covered slopes plunge to the valley floor, which harbors wildflower-adorned meadows and a regal stand of coast redwoods, the planet's tallest living organisms. Located near the dramatic Big Sur coast, this shady sanctuary annually draws thousands of hikers and campers.

Named for the Pfeiffer family, who settled here in the 1860s and later sold its land to the state, the park flanks the river, with camping sites on one side and a picnic area and softball field on the other. Trails trace the river, wending up ridges into the splendid backcountry of the **Ventana Wilderness,** a glorious realm of sharp-crested ridges and V-shaped valleys.

367

What to See and Do
At the heart of the park sits the **Big Sur Lodge,** with its

Big Sur coastline from Ventana Wilderness

McWay Cove, Julia Pfeiffer Burns State Park

368

By the Way

Just 12 miles south of Pfeiffer Big Sur, **Julia Pfeiffer Burns State Park** (408-667-2315. *Entrance fee*) is not to be missed. While you're here, take the **McWay Creek Trail** to **McWay Cove.** Surrounded by high, rugged cliffs, this pretty cove showcases a 50-foot waterfall that plummets directly into the sea. Look for sea otters and migrating gray whales. The park also features a 1,680-acre underwater park (for experienced divers only) and 1,800 acres of upland forest with trails. **Partington Canyon Trail** passes through several redwood groves flourishing at their southernmost range.

cozy restaurant overlooking the Big Sur River. The nearby **Nature Center** *(June-Aug.)* offers an introduction to the area's natural features.

Short and easy **Pfeiffer Falls Trail** makes for a pleasant, brookside stroll through a lush redwood grove to Pfeiffer Falls, which spills over a fern-banked ledge into a pretty green pool. An observation platform here provides a perfect picnic perch. Return the way you came or make a loop via the 0.7-mile **Valley View Trail,** which climbs among oak, Santa Lucia bristlecone fir, and chaparral to a scenic overlook of the Santa Lucia Mountains and distant Point Sur. You may spot black-tailed deer, gray squirrels, raccoons, wild turkeys, foxes, or possums, but don't worry about bears, mountain lions, coyotes, or belligerent wild boars; they stick mainly to the backcountry.

Next, return to the lodge and walk just south on the park road to pick up the 0.3-mile **Nature Trail,** which interprets the area's diverse plant life. The woodland here is dominated by California bays (whose crushed leaves evoke the aroma of Italian cuisine), Western sycamores, live and tan oaks, and stately redwoods. In spring, dainty forget-me-nots, hedge nettle, and globe lilies brighten the forest floor.

To see one of Big Sur's largest redwoods, drive to the group picnic area, where the **Colonial Tree** (27 feet in circumference) towers. If it's a hot summer day, follow the nearby **Gorge Trail,** an unofficial but well-traveled path to the cooling Big Sur River. A few boulder hops away you'll find one of the area's best swimming holes.

Camping and Lodging

The park has 218 tent and RV sites, with showers; two hike-in group camps (Mem. Day–Sept.); a bike-in camp; and 61 cottages. Reservations advised in season; call 800-424-4787. Camping fee.

Nearby Sights

Head south about a mile on Calif. 1 to **Pfeiffer Beach** *(Via unmarked Sycamore Canyon Rd. Adm. fee),* a beautiful crescent of red and white sands under craggy cliffs. It's a fine spot for picnicking, sunbathing, and watching sunsets, but think twice about swimming here: The water is cold and the surf rough.

❏ *PFEIFFER BIG SUR STATE PARK, BIG SUR, CALIFORNIA 93920*

Año Nuevo

On Calif. 1 between Santa Cruz and Half Moon Bay

● 4,000 acres ● 415-879-2025 ● Year-round ● Entrance fee ● No pets ● Breeding ground of northern elephant seals ● Rocky beaches ● Spring wildflowers ● Hiking, sunbathing, picnicking

The setting is rocky, windswept **Point Año Nuevo,** which juts into the crashing, blue Pacific. Here, coastal mountains, bluffs, dunes, and beaches mingle to create a breathtaking mosaic that looks much as it might have in January 1602, when Spanish explorer Sebastian Viscaino sailed by and named it to honor the new year.

With such diverse terrain, Año Nuevo not surprisingly harbors a great variety of wildlife, including some 300 species of birds, bobcats, black-tailed deer, sea lions, sea otters—and northern elephant seals.

Twice a year hundreds of elephant seals (some weighing as much as a Cadillac) lumber ashore to mate, give birth, and molt (shed their pelts) among the shifting sand dunes. The park's main draw, this biannual rite regularly lures thousands of onlookers, who come to watch one of nature's amazing displays at the tip of the point, about 1.5 miles from the **Visitor Center.**

From December to mid-March (mating and pupping season), park rangers offer 2.5-hour guided hikes (*reservations highly recommended; fee*) to this wildlife protection area, where you walk among harems of bellowing, primordial giants.

The molting season occurs April through August. During this time, you must obtain a hiking permit from the Visitor Center to enter the protected area and use the designated trail.

If it's not elephant seal season, sample one of the park's many hiking trails: The short **Cove Beach Trail** leads to a splendid beach sprinkled with rocks and fossils, while the **Atkinson Bluff Trail** meanders through acres of yellow and blue lupine and orange-gold poppies, in bloom from late March to early June.

❑ *AÑO NUEVO STATE RESERVE, NEW YEARS CREEK RD., PESCADERO, CALIFORNIA 94060*

Marathon Migration

Resembling beached whales, northern elephant seals lounge about the sand dunes, seemingly too lazy to blink an eye, much less eat. You'd lie about, too, if you knew that soon you'd be hauling out to sea, where you'll swim constantly—even while asleep. Indeed, over a period of 250 days, male elephant seals travel some 12,500 miles a year, swimming as far north as the Aleutian Islands, while the females are at sea 307 days a year, averaging 11,000 miles on their journeys west toward Japan. These marathon travels represent the longest known migration of any mammal. Returning twice a year to rookeries along the West Coast, these seals are also the only known animal to undertake an annual double migration.

369

Northern elephant seal

Na Pali Coast

8 miles west of Hanalei at end of Hawaii 560, Kauai

● 6,175 acres ● 808-274-3444 ● Year-round ● No pets
● Ocean conditions unpredictable; swimming not
recommended ● Sea cliffs, river valleys, waterfalls
● Archaeological sites

Kalalau Beach

The name tells it all: Na Pali, "the cliffs." Here the volcanic island of Kauai plunges into the sea. Lush valleys open onto hidden beaches, and the famous Kalalau Trail lives up to its reputation as a pathway to paradise. The daunting terrain

and sheer sea cliffs, which can drop more than 1,000 feet, have prevented road building, so the only way in to Na Pali is by foot trail or boat.

The ocean approach offers a broad perspective of sheer coastal *palis* and waterfalls cascading into the sea—a view that has awed visitors since a British fur trader named George Dixon first sailed along this coast in the late 1780s. The valleys of the Na Pali Coast, with their early agricultural terraces, still seem part of Old Hawaii.

What to See and Do

Suitable for fit hikers, the **Kalalau Trail** (which follows much of the same route trod by early Hawaiians) runs 11 miles, from Haena State Park to Kalalau Beach. It cuts above towering sea cliffs and winds through green valleys, dropping now and then to beaches. (*The trail can be precipitous, muddy, and rutted; in some spots along high cliffs it narrows to barely more than a foot wide. Be aware of the dangers of crossing rain-swollen streams and of swimming in the surf.*)

Honeycreeper

Day hikers can experience a bit of the Kalalau Trail, including fine views of the coast, on the 2-mile section from **Kee Beach** at Haena State Park to **Hanakapai Beach.**

At Hanakapai Beach, a maintained but sometimes rough side trail leads 2 miles up the **Hanakapai Valley,** which receives 75 inches of rain a year—more than anywhere else along the Na Pali Coast. The water creates a paradisiacal forest of guava and kukui, with an understory of ferns and grasses. On the up-valley trail you pass bamboo, wild ginger, and mango trees, as well as old irrigation terraces where early Hawaiians grew taro, which they made into the starchy, pasty dish called poi. You also see traces of a coffee mill from the late 1800s. At the top is a waterfall about 150 feet high, with a pool for swimming—but not directly below the falls, since rocks and debris may be washed over. (*Hike the upper part of this trail only in good weather, as there is danger from flash floods and falling rocks.*)

If you choose to continue along the Kalalau Trail (*hiking permit required beyond this point*), the hike becomes more strenuous in its next 4 miles, with steep switchbacks and two hanging valleys to cross. Climbing away from the sea, it reaches **Hanakoa,** a valley with agricultural terraces, where coffee plants now grow wild. Cool off in the pools of **Hanakoa Stream,** or hike a third of a mile up the east fork of the valley to **Hanakoa Falls.** (*Beware of eroded trail sections and treacherous footing.*)

Around the 7-mile point, the Kalalau Trail returns to the

coast, crossing some dry terrain, formerly cattle country, where sisal and lantana grow. Ahead you see the ridges of Na Pali plunging toward the sea, then the **Kalalau Valley** appears, spreading 2 miles wide between fluted walls. Look for the sites of ancient houses and a *heiau* (temple) on the plateau above the shore. A lacework of creeks feeds into Kalalau Stream; you can take a 2-mile side trip up the valley to a natural water slide and pools at **Big Pond.** On the way you pass terraces covered with guava, Java plum, and mango trees. You'll spy goats around the cliffs.

The Kalalau Trail continues to **Kalalau Beach,** a 600-yard stretch of sand that extends to the small Kolea waterfall. In early days the Hawaiian residents of the Kalalau Valley moved down to the beach in summer, living in sea caves and fishing from canoes. Today, commercial boats (*contact Maui Visitors Bureau 800-245-3971*) drop off travelers at this beach and campers stay in the sea caves in summer. Beware of falling rocks around cliff faces.

Further Adventures

Farther along the coast is **Nualolo Kai,** a coastal flat accessible only by commercial boat; it is isolated by cliffs nearly 2,000 feet high. More than six centuries ago, Hawaiians lived here, no doubt drawn by the coral reef where they caught rudderfish, tangs, parrotfish, and other sea creatures for food; now the reef draws snorkelers. In the 1820s missionaries would stop here to rest as they canoed along the coast. And the cliff above Nualolo Kai was a prime spot for *oahi*—a display of early fireworks, created by throwing burning sticks off the cliff. It's said that in the mid-1800s King Kamehameha III stayed overnight at Nualolo just to see this spectacular light show. Today an **interpretive trail** guides you to early Hawaiian sites on the flat: mounds where sweet potatoes were grown, stone walls, house platforms, and an impressive heiau, where people made offerings to help assure a successful growing season.

Still farther along the coast lies **Milolii,** another coastal flat. Boats bring you through a fringed reef to a white-sand beach. About three-quarters of a mile up the **Milolii Valley Trail,** a waterfall tumbles, and you'll see old house sites and farming terraces.

Camping

The park has primitive camping areas (year-round) at Hanakapiai, Hanakoa, and Kalalau; and at Milolii (mid-May–Labor Day). Permit required; available from park office in Lihue. Reservations advised in season; call 808-274-3444. Only 60 campers total allowed per night. Each campsite is located near a stream; bring some means to purify water.

❏ *Division of State Parks, 3060 Eiwa St., Rm. 306, Lihue, Kauai, Hawaii 96766*

Getting Away From It All

During the flower-power 1960s, young people drifted into the Eden of Kalalau Valley to mellow out and live on nature's bounty, such as the orange, papaya, and banana trees growing there. They weren't the first people to seek escape from the outside world: In 1893 a young Hawaiian named Koolau, who had contracted leprosy, hid here with his wife and small son, rather than be forced to leave them and live at the leper colony on Molokai. Neither sheriff nor soldiers could dislodge him from the valley—even with a cannon. The hippie residents of later years were evicted in 1974, when the area was established as a wilderness park.

Waimea Canyon and Kokee

8 miles north of Waimea on Hawaii 550, Kauai

- 1,866 acres (Waimea Canyon), 4,345 acres (Kokee)
- 808-335-9975 ● Year-round ● Dirt roads very slick in wet weather ● Spectacular gorge ● Rain forest ● Dramatic views ● Hiking

Mark Twain dubbed the 3,600-foot-deep gorge at Waimea Canyon State Park the "Grand Canyon of the Pacific."

It was once an ancient volcano, but part of its flank collapsed along a geological fault, creating a pathway for the Waimea River to cut the canyon. For five million years water has sculptured the gorge. Erosion has exposed colorful layers of lava in the canyon walls, showing how many volcanic eruptions it took to build Kauai. The canyon has a red tinge because water has rusted the iron in the soil.

373

Adjacent Kokee State Park protects an island-top, native forest of koa and red-blossoming ohia lehua trees, and streams edged with ferns. Here you'll discover panoramic views of the remote Kalalau Valley, where green ridges plunge toward the blue sea at the Na Pali Coast. There is no foolproof method for avoiding the view-obscuring fogs that come and go. They do, however, come *and* go.

Waimea Canyon

What to See and Do

After driving up Hawaii 550 into Waimea, stop at the .25-mile **Iliau Nature Loop** (*Between Mileposts 8 and 9*). Skirting the canyon rim, this trail offers dramatic views. It also introduces you to native plants, including pukiawe; in Old Hawaii, when high chiefs wanted to socialize with their people, they would walk through the smoke of burning pukiawe to temporarily nullify a taboo that required common folk to prostrate themselves. From here you can hike the steep, 2.5-mile **Kukui Trail,** which drops 2,000 feet to the Waimea River.

Continue driving up Hawaii 550 to the **Waimea Canyon Lookout** *(Between Miles 10 and 11).* Along with the fantastic formations, spires, and amphitheaters of the gorge, you'll see three side canyons opening into the main chasm. At times mists drift across these canyons like wraiths.

Just ahead, stop at the railing at **Puu Ka Pele** to look across the canyon at **Waipoo Falls,** which makes an 800-foot plunge—if there's been any rain. Drive on to **Puu Hinahina Lookout** *(Between Miles 13 and 14),* which offers two very different vistas: down 10-mile-long Waimea Canyon and toward the sea and Niihau Island. At the lookout, you'll spy white-tailed tropicbirds, which soar on updrafts in the canyon and nest on rocky perches.

Wild ginger blossoms

374

Ahead on the left you can take a side trip on paved Makaha Road, a very steep route that leads to remote picnic areas and ends at a Navy radar station.

Or continue on the main road until you reach the **Kokee Natural History Museum** *(808-335-9975).* Tiptoe among the wild jungle chickens, called *moa,* to the door of this small institution that has been providing visitors with free information since 1953. (Ask the helpful museum staff for a trail map and the latest road conditions.) A three-dimensional model gives you a clear overview of Waimea Canyon, and an exhibit tells about hurricanes, which have thrashed Kauai repeatedly, most recently with Hurricane Iniki in 1992. Other displays look at island flora and fauna, including a humpback whale's vertebra and a Pacific green sea turtle, or *honu,* long valued for its shell and meat but now a threatened species. And those jungle chickens outside? You'll learn they're descended from fowl brought by early Polynesian voyagers to Hawaii.

Near the museum the gentle, 0.1-mile **Nature Trail** takes you through a forest where plaques identify native plants, such as the hahalua, whose stalks rise as high as 40 feet. Another popular walking route is the 1.8-mile **Canyon Trail,** which crosses **Kokee Stream** and has awe-inspiring views of Waimea Canyon.

Continue on Hawaii 550, perhaps stopping to hike the 3.25-mile **Awaawapuhi Trail,** which overlooks green valleys above the Na Pali Coast. Next, the main road winds among ohia trees, begonias, and tree ferns to **Kalalau Lookout** *(Mile 18).* Don't be surprised if the view is blocked by clouds; you're at an elevation of 4,000 feet, where clouds form on Kauai. Wait a bit in case the mists clear, allowing you to see into the Kalalau Valley. The biggest valley along the Na Pali Coast, it was once the home of farmers and taro fields, but the last residents moved out in 1919, leaving it to the goats. The ruins of stone irrigation ditches and house foundations remain in the valley.

Drive on until the road ends at **Puu O Kila Lookout.** Below you the Kalalau Valley spreads 2 miles wide, between furrowed walls of green and brown—one of the finest views in the Hawaiian Islands. From here the 3.7-mile **Pihea Trail** leads along the valley's edge, among ohia trees and ferns, to the 3.5-mile **Alakai Swamp Trail.**

Alakai Swamp consists of 30 square miles of bogs and ridges. Why all this moisture? The swamp lies just below one of the world's wettest spots, Mount Waialeale (5,148 feet), which receives an average of 451 inches of rain annually. (One year 681 inches fell—more than 56 feet of water.) A wooden boardwalk along much of the trail saves you from bogging down on the muddy, often slippery ground. The trail brings you to the **Kilohana Lookout,** on the edge of a cliff. From here you can see the sweep of the Wainiha Valley, with lovely Hanalei Bay beckoning on the distant coastline.

Camping

Kokee State Park offers tent sites for up to 75 campers per night. Reservations advised in season; call 808-274-3444.
❏ *Div. of State Parks, 3060 Eiwa St., Rm. 306, Lihue, Kauai, HI 96766*

Kealakekua

12 miles S of Kailua, off Napoopoo Rd., Hawaii

● 808-974-6200 ● Year-round ● No pets ● No camping
● Site of early foreign contact ● Temple ruins ● Captain Cook's Monument ● Snorkeling

In this picturesque bay, Hawaiians and Europeans had their first prolonged encounter when Capt. James Cook visited in 1779. Kealakekua was a Hawaiian political and religious center, and the chiefs and priests may have believed that Cook was the god Lono. (After all, Cook arrived under full sail, and legends foretold that Lono would appear on a "floating island" under streamers of white tapa cloth.)

During a month-long stay, Cook's scientists and artists

Legend of Kokee Meadow

Why should there be an open meadow in front of the Kokee Natural History Museum, while dense forests grow all around? Legend tells us that the meadow was once filled with trees, where an unpleasant *akua* (spirit) lurked. He liked to bedevil fatigued travelers walking the trail to Kalalau Valley. Finally, in response to people's prayers, the god Kanaloa tore out all the trees. Now the evil *akua* had no place to hide. Today the only mischievous spirits you might see around the meadow are mynah birds.

documented early Hawaiian villages, ceremonies, and crafts. But local hospitality ran out when Cook later had to return to Kealakekua to repair a broken mast. The Hawaiians stole a small boat, and Cook, hoping to persuade them to return it, tried to take an important chief hostage. In the ensuing fight, Cook was killed on the shore.

Most visitors come simply to stand for a moment where these momentous historical events occurred. Motorists arrive at Napoopoo, a tiny community whose "beach" now consists of boulders deposited by hurricanes. Near the parking area is the stone platform of **Hikiau Heiau,** a temple that was once the scene of human sacrifices.

Along the bay rises **Pali Kapu O Keoua,** a 600-foot-high sea cliff pocked with lava tubes in which Hawaiian chiefs were buried. On the far side is **Kaawaloa,** a flat, lava peninsula where top chiefs resided. Cook was killed here, and the white obelisk of Captain Cook's Monument stands among kiawe trees. The best way to reach this side of the bay is by boat or kayak. (*Locals rent out kayaks at Napoopoo Landing, next to the park. For information call 808-329-7787.*)

Calm **Kaawaloa Cove** is popular with snorkelers because its shallow coral reef harbors many species of colorful fish. A playful school of spinner porpoises also lives in the bay. Kayakers often paddle out for a look, but regulations prohibit anyone from approaching or bothering the porpoises. The bay's pristine waters and spectacular setting should be enough for anyone.

❏ Division of State Parks, P.O. Box 936, Hilo, Hawaii 96721

376

Iao Valley

5 miles west of Wailuku on Iao Valley Rd. (Hawaii 32), Maui

● 6 acres ● 808-984-8109 ● Year-round ● Historic site ● Lush valley ● Rock spire

This green valley in the West Maui Mountains was named after the demigod Maui's daughter, Iao ("Cloud Supreme"). Long considered a spiritual place, it also makes an important claim on history: Here in 1790, during the Battle of Kepaniwai, the island's defenders under Kalanikupule were trapped by the invading forces of King Kamehameha I who sought to unite the Hawaiian Islands into a kingdom. So terrible was the slaughter that **Iao Stream** ran red with blood and bodies choked the water. (Kepaniwai means "damming of the waters.")

A 0.6-mile walkway offers vistas of the valley and velvet-green **Kukaemoku,** or **Iao Needle**—an eroded basalt spire that rises 1,200 feet from the valley floor. Stairs climb to a lookout shelter—welcome in case some of the valley's annual 150 inches of rain falls. The walkway also dips down to **Iao Stream,** where a dirt path leads among ginger plants to pretty pools.

Just below the bridge, a trail winds through a colorful **botanical garden** of native Hawaiian and Polynesian plants, including a demonstration taro field.

❑ *DIVISION OF STATE PARKS, 54 SOUTH HIGH ST. # 101, WAILUKU, HI 96793*

Iolani Palace

King and Richards Sts., downtown Honolulu, Oahu

- **11 acres** ● **808-522-0832**
- **Year-round** ● **No camping**
- **Royal residence and grounds**

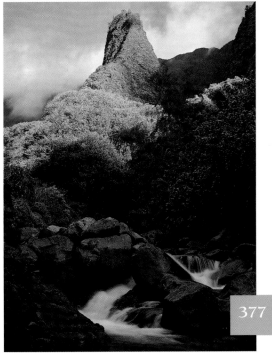

377

Iao Needle

America's only royal residence, this was the home of Hawaii's last monarchs. Island rulers lived here from 1882, when King Kalakaua moved in, until his sister and successor Liluokalani was overthrown in 1893 by those who wanted Hawaii annexed to the United States. The palace's Italian Renaissance-style architecture and eclectic furnishings are evidence of Kalakaua's love affair not only with Europe, but with the rest of the world. Thoroughly modern, he installed one of Hawaii's first telephones and wired the palace for electricity—even before the White House did. After 1893, the palace served as capitol of the Republic of Hawaii and later of the American territory and state.

The guided tour *(fee)* takes in the Grand Hall, with its gleaming native woods and royal portraits; the Throne Room; and the State Dining Room. On the second floor are royal bedrooms, the King's library, and the family music room.

Iolani Palace—the name means "royal or heavenly hawk"—stands on well-tended grounds. Also on the property are the copper-domed **Coronation Pavilion** and the **Iolani Barracks,** which housed the royal guard. The Royal Hawaiian Band *(808-922-5331)* gives concerts most Fridays at noon.

❑ *THE FRIENDS OF IOLANI PALACE, P.O. BOX 2259, HONOLULU, HI 96804*

MORE INFORMATION

State Park Agencies

Alabama – Division of Parks, 64 North Union St., Montgomery, AL 36130; (334) 242-3333; (800) ALA-PARK; http://www.vten.com

Alaska – Division of Parks & Outdoor Rec., 3601 C St., Suite 1200, Anchorage, AK 99503; (907) 269-8700 http://www.state.ak.us

Arizona – Arizona State Parks Office, 1300 W. Washington, Ste. 104, Phoenix, AZ 85007; (602) 542-4174; http://www.pr.state.az.us

Arkansas – Arkansas Dept. of Parks & Tourism, 1 Capitol Mall, Little Rock, AR 72201; (800) 828-8974; http://www.state.ar.us/html/ark_parks.html OR; http://www.yournet.com/sps.html

California – California State Park System, Department of Parks & Recreation, P.O. Box 942896, Sacramento, CA 94296-0001; (916) 653-6995; http://www.ceres.ca.gov/parks

Colorado – Colorado Parks & Outdoor Recreation, 1313 Sherman St., Room 618, Denver, CO 80203; (303) 866-3437; http://www.dnr.co.state.us/parks

Connecticut – Connecticut Division of Parks, State Office Building, 79 Elm Street, Hartford, CT 06102; (860) 424-3200; http://dep.state.ct.us

Delaware – Delaware Division of Parks & Recreation, 89 Kings Highway, P.O. Box 1401, Dover, DE 19903; (302) 739-4702; http://www.state.de.us

Florida – Division of Recreation & Parks, Marjory Stoneman Douglas Bldg., 3900 Commonwealth Blvd. Mail Station 535, Tallahassee, FL 32399; (904) 488-9872; http://www.dep.state.fl.us/parks/index.html

Georgia – Department of Natural Resources; 205 Butler St. SE, Suite 1352; Atlanta, GA 30334; (404) 656-3530; http://www.ga-travel.com/ga/parks/index.html

Hawaii – Division of State Parks, Room 131, 1151 Punchbowl St., Honolulu, HI 96813; (808) 587-0300; http://www.hawaii.gov

Idaho – Idaho Parks & Recreation Department, P.O. Box 83720, Boise, ID 83720-0039; (800) 635-7820; http://www.visitid.org/

Illinois – Illinois Division of Tourism & Parks, DCCA 620 E. Adams St., Springfield, IL 62701; (800) 223-0121; http://dnr.state.il.us/parks/natlpage.htm

Indiana – Indiana Dept. of Natural Resources, 402 W. Washington St., Rm. W298, Indianapolis, IN 46204; (317) 232-4124; http://www.ai.org/dnr/recguide/rec-stat.html

Iowa – Department of Natural Resources, Wallace State Office Building, East 9th St. & Grand Ave., Des Moines, IA 50319-0034; (515) 281-5918; (515) 281-5145; http://www.state.ia.us/parks

Kansas – Kansas Dept. of Wildlife & Parks, 512 S.E. 25th Ave., Pratt, KS 67124-9599; (316) 672-5911 http://www.ink.org/public.kdwp/parks/parks.html

Kentucky – Kentucky Department of Parks, 500 Mero St., Suite 1000, Frankfort, KY 40601; (800) 255-7275 http://www.state.ky.us/agencies/parks/parkhome.htm

Louisiana – Louisiana Office of State Parks, P.O. Box 4426, Baton Rouge, LA 70804; (504) 342-8111; http://crt.state.la.us/crt/spintro.htm

Maine – Bureau of Parks & Lands, 22 State House Street, Augusta, ME 04333; (207) 287-3821 http://www.visitmaine.com

Maryland – Maryland Dept. of N.R. & Parks Service, 580 Taylor Ave., Annapolis, MD 21401; (410) 974-3771; http://gacc.com/dnr/index3.html

Massachusetts – Bureau of Rec. & Div. of Parks, 100 Cambridge St., Boston, MA 02202; (617) 727-3180; http://www.state.ma.us/dem/toc.htm

Michigan – Dept. of Natural Resources & Parks, P.O. Box 30257, Lansing, MI 48909; (517) 373-9900 http://www.dnr.state.mi.us/www/parks/index.htm

Minnesota – Minnesota Dept. of Natural Resources Information Center, 500 Lafayette Rd., Box 40, St. Paul, MN 55155-4040; http://www.dnr.state.mn.us/outdoor/parks/parks.htm

Mississippi – Department of Parks, P.O. Box 451, Jackson, MS 39205; (601) 362-9212; http://www2.msstate.edu/~rex/parks.html

Missouri – Missouri Dept. of Natural Resources Division of Parks, P.O. Box 176, Jefferson City, MO 65102; (314) 751-3443; (800) 334-6946; http:// www.state.mo.us/dnr/dsp/homedsp.htm

Montana – Montana Dept. of Fish, Wildlife & Parks, 1420 E. 6th Ave., Helena, MT 59620-0701; (406) 444-2535; (406) 444-1200; http://fwp.mt.gov/parks/parks.htm

Nebraska – Nebraska Game & Parks Commission; P.O. Box 30350; Lincoln, NE 68503; (402) 471-0641; http://www.ngpc.state.ne.us/

Nevada – Nevada Division of State Parks, Capitol Complex, Carson City, NV 89710; (800) 237-0774 http://www.travelnevada.com/parks.html

New Hampshire – Dept. of Parks, P.O. Box 1856, Concord, NH 03302; (603) 271-3254; (800) 258-3608; http://www.nhparks.state.nh.us

New Jersey – Division of Parks & Forestry, State Park Service, 501 E. State St., CN 404, Trenton, NJ 08625; (800) 843-6420; (609) 292-2797; http://www.nj.com/outdoors/park.html

New Mexico – State Park & Recreation Div., 2040 South Pacheco St., Santa Fe, NM 87505-1147; (505) 827-7173; http://164.64.101.8:80/nmparks/

New York – New York State Office of Parks, Agency Building # 1, Empire State Plaza, Albany, NY 12238; (518) 474-0456

North Carolina – North Carolina Division of Parks & Rec., P.O. Box 27687, Raleigh, NC 27611; (919) 733-7275; (919) 733-4181 http://ils.unc.edu/parkproject/ncparks.html

North Dakota – North Dakota Parks & Recreation, 1835 E. Bismarck Expressway, Bismarck, ND 58504; (701)328-5357; http://www.ndtourism.com

Ohio – Division of Parks & Rec. Dept. of Natural Resources, 1952 Belcher Dr., Columbus, OH 43224-1368; (614) 265-6561; http://www.dnr.state.oh.us/odnr/parks/

Oklahoma – Oklahoma Tourism & Recreation, P.O. Box 60789, Oklahoma City, OK 73146-0789; (405) 521-2409; (800) 652-6552; http://www.otrd.state.ok.us/stateparks.html

Oregon – Oregon Dept. of Parks & Rec., 1115 Commercial St. N.E., Salem, OR 97310-1001; (503) 378-6305; http://www.ohwy.com/or/o/oprd.htm

Pennsylvania – Pennsylvania Bureau of State Parks, P.O. Box 8551, Harrisburg, PA 17105-8551; (800) 63-PARKS; http://www.dcnr.state.pa.us/dcnr/deputate/pksfor/stateparks/spintro.htm

Rhode Island – Division of Parks & Recreation, 2321 Hartford Ave., Johnston, RI 02919; (401) 277-2632

South Carolina – Dept. of Parks, Rec. & Tourism, P.O. Box 71, Columbia, SC 29202; (803) 734-1000; http://www.sccsi.com:80/sc/parks/index.html

South Dakota – South Dakota Game, Fish & Park

Dept., 523 E. Capitol, Pierre, SD 57501; (605) 773-3485; http://www.state.sd.us/gfp/

Tennessee – Bureau of State Parks, 7th Floor, L & C Tower, 401 Church Street, Nashville, TN 37243-0446; (615) 532-0001; (800) 421-6683; http:// www.tnstateparks.com

Texas – State Parks Division, 4200 Smith School Rd. Austin, TX 78744; (800)792-1112; (512) 389-8900; http://www.tpwd.state.tx.us/park/parks.htm

Utah – Division of Parks & Rec., 1594 W. North Temple, Salt Lake City, UT 84114-6001; (801) 538-7220; http://www.nr.state.ut.us/parks/utahstpk.htm

Vermont – Dept. of Parks & Rec., 103 S. Main St., Waterbury, VT 05676; (802) 241-3655; http:// www.state.vt.us/anr/fpr/parks

Virginia – Virginia State Parks, Dept. of Conserv. & Recreation, 203 Governor St., Suite 302, Richmond, VA 23219; (804) 225-3867; (800) 933-PARK; http://www.state.va.us/~dcr/parks/parkindx.htm

Washington – State Parks Recreation Commission, 7150 Clearwater Ln., Olympia, WA 98504; (360) 902-8563; (800) 233-0321; http://www.parks.wa.gov

West Virginia – Division of Tourism & Parks, State Capitol Complex, Charleston, WV 25305; (800) 225-5982; http://wvweb.com/www/travel_recreation/state_parks/state_parks_menu.html

Wisconsin – Dept. of Parks & Natural Resources, P.O. Box 7921, Madison, WI 53707; (608) 266-2181; http://www.dnr.state.wi.us/parks/

Wyoming – Division of State Parks & Historical Sites, 122 West 25th, 1st Floor, NE, Herschler Building, Cheyenne, WY 82002; (307) 777-6323; http://commerce.state.wy.us/sphs

Illustrations Credits

Cover, Frans Lanting/Minden Pictures; 1, Johnny Johnson/Alaska Stock Images; 2-3, Phil Schermeister; 4, Kindra Clineff/The Picture Cube; 5, George H.H. Huey; 7, John Moran/ Silver Image; 8, Jonathan Wallen; 10, José Azel; 12-14, Stephen G. Maka/The Picture Cube; 16, E.R. Degginger/Bruce Coleman, Inc.; 17-20, William H. Johnson; 22, Dennis Welsh; 23, David Muench; 25, William H. Johnson; 26, Diane Cook & Len Jenshel; 27, Bill Ballenberg; 28, Paul O. Boisvert; 31, William H. Johnson; 32, Ken Sherman; 33, William H. Johnson; 34 Paul Skillings/f-Stop Pictures; 35, Tom Till; 36, Jonathan Wallen; 38, Steve Dunwell; 39, Kindra Clineff/The Picture Cube; 40, Jim McElhom/Newport County Convention & Visitors Bureau; 42, Thomas Mark Szelog; 43, William H. Johnson; 45, Tom Till; 46, William H. Johnson; 48, Eliot Cohen; 49, A. Blake Gardner; 50, Pat & Chuck Blackley; 52-53, Wolfgang Kaehler; 54, Kenneth Garrett; 56, Jeff Gnass; 57, Scott Barrow; 58, Hardie Truesdale; 59, New York State Travel Commission; 60, Jonathan Wallen; 62, Ohio Bureau of State Parks; 63, Jonathan Wallen; 64, Dwight L. Dyke; 65-67, Jonathan Wallen; 68, Jeff Gnass; 70, Jonathan Wallen; 72-73, Scott Barrow; 74, Hardie Truesdale; 74-75, Stephen G. St.

John/NGS; 77, David Muench; 78, Bates Littlehales; 79, Jonathan Wallen; 80-81, Robert W. Madden/NGS; 82, Jonathan Wallen; 83-84, C.M. Glover; 85, Bates Littlehales; 86, Gene Ahrens; 88, Richard A. Cooke III; 89, Dwight L. Dyke; 90, John Henley; 91, Catherine Ursillo/Folio, Inc.; 92, John Henley; 93, Jonathan Wallen; 94-96, Steve Shaluta, Jr./West Virginia Division of Tourism; 97, Kenneth Garrett; 99, John Henley; 100, Bates Littlehales; 101, James P. Blair; 102, Ed Cooper Photo; 104, Tom Till; 106, Kelly Culpepper/Transparencies, Inc.; 108, North Carolina Tourism Dept.; 109, Jonathan Wallen; 110, Tom Till; 112, Hardie Truesdale; 113, William H. Johnson; 114, Zandria Beraldo; 116, Tom Till; 117, Dwight L. Dyke; 118, William H. Johnson; 120, Fred Hirschmann; 121, J. Faircloth/Transparencies, Inc.; 123-125, Tom Till; 126, John J. Lopino/Silver Image; 129, A. Blake Gardner; 132, Bruce Borich/Silver Image; 133, A. Blake Gardner; 134, Michael Warren/Silver Image; 135, A. Blake Gardner; 136, David Muench; 139, Tom Till; 141, Robert P. Falls, Sr.; 142-144, Raymond Gehman; 146, John Lewis Stage/The Image Bank; 147, Tria Giovan; 148-151, David Muench; 152, Robert P. Falls, Sr.; 153, Leonard Lee Rue III/Bruce Coleman, Inc.; 155, David Muench; 156-157, Randi Hirschmann; 158, David Muench; 161, Bates Littlehales; 162, Balthazar Korab; 164, David Muench;

166, Thomas R. Fletcher; 167, J. Miles Wolf; 169, Kent & Donna Dannen; 170, Declan Haun; 172, Gary Bublitz/DPA; 174, Fred Hirschmann; 176, Erwin & Peggy Bauer/Bruce Coleman, Inc.; 178, Rob Torreson; 179, Balthazar Korab; 180, Dan Dempster/DPA; 182, J. Miles Wolf; 183, Balthazar Korab; 185, L. West/Bruce Coleman, Inc.; 187, Dan Dempster/DPA; 188, Willard Clay/DPA; 189, Jim Emery/Folio, Inc.; 190, Willard Clay/DPA; 191, Terry Donnelly/DPA; 192, Bates Littlehales; 195, Tom Bean; 196, Terry Donnelly/DPA; 198, Balthazar Korab; 199, Clint Farlinger; 200-203, Greg Ryan-Sally Beyer; 205, Tom Bean; 207, Greg Ryan-Sally Beyer; 208, Annie Griffiths Belt; 210-213, Tom Bean; 215, Stephen G. Maka/The Picture Cube; 216, Tom Bean; 218, Clint Farlinger; 219, Annie Griffiths Belt; 220, Tom Bean; 221-223, Annie Griffiths Belt; 225, Greg Ryan-Sally Beyer; 226, Tom Till; 229, Clint Farlinger; 230, Ken Formanok; 231, Wayne Frantzen; 232-233, Annie Griffiths Belt; 235, Tom Till; 237, Nick Decker/Missouri Dept. of Natural Resources; 238, Kent & Donna Dannen; 240, Tom Bean; 241, Kent & Donna Dannen; 242, Bruce Dale; 244, David G. Fitzgerald; 246, Greg Ryan-Sally Beyer; 248, Tom Till; 249, Fred W. Marvel/Oklahoma Tourism; 250-253, Greg Ryan-Sally Beyer; 255, Tim Schick/Arkansas Dept. of Parks & Tourism; 256-257, A.C. Haralson/Arkansas Dept. of Parks &

Index

Composition for this book by
the National Geographic Society Book Division.
Printed and bound by Quebecor Printing-Hawkins,Kingsport,Tn.
Color separations by World Color Digital Services,Washington,D.C.
Paper by Consolidated/Alling & Cory, Willow Grove, Pennsylvania.
Cover printed by Miken Companies, Inc. Cheektowaga, New York.

Library of Congress Cataloging-in-Publication Data

National Geographic's guide to the state parks of the United States /
prepared by the Book Division, National Geographic Society.
    p.   cm.
    Includes index.
    ISBN 0-7922-7029-0 (reg.). —ISBN 0-7922-7024-X (dlx)
    1. Parks—United States—Guidebooks. 2. United States-
Guidebooks.   I. National Geographic Society (U.S.). Book
Division.
    E160.N2442   1997
    917.304′929—dc21

                                        97-14297